A+ Certificatio Core Hardware

Student Manual

THOMSON

COURSE TECHNOLOGY

Australia • Canada • Mexico • Singapore
Spain • United Kingdom • United States

A+ Certification: Core Hardware

VP and GM of Courseware:	Michael Springer
Series Product Managers:	Caryl Bahner-Guhin, Charles G. Blum, and Adam A. Wilcox
Developmental Editor:	Don Tremblay
Project Editor:	Josh Pincus
Series Designer:	Adam A. Wilcox
Cover Designer:	Steve Deschene

For more information contact:

Course Technology
25 Thomson Place
Boston, MA 02210

Or find us on the Web at: www.course.com

For permission to use material from this text or product, contact us by

- Web: www.thomsonrights.com
- Phone: 1-800-730-2214
- Fax: 1-800-730-2215

Trademarks

Course ILT is a trademark of Course Technology.

Some of the product names and company names used in this book have been used for identification purposes only and may be trademarks or registered trademarks of their respective manufacturers and sellers.

Disclaimer

Course Technology reserves the right to revise this publication and make changes from time to time in its content without notice.

ISBN 0-619-17104-9

Printed in the United States of America

1 2 3 4 5 PM 04 03 02 01

Contents

Introduction   **iii**
    Topic A: About the manual...iv
    Topic B: Setting your expectations vii
    Topic C: Re-keying the course xi

Starting the computer   **1-1**
    Topic A: Overview of computer components............................... 1-2
    Topic B: The boot process... 1-12
    Topic C: How software manages hardware resources................... 1-19
    Unit summary: Starting the computer 1-33

The system board   **2-1**
    Topic A: System board components... 2-2
    Topic B: The CPU and the chip set 2-9
    Topic C: ROM BIOS and RAM 2-30
    Topic D: Buses and expansion slots 2-39
    Unit summary: The system board 2-58

Memory   **3-1**
    Topic A: Understanding memory 3-2
    Topic B: Upgrading memory.. 3-15
    Unit summary: Memory 3-22

Floppy drives   **4-1**
    Topic A: Storing data on a disk 4-2
    Topic B: Supporting floppy drives 4-13
    Unit summary: Floppy drives... 4-26

Hard drives   **5-1**
    Topic A: Overview of hard drives 5-2
    Topic B: How a hard drive is logically organized........................ 5-17
    Topic C: Installing hard drives 5-31
    Topic D: Troubleshooting hard drives... 5-51
    Unit summary: Hard drives 5-62

Troubleshooting fundamentals   **6-1**
    Topic A: Introduction to troubleshooting 6-2
    Topic B: Isolating problems and designing action plans.............. 6-8
    Topic C: Problems after a successful boot 6-14
    Topic D: Preventive maintenance.. 6-34
    Unit summary: Troubleshooting fundamentals............................ 6-39

Supporting I/O devices   **7-1**
    Topic A: Overview of peripheral devices..................................... 7-2
    Topic B: Ports and expansion slots for add-on devices............... 7-10
    Topic C: SCSI devices.. 7-23
    Topic D: Keyboard, mouse, and monitor devices 7-28
    Unit summary: Supporting I/O devices.. 7-45

Multimedia technology   8-1

Topic A: Overview of multimedia 8-2
Topic B: CD-ROM drives..8-11
Topic C: Sound cards 8-24
Topic D: Digital cameras and DVD 8-38
Unit summary: Multimedia technology 8-43

Electricity and power supplies   9-1

Topic A: Measuring the voltage of a power supply 9-2
Topic B: Problems with the power supply 9-13
Topic C: Surge protection and battery backup...9-18
Topic D: Energy Star (Green Star) computers 9-26
Unit summary: Electricity and power supplies..9-30

Communicating over phone lines   10-1

Topic A: Modem basics..10-2
Topic B: Modem troubleshooting guidelines..10-18
Topic C: Other communication technologies..10-24
Unit summary: Communicating over phone lines 10-29

Networking fundamentals   11-1

Topic A: Network architectures 11-2
Topic B: Networking hardware 11-14
Topic B: Networking hardware 11-14
Topic C: Networking software overview 11-20
Unit summary: Networking fundamentals..11-25

Printers and notebook computers   12-1

Topic A: Printers 12-2
Topic B: Notebook computers 12-20
Unit summary: Printers and notebook computers..12-34

Course summary   S-1

Topic A: Course summary...S-2
Topic B: Continued learning after class S-4

Glossary   G-1

Index   I-1

A+ Certification: Core Hardware

Introduction

After reading this introduction, you'll know how to:

A Use Course Technology ILT manuals in general.

B Use prerequisites, a target student description, course objectives, and a skills inventory to properly set your expectations for the course.

C Re-key this course after class.

Topic A: About the manual

Course Technology ILT philosophy

Course Technology ILT manuals facilitate your learning by providing structured interaction with the software itself. While we provide text to explain difficult concepts, the hands-on activities are the focus of our courses. By paying close attention as your instructor leads you through these activities, you'll learn the skills and concepts effectively.

We believe strongly in the instructor-led classroom. During class, focus on your instructor. Our manuals are designed and written to facilitate your interaction with your instructor, and not to call attention to the manuals themselves.

We believe in the basic approach of setting expectations, delivering instruction, and providing summary and review afterwards. For this reason, lessons begin with objectives and end with summaries. We also provide overall course objectives and a course summary to provide both an introduction to and closure on the entire course.

Manual components

The manuals contain these major components:

1   Table of contents
2   Introduction
3   Units
4   Course summary
5   Glossary
6   Index

Each element is described below.

Table of contents

The table of contents acts as a learning roadmap.

Introduction

The introduction contains information about our training philosophy and our manual components, features, and conventions. It contains target student, prerequisite, objective, and setup information for the specific course.

Units

Units are the largest structural component of the course content. A unit begins with a title page that lists objectives for each major subdivision, or topic, within the unit. Within each topic, conceptual and explanatory information alternates with hands-on activities. Units conclude with a summary comprising one paragraph for each topic, and an independent practice activity that gives you an opportunity to practice the skills you've learned.

The conceptual information takes the form of text paragraphs, exhibits, lists, and tables. The activities are structured in two columns, one telling you what to do, the other providing explanations, descriptions, and graphics.

Course summary

This section provides a text summary of the entire course. It's useful for providing closure at the end of the course. The course summary also indicates the next course in this series, if there is one, and lists additional resources you might find useful as you continue to learn about the software.

Glossary

The glossary provides an alphabetical list of common terms and their definitions used in this course.

Index

The index enables you to quickly find information about a particular feature or concept of the software.

Manual conventions

We've tried to keep the number of elements and the types of formatting to a minimum in the manuals. This aids in clarity and makes the manuals more classically elegant looking. But there are some conventions and icons you should know about.

Convention/Icon	Description
Italic text	In conceptual text, indicates a new term or feature.
Bold text	In unit summaries, indicates a key term or concept. In an independent practice activity, indicates an explicit item that you select, choose, or type.
Code font	Indicates code or syntax.
Select **bold item**	In the left column of hands-on activities, bold sans-serif text indicates an explicit item that you select, choose, or type.
Keycaps like ⏎ ENTER	Indicate a key on the keyboard you must press.

Hands-on activities

The hands-on activities are the most important parts of our manuals. They're divided into two primary columns. The "Here's how" column gives short instructions to you about what to do. The "Here's why" column provides explanations, graphics, and clarifications. Here's a sample:

Do it!

A-1: Creating a commission formula

Here's how	Here's why
1 Open Sales	This is an oversimplified sales compensation worksheet. It shows sales totals, commissions, and incentives for five sales reps.
2 Observe the contents of cell F4	F4 ▼ = =E4*C_Rate
	The commission rate formulas use the name "C_Rate" instead of a value for the commission rate.

Topic B: Setting your expectations

Properly setting your expectations is essential to your success. This topic will help you do that by providing:

- Prerequisites for this course
- A description of the target student at whom the course is aimed
- A list of the objectives for the course
- A skills assessment for the course

Course prerequisites

Before taking this course, you should be familiar with personal computers and the use of a keyboard and a mouse. There are no other specific prerequisites for this course.

Target student

This course is aimed at those of you who are interested in what is happening "behind the scenes" in order to install new hardware, diagnose problems, and make decisions about purchasing new hardware. You'll get the most out of this course if you are a PC technician who is interested in pursuing A+ Certification.

Course objectives

These overall course objectives will give you an idea about what to expect from the course. It's also possible that they will help you see that this course is not the right one for you. If you think you either lack the prerequisite knowledge or already know most of the subject matter to be covered, you should let your instructor know that you think you are misplaced in the class.

After completing this course, you'll know how to:

- Start the computer and identify the hardware components, explain the boot process, and understand how system resources are assigned.
- Identify the components of the system board by examining the CPU and chip set, discussing ROM BIOS and RAM, and installing and removing expansion cards.
- Manage memory by defining the different types of memory and installing RAM.
- Support floppy drives by understanding the formatting process, creating an Emergency Startup Disk, and removing and installing a floppy drive.
- Support hard drives by comparing IDE and SCSI technologies, creating partitions, install hard drives, and troubleshoot installation problems.
- Isolate problems and design troubleshooting action plans by using basic troubleshooting guidelines and tools, and protect and maintain a system by developing a preventative maintenance plan.

- Support I/O devices by examining device drivers, working with serial and parallel ports, installing a SCSI device, and discussing keyboard, mouse, and monitor technologies.

- Examine multimedia technology by installing CD-ROM drives and sound cards, and discussing digital cameras and DVDs.

- Define basic electricity concepts by measuring the voltage of the power supply and protecting against power surges.

- Enable communications over phone lines by installing and configuring modems, troubleshooting modem problems, and discussing other communication technologies.

- Define networking fundamentals by discussing network architectures and identifying the hardware and software required for networking.

- Support printers and notebook computers by defining the components and issues that are involved with printers and laptop computers.

Skills inventory

Use the following form to gauge your skill level entering the class. For each skill listed, rate your familiarity from 1 to 5, with five being the most familiar. *This is not a test.* Rather, it's intended to provide you with an idea of where you're starting from at the beginning of class. If you're entirely unfamiliar with all the skills, you might not be ready for the class. If you think you already understand all of the skills, you might need to move on to the next course in the series. In either case, you should let your instructor know as soon as possible.

Skill	1	2	3	4	5
Identifying computer components					
Defining the boot process					
Identifying system board components and their functions					
Defining ROM BIOS					
Installing an expansion card					
Using memory management strategies					
Installing RAM					
Formatting a floppy disk					
Installing a floppy drive					
Describing how a hard drive works					
Creating partitions					
Installing a hard drive					
Identifying troubleshooting tools and guidelines					
Isolating computer problems and resolving them					
Defining serial and parallel ports					
Installing a SCSI device					
Describing how a keyboard, a mouse, and a monitor work					
Identifying multimedia devices					
Installing a CD-ROM drive					

Skill	1	2	3	4	5
Installing a sound card					
Measuring the voltage of a power supply					
Installing and configuring a modem					
Identifying network architectures and network hardware					
Supporting printers					
Supporting notebook computers					
Developing a preventive maintenance plan					

Topic C: Re-keying the course

If you have the proper hardware and software, you can re-key this course after class. This section explains what you'll need in order to do so, and how to do it.

Computer requirements

This course is hardware intensive. It contains activities that require you to install hardware and some software. We recommend that you create a lab workstation with two computers; one machine should have Windows 98 Second Edition, while the other will be a "work" computer and will remain open most of the time for exercises and observation. Some tasks, such as partitioning the hard drive, should only be done on the work computer, while others may be safely done on both computers. Activities that involve installing drivers or checking properties will have to be done on the Windows 98 machine.

Each lab workstation computer should have:

- A Pentium-class processor
- 32 MB RAM or more
- 200 MB hard drive
- One floppy disk drive (either a 3½" or 5¼")
- CD-ROM drive and drivers (if you plan to install software from a CD-ROM)
- Network card and cable
- A keyboard and a mouse
- Super VGA monitor
- Windows 98 Second Edition
- Printer and the appropriate drivers
- An Internet connection (optional) for research

Additional hardware to be used throughout the course

- PC tool kit and any other tools necessary to open each lab workstation's case
- One grounding strap and grounding mat for each lab workstation
- DOS boot system disk
- PCI expansion card
- SCSI host adapter
- One sound card
- Unformatted floppy disk for each lab workstation
- SIMM memory module

- One standard IDE data cable (Master/Slave)
- One multimeter
- One UPS
- Surge protector
- Internal modem card
- One removable (Zip or similar) tape drive and drivers
- Two hard drive jumpers (normally already on the hard drives)
- Audio CD's to test the computer sound system

Setup instructions to re-key the course

Before you re-key the course, you'll need to perform the following steps.

1 On one lab workstation computer, install Windows 98 Second Edition with the default installations. Connect to the Internet, if possible

2 Gather the additional hardware devices that you'll use throughout the course.

Unit 1

Starting the computer

Unit time: 90 minutes

Complete this unit, and you'll know how to:

A Identify the functions performed by different hardware components of a computer.

B Describe what happens when a computer boots.

C Define how hardware interacts with the system and how software manages hardware resources.

Topic A: Overview of computer components

Explanation   Over the past few years, the work done by PC technicians has increasingly been viewed as a profession, and certification for PC technicians has become more desirable. A good PC technician needs to know the major hardware components of a microcomputer system. In performing a computing task, software uses hardware for four basic functions: input, processing, output, and storage. Also, hardware components must communicate both data and instructions among themselves, and, since these components are electrical, an electrical system is required.

Although this book is concerned with the hardware side of being a PC technician, you will deal with some software topics, especially where software interfaces closely with hardware.

Input and output devices

Most input and output devices are outside the computer case, and most processing and storage is done inside the case. The most important hardware device in a computer is the central processing unit (CPU)—the microprocessor or processor. As its name implies, this device is central to all processing done by the computer. Data received by input devices goes to the CPU, and output travels from the CPU to output devices. The CPU stores data and instructions in storage devices and performs calculations and other processing of data as well. Whether inside or outside the case, and regardless of the function the device performs, each device requires these things to operate:

- A method for the CPU to communicate with the device. The device must send data to and/or receive data from the CPU. The CPU might need to control the device by passing instructions to it, and/or the device might need to request service from the CPU.

- Software to instruct and control the device. A device is useless without software to control it. The software must know how to communicate with the device at the detailed level of that specific device, and the CPU must have access to this software in order to interact with the device.

- Electricity to power the device. Electronic devices require electricity to operate. Devices can either receive power from the power supply inside the computer case, or they can have their own power supply by way of a power cable to an electrical outlet.

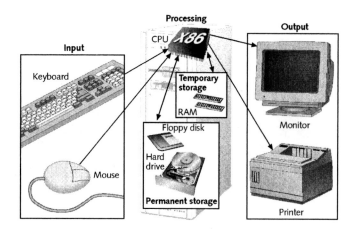

Exhibit 1-1: The central processing unit (CPU) is central to all computer activity

Basic computer terminology

The following table defines several terms that are used throughout the course.

Term	Definition
Hardware	The physical components that constitute a computer system, such as the monitor, keyboard, system board, and printer.
Software	Computer programs or instructions that perform a specific task.
Firmware	Software that is stored permanently in a chip.
Input devices	Components used to send messages to a computer, such as the keyboard and mouse.
Output devices	Components used to display the results of a computer's actions, such as a monitor and printer.
Port	Connection point on a computer case where input and output devices are attached to the computer.
Parallel and serial cables	Cables used to connect the input and output devices to the computer ports on the outside of a computer case.

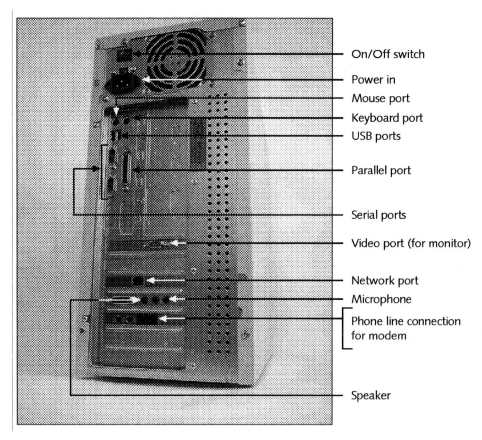

Exhibit 1-2: Input and output devices connect to the back of the computer case

Do it! **A-1: Verifying that the computer is properly connected**

Question	Answer
1 How many cables and cords are connected to the system unit, and to which devices are they connected?	
2 You are employed as a desktop PC support technician. A customer named Matt calls you with a problem. He explains that he just finished moving his PC and reconnecting all of the cables, but now he is getting error messages and both the keyboard and mouse won't work. What is the most likely cause of Matt's problem?	
3 Another customer, Judy, also has just moved her PC, but now the monitor screen is blank. She explains that the power light for the monitor is turned on and that the system unit power light is also on. Which cables would you ask Judy to check first?	

Inside the computer case

Explanation

Most storage and all processing of data and instructions are done inside the computer case. Within their cases, most computers contain the following devices:

- A system board containing the central processing unit (CPU), memory, and chip sets that are used primarily for processing.
- Random access memory (RAM) and cache memory used for temporary storage of data and instructions.
- A floppy drive, hard drive, and CD-ROM drive used for permanent storage.
- Circuit boards used by the CPU to communicate with devices inside and outside the case.
- A power supply with power cables providing electricity to the system board and expansion cards.
- Cables connecting devices to circuit boards and the system board.

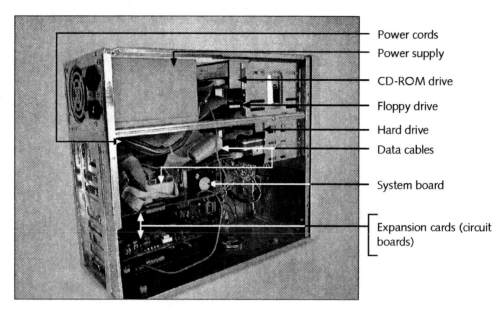

Exhibit 1-3: Inside the computer case

The following table describes the devices generally found inside a computer case:

Item	Description
Central processing unit (CPU)	The heart and brain of the computer. It receives data input, processes information, and executes instructions.
Chip set	A group of chips on the system board that relieves the CPU of some processing tasks, thus increasing the system's overall speed and performance.
Memory	Physical microchips that can hold data and programming located on the system board or expansion cards.
Primary storage	Temporary storage on the system board that the CPU uses to process data and instructions. Random access memory (RAM) chips are an example of primary storage. Cache memory speeds up memory access by providing a holding area for data or instructions that are frequently accessed. Cache memory can be stored on a memory chip inside the CPU housing or, in older systems, on system board memory modules called cache on a stick (COAST).
Secondary storage	Storage that is remote to the CPU and permanently holds data even when the computer is turned off. Four popular secondary storage devices are hard drives, floppy disks, Zip drives, and CD-ROMs.
System board	The main board inside the computer (also called the motherboard) that contains the CPU, memory, and interface cards. The system board is the most complicated piece of equipment inside the case.

Item	Description
Circuit board	A board that holds microchips or integrated circuits (ICs) and the circuitry that connects these chips. All circuit boards contain microchips, which are manufactured in one of two ways: CMOS (complementary metal-oxide semiconductor) chips or TTL (transistor-transistor logic) chips. CMOS chips require less electricity, hold data longer after the electricity is turned off, are slower, and produce less heat than TTL chips do. Most CPUs are CMOS chips.
Interface card	A circuit board that is inserted into a slot on the system board to enhance the capability of the computer. Common interface, or expansion, cards are video cards, a hard drive adapter card, and a multipurpose input/output controller card.
Basic input/output system (BIOS)	Firmware that controls much of a computer's input/output functions, such as communication with the floppy drive, memory chips, and the monitor.
ROM chips	Read-only memory chips that contain programming code and can't be erased.
CMOS	An acronym that stands for complementary metal-oxide semiconductor. A technology used to manufacture microchips. The computer's configuration and setup chip is usually a CMOS chip.
Data cables	Typically flat and wide, these cables connect devices to each other inside the computer.
Power cable	Typically round and small, these cables connect devices to the power supply inside the computer.

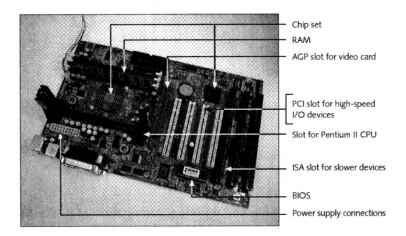

Exhibit 1-4: An example of a Pentium system board

Do it!

A-2: Defining components inside the computer

Question	Answer
1 What is the difference between primary storage and secondary storage?	
2 Name four common secondary storage devices.	
3 What is another name for the system board?	
4 What does the acronym BIOS represent?	
5 What is commonly stored on a CMOS chip?	
6 How can you usually tell the difference between a data cable and a power cable?	

Three types of software

Explanation

Software consists of programs written by programmers that instruct computers to perform specific tasks. Almost all PC software falls into one of three categories: firmware (BIOS), operating system (OS), and applications software. The BIOS and OS perform tasks at startup that determine the overall health and functionality of the computer, just as a mechanic is responsible for the condition of a car before it is turned over to the driver. After startup, the OS, working with applications software and the BIOS, provides instructions to the hardware to perform tasks.

As seen in Exhibit 1-5, first the BIOS and then the OS is in control of preparing the computer for user interaction when it's first turned on. The user can then interact directly with the OS to perform simple tasks such as copying files from the hard drive to a disk or installing applications software. Or the user can use applications software to perform higher-level tasks such as word processing or database management. In this case, the OS is still working behind the scenes, serving as a middle layer between the applications software and the hardware.

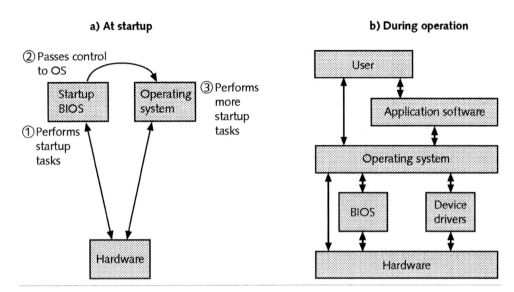

Exhibit 1-5: How software relates to other software and ultimately hardware

Firmware or BIOS

The BIOS on the system board and other circuit boards provides some fundamental instructions to hardware and often serves as the interface between higher-level software and hardware. The BIOS programs stored on the system board are together referred to as the *system BIOS*, or *on-board BIOS*. Part of the system BIOS is the *startup BIOS*, which runs many computer startup functions and brings the computer to a state in which it can be managed by the OS. Once the startup BIOS completes its tasks, it turns control over to the OS, which stays in control as long as the PC is turned on. The process of powering up and bringing the PC to a ready state is called *booting* and is discussed in detail later.

Software layers

Once the computer is running, a hierarchy determines how software interacts so that high-level software can depend on low-level software to manage the hardware for it. Applications software depends on the OS to interface with hardware. The OS might instruct the hardware directly, use the BIOS to provide the instructions, or use special software designed to interface with specific hardware devices. These special software programs are called device drivers and serve the same functions as BIOS programs, but they're stored on secondary storage devices, such as a hard drive, rather than on ROM chips, as the BIOS is. Some device drivers are provided by the OS, and some are provided by the manufacturer of the specific hardware device with which they are designed to interface.

One advantage of using the BIOS and device drivers to interface with hardware is that it frees the OS or applications software from knowing the specifics of how to communicate with a device. For example, different printers understand data and commands according to different sets of rules and standards called protocols. Applications software and the OS can pass print requests to the printer driver, which communicates with the printer. With the device drivers doing the interpreting, applications software developers don't have to include the specific protocol and standards for every printer that might be used by the applications they write.

The applications software doesn't even need to know which printer is being used because Windows keeps track of the default printer, or the currently selected printer. The application sends print jobs to Windows for printing. Windows uses the default printer unless the user selects a different one from the Windows printer list. Windows knows which device driver to call to execute the print job because the device driver was assigned to that printer when the printer was installed.

How software manages and shares information

Before the CPU can process data or follow software instructions, the data or instructions must first be stored in RAM. The CPU tracks where this information is stored in RAM by assigning an address to each unit of RAM that can hold one byte of information. These addresses are called memory addresses and are most often displayed on the screen as hexadecimal (base 16) numbers in segment/offset form (for example, C800:5).

The BIOS, device drivers, OS, and applications software are all working when a computer is running. During output operations, applications software must pass information to the OS, which in turn passes that information to a device driver or to the BIOS. The BIOS and device drivers managing input devices must pass information to the OS, which passes it to the applications software.

By using the CPU, software processes and shares data by referring to the memory address of the data. For example, if applications software wants to print data, rather than instructing the OS, "Please print data ABC," it instructs the OS, "Please print the data at memory address 123." The OS then turns to the printer device driver and instructs, "Please send data at memory address 123 to the printer you control."

Do it!   ## A-3:   Discussing software

Question	Answer
1 Name the three types of software.	
2 How does firmware differ from a software program stored on the hard drive?	
3 What is the difference between the startup BIOS and the operating system?	
4 Give an example of software that doesn't interact directly with the hardware.	
5 What task is performed by using the system BIOS?	

Topic B: The boot process

Explanation

The *boot process* is partly performed by the startup BIOS and then completed by the OS. The BIOS Startup program checks the hardware to make sure it's ready to be used; the user provides specific instructions to the software on what to do; and the software interacts directly with the CPU, which controls the various underlying mechanisms that make the computer work as intended.

System resources

Software has resources to control hardware, and hardware has resources to alert software that it needs attention. Think of a system resource as a tool that's used by either the hardware or software to communicate with one another.

There are four types of system resources: memory addresses, input/output (I/O) addresses, interrupt request numbers (IRQs), and direct memory access (DMA) channels.

Item	Description
IRQ	A line of a system-board *bus* (the circuits that connect all the components to each other). A hardware device can use an IRQ to signal the CPU that the device needs attention. Some lines have a higher priority for attention than others. Each IRQ line is identified by a single number.
I/O addresses	Numbers assigned to hardware devices that software uses to get the devices' attention and to interact with them. Each device "listens" for these numbers and responds to the ones assigned to it.
Memory addresses	Numbers that are assigned to physical memory located in either RAM or ROM chips. Software can then access this memory by using these addresses.
DMA channel	A number designating a channel through which the device can pass data to memory without involving the CPU. Think of a DMA channel as a shortcut for moving data to and from the device and memory.

All of these four resources are used for communication between hardware and software. Hardware devices signal the CPU for attention by using an IRQ. Software addresses a device by one of its I/O addresses. Software looks at memory as a hardware device and addresses it with memory addresses. DMA channels are used to pass data back and forth between a hardware device and memory.

Overview of the boot process

The processes that occur when a computer is booted are vital to ensuring that it operates as desired. The functions performed during the boot are:

1 The startup BIOS tests the essential hardware components. This test is called the *power-on self test (POST)*.

2 Setup information is used to configure both hardware and software.

3 Hardware components are assigned the system resources that they will later use for communication.

4 The OS is loaded, configured, and executed.

5 Hardware devices are matched up with the BIOS and device drivers that control them.

6 Some applications software may be loaded and executed.

The term "booting" comes from the phrase "lifting yourself up by your bootstraps," and refers to the computer bringing itself up to an operable state without user intervention. A *hard boot*, or *cold boot*, involves turning on the power with the on/off switch. A *soft boot* or *warm boot* involves pressing three keys at the same time: Ctrl, Alt, and Del.

A hard boot is more stressful on your machine than a soft boot because of the initial power surge through the equipment. Always use the soft boot method to restart your computer unless the soft boot method won't work. If you must power down, avoid turning off the power switch and immediately turning it back on without a pause, because this can damage the machine. Most PCs have a reset button on the front of the case. Pressing the reset button starts the booting process at an earlier point than does the Ctrl+Alt+Del method and is, therefore, a little slower. However, this method might work when the Ctrl+Alt+Del method fails. For newer system boards, pressing the reset button is the same thing as powering off and on except that there is no stress to the system caused by the initial power surge.

The boot process can be divided into four main steps:

1 POST: The ROM BIOS startup program surveys hardware resources and needs, and assigns system resources to meet those needs.

2 The ROM BIOS startup program searches for and loads an OS. Most often the OS is loaded from logical drive C on the hard drive.

3 The OS configures the system and loads the necessary device drivers.

4 The user opens applications software. The OS first finds the application software, copies it into memory, and then turns control over to it. You command the applications software, which makes requests to the OS, which, in turn, uses the system resources, system BIOS, and device drivers to interact with and control the hardware.

Access to a computer can be controlled by using *startup passwords*, or *power-on passwords*. During booting, the computer asks for a password. If the entered password is incorrect, the booting process is terminated. The password is stored on the CMOS chip and is changed by accessing the setup screen.

Power-on self test (POST)

When you turn on the power to a PC, the CPU begins the process by initializing itself and then turning to the ROM BIOS for instructions. The ROM BIOS startup program begins the startup process by reading configuration information stored in DIP switches, jumpers, and the CMOS chip and comparing that information to the hardware present—the CPU, video card, disk drive, hard drive, and so on. Some hardware devices have a BIOS of their own that requests resources from the startup BIOS, which attempts to assign these system resources as needed.

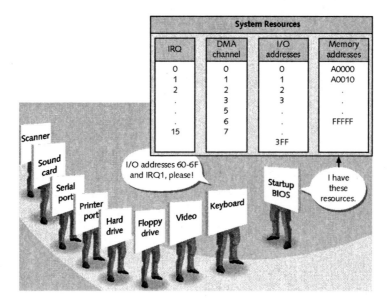

Exhibit 1-6: Step 1 of the boot process

1 When the power is first turned on, the system clock begins to generate clock pulses.

2 The CPU begins working and initializes itself (resetting its internal values).

3 The CPU turns to memory address FFFF0h, which is the memory address always assigned to the first instruction in the ROM BIOS startup program.

4 This instruction directs the CPU to run the POST tests.

5 POST first checks the BIOS program operating it and then tests CMOS RAM.

6 A test is done to determine that there hasn't been a battery failure.

7 Hardware interrupts are disabled (this means that pressing a key on the keyboard or using another input device at this point will not affect anything).

8 Tests are run on the CPU and it's further initialized.

9 A check is done to determine if this is a cold boot. If so, then the first 16 KB of RAM is tested.

10 Hardware devices installed on the computer are inventoried and compared to configuration information.

11 Video, memory, keyboard, floppy disk drives, hard drives, ports, and other hardware devices are tested and configured. Then IRQ, I/O addresses, and DMA assignments are made. The OS will later complete this process.

12 Some devices are set up to go into "sleep mode" to conserve electricity.

13 The DMA controller is checked.

14 Interrupt vectors are moved into the interrupt vector table.

15 The interrupt controller is checked.

16 CMOS setup (a BIOS program to change CMOS configuration data) is run and the BIOS then begins its search for an OS.

During POST, before the CPU has checked the video system, any errors that are encountered are communicated to you by a beeping sound. Short and long beeps indicate an error. After POST checks the video controller card and it passes inspection (note that POST doesn't check to see if a monitor is present or working), POST can use the monitor to display its progress. After video is checked, POST then checks RAM by writing and reading data. A running count of RAM is displayed on the monitor during this phase.

Next, the keyboard is checked, and if you hold any keys down at this point, an error occurs. Secondary storage, including floppy disk drives and hard drives, is checked. The hardware that POST finds is checked against the data stored in the CMOS chip, jumpers, and DIP switches to determine if they agree.

System resources are assigned to devices by more than one method. Jumpers and DIP switches might be set to request a resource (for example, a jumper might be set to "on" if IRQ 5 is requested or "off" if IRQ 7 is requested), or the resources needed might simply be "hard coded" into the BIOS. *Hard coded* means that the values of resources are part of the ROM programming and can't be changed.

In earlier computers, system resources were always assigned to the device during the booting process. Think of the process as a dialog that might go something like this: The startup BIOS recognizes that a hardware device is present. The BIOS asks the device, "What resources do you need?" The device says, "I need this IRQ, these I/O addresses, this DMA channel, and these addresses in upper memory for my BIOS." In almost all cases, a device would be the sole owner of these resources. Problems would occur when more than one device attempted to use the same resource.

Today, more cooperative Plug and Play devices simply say, "I need one IRQ, some I/O addresses, and this many memory addresses for my BIOS. Please tell me the resources I can use."

BIOS finds and loads the OS

Once POST is complete, the next step is to load an OS. Most often, the OS is loaded from the hard drive. On the hard drive, the minimum amount of information required to load an OS is:

- A small program at the very beginning of the hard drive called the master boot program. This program is needed to locate the beginning of the OS on the drive.

- A table that contains a map to the logical drives on the hard drive, including the drive that is the boot drive. This table is called the partition table.

- At the beginning of the boot drive (usually drive C), the DOS boot record that loads the first program file of the OS. For DOS, that program is IO.SYS.

- MSDOS.SYS is needed next, followed by COMMAND.COM. These two files plus IO.SYS are the core components of DOS.

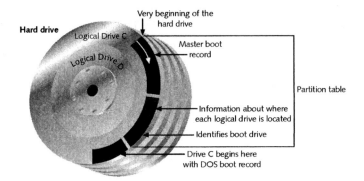

Exhibit 1-7: The master boot record on the boot drive

Often a hard drive is partitioned into more than one logical drive. Regardless of the number of logical drives on a hard drive, the drive always contains a single partition table located at the very beginning of the drive. At the beginning of the table is the master boot program, or *master boot record* (MBR), a small program used to start the boot process. One logical drive on the hard drive is designated as the boot drive, and the OS is stored on it. At the beginning of this logical drive is the DOS boot record, which knows the names of the files that contain the core programs of the OS.

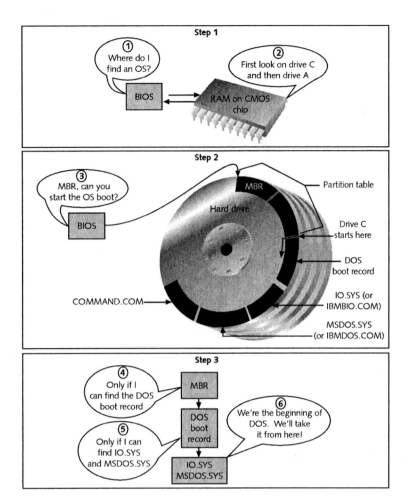

Exhibit 1-8: Step 2 of the boot process

The process for the BIOS to load the OS begins with the BIOS looking to CMOS setup to find out which secondary storage device should have the OS. Setup might instruct the BIOS to first look to drive C, and, if no OS is found there, to then try drive A, or visa versa. If the BIOS looks to drive A and does not find a disk in the drive, it turns to drive C. If it looks to drive A and finds a disk in the drive, but the disk doesn't contain the DOS boot record, IO.SYS, MSDOS.SYS, and COMMAND.COM files, then the following error message is displayed:

```
Non system disk or disk error, replace and press any key
```

You must replace the disk with a disk that contains the OS. Or, you can simply remove the disk to force the BIOS to continue on to drive C to find the OS.

Do it!   **B-1:   Discussing the boot process**

Question	Answer
1 What four types of system resources allow communication between hardware and software?	
2 What does POST stand for, and what is it for?	
3 What small program, necessary for booting, is at the very beginning or a hard drive?	

Topic C: How software manages hardware resources

Explanation The four system resources (IRQs, I/O addresses, memory addresses, and DMA channels) are dependent on certain lines on a bus on the system board. Some lines on the bus are devoted to IRQs, some to addresses (both memory I/O), and some to DMA channels.

The 8-bit and 16-bit ISA bus

All devices are in some way connected to the system board—either directly or indirectly—because they all depend on the CPU for processing their data. A device connects to the system board by a data cable, slot, or port coming directly off the system board. The device always connects to a single bus on the system board. Although there are several different buses on a system board, our discussions here will be limited to only one bus, an older bus used on the early PCs of the 1980s, called the *ISA* (Industry Standard Architecture) bus. The first ISA bus had only eight lines for data and was called the 8-bit ISA bus.

Some of the lines on the bus are used for data, addresses, and voltage; the others are a variety of control lines. You can see that eight lines are used for data, and 20 lines are used for addresses. These 20 lines can carry either memory addresses or I/O addresses. The CPU determines which type of address is using these lines by setting control lines B11 through B14 (memory read/write and I/O read/write). Because only 20 address lines are present when using this bus, the largest address value that can travel on the bus is 1111 1111 1111 1111 1111 or 1,048,576 or 1024K.

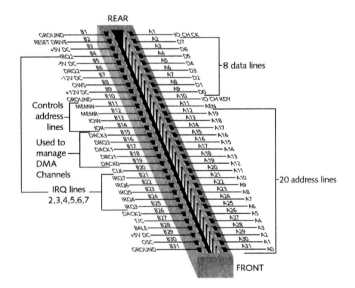

Exhibit 1-9: A 62-pin expansion slot for the 8-bit ISA bus

Two lines are required to manage a DMA channel: DRQ (Direct Request) and DACK (Direct Acknowledge). There are four DMA channels (0, 1, 2, and 3) on the 8-bit ISA bus.

With the improvement of computer technology came an increased desire for more memory, more devices to be operating at the same time, and faster data transfer, which made it necessary to provide more memory addresses, DMA channels, and IRQs. So, the 16-bit ISA bus was invented. The 16-bit ISA bus added an extra extension to the 8-bit slot allowing for eight additional data lines (for a total of 16), five additional IRQ lines, four more DMA channels, and four additional address lines (for a total of 24). Today, the 16-bit ISA bus is still used on system boards. An 8-bit expansion card (an expansion card that processes only eight bits of data at one time) can use the 16-bit ISA expansion slot. However, it uses only the first part of the slot.

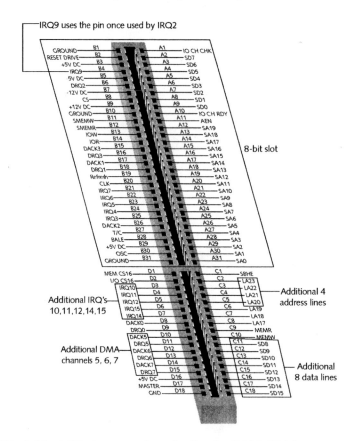

Exhibit 1-10: A 98-pin expansion slot for the 16-bit ISA bus

There are now several newer buses on system boards that are faster and provide more options, but the basics haven't changed. You can still find lines on these buses for data, addresses, IRQs, and DMA channels, although it's common practice today for a line to perform several functions. This makes it somewhat more difficult to study the bus.

Interrupt request number (IRQ)

When a hardware device needs the CPU to do something, such as when the keyboard needs the CPU to process a keystroke after a key is pressed, there must be a way for the device to get the CPU's attention and for the CPU to know what to do once its attention is turned to the device. These interruptions to the CPU are called *hardware interrupts.* The device handles them by placing a voltage on a designated line on the bus to which it is connected. These lines are numbered, and a line is referred to as an *interrupt request number*, or *IRQ*. The voltage on the line serves as a signal to the CPU that the device has a request that needs to be processed. Often, a hardware device that needs attention from the CPU is referred to as "needing servicing."

The following table lists the common uses for IRQs. There are eight IRQs built into this particular bus, but IRQs 0 and 1 aren't available for expansion cards (because they're used for the system timer and keyboard), so they're not given a pin on the expansion slot. IRQ 2 was reserved in the early days of PCs because it was intended to be used as part of a link to mainframe computers. Only five IRQs were actually available for devices, and each device had to have its own IRQ. This made it difficult for more than five devices to be connected to a PC at any one time. COM1 and COM2 are preconfigured assignments that can be made to serial devices such as modems. LPT1 and LPT2 are preconfigured assignments that can be made to parallel devices such as printers.

IRQ numbers for devices using the 8-bit ISA bus

0 System timer	4 COM1
1 Keyboard controller	5 LPT2
2 Reserved (not used)	6 Floppy drive controller
3 COM2	7 LPT1

On early system boards, the eight IRQs were managed by an Intel microchip called the *interrupt controller chip* and labeled the Intel 8259 chip. This chip had a direct connection to the CPU and would signal the CPU when an IRQ was activated. The CPU actually didn't know which IRQ was "up" because the interrupt controller managed that for the CPU. If more than one IRQ was up at the same time, the interrupt controller selected the IRQ that had the lowest value to process first. For example, if the user pressed a key on the keyboard at the exact same time that he or she moved the mouse installed on COM1, then the keystroke was processed first because the keyboard was IRQ 1 and the mouse on COM1 was IRQ 4.

When the 16-bit ISA bus appeared, more IRQs became available. A second interrupt controller chip was added to the system-board chip set, which hooked to the first controller. The second controller used one of the first controller's IRQ values (IRQ 2) to signal the first controller. This was problematic because there were some devices that used IRQ 2. Tying the new IRQ 9 to the old IRQ 2 pin on the 16-bit ISA bus solved the problem. The result was that a device could still use the pin on the expansion slot for IRQ 2, but it was really IRQ 9. As a result, the priority level became 0, 1, (8, 9, 10, 11, 12, 13, 14, 15), 3, 4, 5, 6, 7. Newer buses are designed so that more than one device can share an IRQ.

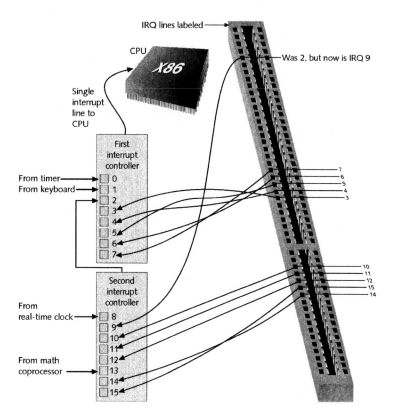

Exhibit 1-11: IRQs 8-15 cascade to IRQ 2

To see how the IRQs are assigned on your computer, use the Device Manager in Windows 9x. Choose Start, Settings, Control Panel, and double-click System. Click the Device Manager tab. Select Computer and click Properties. Notice that IRQ 2 is assigned to the programmable interrupt controller, and IRQ 9 is used by the video card.

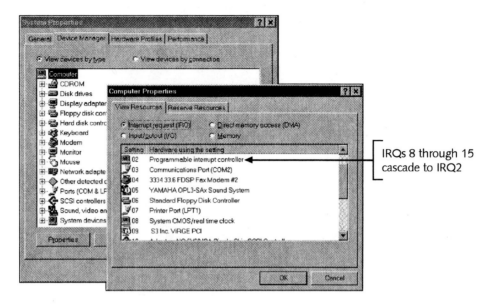

Exhibit 1-12: Using Device Manager to see how your system uses IRQs

Many processes that the CPU carries out are initiated by interrupts and are said to be "interrupt driven." With interrupts, either the hardware device or the software initiates communication by sending a signal to the CPU. However, there is a second way that a device can be serviced called polling. With polling, software that has the CPU periodically check the hardware device to see if service is needed runs constantly. Few devices use polling as the method of communication. A joystick is one example of such a device. Software that is written to manage a joystick has the CPU check the joystick periodically to see if the device has data to communicate, which is why a joystick does not need an IRQ to work. Most hardware devices use interrupts to perform this function.

Do it!

C-1: Recording your workstation's IRQ settings

Here's how	Here's why
1 Start your workstation	You can let it to boot into Windows 9x.
2 Choose **Start**, **Settings**, **Control Panel**	
Double-click the **System** icon	
3 Click the **Device Manager** tab	
Click the **Properties** button	
4 Verify that Interrupt request (IRQ) is selected	

Record the device name for each IRQ from IRQ 00 through IRQ 15

IRQ 00	IRQ 08
IRQ 01	IRQ 09
IRQ 02	IRQ 10
IRQ 03	IRQ 11
IRQ 04	IRQ 12
IRQ 05	IRQ 13
IRQ 06	IRQ 14
IRQ 07	IRQ 15

Memory addresses

Explanation

After the IRQ has gotten the attention of the CPU, its job is done, but memory addresses are used as the device is serviced. *Memory addresses* are numbers assigned to both ROM and RAM memory so that the CPU can access that memory. Think of memory addresses as a single long list of hexadecimal numbers. The CPU has a fixed number of memory addresses available to it, which are determined by the CPU and the bus it's using. These memory addresses can be assigned to any type of physical memory in the system that needs to be addressed by the CPU. This includes ROM and RAM chips on expansion cards on the system board, which can hold either data or instructions. After addresses have been assigned, the CPU sees this physical memory as a single list that can be accessed by using the memory addresses.

Before the CPU can process either data or instructions, both must be in physical memory, and the physical memory must be assigned memory addresses. In the case of the ROM BIOS, these programs are already located on a memory chip. The only thing needed is for memory addresses to be assigned to them. Software stored on a hard drive or another secondary storage device must first be copied into RAM before processing, and memory addresses must be assigned to that RAM. Data coming from an input device or stored in data files on a hard drive must also be copied into RAM before processing, and memory addresses must be assigned to that RAM. The CPU needs both RAM and memory addresses to load a program stored on the hard drive into memory before executing that program.

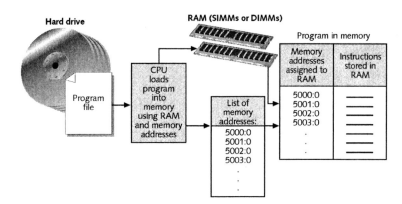

Exhibit 1-13: RAM and memory addresses are used when software is loaded

How memory addresses are used

The startup BIOS and *system BIOS*—also called *on-board BIOS*—stored in the ROM-BIOS chip on the system board must be assigned memory addresses so that the CPU can access these programs. RAM makes up the bulk of memory that is used by the CPU and uses the lion's share of available memory addresses. RAM is stored in SIMMs and DIMMs (which are circuit boards) on the system board. Many programs and data are copied into this RAM, including device drivers, portions of the OS and applications software, and data.

Some ways memory addresses are used

ROM BIOS chip on system board	Startup BIOS program
	System BIOS programs
RAM stored on SIMMs and DIMMs on system board	Parts of the OS permanently stored on the hard drive
	Applications software permanently stored on the hard drive
	Device drivers permanently stored on the hard drive
	Data used by the OS, device drivers, and applications software, either coming from input devices or copied from secondary storage devices
Video RAM stored on memory chips on a video card	Video data
Video ROM BIOS chip on video card	Programs to control video (video BIOS)
RAM and ROM chips on other expansion cards	BIOS and data used by the peripheral devices that the card supports (network card, sound card)

In Exhibit 1-14, some device drivers and BIOSs are labeled 16-bit and some are labeled 32-bit. By using Windows 9x and DOS, all 16-bit programs, including device drivers and BIOSs, must be assigned memory addresses in the first 1024K of addresses. Faster 32-bit programs can be assigned addresses in extended memory. DOS can't support 32-bit programs without the help of Windows, so a pure DOS-based system can use only 16-bit programs. One goal of Windows 9x is to replace all older 16-bit device drivers with newer 32-bit versions. Also, a newer device might contain a BIOS that's written using 32-bit code rather than 16-bit code. Therefore, in a Windows 9x environment, most of the memory addresses below 1024K aren't used.

Finally, note that Exhibit 1-14 applies to only DOS and Windows 9x. Windows NT and Windows 2000 use an altogether different memory-mapping design where there is no conventional, upper, or extended memory—it's all just memory. With this new approach to memory management, the BIOS and device drivers have no say as to what memory addresses they're assigned.

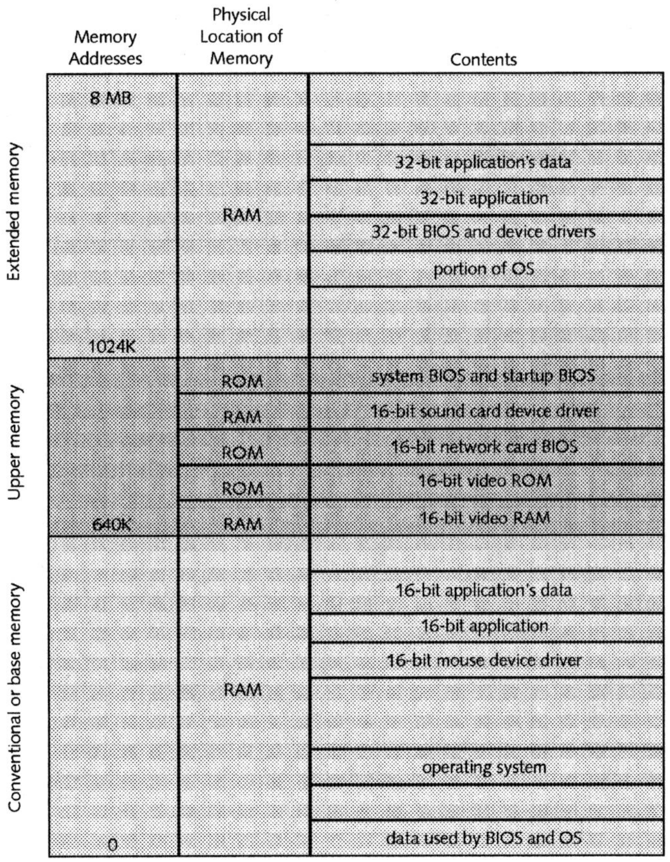

Memory Addresses	Physical Location of Memory	Contents
8 MB		
	RAM	32-bit application's data
		32-bit application
		32-bit BIOS and device drivers
		portion of OS
1024K		
	ROM	system BIOS and startup BIOS
	RAM	16-bit sound card device driver
	ROM	16-bit network card BIOS
	ROM	16-bit video ROM
640K	RAM	16-bit video RAM
		16-bit application's data
		16-bit application
		16-bit mouse device driver
	RAM	
		operating system
0		data used by BIOS and OS

(Left axis labels: Extended memory, Upper memory, Conventional or base memory)

Exhibit 1-14: Memory map showing how ROM and RAM might be mapped to memory addresses

Every computer system has video. A *video controller card*, also called a *video card* or *display adapter,* might have RAM on it with which the CPU must communicate when the CPU passes data to the video card to be sent to the monitor. In addition to RAM, the video card also contains some programming to manage video stored in ROM chips on the card. This video BIOS requires some memory addresses so that the CPU can access the BIOS.

Expansion cards most often contain ROM chips with BIOSs to control the peripheral devices they support. In addition, some of these cards might have RAM chips that also need memory addresses.

How memory addresses are assigned

For the most part, memory addresses are assigned during the boot process. The boot process begins with the startup BIOS on the ROM BIOS chip. This program in ROM is assigned addresses, as is the portion of ROM that contains the system BIOS. Video ROM and RAM get their address assignments early in the boot process so that the startup BIOS has the use of video while booting. Any other ROM or RAM chips on expansion cards also can request memory addresses during the boot process. Also during booting, addresses are assigned to RAM stored on DIMMs and SIMMs on the system board. Some of this RAM is used to hold the OS, device drivers, and data used by both. Most of this RAM isn't used until after booting when applications and their data are loaded.

BIOS and device drivers that request specific memory addresses

Today's BIOSs and software don't expect a specific group of addresses to be assigned to them. However, older BIOSs and device drivers designed to run in a DOS real-mode environment sometimes required a specific group of memory addresses in order to load. BIOS or real-mode device drivers might work if they are given only a specific group of addresses. These addresses are usually in the upper memory address range between 640K and 1024K.

Input/output addresses

Another system resource that is available to hardware devices is input/output addresses (or I/O addresses). *I/O addresses* or *port addresses*—sometimes simply called *ports*—are numbers that the CPU can use to access hardware devices, in the same way it uses memory addresses to access physical memory. If the address bus has been set to carry I/O addresses, then each device is "listening" to this bus. If the address belongs to it, then it responds; otherwise the bus ignores the request for information. In short, the CPU "knows" a hardware device as a group of I/O addresses. If it wants to know the status of a printer or a floppy drive, for example, it will pass a particular I/O address down the address bus on the system board.

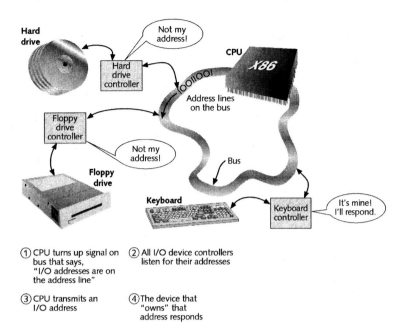

Exhibit 1-15: I/O address lines on a bus work like an old telephone party line

The following table lists a few of the common assignments for I/O addresses. Because IBM made many address assignments when the first PCs were manufactured in the late 1970s, common devices such as a hard drive, a floppy drive, or a keyboard have no problem with I/O addresses. Their BIOS can simply be programmed to use these standard addresses. Devices such as scanners or network cards that were not assigned I/O addresses in the original IBM list can be configured to use more than one group of addresses, depending on how they are set up during either the installation process or the boot process.

IRQ	I/O addresses	Description
0	040–05F	System timer
1	060–06F	Keyboard controller
2	0A0–0AF	Access to IRQs above 7
3	2F8–2FF	COM2
3	2E8–2EF	COM4
4	3F8–3FF	COM1
4	3E8–3EF	COM3
5	278–27F	Sound card or parallel port LPT2

IRQ	I/O addresses	Description
6	3F0–3F7	Floppy drive controller
7	378–37F	Printer parallel port LPT1
8	070–07F	Real time clock
9-10		Available
11		SCSI or available
12	238–23F	System-board mouse
13	0F8–0FF	Math coprocessor
14	1F0–1F7	IDE hard drive
15	170–170	Secondary IDE hard drive or available

Direct memory access (DMA) channels

Another system resource used by hardware and software is a *DMA* (direct memory access) channel, a shortcut method whereby an I/O device can send data directly to memory, bypassing the CPU. A chip on the system board contains the DMA logic and manages the process. Earlier computers had four channels numbered 0, 1, 2, and 3. Channels 5, 6, and 7 were added when the 16-bit ISA bus was introduced. Each channel requires two lines to manage it, one for the DMA controller to request clearance from the CPU and the other for the CPU to acknowledge that the DMA controller is free to send data over the data lines without interference from the CPU.

DMA channel 4 is used as IRQ 2 was used, to connect to the higher IRQs. Channel 4 is used to cascade into the lower DMA channels. DMA channels 0–3 use the 8-bit ISA bus, and DMA channels 5, 6, and 7 use the 16-bit ISA bus. This means that the lower four channels provide slower data transfer than the higher channels, because they don't have as many data paths available. Also, an 8-bit expansion card that uses only the 8-bit ISA bus can't access DMA channels 5, 6, or 7 because it can't get to these pins on the extended expansion slot.

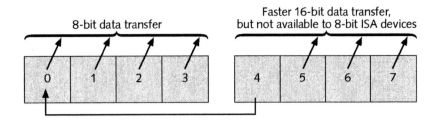

Exhibit 1-16: DMA channel 4 is used to cascade into the lower DMA channels

Some devices, such as a hard drive, are designed to use DMA channels. Others, such as the mouse, are not. Those devices that use channels might be able to use only a certain channel, say channel 3, and no other. Or, the BIOS might have the option of changing a DMA channel number to avoid conflicts with other devices. Conflicts occur when more than one device uses the same channel. DMA channels aren't as popular as they once were. Their design is such that they are slow in comparison to newer methods. However, slower devices such as floppy drives, sound cards, and tape drives might still use DMA channels.

System resources summary

To summarize, a hardware device is assigned the following things at startup:

- An IRQ by which it can signal the CPU that it needs attention
- I/O addresses by which the CPU and the device can communicate
- Memory addresses that indicate where the program to manage the device can be stored
- A DMA channel to speed up sending its data to memory

When a hardware device needs attention from the CPU, the device raises its IRQ line to the CPU. When the CPU senses the IRQ, it stops what it's doing and handles the interrupt. The CPU looks at the location in memory where the device driver or BIOS program that services the device is stored. The CPU then executes this program, which will use the I/O addresses to communicate with the device.

Do it!

C-2: Observing I/O and DMA settings

Here's how	Here's why
1 Verify that the Computer Properties window is still open	
2 Select **Input/output (I/O)**	To open the Control Panel.
Observe the assigned I/O addresses	To see which devices use which I/O addresses.
3 Select **Direct memory access (DMA)**	
Observe the DMA settings	
4 Click **Cancel**	To close the Computer Properties window.
Click **Cancel**	To close the System Properties window.
5 Close the Control Panel	

Unit summary: Starting the computer

Topic A   You reviewed basic computer terminology and learned that the four basic functions of a microcomputer are **input**, **output**, **processing**, and **data storage**. You reviewed the internal and external computer components by defining **hardware**, port, chip set, and cables. You learned about the **system board,** which contains the **CPU** as well as access to other circuit boards and **peripheral devices**.

Topic B   You examined the details of the **boot process**. You learned about the **POST** and how the **BIOS** find the **operating system (OS)**.

Topic C   In this topic, you examined the **four system resources: IRQs, memory addresses, I/O addresses, and DMA channels**. You discovered how they work together with software and hardware devices.

Independent practice activity

1 Use an operational computer. If your computer has a Reset button, press it, and then watch what happens. If your computer doesn't have a Reset button, turn it off, wait a few seconds, and then turn it back on. Write down every beep, light on/off, and message on the screen that you notice. Compare your notes to others' to verify that you aren't overlooking something.

2 Unplug the keyboard and repeat the step 1 above. Write down what happens that's different.

3 Plug the keyboard back in, unplug the monitor, and repeat the step 1 again. After you reboot, plug the monitor in. Did the computer know the monitor was missing?

4 Put a disk that doesn't contain DOS in drive A, and then press the Reset button. If you don't have a Reset button, press Ctrl+Alt+Del to soft boot. Write down what you observe.

5 Use the System Properties in the Control Panel to observe your computer's memory settings.

Unit 2

The system board

Unit time: 120 minutes

Complete this unit, and you'll know how to:

A Identify the physical components on a system board.

B Define the CPU and chip set.

C Identify the types of ROM and RAM.

D Upgrade some components on a system board.

Topic A: System board components

Explanation The system board is the central site of computer logic circuitry and the location of the most important microchip in the computer, the central processing unit (CPU). A system board's primary purpose is to house the CPU so that all devices can communicate with it and with each other.

Types of system boards

There are two popular types of system boards, the older AT and the newer ATX. The differences between the two types of boards has nothing to do with their overall performance; they differ only in size, convenience features, the type of case into which they fit, and the type of power connections they have. The AT system board has a power connection for 5- and 12-volt lines coming from the power supply. The ATX has lines for 5, 12, and 3.3 volts from the power supply so that it can accommodate the newer CPUs that use less voltage. Each of the two types of boards comes in two different sizes. The following table summarizes these different boards and their form factors. The term *form factor* refers to the size and shape of the board.

System board type	Description
AT	Oldest type of system board still commonly used
	Uses P8 and P9 power connections
	Measures 30.5 cm × 33 cm
Baby AT	Smaller version of AT. Small size is possible because system board logic is stored on a smaller chip set.
	Uses P8 and P9 power connections
	Measures 33 cm × 22 cm
ATX	Developed by Intel for Pentium systems
	Has a more conveniently accessible layout than AT boards
	Includes a power-on switch that can be software-enabled and extra power connections for extra fans
	Uses a single 20-pin power connection called a P1 connector
	Measures 30.5 cm × 24.4 cm
Mini ATX	An ATX board with a more compact design
	Measures 28.4 cm × 20.8 cm

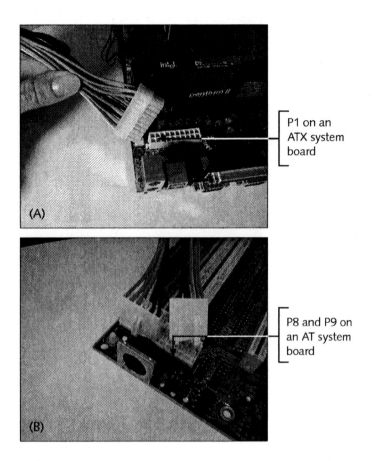

Exhibit 2-1: Power connections on ATX and AT system boards

System board components

The main components on a system board include:

- A CPU and its accompanying chip set
- A system clock
- ROM BIOS
- A CMOS configuration chip and its battery
- RAM
- RAM cache
- A system bus with expansion slots
- Jumpers
- Ports that come directly off the board
- Power supply connections

Of the components listed above, only five can be replaced or upgraded: the CPU, the ROM BIOS chip, the CMOS battery, RAM, and RAM cache. Because these items can be exchanged without returning the system board to the manufacturer, they are called *field replaceable units*.

Do it!   **A-1:   Examining the system board**

Here's how	Here's why
1 Looking at the back of your computer, list the ports that you believe to be coming directly from the system board	
2 Turn off the computer and unplug it	To prepare to remove the cover.
3 Unplug the monitor, mouse, and keyboard	Move the cords out of the way.
4 Remove the cover screws	For a desktop case or tower case, locate and remove the screws on the back of the case. Look for the screws in each corner and one in the top center. Be careful that you don't unscrew any other screws.
5 Slide the cover off	For desktop cases, you need to slide it forward and then up. For tower cases, slide the cover back slightly before lifting it up to remove it. You might also need to remove the panel screws in the back of the case.

6 Identify these components:
    Power supply
    Floppy disk drive
    Hard drive
    System board	

7 List the different circuit boards in the expansion slots	Did you guess correctly about which ports come from the system board?

8 Locate the following components of the system board:
    CPU
    RAM
    Cache memory
    Expansion slots
    Ports
    Power supply connections
    ROM BIOS chip
	You might need to remove some expansion boards if they're blocking your view of the system board. To make reassembling easier, be sure to take notes before removing anything.

9 Reassemble the computer	Replace the cables and any expansion cards you removed. Plug in the keyboard, monitor, and mouse.
10 Turn on the computer	To verify that it's working properly before you put the cover back on. Don't touch the inside of the computer while the power is on.
Turn off the computer	When it's working properly.
11 Replace the cover and screws	

Choosing a system board

Explanation

Selecting a system board is an important decision when you purchase a computer or assemble one from parts, because the system board determines so many of your computer's features.

Depending on which applications and peripheral devices you plan to use with the computer, you can take one of three different approaches to selecting a system board. The first option is to select the board that provides the most room for expansion so you can upgrade and exchange components and add-on devices easily. A second approach is to select the board that best suits the needs of the computer's current configuration, knowing that when you need to upgrade, you'll likely switch to new technology and a new system board. The third approach is to select a system board that meets your present needs with moderate room for expansion.

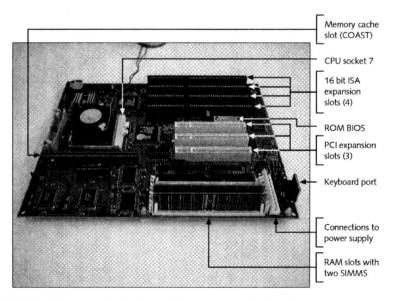

Exhibit 2-2: A typical classic Pentium system board

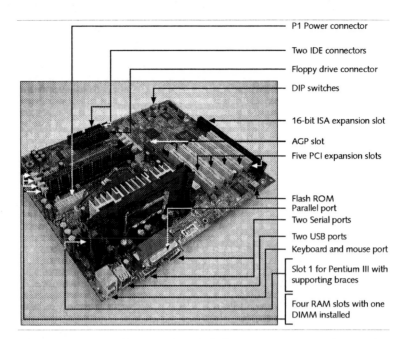

P1 Power connector

Two IDE connectors

Floppy drive connector

DIP switches

16-bit ISA expansion slot

AGP slot

Five PCI expansion slots

Flash ROM
Parallel port
Two Serial ports

Two USB ports
Keyboard and mouse port

Slot 1 for Pentium III with
supporting braces

Four RAM slots with one
DIMM installed

Exhibit 2-3: An ATX system board with a Pentium III and one DIMM module

When you buy a system board, your selection will affect many other factors, including:

- What types and speeds of CPU you can use
- The chip set on the board (which is always already installed)
- Memory cache type and size
- The types and number of expansion slots: EISA, PCI, and AGP
- The type of memory: ECC, EDO, SDRAM, SIMMs, or DIMMs
- The maximum amount of memory you can install on the board and the incremental amounts by which you can upgrade memory
- The type of case you can use
- ROM BIOS, which is already installed
- The type of keyboard connector
- The presence or absence of different types of proprietary video and proprietary local bus slots
- The presence or absence of IDE adapters and a SCSI controller (explained below)
- The presence or absence of COM ports, LPT ports, and a mouse port

Embedded components

Sometimes a system board contains a component that's more commonly offered as a separate device. A component on the board is called an embedded component. One example is support for video. The video port might be on the system board or might require a video card. The cost of a system board with an embedded component is usually less than the combined cost of a system board with an expansion card but no component. If you plan to expand, be cautious about choosing a proprietary board that has many embedded components. A proprietary design using many embedded devices often doesn't easily accept add-on devices from other manufacturers. For example, if you plan to add a more powerful video card, avoid a system board that contains an embedded video controller.

Even though you can often set a switch on the system board to disable the proprietary video controller, there's little advantage to paying the extra money for the on-board video controller.

If you have an embedded component, make sure you can disable the component so that you have the option of using another external component if needed. Disabling a component on the system board is done through jumpers on the board or through CMOS setup.

The following table lists the names and Web addresses of several system board manufacturers.

Manufacturer	Web address
Abit	www.abit.com
American Megatrends, Inc.	www.megatrends.com
ASUS	www.asus.com
Diamond Multimedia	www.diamondmm.com
First International Computer, Inc.	www.fica.com
Giga-Byte Technology Co., Ltd.	www.giga-byte.com
Intel Corporation	www.Intel.com
Supermicro Computer, Inc.	www.supermicro.com
Tyan Computer Corporation	www.tyan.com

System clock

The system board contains a system clock that keeps the beat for many system board activities. Units called megahertz measure clock frequency. One megahertz (MHz) is equal to 1,000,000 beats, or cycles, of the clock per second. A single clock beat or cycle was once the smallest unit of processing the CPU or another device could execute, meaning that it could only do one thing for each beat of the clock. Some CPUs today can perform two activities per clock cycle. Even though how fast a CPU can operate is often referred to as the CPU speed, it's more accurate but less common to speak of the CPU frequency. For example, you might say that a CPU can operate at a frequency of 550 MHz.

A wait state occurs when the CPU must wait for another component, for example when slower dynamic RAM reads or writes data. To allow time for the slow operation, CMOS setup information specifies that the CPU maintain a wait state. If the CPU normally can do something in two clock beats, for example, it's told to wait an extra clock beat, meaning its cycle takes a total of three clock beats. It works for two beats and then waits one beat, which slows performance by 50%. Wait states might be incorporated to slow the CPU so that the rest of the system-board activity can keep up. Wait states are initially set as part of the system board's default settings and are changed in only rare circumstances, such as when the board becomes unstable.

Do it!

A-2: Discussing system boards

Question	Answer
1 What are the two most popular types of system board form factors?	
2 Name 10 components that are contained on a system board.	
3 When is it appropriate to have a Slot 1 on a system board?	
4 Why would you want both ISA and PCI expansion slots on a system board?	
5 What characteristics of the system board architecture determine the amount of memory that a CPU can address?	

The system board 2–9

Topic B: The CPU and the chip set

Explanation IBM and IBM-compatible computers manufactured today use a microprocessor chip made by Intel or one of its competitors. Early CPUs by Intel were identified by model numbers: 8088, 8086, 80286, 386, and 486. The next CPU introduced after the 486 was named the Pentium, and all Intel CPUs after that include Pentium in their names. The model numbers can be written with or without the 80 prefix and are sometimes preceded with an "i" as in 80486, 486 or i486.

Attributes of CPU chips

You need to know how to identify a CPU installed in a system and what performance to expect from that CPU. The following attributes are used to rate CPUs:

- *CPU speed measured in megahertz.* The first CPU used in an IBM PC was the 8088, which worked at about 4.77 MHz, or 4,770,000 clock beats per second. An average speed for a new CPU today is about 550 MHz, or 550,000,000 beats per second.

- *Efficiency of the programming code.* Permanently built into the CPU chip are numerous programs that accomplish fundamental operations, such as how to compare two numbers or how to add two numbers. Less efficient CPUs require more steps to perform these simple operations than more efficient CPUs. These groups of instructions are collectively called the *instruction set.*

- *Word size, sometimes called the internal data path size.* Word size is the largest number of bits the CPU can process in one operation. Word size ranges from 16 bits (2 bytes) to 64 bits (8 bytes).

- *Data path.* The *data path*, sometimes called the external data path size, is the largest number of bits that can be transported into the CPU. The size of the data path is the same as the system bus size, or the number of bits that can be transported along the bus at one time. (The data path ranges from 8 bits to 64 bits.) The word size need not be as large as the data path size; some CPUs can receive more bits than they can process at one time.

- *Maximum number of memory addresses.* A computer case has room for a lot of memory physically housed within the case, but a CPU has only a fixed range of addresses that it can assign to this physical memory. The number of memory addresses that the CPU can assign limits the number of physical memory chips that can be used effectively by a computer. The minimum number of memory addresses a CPU can use is one megabyte (where each byte of memory is assigned a single address). One megabyte is equal to 1024 kilobytes, which is equal to 1024×1024 bytes, or 1,048,576 memory addresses. The maximum number of memory addresses for Pentium CPUs is 4096 megabytes, which is equal to 4 gigabytes.

- *The amount of memory included with the CPU.* Some CPUs have storage for instructions and data built right inside the chip housing. This is called *internal cache*, primary cache, level 1, or L1 cache.

- *Multiprocessing ability.* Some microchips are really two processors in one and can do more than one thing at a time. Others are designed to work in cooperation with other CPUs installed on the same system board.

- *Special functionality.* An example of this is the Pentium MMX CPU, which is designed to manage multimedia devices efficiently.

Of the eight criteria listed above, the three most popular ways of measuring CPU power are speed measured in megahertz, and word size and data path size measured in bits. The criteria for measuring the power of a CPU have changed since the introduction of the Pentium. The words "size" and "path size" are no longer distinguishing qualities because these sizes haven't changed significantly over the last few years. Instead, the criteria generally taken into account when measuring a CPU's power include clock speed, bus speed, internal cache, and, most importantly, the intended functionality of the chip; for example, its ability to handle graphics well (MMX technology).

Relating CPU attributes to bus architecture

Two of the CPU attributes listed above work in relation to the bus architecture. These attributes are the number of memory addresses and data path size. The *data path* size is determined by the width of the bus data path, or the number of parallel wires in the bus data path. The number of memory addresses is determined by the number of traces, or wires, on the bus that are used for memory addresses.

If a data path is 16 bits wide, then there are 16 wires on the bus, each of which is used to transmit one bit. There also are 16 pins connecting to the CPU that can input and output single bits. If a bus has 20 wires dedicated to memory addresses transmitted over the bus, then the CPU can transmit a maximum of 20 bits to define one memory address. Thus, the largest 20-bit base 2 number possible is the maximum number of memory addresses the CPU can use. That number is 1111 1111 1111 1111 1111 in binary, or 1 MB of memory addresses (1,048,576 unique addresses).

Earlier Intel CPUs

The 80386SX chip had a smaller path size than the 80386DX although it was developed later. At the time Intel first manufactured the 80386DX with its 32-bit path size, system board manufacturers could produce at a reasonable cost a system board with a path size of only 16 bits, or 2 bytes. Therefore the system board manufacturers couldn't take advantage of the DX's 32-bit path size and chose not to use the first 80386DX chips. In response to this, Intel produced the cheaper 80386SX chip, which accommodated the smaller path size and kept the cost of the system more reasonable for personal computer users. The 80386SX chip used an internal 32-bit word size but an external 16-bit path size. (Internal refers to operations inside the CPU, and external refers to operations between the inside and outside of the CPU, such as on the bus.) The smaller path size of the 80386SX is the reason it's slower than the 80386DX chip (S stands for single and D for double).

The following table lists the earlier CPUs chronologically based on their introduction in the marketplace. If you look at one of these CPUs, you see it's labeled as 80386SX-16, 80486DX2-50, or another number using a similar convention. The number at the end of the model number, 16 or 50 in the examples, refers to the speed of the CPU in megahertz. The 2 following the 486DX CPU indicates that the chip can work in overdrive mode, which doubles the clock speed to increase the overall speed of the computer. (On some older computers, doubling the clock speed was called turbo mode and was accomplished by pressing a button on the computer case.) Sometimes, system boards and CPUs that work in this overdrive mode overheat, and heat sinks and/or fans must be mounted on top of the CPU.

Model	Approx. speed (MHz)	Word size (bits)	Path size (bits)	Memory addresses (MB)
80386DX	40	32	32	4096
80386SX	33	32	16	16
486DX	60	32	32	4096
486SX	25	32	32	4096
First Pentium	60	32×2	64	4096

For notebook computers, the CPU model number often has an L in it, as in 486SL-20. The L indicates that this microchip is a 486SX that requires a lower voltage than the regular SX; the 20 indicates that the speed is 20 megahertz.

Voltages used by CPUs

Early CPUs—including the 486DX, 80486SX, 80487SX, and 80486DX2—all used 5 volts of electrical current to operate. Later versions of the 80486SX and the 80486DX4 CPUs ran on 3.3 volts. Because the power supply to the system board supplied only 5 and 12 volts, a voltage regulator was used to provide the 3.3 volts. The first Pentium running 60/66 MHz used 5 volts. All other Pentiums, including the Pentium Pro and Pentium II, use 3.3 volts and 2.8 volts.

Coprocessors used with older CPUs

Some older CPU microchips were designed to work hand-in-hand with a secondary microchip processor called a coprocessor. The coprocessor performed calculations for the CPU at a faster speed than the CPU. The coprocessor for the 80386 chip is the 80387. The 486DX has the coprocessor built into the CPU housing. The 486SX has the coprocessor portion of the chip disabled. Software must be written to make use of a coprocessor. Most software today assumes you have a 486DX or Pentium chip and writes its code to take advantage of this coprocessor capability.

The Pentium and its competitors

The latest CPU microchips by Intel are the Pentium series of chips. A Pentium chip has two arithmetic logic units, meaning that it can perform two calculations at the same time; it's therefore a true multiprocessor. Pentiums have a 64-bit external path size and two 32-bit internal paths, one for each arithmetic logic unit.

Comparing chips

To compare the Pentium family of chips and the Pentium competitors, you need some background on bus speed, processor speed, multiplier, and memory cache.

Bus speed is the speed at which data moves on a *bus*. Each bus runs at a certain speed, some faster than others. Only the fastest bus connects directly to the CPU. This bus goes by many names, including

- System board bus, or the system bus, because it's the main bus on the system board and connects directly to the CPU
- Pentium bus because it connects directly to the Pentium
- Host bus because other buses connect to it to get to the CPU
- *Memory bus* because it connects the CPU to RAM

The three most common speeds for the memory bus are 66 MHz, 75 MHz, 100 MHz, 133 MHz, and 200 MHz, although the bus can operate at several other speeds, depending on how jumpers are set on the system board. Sometimes, the memory bus speed is called the bus clock because the pulses generated on the clock line of the bus determine its speed. Other slower buses connect to the memory bus, which serves as the go-between for other buses and the CPU.

Tip: When you read that Intel supports a system board speed of 66 and 100 MHz, and that its competitors support bus speeds of 75 MHz, these speeds all refer to the memory bus speed.

Processor speed is the speed at which the CPU is operating internally. If the CPU operates at 150 MHz internally, but 75 MHz externally, the processor speed is 150 MHz and the memory bus speed is 75 MHz. The CPU is operating at twice the speed of the bus. This factor is called the *multiplier*. If you multiply the memory bus speed by the multiplier, you get the processor speed or the speed of the CPU.

```
Memory bus speed × multiplier = processor speed
```

Jumpers on the system board are used to set the memory bus speed or bus clock. Jumpers are then used to set the multiplier, which in turn determines the CPU speed or processor speed. Common multipliers are 1.5, 2, 2.5, 3, 3.5, and 4.

A *memory cache* is a small amount of RAM (referred to as static RAM or SRAM) that's much faster than the rest of RAM, which is called dynamic RAM (DRAM) because it loses its data rapidly and must be refreshed often. Refreshing RAM takes time. SRAM doesn't need refreshing because it can hold its data as long as power is available. Therefore, both programming code and data can be stored temporarily in this faster static RAM cache to speed up the CPU processing of both. The size of the cache a CPU can support is a measure of its performance, especially during intense calculations.

A memory cache that's included on the CPU microchip itself is called *internal cache*, primary cache, Level 1, or L1 cache. A cache outside of the CPU microchip is called *external cache,* secondary cache, Level 2, or L2 cache. L2 caches are usually 128K, 256K, 512K, or 1 MB in size. In the past, all L2 cache was contained on the system board. Beginning with the Pentium Pro, some L2 cache has been included inside the Pentium physical housing—not on the CPU microchip as with L1 cache—but on a tiny circuit board with the CPU chip, within the same housing. The bus between the processor and the L2 cache is called the *backside bus* or cache bus and isn't visible, because it's completely contained inside the CPU housing. On the Pentium Pro and Pentium III, this cache bus runs at half the speed of the processor.

In contrast, the bus that connects the CPU to memory outside the housing is called the *frontside bus,* and can be seen on the system board. The frontside bus is the same bus as the memory bus. (Now the memory bus has one more name!)

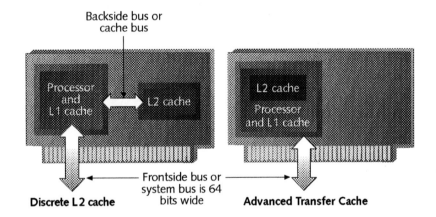

Exhibit 2-4: Comparing discrete L2 cache and advanced transfer cache

More recently, some Pentium III CPUs contain L2 cache directly on the same die as the processor core that's called Advanced Transfer Cache (ATC), making it difficult to distinguish between L1 and L2 cache. ATC makes it possible for the Pentium III to fit on a smaller and less expensive form factor (the shape and size of a device). Pentium III L2 cache stored on a separate microchip within the CPU housing is called discrete L2 cache. With discrete L2 cache, the Pentium III cache bus is 256 bits wide and runs at the same speed as the processor. All Pentium III processors have either 512K of discrete cache or 256K of ATC cache.

The following table lists the five types of Pentium CPUs on the market today. Variations of the Pentium II processor include the Celeron and Xeon.

Processor	Current processor speeds (MHz)	Primary L1 Cache	Secondary L2 Cache	System Bus Speeds (MHz)
Classic Pentium	60, 66, 75, 90, 100, 120, 133, 150, 166, 200	16K	None	66
Pentium MMX	133, 150, 166, 200, 233, 266	32K	None	66
Pentium Pro	150, 166, 180, 200	16K	256K, 512K, or 1MB	60, 66
Pentium II	233, 266, 300, 333, 350, 366, 400, 450	32K	256K, 512K	66, 100
Celeron	266, 300, 333, 366, 400, 433, 450 (mobile), 466, 500, 533, 566, 600	32K	Some have 128K	66, 100 (mobile only)
Pentium II Xeon	400, 450	32K	512K, 1 MB, or 2 MB	100
Pentium III	400, 450, 500, 533, 550, 600, 650, 667, 700, 733, 750, 800, 850, 866, 933, 1 GHz	32K	256K, 512K	100, 133
Pentium III Xeon	500, 550, 600, 667, 700, 733, 800, 866	32K	256K to 2 MB	100, 133

Classic Pentium

The first Pentium chip was introduced in March 1993, and has now become affectionately known as the Classic Pentium. Early problems with this first Pentium (which Intel later resolved) could cause errors such as wrong calculations on spreadsheets. The Classic Pentium is no longer manufactured.

Pentium MMX

The Pentium MMX (Multimedia Extension) targets the home market. It speeds up graphical applications and performs well with games and multimedia software.

Pentium Pro

Intel recommends the Pentium Pro for 32-bit applications that rely heavily on fast access to large amounts of cache memory. It was the first Pentium to offer Level 2 cache inside the CPU housing, as well as other features not available on the Classic Pentium. The Pentium Pro is popular for computing-intensive workstations and servers but, because it doesn't perform well in real mode, it doesn't perform well with older 16-bit applications software written for DOS or Windows 3.x.

Pentium II

The Pentium II is designed for graphics-intensive workstations and servers, and works well with 3-D graphic manipulation, CAD (computer-aided design), and multimedia presentations. The Pentium II is the first Pentium to use a slot (Slot 1) instead of a socket to connect to the system board. Intel chose to patent Slot 1, and, in doing so, forced its competitors to stay with the slower socket technology as they developed equivalent processors. The Pentium II can use the 100-MHz memory bus with processor speeds up to 450 MHz.

The Celeron processor is a low-end Pentium II processor that targets the low-end multimedia PC market segment. It uses Level 2 cache within the processor housing and works well with Windows 9x and the most common applications.

The Xeon processor is a fast, high-end Pentium II processor designed exclusively for powerful servers and workstations. It can support up to eight processors in one computer and is recommended for use with Windows NT and UNIX operating systems.

Pentium III

The Pentium III uses either a slot or a socket and runs with the 100-MHz or 133-MHz memory bus with a processor speed up to 1 GHz. The Pentium III introduced Intel's new performance enhancement called SSE, for Streaming SIMD Extensions. (SIMD stands for single instruction multiple data, and is a method used by MMX to speed up multimedia processing.) SSE is a new instruction set designed to improve multimedia processing even further. SSE will be an improvement over MMX as soon as operating systems and applications software are written to use it.

The Pentium III Xeon is a high-end Pentium III processor that runs on the 133 MHz system bus and is designed for mid-range servers and high-end workstations. It uses a 330-pin slot called the SC330 (slot connector 330), sometimes called Slot 2, and is contained within a cartridge called a Single Edge Contact Cartridge (SECC).

Exhibit 2-5: Pentium III contained in a SECC cartridge in Slot 1

The Pentium competitors

Intel's two primary competitors are AMD and Cyrix. Both companies have advertised goals to produce CPUs that are just as fast and powerful as Intel's, but at a lower cost. For the latest information about the Pentium and its competitors, see these Web sites: www.amd.com, www.cyrix.com, and www.intel.com.

The following table lists the two early processors that competed with Intel's Classic Pentium. Neither of these processors is manufactured today, although plenty of them are still in use.

Processor	Current processor speeds (MHz)	Bus speeds	Multiplier	Internal or primary cache
Cyrix 6x86 or M1	150	75	2	16K
AMD K5	75, 90, 100, 116, 133	50, 60, 66	1.5 or 1.75	24K

The AMD K5 offers an unusual assortment of clock speeds and bus speeds. One disadvantage of the Cyrix 6x86 is that it uses an external bus speed of 75 MHz, which isn't supported by Intel for its chip set (that is, Intel doesn't guarantee this bus speed to be stable). Therefore, if a system uses this Cyrix chip, the system board must use another brand of chip set other than the popular Intel brand or, if the Intel chip set is used, the system board must be set to run at a bus speed that isn't guaranteed by Intel to be stable.

Running a system board at a higher speed than that suggested by the manufacturer is called *overclocking* and isn't recommended, because the speed isn't guaranteed to be stable by Intel. VIA and SiS both have chip sets that support the memory bus speeds needed by the Cyrix CPUs.

Competitors of the advanced Pentiums

The following table shows the performance ratings of five competitors of the Pentium advanced processors. Cyrix processors such as the Cyrix III shown in Exhibit 2-6 use sockets that also can be used by Intel Pentium processors, but AMD takes a different approach. AMD processors that can run on a 100 MHz system bus use a special type of socket called Super Socket 7 that supports an AGP video slot and 100 MHz system bus. AGP refers to a special port for video cards called the accelerated graphics port (AGP), which is discussed later in the chapter. The AMD Athlon uses a proprietary 242-pin slot called Slot A that looks like the Intel Slot 1, also with 242 pins.

Processor	Current clock speeds (MHz)	Compares to	System bus speed (MHz)	Socket or slot
Cyrix M II	300, 333, and 350	Pentium II, Celeron	66, 75, 83, 95, 100	Socket 7
Cyrix III	433, 466, 500, 533	Pentium III, Celeron	66, 100, 133	Socket 370
AMD-K6-2	166, 200, 266, 300, 333, 350, 366, 380, 400, 450, 475	Pentium II, Celeron	66, 95, 100	Socket 7 or Super Socket 7
AMD-K6-III	350, 366, 380, 400, 433, 450	Pentium II	100	Super Socket 7
AMD Athlon	600, 650, 700, 750, 800, 850, 900, 950, 1 GHz	Pentium III	200	Slot A

Exhibit 2-6: The Cyrix III

Intel's Itanium: The next generation processor

The next processor scheduled to be released by Intel before this book goes to print is the Itanium, Intel's first 64-bit processor for microcomputers. Earlier computers always operated in real mode, which used a 16-bit data path. Later, protected mode was introduced, which uses a 32-bit data path. Almost all applications written today use 32-bit protected mode because all CPUs manufactured today for microcomputers use a 32-bit data path. The Itanium will change all that. To take full advantage of the Itanium's power, software developers must redo their applications to use 64-bit processing, and operating systems must be written to use 64-bit data transfers. Microsoft is expected to provide a 64-bit version of Windows 2000 when Itanium becomes available. Intel has promised that the Itanium will provide backward compatibility with older 32-bit applications.

CPUs that use RISC technology

In addition to CPUs becoming faster and using a wider data path, another trend in chip design is the increased use of RISC (reduced instruction set computer) technology. RISC chips are challenging the monopoly in the chip market held by CISC (complex instruction set computer) chips. (CISC is the name given to traditional chip design.) The difference between the RISC and CISC technologies is the number of instructions (called the instruction set) contained directly on the CPU chip itself. With RISC technology, the CPU is limited to a very few instructions that can execute in a single clock cycle. One advantage that RISC chips have over CISC chips is that, because they have only a small number of operating instructions to perform, they can process much faster when few complex calculations are required. This feature makes RISC chips ideal for video or telecommunications applications. They also are easier and cheaper to manufacture.

Most Intel chips use the CISC technology to maintain compatibility with older systems and software, although the Pentium II uses a combination of both technologies. The K6 by AMD use the RISC technology. Cyrix, on the other hand, has chosen to stay with CISC technology, contending that it's better than RISC. Most CPU manufacturers for high-end servers have a version of a RISC chip. Sun Microsystems has the SPARC chip, Digital Equipment Corporation (DEC) has the MIPS and Alpha, and IBM Corporation has the RS 6000.

CPU cooling fans

Because a CPU generates so much heat, most computer systems use a cooling fan to keep the temperature below the Intel maximum allowed limit of 185° F. Good CPU cooling fans can maintain the temperature at 90 to 110° F. Use cooling fans to prevent system errors and to prolong the life of the CPU. The ball-bearing cooling fans last longer than other kinds.

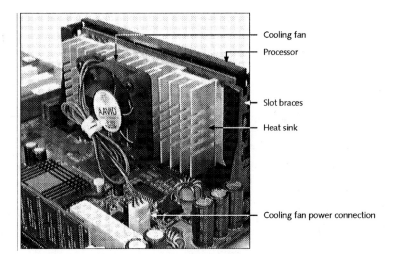

Exhibit 2-7: A CPU cooling fan

The cooling fan usually fits on top of the CPU with a wire or plastic clip. A cream-like thermal compound made of silicon is placed between the fan and the CPU. This compound draws heat from the CPU and passes it to the fan. The thermal compound transmits heat better than air and makes the connection between the fan and the CPU airtight. The fan is equipped with a power connector that connects to one of the power cables coming from the power supply.

Some newer CPUs generate so much heat that they need extra cooling. The chips might have a heat sink attached to them and a large fan attached on top of the sink or to the side of the case, blowing over the heat sink. A *heat sink* is a clip-on device that mounts on top of the CPU. Fingers or fins at the base of the heat sink pull the heat away from the CPU.

Some system boards feature a power connection for the cooling fan that sounds an alarm if the fan stops working. Because the fan is a mechanical device, it's more likely to fail than the electronic devices inside the case. To protect the expensive CPU, you can purchase a heat sensor for a few dollars. The sensor plugs into a power connection coming from the power supply and is mounted on the side of the case. It sounds an alarm when the inside of the case gets too hot.

CPU form factors

Intel currently has five form factors used to house its processors:

- SEP (Single Edge Processor): The processor isn't completely covered by the black plastic housing, making the circuit board visible at the bottom of the housing. The first Celeron processors used the SEP form factor in Slot 1.
- SECC (Single Edge Contact Cartridge): The processor is completely covered with a black plastic housing and a heat sink and fan is attached to the housing. You can't see the circuit board or edge connector in a SECC form factor. The Pentium II and Pentium III use a SECC form factor in Slot 1.
- SECC2 (Single Edge Contact Cartridge, version 2): The SECC2 processor has a heat sink and fan similar to the SECC, but the edge connector on the processor circuit board is visible at the bottom of the housing. Pentium II and Pentium III use the SECC2 form factor.
- PPGA (Plastic Pin Grid Array): The processor is housed in a square box designed to fit flat into Socket 370. Pins are on the underside of the flat housing and heat sinks or fans can be attached to the top of the housing using a thermal plate or heat spreader. Current Celeron processors use this form factor.
- FC-PGA (Flip Chip Pin Grid Array): This form factor looks like the PPGA form factor and uses Socket 370. Heat sinks or fans can be attached directly to the top of the package. The Pentium III uses FC-PGA as one of its two form factors.

Exhibit 2-8: The Intel Celeron processor is housed in the PPGA form factor that has pins on the underside that insert into Socket 370

CPU slots and sockets

A *slot* or socket is the physical connection used to connect a device (the CPU) to the system board. The type of socket or slot supplied by the system board for the processor must match that required by the processor. The following table lists several of the types of sockets used by CPUs.

Connector name	Used by CPU	Number of pins	Voltage
Socket 4	Classic Pentium 60/66	273 pins 21 × 21 PGA grid	5 V
Socket 5	Classic Pentium 75/ 90/ 100/ 120	320 pins 37 × 37 SPGA grid	3.3 V
Socket 6	Not used	235 pins 19 × 19 PGA grid	3.3 V
Socket 7	Pentium MMX, Fast Classic Pentium, AMD K5, AMD K6, Cyrix M	321 pins 37 × 37 SPGA grid	2.5 V to 3.3 V
Super Socket 7	AMD K6-2, AMD K6-III	321 pins 37 × 37 SPGA grid	2.5 V to 3.3 V
Socket 8	Pentium Pro	387 pins 24 × 26 SPGA grid	3.3 V
Socket 370 or PGA370 Socket	Pentium III FC-PGA, Celeron PPGA, Cyrix III	370 pins SPGA grid	1.5 V or 2 V

Connector name	Used by CPU	Number of pins	Voltage
Slot 1or SC242	Pentium II, III	242 pins in 2 rows Rectangular shape	2.8 V to 3.3 V
Slot A	AMD Athlon	242 pins in 2 rows Rectangular shape	1.3 V to 2.05 V
Slot 2 or SC330	Pentium II Xeon, Pentium III Xeon	330 pins in 2 rows Rectangular shape	1.5 V to 3.5 V

The 486 and earlier Pentiums used a *pin grid array (PGA)* socket where the pins were aligned in uniform rows around the socket. Later sockets use a *staggered pin grid array (SPGA)* where pins are staggered over the socket to squeeze more pins into a smal l space. Socket 7 is used on system boards that run at 66 MHz, and Super Socket 7 is used on the newer 100-MHz system boards. Super Socket 7 was designed for AMD CPUs, which compete with the Intel Pentium II.

Socket 370 is used by two types of processors w ith two types of package form factors: PPGA (Plastic Pin Grid Array) and FC-PGA (Flip Chip Pin Grid Array). Both form factors have pins on the underside of the processor that insert into the pin holes on the Socket 370. Socket 370 also is used by the Cyrix III and a version of the Pentium III designed for smaller computer cases called the Pentium III FC -PGA. The following exhibit shows socket comparisons.

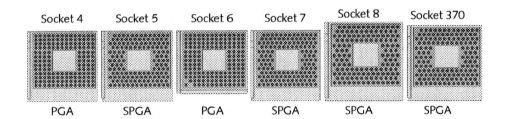

Exhibit 2-9: Examples of the CPU socket design

Earlier CPU sockets, called *dual inline pin package* (DIPP) sockets, were rectangular with two rows of pins down each side. PGA and SPGA sockets are a ll square or close to it. DIPP and some PGA sockets, called *low insertion force (LIF)* sockets, were somewhat troublesome to install because it was difficult to apply even force when inserting them. Current CPU sock ets are called *zero insertion force (ZIF)* sockets and have a small lever on the side of the socket that lifts the CPU up and out of the socket. If you push the lever down, the CPU moves into its pin connectors wit h equal force over the entire housing. The heat sink or fan clips on to the top of the CPU. With this method, you can easily remove the CPU and replace it with another if necessary.

Slot 1, Slot A, and Slot 2 are all designed to accommodate processors using the SEP or SECC housing that stand on their end much like an expansion card. The CPU is secured in the slot with clips on each side of the slot. You can attach a heat sink or cooling fan to the side of the CPU case. The Pentium II and Pentium III use Slot 1 and the Xeon versions of these processors use the longer Slot 2. AMD processors use Slot A.

The Celeron processor uses the PPGA form factor and Socket 370. Some system boards that have a Slot 1 can accommodate the Celeron processor by using a riser CPU card. The riser card inserts into Slot 1 and the Celeron processor inserts into Socket 370 on the riser card. With this feature you can upgrade an older Pentium II system to the faster Celeron.

The Pentium III processor uses two types of form factors: the SECC 2 and the FC-PGA. The SECC 2 is inserted into Slot 1 and the FC-PGA uses Socket 370. However, some older system boards that have a Socket 370 aren't designed to support the Pentium III FC-PGA. The Celeron processor uses 2.00 volts and the Pentium III FC-PGA uses either 1.60 or 1.65 volts. A system board built to support only the Celeron might not recognize the need to decrease the voltage for the Pentium III FC-PGA processor. This overvoltage can damage the Pentium III. Always consult the system board documentation to know what processors the board can support.

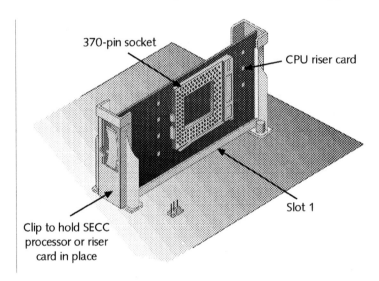

Exhibit 2-10: A riser card can be used to install a Celeron processor into a system board with Slot 1

CPU voltage regulator

Different CPUs require different amounts of voltage on the system board. Some CPUs require one voltage amount for external operations and another amount for internal operations. CPUs that require two different voltages are called *dual voltage CPUs.* The others are called *single voltage CPUs.* A CPU voltage regulator controls the amount of voltage on the system board. Some CPUs require that you set the jumpers on the system board to control the voltage, and other CPUs automatically control the voltage without your involvement.

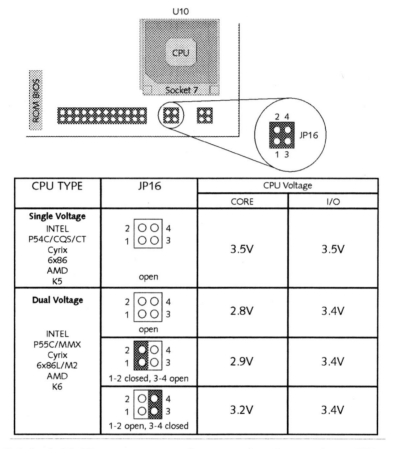

CPU TYPE	JP16	CPU Voltage	
		CORE	I/O
Single Voltage INTEL P54C/CQS/CT Cyrix 6x86 AMD K5	2 ☐☐ 4 1 ☐☐ 3 open	3.5V	3.5V
Dual Voltage INTEL P55C/MMX Cyrix 6x86L/M2 AMD K6	2 ☐☐ 4 1 ☐☐ 3 open	2.8V	3.4V
	2 ■☐ 4 1 ■☐ 3 1-2 closed, 3-4 open	2.9V	3.4V
	2 ☐■ 4 1 ☐■ 3 1-2 open, 3-4 closed	3.2V	3.4V

Exhibit 2-11: Using jumpers on the system board to configure CPU voltage regulator

B-1: Defining CPU components

Question	Answer
1 All CPUs are the same size. True or false?	
2 How many power connectors attach to a Baby AT system board?	
3 CPU voltage varies depending on the generation and brand name of the CPU. True or false?	
4 Chip pullers are used to remove the heat sink from the top of the CPU. True or false?	
5 ZIF sockets are used to connect the memory to the system board. True or false?	
6 Which is faster: the 8088 processor or the 486 processor?	
7 You are currently employed as a PC support technician at the Heavenly Palace Factory. Your supervisor wants to upgrade his 486 computer to a Pentium 166. He asks you to tell him what parts he will need to purchase for this upgrade. List the minimum parts your supervisor needs.	
8 You are at your local computer store and are considering upgrading your home PC to a Pentium Pro. Will you be able to use the CPU cooling fan from your 486 at home if you purchase the Pentium Pro chip?	

The chip set

Explanation

A *chip set* is a set of chips on the system board that collectively controls the memory cache, external buses, and some peripherals. Intel makes the most popular chip sets, which are listed in the following table.

The Intel 440BX chip set is the first PC chip set to offer a memory bus that runs at 100 MHz, which enables the Pentium II running at 350 MHz or 400 MHz to reach its full potential for performance in desktop PCs. Before this chip set, the memory bus slowed the CPU speed down. The 440BX chip set also is the first chip set to use the mobile version of the Pentium II processor for notebooks. You will often see this chip set advertised with AGP in the name; for example, the Intel 440BX AGP chip set. AGP refers to a special port for video cards called the *accelerated graphics port (AGP)*. The 440GX chip set is an evolution of the 440BX

Common name	Model #	Comments
Intel i800 Series	840	Designed for multiprocessor systems using Pentium II Xeon for Pentium III Xeon processors
	820	Designed for Pentium II and Pentium III systems
	810	First Intel chip set to eliminate the PCI bus as the main device interconnection
Orion	450GX, KX	Supports the Pentium Pro (includes support for multiprocessors)
	450NX	Designed for servers with multiple Pentium II or Pentium III Xeon processors
Natoma	440FX	Supports the Pentium Pro and Pentium II
	440BX	Designed for servers and workstations
	440GX	Designed for servers and workstations using the Pentium II Xeon and Pentium III Xeon processors
	440ZX	Designed for entry-level PCs using the Pentium II
	440LX	Designed for the Celeron processors
	440MX	Designed for notebook computers (M=mobile)
	440EX	Designed for smaller system boards, such as the mini-ATX

Common name	Model #	Comments
Triton III	430VX	Value chip set, supports SDAM
	430MX	Used for notebooks (M = mobile)
	430TX	Supports SDRAM, ultra DMA; replaced the VX and MX
Triton III	430VX	Value chip set, supports SDAM
	430MX	Used for notebooks (M = mobile)
	430TX	Supports SDRAM, ultra DMA; replaced the VX and MX
Triton II	430HX	High performance, supports dual CPUs
Triton I	430FX	The oldest chip set, no longer produced

The 400 series of Intel chip sets use the PCI bus as the interconnection between slower buses and the system bus. The Intel i800 series of chip sets introduces a new way for I/O buses to relate to the faster system bus and ultimately to the CPU. With the i800 series, the interconnection between buses is done using a hub interface architecture whereby all I/O buses connect to a hub that connects to the system bus. This hub is called *Hub Interface* and the architecture is called the *Accelerated Hub Architecture*. The fast end of the hub that contains the graphics and memory controller (GMCH) connects to the system bus and is called the hub's North Bridge. The slower end of the hub, called the South Bridge, contains the I/O Controller Hub (ICH). All I/O devices except display and memory connect to the hub using the slower South Bridge.

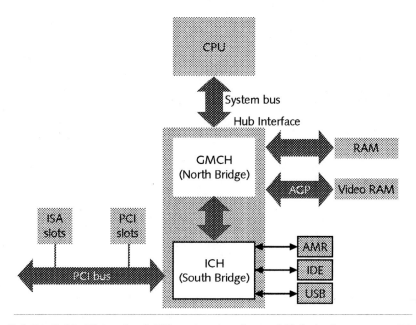

Exhibit 2-12: Using Intel 800 series Accelerated Hub Architecture, a Hub Interface is used to connect slower I/O buses to the system bus

The following companies manufacture chip sets:

- Intel Corporation
- AMD, Inc.
- Cyrix Corporation
- Silicon Integrated Systems Corp. (known as SiS)
- Ali, Inc.
- Standard Microsystems Corp.
- United Microelectronics Corp.
- VIA Technology, Inc.
- VLSI Technology, Inc.

Chip sets that compete with Intel

SiS uses a faster North Bridge and slower South Bridge approach to managing slower I/O buses interconnecting with a faster system bus. The SiS620 chip set includes a digital video interface for digital flat panel display screens, and supports a 100MHz system bus and an advanced hard drive interface called Ultra DMA.

The Aladdin V chip set from Ali supports Socket 7 processors and the 100MHz system bus speed. VIA in combination with AMD has the Apollo MVP3 chip set that supports AGP, 100-MHz bus speed, and Socket 7.

Currently, Intel dominates the chip set market for several reasons. The major advantage that Intel has over other chip set manufacturers is that the company knows more about their Intel CPUs than anyone else, and the chip sets are therefore more compatible with the Pentium family of CPUs. Intel's investment in research and development has enabled their engineers to invent the PCI bus, the universal serial bus, the advanced graphics port (AGP), and more recently the Accelerated Hub Architecture.

Do it!

B-2: Removing and reinstalling the CPU

Here's how
1 Power off your lab workstation
Unplug the system unit's power cord
Verify that you are properly grounded
2 Remove the case from your lab workstation
3 Locate the CPU
4 If the computer has a heat sink, release the heat sink from the top of the CPU (If the heat sink doesn't come off with ease, leave it on top of the CPU.)
5 Release the ZIF lever
6 Note how the CPU is currently installed (This will be important when you try to reinstall the CPU. Specifically, note the orientation of the writing on the CPU.)
7 Use the chip pulling tool to remove your CPU (*Warning*: When removing your CPU, pull evenly straight up on the CPU; don't bend it from side to side.)
8 Stand clear of the case and plug in the power cord
9 Power on the PC and observe what happens to the PC without a CPU
10 Power off the workstation

11 Remember which direction the CPU should be facing and gently slide it back into the correct position

Lock the CPU into position by using the ZIF lever

If necessary, replace the heat sink on top of the CPU

12 Stand clear of the case and plug in the power cord

Power on the PC and verify that the system boots properly

13 Power off the PC and unplug the power cord

14 Replace the case

15 Plug in the system unit and power it on

16 Power off the PC

Topic C: ROM BIOS and RAM

Explanation

There is one ROM chip on the system board that contains BIOS, which manages the startup process (startup BIOS) and many basic I/O functions of the system (system BIOS). Phoenix Software, Award Software, and American Megatrends, Inc. (AMI) write the most well-known and dependable ROM code for PCs. When selecting a PC clone, make sure you know who wrote the ROM BIOS code. If you select code written by one of these companies, your ROM BIOS will be compatible with most software.

Identifying the BIOS manufacturer

An easy way to identify the name of the BIOS manufacturer without having to remove the case cover is to watch the boot process. The name of the BIOS manufacturer appears at the beginning of this process. You also can look for identifying information written on top of the chip. The ROM BIOS chip is easy to spot because it's larger than most chips and often has a shiny plastic label on it, which lists the manufacturer's name, the date of manufacture, and the serial number of the chip. This information is important on occasions when you need to identify the chip precisely, such as when selecting the correct upgrade for the chip.

In the past, if the ROM BIOS needed upgrading—either because of new hardware or software added to the system or because the BIOS was causing errors—this meant exchanging the chip. The chip is usually socketed in, not soldered, for easy exchange. A newer kind of ROM, called Flash ROM, is becoming increasingly popular because upgraded versions of the BIOS can be written to it without having to physically replace the chip.

You need to know the following things about your BIOS:

- Does it support Plug and Play?
- Does it support large hard drives?
- Is the BIOS chip a Flash ROM chip?

The single ROM BIOS chip on the system board contains only a portion of the total BIOS code needed to interface with all the hardware components in the system. Understanding that BIOS programs can come from several sources helps in solving memory problems and other problems that arise from resource conflicts.

The total BIOS in your system

Some expansion cards, such as a network interface card (NIC) or a video/graphics card, also have ROM chips on them containing BIOS code. The operating system uses the programs stored on these ROM chips to communicate with the peripheral devices. During the boot process, the expansion card tells the startup program the memory addresses that it requires to access its ROM code, usually in the upper memory area between 640K and 1024K when running in real mode. The ROM code from these boards becomes part of the total BIOS that the OS uses to communicate with peripherals. Usually these boards reserve certain addresses of upper memory for their exclusive use. Problems referred to as *hardware configuration conflicts* can occur if two boards request the same addresses in upper memory.

Exhibit 1-13 shows how the programming code from various ROM BIOS chips can be mapped onto the memory addresses managed by the CPU. The areas of upper memory are labeled the F range and the C range. In hex notation, upper memory addresses are numbered A0000 to FFFFF. Because of these hex numbers, the divisions of upper memory are often referred to as the A range, B range, C range, and so on up to F range.

Memory is viewed logically as a series of memory addresses that can be assigned to physical memory devices, such as a SIMM on the system board, a ROM BIOS chip on the system board, or a ROM chip on a network card. After booting is complete, most if not all of the BIOS on the system is shown to exist and has requested memory addresses. Each memory device is assigned a different address in upper memory.

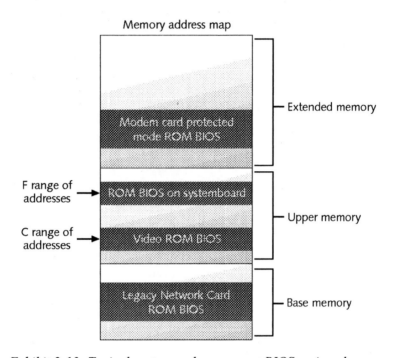

Exhibit 2-13: Typical system and component BIOS assigned memory addresses

If the programming code from the ROM BIOS chips also is copied into RAM, this is called *shadowing ROM* or sometimes Shadow RAM. The terms indicate that RAM is shadowing ROM code. In the setup of your computer, you usually have the choice of whether to shadow System BIOS. For DOS and Windows 9x, accept the default setting for this option.

Plug and Play BIOS

Plug and Play (PnP) is a term that applies to both the Windows 9x OS and to some ROM BIOS. It means that rather than resetting DIP switches and jumpers, the OS and the BIOS automatically configure hardware devices to reduce or eliminate conflicting requests for system resources, such as I/O addresses, IRQs, DMA channels, or upper memory addresses. Windows 9x Plug and Play assigns these resources to a device only if the device allows it. For example, if a legacy sound card requires a certain group of upper memory addresses that are hard coded into its on-board BIOS, then Windows 9x Plug and Play can't change the code. *Hard coded* means the code can't be changed. Plug and Play simply tries to work around the problem as best it can. If two non-Plug-and-Play hardware devices require the same resource and their BIOS doesn't provide for accepting a substitute, these two devices can't coexist on the same PC.

Newer devices that are Plug and Play compliant are more cooperative. At startup, they simply request to work and then wait for the OS to assign the resources they need. Windows 9x tries to do that even if the system BIOS is Plug and Play BIOS. Plug and Play BIOS does some of the upfront work for Windows, the way that an efficient secretary organizes a boss's work for the day. At startup, it's the Startup BIOS that examines the hardware devices present, takes inventory, and then loads the OS. Part of the job of Plug and Play BIOS is to collect information about the devices and the resources they require and later to work with Windows 9x to assign the resources.

ESCD (extended system configuration data) Plug and Play BIOS goes even further, creating a list of all the things you have done manually to the configuration that Plug and Play doesn't do on its own. This ESCD list is written to the BIOS chip so that the next time you boot, the Startup BIOS can faithfully relate that information to Windows 9x. The BIOS chip for ESCD BIOS is a special RAM chip called Permanent RAM, or PRAM, that can hold data written to it without the benefit of a battery, which the CMOS setup chip requires.

Most ROM BIOS chips made after the end of 1994 are Plug and Play. Windows 9x can use most—but not all—of its Plug and Play abilities without Plug and Play BIOS. If you are buying a new PC, accept nothing less than Plug and Play BIOS. As more and more devices become Plug and Play compliant, the time will come when installing a new device on a PC will be just as error-free and easy to do as it is on a Mac. For years, Apple has known about and used the same concepts that are used in Plug and Play.

When BIOS is incompatible with hardware or software

BIOS is a hybrid of two worlds. Technically, it's both hardware and software—it's really the intersection point of the two—and must communicate with both well. When hardware and software change, BIOS might need to change too. In the past, most users upgraded BIOS because new hardware was incompatible with it. Sometimes, however, you need to upgrade BIOS to accommodate new software, such as Plug and Play.

Historically, when a new device became available, such as the 3½-inch floppy disk drive, PCs sometimes could not use the new device until the BIOS was upgraded. This was done by replacing the old BIOS chip with a new chip that supported the new device. Now, however, it's much easier. Most of today's new devices aren't supported by the System BIOS at all, but by device drivers that are software programs installed on the hard drive as add-on parts of the OS. But, if some new feature does require an upgrade to BIOS, you can do the upgrade with Flash ROM. Installing a larger hard drive is an example of a hardware upgrade that might require a BIOS upgrade because the hard drive is incompatible with the existing BIOS. Older BIOS supports only those hard drives with a 504 MB capacity. If you have this problem—large drive, old BIOS— you can solve it in one of two ways: either upgrade BIOS or use special software designed to get around the problem. Often the device manufacturer supplies the software.

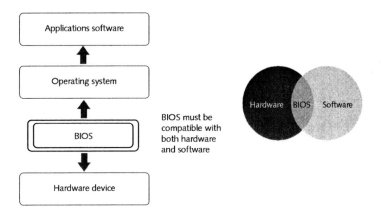

Exhibit 2-14: BIOS can serve as the hardware/software interface

Flash ROM

Technically speaking, *Flash ROM* is called EEPROM (electronically erasable programmable read-only memory), which means you can change the programming on the chip through software on your PC. The updated programming will be retained— even when you turn off your PC for long periods of time—until you change it again. With Flash ROM, you can upgrade system BIOS without having to replace the ROM chip.

As more devices become Plug and Play compliant, Plug and Play BIOS will become more sophisticated. Expect to upgrade to Plug and Play BIOS over time. Additionally, makers of BIOS code are likely to change BIOS frequently because it's so easy for them to provide the upgrade on the Internet. You can get upgraded BIOS code from manufacturers' Web sites or disks or from third-party BIOS resellers' Web sites or disks.

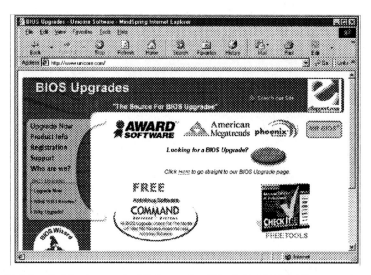

Exhibit 2-15: A sample Web site for Flash ROM BIOS upgrades

To upgrade Flash ROM, follow the directions that came with your system board and the upgrade software itself. Generally, you'll perform these tasks:

1　Set a jumper on the system board telling the BIOS to expect an upgrade of itself.

2　Copy the BIOS software upgrade to a bootable disk.

3　Boot from the disk and follow the menu options to upgrade the BIOS.

4　Set the jumper back to its original setting, reboot the system, and verify that everything is working.

Be very careful that you upgrade the BIOS with the correct upgrade and that you follow the manufacturer instructions correctly. Upgrading incorrectly could make your system BIOS useless. If you're not sure you're using the correct upgrade, don't guess. Check with technical support for your BIOS before moving forward. Before you call technical support, have the information that is written on the BIOS chip label available.

Do it!

C-1:   Discussing ROM BIOS

Question	Answer
1 How can you identify the manufacturer of a BIOS chip?	
2 Why do you need to know the manufacturer's name?	
3 What is PnP BIOS?	
4 Why is it said that BIOS is both hardware and software?	
5 What is Flash ROM?	

RAM (Random Access Memory)

Explanation

In older machines, RAM existed as individual chips socketed to the system board in banks or rows of nine chips each. Each bank held one byte by storing one bit in each chip, with the ninth chip holding a *parity* bit. On older PCs, the parity chip was separated a little from the other eight chips. Parity refers to an error-checking procedure whereby either every byte has an even number of ones or every byte has an odd number of ones. The use of a parity bit means that every byte occupies nine rather than eight bits.

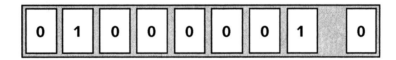

Exhibit 2-16: Eight chips and a parity chip represent the letter A in ASCII with even parity

Dynamic memory

There are two types of RAM: *dynamic RAM (DRAM)* and *static RAM (SRAM)*. Dynamic RAM chips hold data for a very short time; static RAM chips hold data until the power is turned off. Because DRAM is much less expensive than SRAM, most of the RAM on the system board is DRAM. DRAM comes in three types: parity, non parity, or an altogether new method of error checking called ECC (error checking and correction) that not only can detect an error but also correct it.

Parity is a method of testing the integrity of the bits stored in RAM or some secondary medium, or of testing the integrity of bits sent over a communications device. When data is written to RAM, the computer calculates how many ON bits (binary 1) there are in the 8 bits of a byte. If the computer uses odd parity, it makes the ninth or parity bit either a 1 or a 0 to make the number of 1s in the 9 bits odd. Likewise, if the computer uses even parity, it makes the parity bit a 1 or 0 to make the number of 1s in the 9 bits even.

Later, when the byte is read back, the computer checks the odd or even state. If the number of bits isn't an odd number for odd parity or an even number for even parity, a *parity error* occurs. A parity error always causes the system to halt. On the screen, you'll see the error message "Parity Error 1" or "Parity Error 2" or a similar error message about parity. Parity Error 1 is a parity error on the system board; Parity Error 2 is a parity error on a memory expansion board. Parity errors can be caused by RAM chips that have become undependable and that are unable to hold data reliably. Sometimes this happens when the chips overheat or power falters. If the parity errors continue to occur, you can use diagnostic software to identify the chip that is causing the parity error so that you can replace it. In older systems, when RAM was stored as individual chips, sometimes the faulty chip could be spotted by determining which chip felt warmer to the touch than the others after the computer had been running for some time.

Later, computers were made to hold RAM on a group of chips stored in a single physical unit called a *SIMM* (single inline memory module). A SIMM is a miniboard that stores an entire bank or banks of RAM. A SIMM can have several chips with 30 or 72 pins on the edge connector of the tiny board. RAM is then upgraded or changed by unplugging and plugging in SIMMs, which are much easier to work with than single chips. RAM chips or SIMMs are located either on the system board or on memory expansion cards. SIMMs hold from 8 MB to 64 MB of RAM on one board.

All new system boards today use *DIMMs* (dual inline memory module), which have 168 pins on the edge connector of the board. A DIMM can hold from 8 MB to 256 MB of RAM on a single board.

Most system boards today use 168-pin DIMMs. However, memory can be managed by using several technologies that involve how memory is accessed, how timing the access is managed, and how the system board and the CPU relate to the memory modules. The more prevalent memory technologies (and some variations of each) used by the industry are listed in the following table. The technology used by the memory modules must match the technology supported by the system board.

Technology	Description
Conventional	Used with earlier PCs but currently not available.
Fast Page Memory (FPM)	Improved access time over conventional memory. FPM might still be seen on older system boards.
Extended Data Out (EDO)	Refined version of FPM that speeds up access time. Still seen on older system boards.
Burst EDO (BEDO)	Refined version of EDO that significantly improved access time over EDO. BEDO is seldom used today because Intel chose not to support it.
Synchronous DRAM (SDRAM)	SDRAM runs in sync with the system clock and is rated by clock speed, whereas other types of memory run independently of (and slower than) the system clock.
Rambus DRAM (RDRAM)	RDRAM uses a faster memory bus (up to 800 MHz), but has only a 16-bit data path. The Intel Itanium processor will use RDRAM.
Double Data Rate (DDR) SDRAM	A faster version of SDRAM that can run at 200 MHz.

Regardless of the type, dynamic RAM chips don't hold their data very long and must be refreshed about every 3.86 milliseconds. To *refresh RAM* means that the computer must rewrite the data to the chip. Refreshing RAM is done by the DMA (dynamic memory access) chip or sometimes by circuitry on the system board other than the DMA chip.

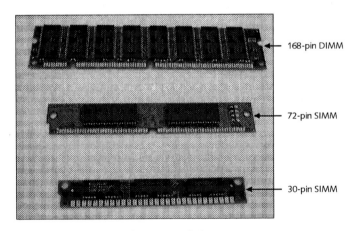

Exhibit 2-17: Types of RAM modules

Do it!

C-2: Discussing RAM

Question	Answer
1 What are two types of RAM?	
2 Name the three types of DRAM.	
3 Define a SIMM and DIMM.	

Topic D: Buses and expansion slots

Explanation

As microcomputer systems have evolved, so too have their "transportation" systems. The earliest PC had only a single and simple bus. Today's PCs have four or five buses, each with different speeds, access methods, and protocols. Backward compatibility dictates that older buses still be supported on a system board, even when faster, better buses exist. All this makes for a maze of many buses on a system board.

Bus evolution

Buses have evolved around the issues of data path and speed. Traffic on a computer's bus travels in a digital (on and off) manner rather than in an analog (continuous) manner. For this reason, it's more accurate to refer to CPU or bus frequency rather than CPU or bus speed when describing how fast a bus or CPU is operating. The system clock, which runs by a crystal on the system board, occupies one line of a bus and keeps the beat for components. Do something. Stop. Do something. Stop. Do something. Stop. With each beat, called a clock cycle, something can happen. Everything stops between beats, waiting for the next beat. The CPU listens to this beat and works on these clock cycles. If another component on the system board also works by the beat or clock cycle, then it's synchronized with the CPU. For example, the backside bus of the Pentium II works at half the speed of the CPU. This means that the CPU does something on each clock cycle, but the backside bus does something on every other clock cycle.

Some components don't attempt to keep in sync with the CPU, even to work at a half or a third of the clock cycles. These components are said to be working asynchronously with the CPU. They might be working at a rate determined by the system clock or by another crystal on or off the system board. Either way, the frequency is much slower than the CPU and not in sync with it. If the CPU requests something from one of these devices and the device isn't ready, it will issue wait states to the CPU until it can catch up.

Devices attached to an 8-bit or 16-bit ISA bus are an example of these slower devices. The 16-bit ISA bus works at a rate of 8.33 MHz, compared to memory bus speeds of 66 MHz to 100 MHz. Buses that work in sync with the CPU and the system clock are called *local buses* (sometimes called *system buses*). Buses that work asynchronously with the CPU at a much slower rate are called *expansion buses*. For example, the memory bus is a local bus and the ISA bus is an expansion bus.

Bus	Bus type	Data path in bits	Address lines	Bus speed in MHz	Throughput
Memory	Local	64	32	66, 75, 100 …	Up to 528 MB/sec
AGP	Local video	32	NA	66, 75, 100 …	Up to 528 MB/sec
PCI	Local I/O	32	32	33, 66	Up to 264 MB/sec
VESA or VL	Local video or expansion	32	32	Up to 33	Up to 250 MB/sec
MCA	Expansion	32	32	12	Up to 40 MB/sec
EISA	Expansion	32	32	12	Up to 32 MB/sec
16-bit ISA	Expansion	16	24	8.33	8 MB/sec
8-bit ISA	Expansion	8	20	4.77	1 MB/sec
FireWire	Local I/O or expansion	1	Addresses are sent serially	NA	Up to 400 Mbps
USB	Expansion	1	Addresses are sent serially	3	1.5 or 12 Mbps

Types of buses

When the first PCs were introduced in the early 1980s, there was only one bus on the system board, called the system bus, which ran at the same speed as the CPU (4.77 MHz). Everything on the system board worked with the CPU and the bus would simply keep the same beat, following the pulses of the one system clock. (This first bus is now called the 8-bit ISA bus.) Things today aren't as simple. With the speeds of different hardware components evolving at different rates, a single speed for all components is no longer practical. The CPU works at one speed, while the bus connecting the CPU to memory works at a slower speed, and the bus communicating with I/O devices must work at an even slower speed. In fact, there might be as many as five or six different buses working at different speeds on the same system board. Each bus has a set speed for all connected components. The system board contains components that convert data moving from bus to bus to the speed of the new bus.

The previous table lists the system board buses in common use today, from fastest to slowest. Historically, the 8-bit ISA (Industry Standard Architecture) bus came first, later revised to the 16-bit ISA bus to keep up with the demand for wider data path sizes. Then, in 1987, IBM introduced the first 32-bit bus, the MCA (Microchannel Architecture) bus, and competitors followed with the 32-bit EISA (Extended Industry Standard Architecture) bus. Because these buses aren't synchronized with the CPU, they're all expansion buses. Of these buses, the only one still in use today is the 16-bit ISA. A relatively new expansion bus is the USB bus, which targets slow I/O devices such as the mouse, digital camera, and scanner. The advantage of using this bus is that USB devices are easily installed and configured.

A local bus is synchronized with the CPU. In the sense that a local bus is a bus that is close to or "local to" the CPU, there's only one "true" local bus—the memory bus—that connects directly to the CPU. All other buses must connect to the memory bus to get to the CPU. A *local I/O bus* is a bus designed to support fast I/O devices such as video and hard drives. It runs synchronously with the system clock, which means that it's also synchronized with the CPU. Local I/O buses didn't always exist on a PC but were created as the need arose for a bus that was synchronized with the system clock, and that wasn't as fast as the memory bus but faster than an expansion bus. The evolution of local I/O buses includes earlier proprietary designs, the VESA bus, the PCI bus, and the newer AGP bus. Of these, only the PCI and AGP bus are still sold. The most current local I/O bus is the FireWire bus, which isn't readily available as yet. It can work either synchronously or asynchronously and so is classified as either a local or expansion bus. The VESA bus also could be set to work either way.

What a bus does

Look on the bottom of the system board and you will see a maze of circuits that make up a bus. These embedded wires are carrying four kinds of cargo:

- *Electrical power*. Chips on the system board require power to function. These chips tap into a bus's power lines and draw what they need.
- *Control signals*. Some of the wires on a bus carry control signals that coordinate all the activity.
- *Memory addresses*. Memory addresses are passed from one component to another as these components tell each other where to access data or instructions. The number of wires that make up the memory address lines of the bus determines how many bits can be used for a memory address. The number of wires thus limits the amount of memory the bus can address.
- *Data*. Data is passed over a bus in a group of wires, just as the memory addresses are. The number of lines in the bus used to pass data determines how much data can be passed in parallel at one time. The number of lines depends on the type of CPU and determines the number of bits in the data path. (A data path can be 8, 16, 32, or 64 bits wide.)

When comparing buses, users most often focus on the width of the data path and the overall bus speed. But you also should consider the type of expansion slot the bus can use. The number of fingers on the edge connector of the expansion card and the length of the edge connector are determined by the bus that controls that expansion slot.

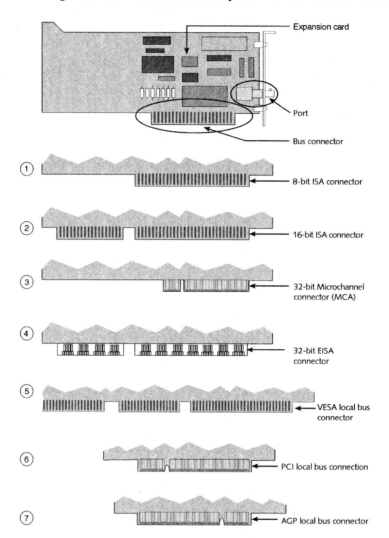

Exhibit 2-18: Seven bus connections on expansion cards

The ISA bus

Used on the first IBM 8088 PCs in the early 1980s, the *ISA bus* had an 8-bit data path. Later, IBM revised the ISA bus to have a 16-bit path size. The IBM AT personal computer used this bus and the 80286 chip, which is why the 16-bit bus is sometimes called the AT bus. IBM wanted this bus to be backward compatible with the older 8-bit ISA bus so that the older 8-bit circuit boards would fit into the newer AT computers. To maintain compatibility, IBM kept the old 62-line slot connector and added another slot connector beside it to provide the extra 8 bits. Slots with both connectors are called 16-bit slots. A new system board today usually has at least one 16-bit slot that can be used by either an 8-bit or 16-bit ISA card.

Microchannel Architecture (MCA) bus

With the introduction of the line of PS/2 computers in 1987, IBM introduced the first 32-bit bus for personal computers, the Microchannel Architecture (MCA) bus. IBM didn't intend the MCA bus to be compatible with ISA buses. Circuit boards used in older IBM computers couldn't be used in the PS/2 line. (The PS/2 Models 25 and 30 still included the older ISA bus in order to support legacy cards.)

IBM chose to patent the bus so that other companies couldn't economically manufacture and market it. IBM intended to control a subset of the bus market with MCA. In response, Compaq and eight other companies (called the "Gang of Nine") joined to design and build a competing 32-bit bus, the EISA bus

The EISA bus

Compaq and eight other companies (called the "Gang of Nine") joined to design and build a competing 32-bit bus, the EISA bus. Designed to compete with the MCA bus, the *EISA* (Extended ISA) bus (pronounced "ease-sa") has a 32-bit data path. This bus is compatible with older ISA buses so that expansion boards having 8-bit or 16-bit data paths work on the EISA bus. The speed of the EISA bus is about 20 MHz. To accommodate a 16-bit or 8-bit ISA circuit board, the 32-bit EISA has two slots that have the same width as 16-bit ISA slots. However, the EISA bus slots are deeper than 16-bit slots. All 32-bit circuit boards have longer fingers on the edge connectors that go deep into the EISA slot connecting to the 32-bit pins. A 16-bit circuit board reaches only partway down the slot connecting at a shallower level to only the 16-bit pins.

Universal serial bus

A relatively new I/O bus is the *universal serial bus* or USB, originally created by a seven-member consortium including Compaq, Digital Equipment, IBM, Intel, Microsoft, NEC, and Northern Telecom. It's designed to make the installation of slow peripheral devices as effortless as possible. USB is much faster than regular serial ports and much easier to manage, thus eliminating the need to resolve resource conflicts manually because the host controller uses only one set of resources for all devices. It's expected that USB will ultimately replace both serial and parallel ports as the technology matures and more devices are built to use USB.

One or two USB ports are found on most new system boards today, and older system boards that don't have USB ports can be upgraded by adding a PCI-to-USB controller card in a PCI slot to provide a USB port. USB can have two speeds—1.5 MB per second and 12 MB per second—and works well for slow I/O devices.

Exhibit 2-19: A system board with USB ports and a USB cable

A USB host controller, which for the Intel chip set is included in the PCI controller chip, manages the USB bus. As many as 127 USB devices can be daisy-chained together. The host controller manages communication to the CPU for all devices, by using only a single IRQ, I/O address range, and DMA channel. USB allows for *hot-swapping*, meaning that a device can be plugged into a USB port while the computer is running, and the host controller will sense the device and configure it without your having to reboot the computer. One USB device, such as a keyboard, can provide a port for another device, or a device can serve as a *hub* with several devices connecting to it. You also can have a standalone hub into which several devices can be plugged. In USB technology, the host controller polls each device, asking if data is ready to be sent or requesting to send data to the device. The USB cable has four wires, two for power and two for communication. The two power wires (one carries voltage and the other is ground) enable the host controller to provide power to a device.

I/O devices that are now or are soon to be available with a USB connection are the mouse, joystick, keyboard, printer, scanner, monitor, modem, video camera, fax machine, and digital telephone.

For USB to work, it must be supported by the operating system. Windows 95 with the USB update, Windows 98, and Windows 2000 support USB, but Windows NT doesn't. For more information about USB, see the forum Web site at www.usb.org.

FireWire, i.Link or 1394

FireWire and i.Link are the common names for another peripheral bus officially named *IEEE 1394* after the group that designed it: The Institute of Electrical and Electronics Engineers. This group was primarily led by Apple Computer and Texas Instruments during the initial design of the bus. Although FireWire is similar in design to USB, by using serial transmission of data, it's faster. FireWire supports data speeds as high as 1.2 Gbps (gigabits per second), which is much faster than what USB supports. FireWire is a viable option for connecting network cards, camcorders, DVDs, and other high-speed, high-volume devices. Whereas USB is likely to replace slow serial and parallel ports, FireWire is likely to replace SCSI, a very fast, but difficult to configure, peripheral bus.

As with USB, devices can be daisy-chained together and managed by a host controller using a single set of system resources (an IRQ, an I/O address range, and a DMA channel). One host controller can support up to 63 FireWire devices. Also, as with USB, FireWire must be supported by the operating system. Windows 2000, Windows NT and Windows 98 all support FireWire.

Local I/O buses

The primary intent of a local bus is to provide direct access to the CPU for a few fast devices, such as memory and video, that run at nearly the same speed as the CPU. A local I/O bus must connect to the CPU by way of the memory bus.

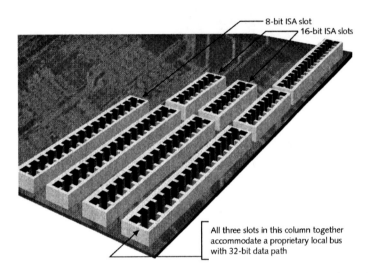

Exhibit 2-20: Three kinds of bus connections on the same board

In an attempt to create a standard for local 32-bit buses, many manufacturers endorsed the *VESA (Video Electronics Standards Association) VL bus*. Many system boards offered the VESA local bus for video and memory circuit boards. The expansion slot for a VESA local bus includes the 16 bits for the ISA slot plus an added extension with another 116 pins. The VESA bus has now been replaced by the PCI bus.

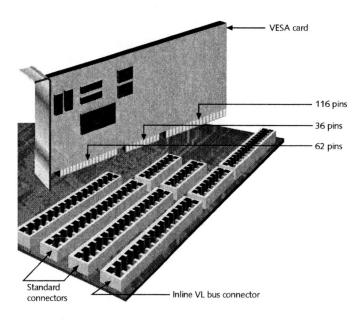

Exhibit 2-21: VESA local bus expansion slot

PCI bus

Another local I/O bus, the *PCI local bus (peripheral component interconnect bus)* is now the standard local I/O bus, not only with Pentium CPUs but also with RISC CPUs. Standard PCI has a 32-bit data path and runs at 33 MHz when the system board runs at 66 MHz. However, the PCI specifications also can use a 64-bit data path and can run at a speed of 66 MHz when the system bus runs at 133 MHz. Also, an addendum to the PCI specifications, called PCI-X, released in September 1999, enables PCI to run at 133 MHz.

One advantage of the PCI local bus is that devices connected to it can run at one speed while the CPU runs at a different speed. Devices connected to the VESA bus must run at the same clock speed as the CPU, which forces the CPU to endure frequent wait states. The PCI bus expansion slots are shorter than ISA slots and set a little farther away from the edge of the system board.

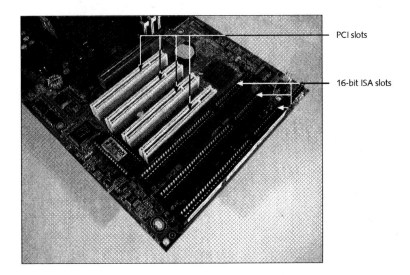

Exhibit 2-22: Comparing PCI bus expansion slots and ISA slots

In addition to supporting the I/O devices connected to it, the PCI bus also serves another function for the Intel 400 series chip. The PCI bus interfaces with the expansion bus and the memory bus, serving as the go-between for the two, controlling the input and output to the expansion bus. The PCI bus isolates the memory bus from the ISA bus. The connection between the two is the PCI bridge. The bridge enables the PCI bus to control the traffic not only from its own local devices but also from the ISA bus.

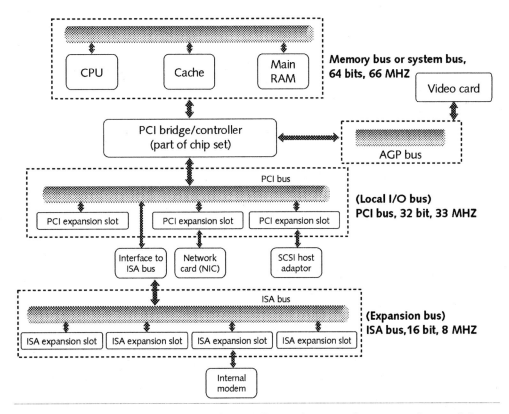

Exhibit 2-23: The PCI bus serves as the middleman between the memory bus and the expansion bus

The SCSI (Small Computer System Interface) host adapter, a network interface card (NIC), and a video card are all connected to the PCI bus. Physically, each card is inserted in a PCI expansion slot. The PCI bridge/controller accesses the local bus where the CPU and memory run at top speed without interference or wait states. For example, if the CPU wants to send data to the video card, it dumps it on the PCI bridge/controller at top speed. The controller puts the data in its own buffer or temporary memory storage and then writes it to video at a pace slower than the local bus. The bridge/controller eliminates interference with the local bus.

The interface from the PCI bus to the ISA bus is a significant feature that distinguishes the PCI bus from other buses. The PCI bus wasn't designed to replace the traditional expansion bus, but to support it. The ISA bus in the previous exhibit passes data through the interface to the PCI bus, which in turn passes the data on to the memory bus, to the CPU, and to memory.

The PCI bus also supports bus mastering. A bus master is an intelligent device (has a microprocessor that manages it) that, when attached to the PCI bus, can gain access to memory and other devices on the bus without interrupting the action of the CPU. The CPU and the bus mastering devices can run concurrently and independently of each other.

Because of the effective design of the PCI bus, the throughput performance, or the data transfer rate per second, is 132 MB when the bus is running at 33 MHz with a 32-bit data path. *Throughput performance,* or data throughput, is a measure of the actual data transmitted by the bus, not including error-checking bits or redundant data.

Accelerated graphics port

The accelerated graphics port (AGP) is designed to provide fast access to video. System boards have a single AGP slot to support an AGP video card. AGP is more of a port than a bus because it's not expandable and can support only a single card. The faster AGP bus has a direct connection to the CPU without having to use the slower PCI bus.

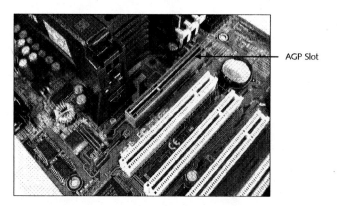

Exhibit 2-24: The AGP slot on the system board

Tip: A slot or socket is the physical connector on a system board for a device and doesn't include logic to support the connected device. A port is a socket or slot but goes a step further and also includes the logic to support that connection (for example, serial and parallel ports). A bus, among other things, provides the logic to support several devices connected to the system board, but doesn't include the physical connection itself. You need an expansion slot for that.

The AGP bus runs at the same speed as the memory bus, connects directly to it, and has a 32-bit-wide data path. AGP runs faster than PCI, running at half the memory bus speed, but it also offers additional features that give it overall better performance for video than PCI. It offers an improved rendering of 3-D images when software is designed to use it.

AGP can share system memory with the CPU to do its calculations and, therefore, doesn't always have to first copy data from system memory to video memory on the graphics card. This feature, known as direct memory execute (DIME) is probably AGP's most powerful feature. The first AGP specification defined AGP 2X, which allowed AGP to transfer two cycles of data during a single AGP clock beat. The AGP 2.0 specification defined AGP 4X whereby four cycles of data can be transferred during a single AGP clock beat yielding an overall data throughput of more than 1 GB/sec (gigabytes per second).

Exhibit 2-24 shows a 132-pin AGP slot on a system board. The latest AGP standard, called the AGP Pro, has provision for a longer slot. The new 188-pin slot has extensions on both ends that each contain an additional 28 pins used to provide extra voltage to the AGP video card in the slot. AGP Pro is used for high-end workstations that require powerful graphic accelerator cards for graphic-intensive applications.

For AGP to work at its full potential, the system board must be running at a minimum of 100 MHz, and the operating system must support AGP. Windows 98 and Windows 2000 both support AGP. See developer.intel.com/technology/agp/ for more information.

Audio Modem Riser

Newer system boards sometimes have an Audio Modem Riser (AMR) slot that can accommodate a small modem card or sound card. These small cards are inexpensive as most of the logic to support audio or the modem is contained within the system board chip set. The AMR slot makes it possible to add the card at a low cost without using up a PCI or ISA slot.

Do it! **D-1: Installing and removing a PCI expansion card**

Here's how
1 Power off your PC
Verify that you're properly grounded
Unplug the system unit's power cord
2 Remove the top of the case
3 Locate the available PCI slot where you plan to install the PCI expansion card
4 Gently install the PCI expansion card into the slot (*Warning*: Don't bend the card from side to side; move the card only back and forth or from end to end.)
Screw the mounting screw into place
5 Replace the top of the case
6 Plug in the system unit
Power on the lab workstation and boot into Windows 9x
7 Power off your PC
Verify that you're properly grounded
Unplug the system unit's power cord
8 Remove the top of the case
9 Unscrew the mounting screw from the frame
Gently remove the PCI expansion card from the PCI slot
10 Replace the top of the case
11 Plug in the system unit and power it on
Boot into Windows 9x

Setting the CPU and bus speeds

Explanation

You can, to some extent, control the speed of your system. There are two ways to change the speed of a computer:

1 Change the speed of the memory bus. Whatever the memory bus speed is, the PCI bus speed is half or one third of that.

2 Change the multiplier that determines the speed of the CPU. The choices for the multiplier normally are 1.5, 2, 2.5, 3, 3.5 and so forth.

Bus or Device	How speed is determined	How controlled
CPU	Processor speed = memory bus speed × multiplier. Typical speeds are 350 MHz, 450 MHz, and 500 MHz	Multiplier is set by jumpers or DIP switches on the system board or in CMOS setup.
Memory bus or system bus	System board manufacturer recommends the speed based on the processor and the processor's rated speed. Typical values are 66 MHz, 100 MHz, and 133 MHz	Set by jumpers, DIP switches or in CMOS setup. Most commonly set by jumpers.
PCI bus	Memory bus speed / 2 (For faster boards, can be divided by 3.)	The speed is set when you set the speed of the memory bus; either 33 MHz or 66 MHz
ISA bus	Runs at only one speed: 8.77 MHz	NA

Studies show that when a multiplier is large, the overall performance of the system isn't as good as when the multiplier is small. This is a reasonable result because you are interested in the overall speed of the computer, which includes the CPU and the buses, not just the speed of the CPU. For example, a bus speed of 60 MHz and a multiplier of 5 yield a relatively fast CPU but a relatively slow bus. It's better to have a bus speed of 80 MHz and a multiplier of 3 so that the bus runs fast enough to keep up with the CPU.

See the system board documentation to learn how to set these speeds by using jumpers, DIP switches, or CMOS setup. Exhibit 2-25 shows the documentation for one system board that uses one bank of jumpers to set the CPU-to-bus multiplier and another jumper bank to set the bus frequency. The steps to do this are:

1 Read the documentation of your CPU to determine its recommended frequency.

2 Read the multiplier from the selected row, which is 3.5x. Find the jumper settings for a multiplier of 3.5 in the possible jumper combinations for the CPU Core: BUS Frequency Multiple (fourth entry in first row).

3   The CPU type and speed also determine the bus frequency, which is 100 MHz. To set the bus frequency to 100 MHz, find the jumper combination for the second jumper bank, which is the fourth entry in the list of selections for the CPU External Clock (Bus) Frequency Selection.

4   Set the jumpers in the two jumper banks. Exhibit 2-27 shows the jumper group for the multiplier set to 3.5.

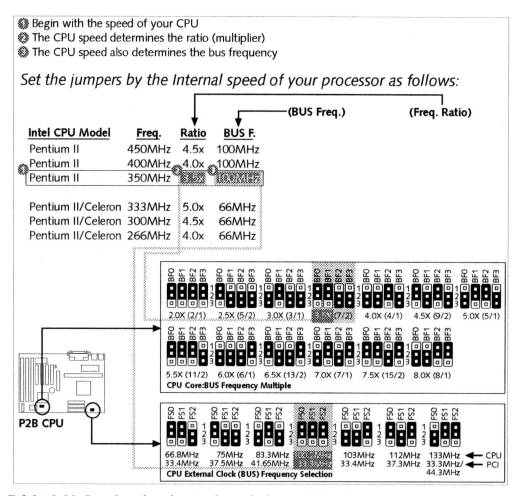

Exhibit 2-25: Based on the advertised speed of your CPU, select the multiplier and the bus frequency from the table to determine which jumper settings to use

Exhibit 2-26: Jumper group that controls the CPU core-to-bus frequency

On-board ports

Many system boards contain *on-board ports* such as a keyboard port and a mouse port. In addition, a parallel printer port and one or two serial ports might be located directly on the system board. Few older system boards contain more ports than these. A few older system boards support video and will contain a video port. Newer system boards contain one or two USB ports.

You don't have to replace an entire system board if one port fails. Most system boards contain jumpers or DIP switches that can tell the CPU to disable one port and look to an expansion card for the port instead. Ports also can be disabled through CMOS setup.

When buying a new computer or system board, look for the ability to disable ports, floppy drive connectors, or hard drive connectors coming directly from the system board by changing the hardware configuration. You can easily tell if ports on the outside of the case are directly connected to the system board without opening the case; the ports are lined up along the bottom of the computer case.

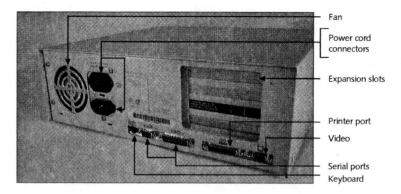

Exhibit 2-27: Ports along the bottom of the computer case

Hardware configuration

Hardware configuration information communicates to the CPU what hardware components are present in the system and how they're set up to communicate with the CPU. Hardware configuration includes information such as how much memory is available, the kind of monitor present, and whether disk drives, hard drives, modems, serial ports, and the like are connected. Remember that during POST, BIOS looks to the system configuration information to determine what equipment it should expect to find and how that equipment communicates with the CPU. The CPU uses this information later to process data and instructions. Configuration information is provided on the system board in three different ways: DIP switches, jumpers, and CMOS.

Setup stored on a CMOS chip

Computers today store most configuration information on one CMOS chip that retains the data even when the computer is turned off. (There are actually many CMOS chips on a system board, used for various purposes.) A battery near the CMOS chip provides enough electricity to enable the chip to maintain its data. If the battery is disconnected or fails, setup information is lost. Password information also is a part of the computer's setup that's stored in CMOS. The program to change the setup information is now stored in ROM, but was once stored on a disk that came with the computer.

System-board manuals should contain a list of all CMOS settings, an explanation of their meanings, and their recommended values. When you purchase a system board or a computer, be sure the manual is included for this purpose. If you don't have the manual, you can sometimes go to the system board manufacturer's Web site and download the information you need to understand the specific CMOS settings of your computer.

Category	Setting	Description
Standard CMOS setup	Date and time	Used to set system date and time (called the real time clock).
	Primary display	Used to tell POST and DOS (but not Windows) the type of video being used.
	Keyboard	Used to tell the system whether the keyboard is installed. Useful if the computer is used as a print or file server and if you don't want someone to change settings.
	Hard-disk type	Used to record the size and mapping of the drive.
	Floppy-disk type	Choices are usually 31□2 inch and 51□4 inch.
Advanced CMOS setup	Above 1 MB memory test	Used to disable POST check of this memory to speed up booting. The OS will check this memory anyway.
	Memory parity error check	If you have a parity system board, this is used to enable parity checking to ensure that memory is correct.
	Numeric processor test	Enabled unless you have an old 386 or 486SX computer
	System boot sequence	Used to establish the drive that the system first looks for an OS. Normally drive A, then C.
	External cache memory	Used to enable if you have L2 cache. A frequent error in setup is to have cache but not use it because its disabled here
	Internal cache memory	Normally enabled; disable only for old 386 computers
	Password checking option	Used to establish a startup password. Use this only if you really have a problem with someone using your PC who can't be trusted
	Video ROM shadow C000, 16K	For DOS and Windows 9x, shadow video ROM is recommended because ROM runs slower than RAM
	System ROM shadow F000, 64K	Enabling shadow system ROM is recommended

Category	Setting	Description
	IDE Multi-block mode	Enables a hard drive to read or write several sectors at a time. Dependent on the kind of hard drive you have.
	Boot sector virus protection	Gives a warning when something is written to the boot sector of the hard drive. Can be a nuisance if your software is designed to write to the boot sector regularly.
Advanced chip set setup	AT bus clock selection	Gives the number by which the CPU speed is divided to get the ISA or EISA bus speed.
	ISA bus speed	Gives the number by which the PCI bus speed is divided to get the ISA bus speed.
	Bus mode	Can be set to synchronous or asynchronous modes. In synchronous mode, the bus uses the CPU clock. In asynchronous mode, its own AT bus clock is used.
	AT cycle wait state	The number of wait states the CPU must endure while it interfaces with a device on the ISA or EISA bus. Increase this if an old and slow ISA card isn't working well.
	Memory read wait state	Number of wait states the CPU must endure while reading from RAM.
	Memory write wait state	Number of wait states the CPU must endure while writing to RAM.
	Cache read option	Sometimes called "cache read hit burst." The number of clock beats needed to load four 32-bit words into the CPU's internal cache. 4-1-1-1 is the usual choice.
	Fast cache read/write	Refers to external cache. Enable it if you have two banks of cache, 64K or 256K.
	Cache wait state	Refers to external cache. The number of wait states the CPU must use while accessing cache.

Category	Setting	Description
Power menu	Power management	Disable or enable all power management features. These features are designed to conserve electricity.
	HDD power down	Disable or enable the feature to shut down the hard drive after a period of inactivity.
	Wake on LAN	Wake on LAN enables your PC to be booted from another computer on the same network. It requires an ATX power supply that supports the feature.
	Wake on keyboard	Power up your PC by pressing a certain key combination.

Do it!

D-2: Reviewing configuration

Question	Answer
1 In what two ways can you change the computer's speed?	
2 How is the multiplier changed?	
3 If an on-board port fails, you need to replace the whole system board. True or False?	
4 How does the CMOS maintain information when the computer is shut off?	

Unit summary: The system board

Topic A In this topic, you learned that the **system board** is the most complicated of all the **components** inside the computer. It contains the CPU and accompanying chip set, the real-time clock, ROM BIOS, CMOS configuration chip, RAM, RAM cache, system bus, expansion slots, jumpers, ports, and power supply connections. The system board you select determines both the capabilities and limitations of your system.

Topic B You learned that the **CPU** is the most important component on the system board. This microprocessor is the heart of a PC system, where almost all operations must ultimately be processed. A **chip set** is a group of chips on the system board that supports the CPU. Intel is the most popular manufacturer of chip sets.

Topic C The total BIOS of a system includes the **ROM BIOS** on the system board as well as BIOS on expansion cards. **Flash ROM** enables the ROM BIOS to be upgraded without having to change the ROM chip. **Dynamic RAM** (DRAM) is slower than **static RAM** (SRAM) because dynamic RAM must be refreshed.

Topic D In this topic, you learned that a **bus** is a path on the system board that carries electrical power, control signals, memory addresses, and data to different components on the board. Some well-known buses are the 16-bit ISA bus, EISA bus, and the two local buses (the VESA bus and the PCI bus). A **local bus** is gives fast devices quicker and more direct access to the CPU than that given by other buses.

Review questions

1 You're employed at Cold Sweet Ice Company as a help desk technician. Jamie wants to install more memory into her PC but doesn't know how to attach it to the system board. Describe the steps Jamie needs to follow to locate the memory slots.

2 You're currently employed as a PC support technician at the Heavenly Palace Factory. Your supervisor wants to upgrade his Pentium computer to a Pentium III. He asks you to tell him the parts that he will need to purchase for this upgrade. List the minimum parts your supervisor needs to complete this upgrade.

3 What is one advantage of using PCI over ISA?

Unit 3

Memory

Unit time: 60 minutes

Complete this unit, and you'll know how to:

A Identify the types of physical memory housed on the system board and expansion boards.

B Upgrade the memory in your computer.

Topic A: Understanding memory

Explanation

In this unit, you'll about different kinds of memory the computer uses. You'll also learn how to upgrade the RAM on your computer. First, let's look at the physical memory to see where it's located, and what kinds of memory chips and modules are found in a computer. There are many different ways memory can be physically installed on the system board and expansion boards.

Physical memory

Computer memory is divided into two categories: ROM and RAM. RAM is called primary memory. It temporarily holds data and instructions as the CPU processes them. All data stored in RAM is lost when the PC is turned off. (There is an exception; remember that the CMOS setup chip doesn't lose its data, because it has its own battery that powers it when the machine is turned off.) RAM is further divided into two categories, *static RAM (SRAM)* and *dynamic RAM (DRAM)*, in order to improve performance. ROM, on the other hand, stores system BIOS and startup BIOS programs in a type of microchip that doesn't lose its data when the power is turned off.

Besides the system board, expansion boards also can have RAM chips to hold their data and ROM chips that provide the programming to drive the devices that they control. For example, a network card contains ROM chips that provide the programming to communicate with a network. Similarly, video cards contain ROM chips that hold the programming that controls the monitor, and RAM chips to hold video data just before it's sent to the monitor.

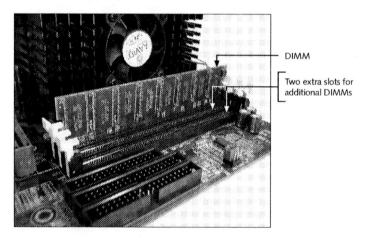

DIMM

Two extra slots for additional DIMMs

Exhibit 3-1: DRAM on most system boards today is stored on DIMMs

ROM on the system board

ROM, or read-only memory, consists of memory chips that contain programs that are acid-etched into the chips at the factory. The programs on a ROM chip (sometimes called firmware) are permanent; they can't be changed. *EEPROM* chips (or Flash ROM) do enable their programs to be changed. On EEPROM chips, a higher voltage is applied to one of the pins to erase its previous memory before a new instruction set or data is electronically written. *EPROM (erasable programmable ROM)* chips also can have their programs changed. They have a special window where the current memory contents can be erased with a special ultraviolet light, so that the chip can be reprogrammed. Many BIOS chips are EPROM chips. They're seen on the system board with shiny tape covering the window. However, for the discussions in this unit, consider the EEPROM, EPROM, and ROM chips as all providing BIOS that isn't erasable during normal PC operations. In addition, when the text refers to ROM chips, they may be EEPROM, EPROM, or ROM chips.

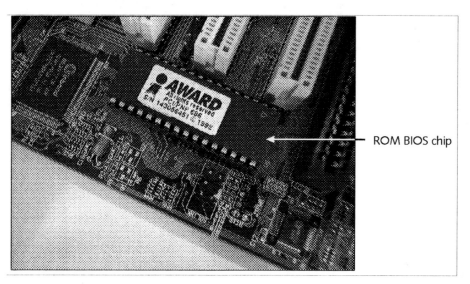

Exhibit 3-2: The ROM BIOS on newer system boards can be upgraded by using software provided by the BIOS manufacturer

When you purchased your computer, it contained several ROM chips on the system board and some on the expansion boards. These ROM chips contain the programming that the computer uses to start up and to do routine utility operations, such as reading from and writing to hardware devices and performing basic data manipulation. The ROM chips on the system board contain much of the BIOS for your computer. System BIOS is a set of programs that perform the basic input/output chores. The operating system calls on the system BIOS programs to interact with input/output devices as needed. Startup BIOS is responsible for the early stages of the boot process.

ROM chips are usually socketed onto the system board. Occasionally, you'll have to replace a ROM chip either because the ROM chip has gone bad or because the ROM programming is outdated and you must upgrade ROM. The chips can be removed easily, and a new ROM chip can be popped into the socket.

Flash memory

Upgrading the programming on an existing chip is much easier than physically exchanging a ROM chip. Flash memory makes this possible. *Flash memory* acts more like secondary storage than like other types of memory, because it doesn't lose its data when the power is turned off. Flash memory is different from a hard drive in that a hard drive holds its data as a magnetized area on a platter, whereas flash memory holds its data electronically. Also, flash memory provides much faster data access than a hard drive does, because a hard drive is a mechanical device, and flash memory is an electronic device. Another difference is that flash memory is much more expensive than hard drive storage.

Flash memory uses EEPROM chips. Flash memory also is used on notebook computers and is often found on PC cards (PCMCIA), which look like thick credit cards and are used to attach peripherals to notebook computers. Flash ROM is one example of the use of this kind of memory on a system board. Flash memory also is used to hold picture data in digital cameras.

RAM on the system board

The other kind of computer memory is RAM, or random access memory. In the 1980s, RAM chips were either socketed or soldered directly on system boards, but today all RAM used as main memory is housed on SIMMs or DIMMs. Memory chips on SIMMs or DIMMs can only hold their data for a few milliseconds. This memory, because it constantly needs refreshing, is called dynamic RAM (DRAM), pronounced "DEE-RAM" (two syllables).

Besides serving as main memory, RAM also provides a memory cache. A system board has a lot of main memory to hold data and instructions as they get processed, and a little memory cache to help speed up the access time to main memory. Cache memory is contained on the system board or inside the CPU housing. On the system board, memory is either on individual chips or on a memory module called a *COAST (cache on a stick)*. These memory chips hold their data for as long as the power is on and are therefore called static RAM or SRAM, pronounced "ESS-RAM" (two syllables). The recent trend is to put all cache memory inside the CPU housing, but there is still some on the system boards.

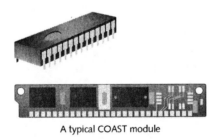

A typical COAST module

Exhibit 3-3: Single SRAM chip and COAST module

Main memory	Cache memory
DRAM, needs constant refreshing	SRAM, doesn't need refreshing
Slower than SRAM because of refreshing time	Faster, but more expensive
Physically housed on DIMMs, SIMMs	Physically housed on the system board on COAST modules or single chips or included inside the processor case

Technologies include:
    FPM
    EDO
    BEDO
    Synchronous DRAM (SDRAM)
    Direct Rambus DRAM
    Double Data Rate SDRAM
	Technologies include:
	    Synchronous SRAM
	    Burst SRAM
	    Pipelined burst
	    Asynchronous SRAM

Memory addresses are assigned	No memory addresses assigned here

SRAM and memory caching

Because data doesn't need to be constantly rewritten to SRAM, it provides faster access than DRAM, since CPU time must be devoted to refreshing data in DRAM every 4 milliseconds or so. SRAM chips are made up of transistors that can hold a charge, but DRAM chips are made up of capacitors that must be recharged. SRAM chips are more expensive than DRAM chips, which is why all RAM is not made up of SRAM chips. As a compromise, most computers have a little SRAM on the system board and a lot of DRAM.

Memory caching is a method used to store data or programs in SRAM for quick retrieval. Memory caching requires some SRAM chips and a cache controller to control the caching. When memory caching is used, the cache controller tries to anticipate what data or programming code the CPU will request next, and copies that data or programming code to the SRAM chips. Then, if the cache guessed correctly, it can satisfy the CPU request from SRAM without having to access the slower DRAM. Under normal conditions, memory caching guesses correctly more than 90% of the time and is an effective way of speeding up memory access.

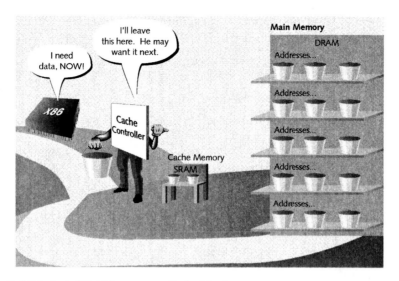

Exhibit 3-4: SRAM temporarily holds data

On older 386 computers, the cache controller was located on a single chip labeled the 385 chip, but 486 and later CPUs have the cache controller chip embedded in the CPU chip, housed together with some static RAM. This SRAM is called an internal cache, level 1 cache, or L1 cache, and is found in all 486 CPUs and higher. However, a system board can have additional static RAM, called an external cache, level 2 cache, or L2 cache. This L2 cache might be on the system board of older computers or inside the CPU housing of newer systems.

If the cache memory is inside the CPU housing, you have no control over how much is present; it's dependent on the type of CPU you use. However, older system boards were usually manufactured with some cache memory already installed, but with the option to add more in order to improve performance.

How much SRAM on a system board is enough without being prohibitively expensive? On most computers 256 KB of SRAM is considered the minimum, and many system boards come with 256 KB already on the board, with additional banks for another 256 KB or more. The second 256 KB of cache doesn't improve performance nearly as much as the first 256 KB does. For system boards running at 66 MHz, more than 512 KB of cache doesn't offer a significant improvement in access time. Newer, faster system boards might hold as much as 2 MB of cache.

SRAM on the system board. SRAM might be on a system board either on individual chips or on a COAST. COAST isn't as prevalent as it once was, because many system boards now use single, socketed chips.

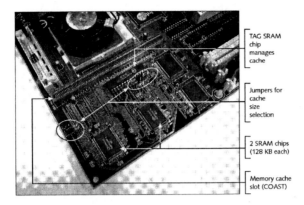

Exhibit 3-5: SRAM on this system board is stored in individual chips, and the board also has a COAST slot

System boards designed to support Pentium II CPUs that contain L2 cache within the CPU housing don't have SRAM on the board. In this case, the CPU has already provided the optimum amount of SRAM, and supporting memory becomes much simpler.

SRAM is installed in increments of 64 KB, 128 KB, 256 KB, or 512 KB. See the documentation for the system board to determine which amounts of cache the board supports and what kind of memory to buy. All RAM sends data and control signals over the system bus. The methods used to coordinate how and when data and control signals are sent and read differ with various kinds of memory. SRAM uses a couple of different methods: synchronous or asynchronous. Synchronous SRAM is more expensive and about 30% faster than asynchronous SRAM.

Synchronous SRAM requires a clock signal to manage or synchronize its control signals. This enables the cache memory to run in step with the CPU. Synchronous SRAM can be either burst or pipelined burst SRAM. Burst SRAM is more expensive than pipelined burst SRAM and only slightly faster. *Burst SRAM* uses the concept that data is sent in a two-step process: the data address is sent, and then the data itself is sent. Burst SRAM sends a burst of data without sending all the addresses of the data; it sends only the first address. With burst, a large amount of data can be sent without interruption. *Pipelined burst SRAM* uses more clock cycles per transfer than does the burst without pipelining, but it doesn't significantly slow down the process and is desirable because of the reduced cost.

Asynchronous SRAM doesn't work in step with the CPU clock speed. It must look up the address sent to it by the CPU and return the data within one clock cycle, which makes it unable to process as much data in one request and results in overall slower memory access.

A system board might be designed to support both asynchronous and synchronous SRAM, but not at the same time. See the documentation for the system board to determine which kinds of SRAM the board can support, and then look to see what kind of SRAM is already present on the board, before you buy new SRAM. You might need to replace the existing SRAM on the board in order to upgrade to a larger or faster cache.

Main memory: SIMMs and DIMMs

In earlier PCs, main memory was stored on the system board as single, socketed chips; but today, RAM is always stored in either SIMMs (single inline memory modules) or DIMMs (dual inline memory modules), which plug directly into the system board. The major difference between a SIMM and a DIMM module is the width of the data path that the module accommodates. A SIMM has a data path of 32 bits, and a DIMM has a data path of 64 bits.

The technology used by SIMM and DIMM microchips has evolved to improve speed and size. SIMMs first used FPM and then EDO technologies. Next came DIMMs using burst EDO, followed by SDRAM technology and Direct Rambus technology. The goal with each new technology is to increase overall throughput. FPM is used on system boards that range in speed from 16 to 66 MHz. EDO is used on system boards rated at about 33 to 75 MHz, and SDRAM and Direct Rambus are used on system boards rated from 66 and higher. The older the system board, the older the memory technology it can use, so, as a PC technician, you must be familiar with all these technologies even though the boards sold today only use the latest.

SIMM technologies

Older SIMMs use FPM technology, have 30 pins on the edge connector, and come in sizes of 256 KB to 4 MB. Later FPM SIMMs had 72 pins on the edge connector and came in sizes up to 16 MB. Newer SIMMs use EDO technology, have 72 pins on the edge connector, are slightly longer, and come in sizes of 1 MB to 64 MB. A SIMM might have three or more chips, but this doesn't affect the amount of memory that the SIMM can hold. SIMMs are also rated by speed, measured in nanoseconds. A nanosecond (ns) is one billionth of a second. Common SIMM speeds are 60, 70, or 80 ns. This speed is a measure of access time, the time it takes for the CPU to receive a value in response to a request. Access time includes the time it takes to refresh the chips. An access time of 60 ns is faster than an access time of 70 ns. Therefore, the smaller the speed rating, the faster the chip.

FPM (fast page mode) memory improved on the earlier memory types by sending the row address just once for many accesses to memory near that row. Earlier memory types required a complete row and column address for each memory access.

EDO (extended data output) memory is an improvement over earlier FPM memory. EDO memory is faster because it enables the memory controller to eliminate the 10-ns delay in the time that it normally waits before it issues the next memory address. When no memory cache is present, computer performance increases 10% to 20% when using EDO memory instead of FPM memory. However, if 256 KB of cache is used, the increased performance from FPM to EDO memory is only 1% to 2%. EDO memory doesn't cost significantly more than FPM memory, but your system board must be able to support it. Check your system board documentation or CMOS setup to determine if you should use EDO memory. If your system board doesn't support EDO memory, you can still use it, but it will not increase system performance. EDO memory is used on SIMMs and video memory, and is often used to provide on-board RAM on various expansion boards.

DIMM technologies

DIMMs also are rated by the amount of memory they hold and their speed. DIMMs have 168 pins on the edge connector of the board and hold from 8 MB to 256 MB of RAM. Most DIMMs use either *burst EDO (BEDO)* or *synchronous DRAM (SDRAM)* technology. BEDO is a refined version of EDO with improved access time over EDO. BEDO isn't widely used today because Intel chose not to support it.

Synchronous DRAM is currently the fastest memory available for PCs. SDRAM is rated by the system bus speed and operates in sync with the system clock, whereas other types of memory (FPM, EDO, and BEDO) all run at a constant speed.

Either 3.3 volts or 5.0 volts can power SDRAM modules. Purchase DIMMs that use the voltage supported by your system board. Your system board also determines whether you can use buffered or unbuffered DIMMs. Buffered memory is faster than unbuffered because adding a buffer enables larger chunks of data to be read or written to memory at a time. To determine which of these features a DIMM has, check the position of the two notches on the DIMM module. The position of the notch on the left identifies the module as buffered or unbuffered memory. The notch on the right identifies the voltage used by the module. The position of the notches not only helps identify the type of module, but also prevents the wrong kind of module from being used on a system board.

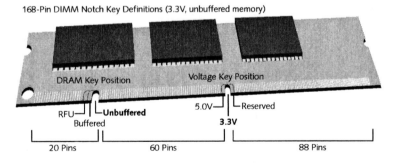

Exhibit 3-6: The positions of two notches identify the type of DIMM

Other RAM technologies

Synchronous DRAM is currently the most popular memory type. SDRAM is rated by the system bus speed and operates in sync with the system clock, whereas older types of memory (FPM, EDO, and BEDO) all run at a constant speed. SDRAM currently comes in three variations: regular SDRAM, SDRAM II (DDR), and SyncLink (SLDRAM).

Regular SDRAM runs at the same speed as the system bus: 66 MHz, 100 MHz, 133 MHz, and so forth. The SDRAM data path is 64 bits wide, making SDRAM about 50% faster than its predecessor, EDO memory.

Double-data rate SDRAM (DDR SDRAM), sometimes called SDRAM II, runs twice as fast as regular SDRAM. Instead of processing data for each beat of the system clock as regular SDRAM does, it processes data when the beat rises and again when it falls, doubling the data rate of memory. If a system board is running at 100 MHz, then SDRAM II is running at 200 MHz with a data path of 64 bits. Future plans for DDR SDRAM include increasing this data path to 128 bits. DDR SDRAM is supported by a consortium of 20 major computer manufacturers. It's an open standard, meaning that no royalties need to be paid to use it. *SyncLink* (SLDRAM) was developed by a consortium of twelve DRAM manufacturers. It improves on regular SDRAM by increasing the number of memory banks that can be accessed simultaneously from four to sixteen. Memory banks are discussed later.

Direct Rambus DRAM (sometimes called RDRAM or Direct RDRAM) is named after Rambus, the company that developed it. The technology uses a narrow 16-bit data path rather than the wider 64-bit SDRAM data path. It works like a packeted network, not a traditional memory bus, and can run at speeds of 400 MHz to 800 MHz. The high speeds are possible because of the narrow bus width; wider buses can't accommodate these high speeds. RDRAM uses a proprietary memory module called a RIMM, not a DIMM. An earlier version of Rambus memory is Concurrent RDRAM, which is not as fast as Direct RDRAM. Manufacturers other than Rambus and Intel must pay licensing fees to use RDRAM, which might cause the industry to turn more toward SDRAM memory advancements over Rambus even though Intel is promoting RDRAM. The Intel 820 and 840 chip sets both support RDRAM. The following table shows a comparison in data throughput of the current contenders for the memory market.

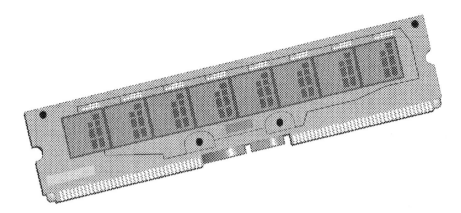

Exhibit 3-7: Direct Rambus DRAM is stored on a RIMM rather than a DIMM

Memory technology	Calculation of throughput	Data throughput
RDRAM	16 bits × 400 MHz	800 MB per second
RDRAM	16 bits × 800 MHz	1600 MB per second
SDRAM on 100 MHz board	64 bits × 100 MHz	400 MB per second
DDR-SDRAM on 133 MHz board	64 bits × 266 MHz	1064 MB per second
DDR-SDRAM on 166 MHz board	128 bits × 332 MHz	2656 MB per second

ECC, Parity, and Nonparity DRAM

Some SDRAM memory modules support a chip set feature called *ECC (error checking and correction)*. DIMMs that support ECC will have a ninth chip on the module (the ECC chip), whereas there are normally only eight chips present. The module is identified as a 72-bit DIMM instead of a 64-bit DIMM. ECC uses an extra 7 bits to verify the integrity of every 64 bits stored on the module and correct any error, when possible. ECC memory costs a little more than regular memory, but is more reliable. To see if your system board supports ECC memory, look for the ability to enable or disable the feature in CMOS setup or check the system-board documentation.

Some older system boards support *parity memory,* and some only use *nonparity memory*. If there are an odd number of chips on a SIMM, most likely the SIMM is parity memory; an even number of chips usually indicates nonparity memory. Parity memory validates the integrity of the data stored in RAM by counting the number of bits set to 1, to determine whether the total is an even or odd number. Parity memory then sets a parity bit either to make the number of 1-bits even (called even parity) or to make the number of 1s odd (called odd parity). When the data is read, the number of 1s is counted. If parity is even but the number of 1s is odd (or vice versa), then a parity error occurs, and the CPU will stop processing this data.

Most manufacturers of PC system boards today use nonparity memory to save processing time, and therefore money.

When a computer first boots up, the system must detect what type of memory is installed. To do so, the systems can use two methods: Parallel Presence Detect (PPD) that uses resistors to communicate the type of memory present, or Serial Presence Detect (SPD) that stores information about the memory type in EPROM. When purchasing memory for a system, you must match the method used by the module to what the system board requires. See the system board documentation to know which type to buy. If the board doesn't specify the method used, assume PPD.

Another feature of memory is called Cas Latency (CL) and reflects the number of clock cycles that passes while data is written to memory. Values are 2 or 3 clock cycles. CL2 (Cas Latency 2) is a little faster than CL3 (Cas Latency 3). Again, use the memory type recommended by the system board manufacturer.

What to look for when buying memory chips and modules

Memory chips and memory modules are sold at different speeds and sizes and use different technologies and features. Chips can be high-grade, low-grade, remanufactured, or used. Poor-quality memory chips can cause frequent *General Protection Fault (GPF) errors* in Windows, application errors, and errors that cause the system to hang. So it's important to know the quality and type of memory you're buying. The following are some guidelines to follow to ensure that you are purchasing high-quality memory chips.

Memory speed — Generally, you want to use the fastest memory that your system board supports. The documentation for a system board states what speed of memory to use on the board. It's possible, but not recommended, to mix the speed of memory modules on a system board, but don't mix the speeds within a single SIMM memory bank.

Tin or Gold leads — Memory modules and the banks that hold them can be made of either tin or gold. On a system board the connectors inside the memory slots are made of either tin or gold, as are the edge connectors on the memory modules. You should match tin leads to tin connectors and gold leads to gold connectors to prevent a chemical reaction between the two different metals, which can cause corrosion. Corrosion can result in intermittent memory errors and can even cause the PC to be unable to boot.

Choosing the correct size of module — Not all sizes of memory modules will fit on any one computer. Use the right number of SIMM or DIMM modules with the right amount of memory on each module to fit the memory banks on your system board.

Remanufactured and used modules — Stamped on each chip of a SIMM or DIMM module is a chip ID that identifies, along with other things, the date the chip was manufactured. Look for the date in the YYWW format, where YY is the year the chip was made and WW is the week of that year. For example, 9910 indicates a chip made in the 10th week of 1999. If you see date stamps on a SIMM or DIMM chip that are older than one year, chances are that these chips are used memory. If some of the chips are old, but some are new, the module is probably remanufactured. When buying memory modules, look for ones on which all chips have dates that are relatively close together and less than a year old.

Re-marked chips — New chips have a protective coating, which gives them a polished, reflective-looking surface. If the surface of the chip is dull or matted, or you can scratch the markings off with a fingernail or knife, suspect that the chip has been re-marked. *Re-marked chips* are chips that have been used and returned to the factory, marked again, and then sold.

Do it!

A-1:   Reviewing physical memory

Question	Answer
1 Where might flash memory be found on a system board?	
2 Name two ways that a SIMM and a DIMM are alike. Name two ways they're different.	
3 How many pins are on a DIMM? What are the two possible numbers of pins on a SIMM?	
4 Which is faster, EDO memory or BEDO memory?	
5 How does a memory cache speed up computer processing?	
6 Explain the difference between a level 1 cache and a level 2 cache.	
7 What type of memory must you use for a 100 MHz system board?	
8 If your system board supports FPM memory, will EDO memory still work on the board?	
9 Looking at an SDRAM DIMM, how can you know for certain the voltage needed by the module?	
10 What are the two major categories of static RAM memory?	

Topic B: Upgrading memory

Explanation

Upgrading memory means to add more RAM to a computer. Many computers, when first purchased, have empty slots on the system board so that you can add SIMMs or DIMMs to increase the amount of RAM. If all the slots are full, sometimes you can take out small-capacity modules and replace them with larger-capacity modules. When you add more memory to your computer, ask yourself these questions:

- How much memory do I need?
- How much memory can my computer physically accommodate?
- What increments of memory does my system board support?
- How much additional memory is cost effective?
- What kind of memory can fit on my system board?
- What memory is compatible with the memory I already have installed?

With the demands today's software places on memory, the answer to the first question is probably, "All I can get." Both Windows 95 and Windows 98 require 24 MB to 32 MB of memory. The minimum requirement is 8 MB, although performance will be slow with this small amount of memory because the system is forced to write working files to the slower hard drive as virtual memory instead of using the much faster RAM.

How much memory can fit on the system board?

To determine how much memory your computer can physically hold, read the documentation that comes with your computer. For example, one manual for a 486 computer explains that the system board can support up to 32 MB of memory, but there are only nine possible memory configurations.

The following table shows that this system board has two banks. A *bank* is a location on the system board that contains slots for memory modules. On this system board, each bank can hold 256 KB, 1 MB, or 4 MB of memory. The first bank always has some memory in it, but the second bank might or might not contain memory. This computer, which is typical of many older 486 boards, uses SIMMs on the system board. A SIMM is a small miniboard that contains memory chips. The SIMMs are inserted into the slots in a bank. This computer can support these sizes: 256 KB, 1 MB, and 4 MB.

SIMM size in Bank 1	SIMM size in Bank 2	Total RAM on system board
256K	0	1 MB
256K	256K	2 MB
1 MB	0	4 MB
1 MB	256K	5 MB
1 MB	1 MB	8 MB
4 MB	0	16 MB
4 MB	256K	17 MB
4 MB	1 MB	20 MB
4 MB	4 MB	32 MB

To determine how many slots are in one bank, you must know the computer's bus size. This 486 computer uses a 32-bit bus. When bits travel down a circuit on the system board to the bank to be stored in RAM, they're moving 32 bits abreast. The bank must receive 32 bits at a time to work with this bus. This system board uses 30-pin SIMMs. Each 30-pin SIMM receives one 8-bit byte at a time. The following exhibit shows that the 32-bit bus directs 8 bits to each of the four SIMMs in the bank. The bank must contain four SIMMs to receive these 32 bits. Since each SIMM receives an equal part of the 4 bytes traveling down the circuit, all SIMMs within one bank must store the same amount of bytes.

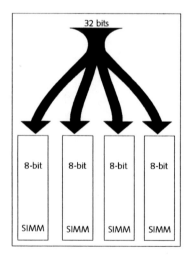

Exhibit 3-8: One bank on a 486 system board that uses a 32-bit bus and 8-bit, 30-pin SIMMs

In the first row of the table, bank 1 contains 256 KB SIMMs and bank 2 is empty. Bank 1 contains four slots, each of which must contain a SIMM in order to accommodate the 32-bit bus. Hence, the amount of memory is 4 × 256 KB or 1 MB of memory. In the second row of the table, each bank contains four 256 KB SIMMs for a total of 2 MB of memory: (4 × 256 KB) + (4 × 256 KB) = 2 MB.

Notice that in the fourth row of the table, bank 1 contains 1 MB SIMMs, and bank 2 contains 256 KB SIMMs for a total of 5 MB of memory on the system board (calculations are left to the reader). The four SIMMs in a bank must be the same size, but the SIMMs can vary in size from one bank to another.

Our second example of a system board is one used by a Pentium, and it supports up to 128 MB of RAM. It has four SIMM sockets divided into two banks. Bank 0 holds SIMMs 1 and 2, and bank 1 holds SIMMs 3 and 4. Memory can be installed using 4 MB, 8 MB, and 16 MB SIMMs using either 72-pin EDO or FPM modules, which must have at least 70 ns speed.

The Pentium memory bus between RAM and the CPU is 64 bits wide. Most 72-pin SIMM modules sold today accommodate a 32-bit data path so two SIMMs must be paired together to receive data from the 64-bit Pentium memory bus. One bank of memory on the Pentium system board must contain two 32 bit SIMMs. The other bank doesn't need to be filled, but, if it's used, both of the two SIMMs must be present in that second bank. Remember that this is the Pentium memory bus connecting the CPU and RAM, not the PCI bus, which is only 32 bits wide.

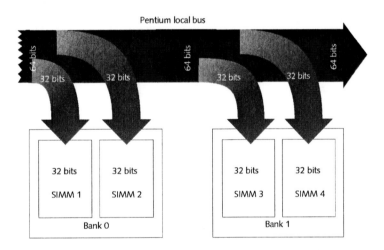

Exhibit 3-9: A Pentium memory bus is 64 bits wide and requires two 32 bit SIMMs to accommodate the bus width

The following table shows half of the memory configurations supported by a Pentium system board using SIMMs.

Pentium system boards that use DIMM modules use only one socket to a bank, since a DIMM module accommodates a data path of 64 bits. Single-sided modules come in 8, 16, 32, 64, and 128 MB sizes, and double-sided modules come in 32, 64, 128, and 256 MB sizes. The following exhibit shows how one, two, or three sockets of DIMMS can be used by a Pentium system board.

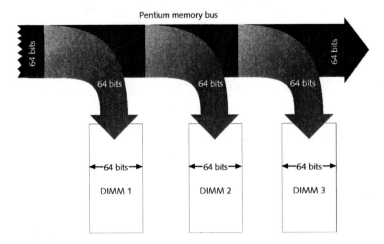

Exhibit 3-10: Only a single DIMM is needed to fill one bank of memory for a Pentium memory bus

SIMM size in bank 0	SIMM size in bank 1	Total memory
4 MB	0	8 MB
4 MB	4 MB	16 MB
4 MB	8 MB	24 MB
4 MB	16 MB	40 MB
4 MB	32 MB	72 MB
8 MB	0	16 MB
8 MB	4 MB	24 MB
8 MB	8 MB	32 MB
8 MB	16 MB	48 MB
8 MB	32 MB	80 MB
16 MB	0	32 MB
16 MB	4 MB	40 MB
16 MB	8 MB	48 MB

Selecting memory types

When you place memory on the system board, match the type of memory to the system board requirements. For example, for the first Pentium system board just discussed, the documentation says that you must use 72-pin SIMMs, which can be either EDO or FPM modules. The speed must be at least 70 ns. Avoid mixing speeds on the same system board. If you use a SIMM having one speed in one bank and a SIMM having another speed in the other bank, your computer will only work as fast as the slower bank. Always put the slower SIMMs in the first bank. However, to ensure the most reliable results, use the same speed of SIMMs in all banks and also buy the same brand of SIMMs.

For the second Pentium system board just discussed, which uses 168 pin DIMM modules, the documentation says to use unbuffered, 3.3V, PC100 DIMM SDRAM modules. The PC100 refers to the speed of the modules, meaning that the modules should be rated to work with a system board that runs at 100 MHz. You have the choice of using ECC modules. If you choose to not use them, then CMOS setup should show the feature disabled. There are three DIMM sockets on the board, and each socket represents one bank.

DIMM Location	168-pin DIMM		Total Memory
Socket 1 (Rows 0&1)	SDRAM 8, 16, 32, 64, 128, 256MB	x1	
Socket 2 (Rows 2&3)	SDRAM 8, 16, 32, 64, 128, 256MB	x1	
Socket 3 (Rows 4&5)	SDRAM 8, 16, 32, 64, 128, 256MB	x1	
	Total System Memory (Max 768MB)	=	

Exhibit 3-11: Possible combinations of DIMM sizes

Installing memory

When installing SIMMs or DIMMs, remember to protect the chips against static electricity. Always use a ground bracelet as you work. Turn the power off and remove the cover to the case. Handle memory modules with care. Ground yourself before unpacking or picking up a card. Don't stack cards, because you can loosen a chip. Usually modules pop easily into place and are secured by spring catches on both ends. Look for the notch on one side of the SIMM module that orients the module in the slot. The module slides into the slot at an angle. Place each module securely in its slot. Turn on the PC and watch the amount of memory being counted by POST during the boot process. If all the memory you expect doesn't count up correctly, remove and reseat each module carefully. To remove a module, release the latches on both sides of the module and gently rotate the module out of the socket at a 45-degree angle.

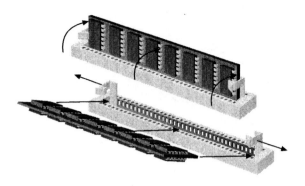

Exhibit 3-12: Installing a SIMM module

For DIMM modules, small latches on either side of the slot hold the module in place. Look for the notches on the DIMM module to orient it into the slot. Insert the module straight down into the slot, just as you would an expansion card.

For RIMM modules, the technology works so that the signal enters one end of the first RIMM socket, comes out the other end, and then moves on to the next socket. For this reason, each socket must be filled so that continuity throughout all sockets is maintained. If the socket doesn't hold a RIMM, then it must hold a placeholder module called a C-RIMM (Continuity RIMM) to assure continuity throughout all slots. The C-RIMM does not contain any memory.

Exhibit 3-13: Installing a DIMM module

Most often, placing memory on the system board is all that's necessary for installation. When the computer powers up, it counts the memory present without any further instruction and senses what features the modules support, such as parity or ECC. For some computers, you must tell the setup how much memory is present.

Do it!   **B-1:   Installing RAM**

Here's how

1 Power off the lab workstation

2 Unplug the power cord

3 Remove the case from the lab workstation

4 Locate the SIMM banks on your system board

   Place the SIMM at a 45-degree angle and then gently snap it in place

5 Replace the case

6 Plug in the power cord

7 Power on your lab workstation

8 Enter the CMOS Setup program

   Verify that Setup recognizes the correct amount of memory

9 Save the changes and reboot the workstation

10 Allow your lab workstation to boot into Windows 9x

11 Right-click the **My Computer** icon

   Choose **Properties**

12 On the General tab, locate the Computer heading

13 Verify that Windows 9x is using all of the installed memory

Unit summary: Memory

Topic A   Memory can be viewed as both **physical memory** installed on the system board and expansion boards and as **logical memory** managed by the operating system. The two kinds of physical memory are **RAM** and **ROM**.

Topic B   This topic addressed **upgrading memory**. **Memory modules** must be installed on a system board in the slots of a memory bank according to the rules specified in the system board documentation. There are a fixed number of memory configurations that a board supports.

Review questions

1 What's the difference between RAM and ROM? What is each used for?

2 What two ways could you update the system BIOS?

3 What's the main difference between SIMMs and DIMMs? What do these acronyms mean?

Unit 4

Floppy drives

Unit time: 60 minutes

Complete this unit, and you'll know how to:

A Explain how data is stored on floppy disks.

B Replace or install a disk drive.

Topic A: Storing data on a disk

Explanation

Some years ago, floppy drives came in two sizes: 5¼ inches and 3½ inches. Today, new computers are equipped with only a 3½-inch drive. However, because there are still a few computers with 5¼-inch floppy disk drives, this section covers some details about those disks as well. Although they're larger, 5¼-inch disks don't hold as much data as 3½-inch disks because 5¼-inch disks don't store data as densely as 3½-inch disks.

Overview of floppy disks

The following table summarizes the capacity of the four common types of floppy disks. You probably will not find the 5¼-inch double-density disks any more because that technology became outdated quite some time ago. The 3½-inch extra-high-density disks also didn't become as popular as first expected. Most disks today are 3½-inch high-density and hold 1.44 MB of data.

Type	Storage capacity	# of tracks per side	# of sectors per side	Cluster type
3½-inch, extra-high-density	2.88 MB	80	36	2 sectors
3½-inch, high-density	1.44 MB	80	18	1 sector
3½-inch, double-density	720K	80	9	2 sectors
5¼-inch, high density	1.2 MB	80	15	1 sector
5¼-inch, double-density	360K	40	9	2 sectors

Regardless of disk size and density, the physical hardware used to access a disk looks and works much the same way. The data cable connects from the floppy drive to a controller for the drive on the system board. In older computers, the controller board was plugged into the expansion bus in an expansion slot. The board then communicated with the CPU, passing data back and forth from the floppy disk. These controller boards often served multiple functions, having connections for a hard drive, floppy drive, and serial and parallel ports, and were called I/O cards. Today, the controller is built into the system board so that the data cable goes directly from the drive to the system board.

A floppy drive is connected to either the controller card or system board by way of a 34-pin data cable. The cable has the controller connection at one end and a drive connection at the other end. A second drive connection is placed somewhere in the middle of the cable to accommodate a second floppy drive. Having two drives share the same cable is a common practice for floppy drives as well as hard drives and CD-ROM drives.

Floppy drives receive their power from the power supply by way of a power cord. The power cord plugs into the back of the drive and has a smaller connection than the power cord for other drives in the system.

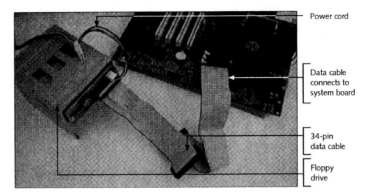

Exhibit 4-1: Floppy drive subsystem: floppy drive, data cable, and power connection

How data is physically stored on a disk

Floppy disks, no matter what density or size, store data in much the same way. When first manufactured, all disks are blank, with sheets of magnetically coated plastic. Before data can be written on a disk, the disk must first be mapped out in concentric circles called *tracks*, and in pie-shaped wedges called *sectors*. This process of preparing the disk to receive data is called *formatting* the disk. There are 80 tracks or circles on the top side of the disk and 80 more tracks on the bottom side of the disk. The tracks are numbered 0 through 79. Each side of the disk has 9 sectors, numbered 1 through 9. Even though the circles or tracks on the outside of the disk are larger than the circles closer to the center, all tracks store the same amount of data. Data is written to the tracks of the disk as bits, either a 0 or a 1. Each bit is a magnetized spot on the disk that's shaped roughly like a rectangle. Between the tracks there's a space that isn't magnetized, and there is space between each spot on a track. This spacing prevents one spot from affecting the magnetism of a nearby spot. The difference between a 0 spot and a 1 spot is the orientation of the magnetization of the spot on the disk surface.

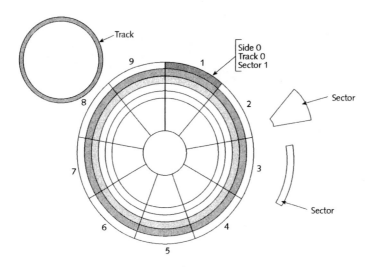

Exhibit 4-2: 3½-inch double-density floppy disk showing tracks and sectors

Data is written to and read from the disk via a magnetic *read/write head* mechanism in the floppy drive. Two heads are attached at the end of an actuator arm that freely moves back and forth over the surface of the disk. The arm has one read/write head above the disk and another read/write head below the disk. Moving in unison back and forth across the disk, the two heads lightly touch the surface of the disk, which is spinning at either 300 rpm (revolutions per minute) or 360 rpm, depending on the type of disk. Data is written first to the bottom and then to the top of the disk, beginning at the outermost circle and going in.

Exhibit 4-3: Inside a floppy disk drive

Eraser heads on either side of the read/write head ensure that the widths of the data tracks don't vary. As the data is written, the eraser heads immediately behind and to the sides of the write head clean up both sides of the magnetized spot, making a clean track of data with no "bleeding" from the track. The magnetized area doesn't spread too far from the track. All tracks are then the same width, and the distance between tracks is uniform.

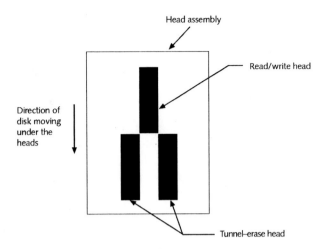

Exhibit 4-4: Uniform track widths are created by floppy drive read/write heads

The disk is actually a piece of Mylar similar to that used for overhead transparencies. Covering the surface of the Mylar is a layer of either cobalt oxide or iron oxide (rust) that can hold a magnetic charge. Some disks have another layer of Teflon on top to protect the oxide layer so that the read/write heads can move more smoothly over the surface. During formatting, the tracks are created by laying down a repeating character, the 3 (division) symbol in ASCII code, which is hex F6 or 1111 0110 in binary. The tracks are divided into sectors, and the sector that starts a new track is marked on each track with a designated code. For 3½-inch floppy disks, the sector address mark written on the disk during formatting marks the beginning sector. After formatting, actual data is written on the disk by overwriting the F6h patterns on the tracks.

The different disk types use varying degrees of magnetic strength when data is written to a disk or when a disk is formatted. For example, a 3½-inch high-density disk can hold more data than a double-density disk, because the data is written closer together. Data on the high-density disk is recorded at about twice the magnetic strength as data on the double-density disk. The high-density disk surface isn't as sensitive to a magnetic field as the double-density is and can, therefore, handle data being written to it with double the magnetic strength.

Many users have discovered that the less expensive double-density disks can be formatted as high-density, and that the format will work, and data can be written to the disk. However, such a disk isn't reliable with important data. The surface of a double-density disk is more sensitive to the magnetic field, and eventually the magnetic spots on the disk will affect each other, corrupting the data. The life span of an incorrectly formatted disk is very short. For this reason, always format a disk by using the density for which it was manufactured.

When data is read from the disk surface, the read/write head changes roles. It passes over a track on the disk, waiting for the right position on the disk to appear. When the correct sector arrives, the controller board opens a gateway, and the magnetic charge on the disk passes voltage to the read/write head. The voltage is immediately amplified and passed on to the controller board, which in turn passes the data to the expansion bus.

How data is stored logically on a disk

The word sector means two different things. A *sector* describes the entire pie-shaped wedge on one side of a disk, as well as the single segment of one track or circle that falls within the wedge. In most of our discussions, we use the term sector to mean the segment of one track, unless we specifically say that we are talking about the entire wedge. A sector, or a segment of a track, always holds 512 bytes of data. This is true for all floppy disks, no matter what the size or density.

In making the transition from how data is stored physically on a disk to how it's stored logically, the discussion turns from sectors to clusters. Sector is a physical term, but *cluster* is a logical term for describing how data is organized. The BIOS manages the disk as physical sectors, but the operating system sees the disk only as a long list of clusters that can each hold a fixed amount of data.

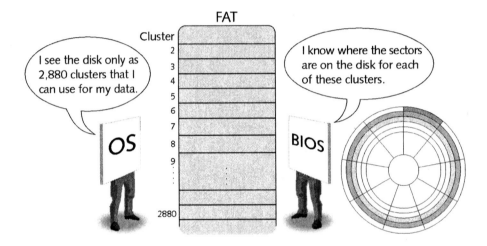

Exhibit 4-5: The operating system manages clusters or file allocation units in the FAT, and BIOS manages clusters as physical sectors on the disk

Because the operating system reads data from and writes data to a disk in fixed-length chunks called clusters, a cluster is defined as the smallest unit of data that can be read from or written to a disk at one time. Because the operating system manages a file on the disk as a group of clusters, a cluster also is called a *file allocation unit*. The operating system sees a disk as a long list of clusters, or file allocation units, and keeps that list in a table called the *file allocation table* or *FAT*.

Look at a single track on the disk in Exhibit 4-2 to see how clusters relate to sectors. Recall that there's a matching track on the bottom of the disk as well. The sector directly underneath the top sector also holds 512 bytes of data. It's written to and read from at the same time as the top sector. These two sectors together make up one cluster. On the 3½-inch double-density floppy disk in Exhibit 4-2, there are 9 sectors to each track, 80 tracks on one side of the disk, and 80 more tracks on the other side. The top and bottom sides each have 720 sectors (80 × 9). Because there are two sectors to a cluster, there are a total of 720 clusters. Each cluster holds 512 bytes × 2 = 1,024 bytes of data. There are, therefore, 1,024 × 720 = 737,280 bytes of storage space on one of these disks. Divide this number by 1,024 bytes per kilobyte and you see that the storage capacity is 720 kilobytes.

A 3½-inch high-density floppy disk has 80 tracks and 18 sectors per track on each side. There are 80 tracks × 18, or 1,440 sectors, on each side. With this type of disk, there's only one sector per cluster, making 1,440 × 2 sides, or 2,880 clusters, on the disk. Because each cluster holds only 512 bytes (one sector) of data, this type of disk has 2,880 × 512 = 1,474,560 bytes of data. Divide this number by 1,024 to convert bytes to kilobytes. The storage capacity of this disk is 1,440 kilobytes. Divide by 1,000 to convert kilobytes to megabytes, and the storage is then written as 1.44 MB.

The formatting process

The formatting of all disks is similar, no matter what size or density. During formatting, the Windows 9x or DOS FORMAT command performs the following steps:

- Creates the tracks and sectors by writing tracks as a series of F6s in hex and, as necessary, writing the sector address mark to identify the beginning sector on a track
- Creates the master boot record
- Creates two copies of the file allocation table (FAT)
- Creates the root directory

Creating the tracks and sectors

The FORMAT command is a DOS and Windows 9x command that prepares a disk for use. The first step in the formatting process erases any data that is on the disk. In its simplest form, without adding any parameters, the FORMAT command always overwrites the data with the F6h character.

The master boot record

During formatting, DOS or Windows 9x prepares the disk so that it can be written to or read from. There is no difference in the way DOS and Windows 9x prepare a disk before writing files to it.

At the beginning of each floppy disk, the first sector contains basic information about how the disk is organized. This information is collectively called the *master boot record (MBR)*. At the end of the MBR is a small program that can be used to boot from the disk. The MBR, sometimes called the DOS boot record, indicates which version of DOS or Windows was used to format the disk, and is always located at the beginning of the disk at track 0, sector 1 (bottom of the disk, outermost track). This uniformity of layout and contents enables any version of DOS or Windows to read any disk. A floppy disk has only one boot record, but a hard drive has at least two. On a floppy disk, the master boot record and the DOS boot record are the same record. On a hard drive, they are two different records, each with a different purpose.

Some disks are bootable, meaning that they contain enough DOS code to load the operating system—whatever it may be—into memory and to boot to the A prompt or B prompt, depending on the drive in which the floppy disk is inserted. To make a disk bootable, certain parts of the operating system must be present. For DOS, this is two hidden files and COMMAND.COM. These files can be loaded on the disk when it's formatted, or they can be loaded with the DOS SYS command. When Windows 9x creates a system disk, it copies Command.com and two hidden files, IO.SYS and MSDOS.SYS, to the disk to make the disk bootable.

All master boot records, however, are the same whether the disk is bootable. When the PC looks for a bootable disk during POST, if a disk is in the drive, the program stored in the master boot record is executed. This program tries to load the startup files of the operating system. On a bootable disk, the boot record contains the names of the two hidden files. For example, for IBM DOS 3.3, the file names of the hidden files are IBMBIO.COM and IBMDOS.COM. The program looks for these two files on the disk. If it doesn't find them, the disk isn't bootable and a message appears, such as the following:

```
Non-system disk or disk error...Replace and strike any key
when ready...Disk boot failure.
```

POST terminates until the user intervenes. Only the program in the master boot record can determine whether the disk is bootable.

Do it!

A-1: Defining boot priority

Question	Answer
1 What is boot priority?	
2 Why does my computer boot from the CD-ROM?	

The file allocation table (FAT)

Explanation

The next item that the FORMAT command writes to the disk is two copies of the file allocation table (FAT). The FAT contains the location of files on the disk. It basically is a one-column table; the width of each entry in the column is 12 bits. Because each entry is 12 bits, the FAT is called a 12-bit FAT or FAT 12. The FAT lists how each cluster or file allocation unit on the disk is currently used. (Remember that a cluster is the smallest unit of disk space allocated to a file.) A file can be contained in one or more clusters. The clusters need not be contiguous on the disk. In the FAT, some clusters might be marked as bad clusters (the 12 bits to mark a bad cluster are FF7h). These bits can be entered in the FAT when the disk is formatted or added later with the DOS RECOVER command. An extra copy of the FAT is kept immediately following the first. If the first is damaged, sometimes you can recover your data and files by using the second copy.

When the operating system wants to write a file to a disk, the process works as follows. The name of the file, its size, and other attributes about the file are written in a directory. A *directory*, in its simplest form, is a list of files on a disk. One of the pieces of information kept in the directory concerning this file is the cluster number where the data begins. Only the first cluster number is kept in the directory. The operating system turns to the FAT to keep track of any additional clusters that are needed to hold the file.

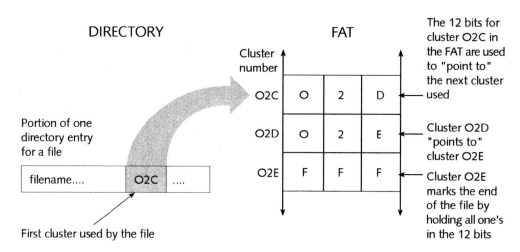

Exhibit 4-6: The operating system keeps track of where a file is stored by using a single entry in a directory and several entries in the FAT

The beginning cluster number is 02Ch and is stored in the directory. The 12-bit FAT entry for cluster 02Ch contains 02Dh, or 0000 0010 1101 binary. This entry is interpreted as the next cluster, the second cluster, used by the file. Look in the FAT entry for cluster 02Dh to see what cluster is used next, if there is one. The entry in the FAT for cluster 02Dh is 02Eh, indicating that the file continues on to a third cluster, which is 02Eh. When we look in the FAT entry for 02Eh, we see FFFh (binary 1111 1111 1111), which is the code that says that this is the last cluster used by the file. The file uses a total of three clusters.

In the following exhibit, the file contains 1,798 bytes. The file is stored beginning in cluster 4, then cluster 5, cluster 1C2, and cluster 1C3. Because this file isn't stored in consecutive clusters, it's called a *fragmented file*. Recall that the beginning cluster number and the size of the file in bytes are stored in the root directory of this disk. The disk is a 3½-inch high-density floppy disk, which has clusters equal to 1 sector, or 512 bytes. Because the file is 1,798 bytes, this file requires four whole clusters or 2,048 bytes of disk space. The first FAT entry for the file tells you that the file starts in cluster 4. The cluster 4 table entry is 005, which points to the table entry for cluster 5. Remember that all disks have 12 bits for each FAT entry. The bits are used to store 3 hex digits of 4 bits each. The location for cluster 5 has the hex numerals 1C2. Looking to cluster 1C2, you see the hex numerals 1C3, which point to cluster 1C3. At cluster 1C3 you see FFF, which marks the end of the file. These four FAT entries are called a cluster chain. The *cluster chain* determines all cluster locations for a file on a disk.

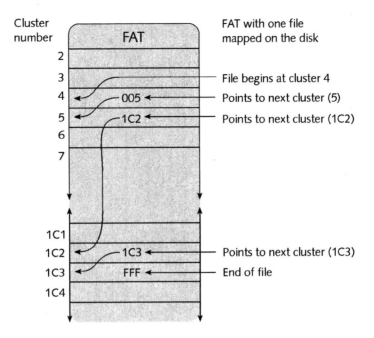

Exhibit 4-7: FAT with one file mapped on the disk

The root directory

After creating the file allocation tables, the formatting process sets up the root directory. Recall that the *root directory*, or *main directory*, is a table listing all the files that are assigned to this table. The root directory contains a fixed number of rows to accommodate a predetermined number of files and subdirectories; the number of available rows depends on the disk type.

Disk type	Number of root directory entries
5¼-inch, double-density	112
5¼-inch, high-density	224
3½-inch, double-density	112
3½-inch, high-density	224

In summary, for DOS, the FORMAT command writes tracks and sectors on a disk, and creates a master boot record, an empty file allocation table, and an empty root directory. If you include the /S option in the FORMAT line, you add the two hidden files and COMMAND.COM that together make a disk bootable. The three files are referenced in the FAT and in the root directory. The two hidden files have their file attribute bit 7, the hidden bit, set to 1 (hidden). When you make a Windows 9x rescue disk, the two hidden files and COMMAND.COM are copied to the disk to make the disk bootable.

Do it!

A-2: Discussing the floppy disk formatting process

Question	Answer
1 What DOS command is used to prepare a floppy disk for use?	
2 Describe the format process.	
3 Describe the difference between a sector and a track.	
4 Why does a floppy disk have only one master boot record while hard drives have two?	
5 What is a file allocation table?	
6 Why are two copies of the FAT created?	
7 What is the root directory?	

Topic B: Supporting floppy drives

Explanation

This section addresses problems that can occur with a floppy drive and its support system, how to replace the drive and controller card, and how to add an additional floppy drive to a computer system. When a floppy drive can't read a disk, the problem might have many causes.

Many computers today come with one 3½-inch floppy drive, a hard drive, and a CD-ROM drive. The machine might have one or two empty bays for a second floppy drive or for a Zip drive. If you don't have an extra bay and want to add another drive, you can attach an external drive that comes in its own case and has its own power supply.

Floppy drives are now so inexpensive that it is impractical to repair one. Once you determine that the drive itself has a problem, simply open the case, remove the drive, and replace it with a new one. This procedure takes no more than 30 minutes, assuming, of course, that you don't damage or loosen something else in the process and create a new reason for troubleshooting.

Using floppy drive testing software

To determine whether a drive is damaged takes only a short time if you have the proper software tools. You can test your floppy drives by using diagnostic utilities like Nuts & Bolts (by Helix Software) and TestDrive (by MicroSystems Development Technologies, Inc.). The explanation below of what the drive-testing software checks will help you solve drive problems and give you some insight into how floppy drives work. By working with floppy drive diagnostic software, you can test these criteria:

- **Azimuth skew:** Does the drive head align itself well with the tracks, or is it at a tangent?
- **Hub centering:** Does the disk wobble as it turns, or does it turn in a perfect circle?
- **Hysteresis:** Can the drive find a track regardless of the direction from which it approaches the track?
- **Radial alignment:** Is the drive head centered correctly on the track, or is it too far to the left or the right?
- **Rotational speed:** Does the drive turn the floppy disk at the proper speed?
- **Sensitivity:** How far from the data must the head be before it can read the data?

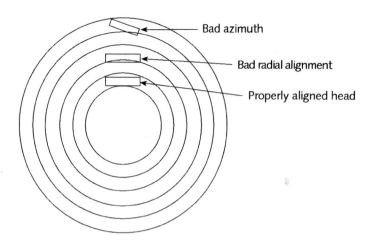

Exhibit 4-8: Alignment of floppy drive heads

Over time, floppy drives can slowly shift out of alignment. A symptom of this problem is that a disk written by one drive can't be read by another drive. To check thoroughly for these kinds of problems, the testing software must have a disk that it can use as its standard to measure the drive. The software determines how the drive reads the data from a disk that it knows to be written perfectly. These disks are known as *digital diagnostic disks* or *DDDs* and can be purchased at computer stores. The TestDrive software uses a DDD for several of its tests. We ask you to do only those tests that don't require the DDD disk.

When a floppy disk drive doesn't work

Sometimes a problem with the floppy drive arises during POST, and BIOS displays an error message. Error messages in the 600 range occur when the floppy drive didn't pass the POST test. These problems can be caused by the power supply, the drive, or the controller board.

Even if POST finds no errors, you might still have a problem. If you put a disk in a faulty drive and issue a command to access the disk, an error message such as the following might appear on the screen:

```
General failure reading drive A: Abort, Retry, Fail?
```

Or, perhaps nothing happens and the computer simply stops working. The problem might come from several sources, including the following:

- The application you're currently running is pointing to a different drive.
- DOS or Windows 9x might have just encountered an unrelated error that has locked up the system.
- The System BIOS or CMOS Setup isn't correctly configured.
- The disk in the drive isn't formatted.
- The floppy drive is bad.
- The shuttle window on the floppy disk isn't able to open fully.

- The floppy drive controller card is loose in the expansion slot or has a bad chip.
- The cable from the controller card to the drive is damaged or poorly connected.
- The edge color on the cable isn't aligned with Pin 1.
- The power supply is bad.
- The power supply cable to the drive is loose or disconnected.
- The command just issued has a mistake or is the wrong command.
- The drive latch isn't closed, or the disk is inserted incorrectly.

When you have any computer trouble, check the simple things first. Here are a few suggestions for solving drive problems:

- Remove the disk. Does the shuttle window move freely? Do you see any debris on the disk's Mylar surface? Does the disk spin freely inside the housing cover? Some new disks simply need a little loosening up. Put the disk back in the drive and try to access it again.
- Does the light on the correct drive go on? Maybe you're trying to access drive B, but the disk is in drive A.
- Does another disk work in the drive? If so, the problem is probably caused by the disk, not the drive. There is an exception to this statement. The drive might be out of alignment. If it is, the drive will be unable to read a disk that it didn't format, although it might read a disk that it formatted with its own alignment. To test this possibility, try several disks, and note whether the drive reads only those disks that it has recently formatted. If so, then you might have identified the problem, and you probably will want to replace the drive.
- Does the drive light come on at all? If not, then the problem might be with the software or the hardware. Try to access the disk with other software. Can DOS access the drive with a simple DIR A: command? Can File Manager or Windows Explorer access the disk? How about using the CHKDSK A: command? If the light doesn't come on even then, consider that the problem might be with the power to the drive or the hardware connections inside the case. Does the other drive work? If both lights refuse to come on, consider the power supply or the floppy drive controller card as the source of your problem.
- Does the light come on and then stay on at boot? This is most likely caused by the cable not being attached correctly to Pin 1. Check the edge color to see that it's aligned with Pin 1.
- Has this drive been used recently? Perhaps the system setup has lost CMOS data. The system might think it has a 720 KB drive when it really has a 1.44 MB drive. Access the setup and check the drive specifications.
- Reboot the machine and try again. Many problems with computers disappear with a simple reboot. If a soft boot doesn't do it, try a hard boot.
- Try cleaning the drive's read/write heads. Use a head-cleaning kit that includes a paper disk and a cleaning solution. Follow the directions that come with the kit. You can purchase a kit at any store that sells computer supplies.

- If the drive still refuses to work with any disk and any software, then you must dig deeper. Inside the case, the hardware that can cause this problem is the drive itself, the data cable from the controller card to the drive, the power supply, the power cable, or the system board. To find the culprit, replace each hardware component with a known good component, one component at a time, until the problem goes away. It's helpful to have access to another working computer from which you can borrow parts.

  Tip: When you're trying to discover which device is causing a problem during a troubleshooting session, you can trade a suspected device for one you know is good (called a *known-good device*). You also can install the device you suspect is bad in a computer system you know works. If the problem follows the device, then you know the device is bad.

- Turn off the computer and open the computer case. Check every connection from the system board to the drive. Check the power cable connection. Remove the controller card. If the second drive works, there is a chance (but not a guarantee) that the problem isn't the card or its connection. Using a clean white eraser, clean the edge connector and reseat the board.

- Take the power cable from the second working floppy drive and put it on the non-working one to eliminate the power cable as the problem.

- Replace the data cable and try the drive again. Make sure to align the cable correctly with Pin 1. Exchange the controller card. If that doesn't work, exchange the drive itself and try again.

- If the drive still doesn't work, suspect the system board or the ROM BIOS on the system board.

Common error messages and their meanings

Here are some common error messages that might be caused by problems with a floppy drive, together with what they mean.

```
Non-system disk or disk error. Replace and strike any key when
ready.
```

This message says that you are trying to boot from a disk that isn't bootable. Remove the disk from the drive and press any key. The computer bypasses the floppy drive and loads the operating system from the hard drive. If you really did intend to boot from the floppy drive, the disk you're using should have been formatted with the /S option, or you should have used the SYS command to place the two hidden DOS system files on the disk together with COMMAND.COM. These three files are necessary to load DOS. To boot from a rescue disk in Windows 9x, first create the rescue disk.

If you had no disk in the floppy drive, then you can assume that some of your critical operating system files are missing from the hard drive. In this case, boot from a bootable floppy disk or rescue disk, and check whether the files have been erased accidentally from your hard drive.

```
Invalid or missing COMMAND.COM
```

This error appears when DOS is loading and the two hidden files are present, but COMMAND.COM isn't present or is corrupt. Boot from a bootable disk that has COMMAND.COM and then copy the file to the disk that you want to be bootable.

```
Incorrect DOS version
```

This message appears when you try to use a DOS command such as FORMAT or BACKUP. These commands are called external commands in DOS, because they require a program to execute that isn't part of COMMAND.COM. DOS contains a number of programs that reside on the hard drive in a directory named \DOS or, in the case of Windows 9x, in a directory named \Windows\Command. When you type the FORMAT or BACKUP command, you're really executing these programs. DOS knows which version of DOS these programs belong to and the error message tells you that the FORMAT or BACKUP program that you're using doesn't belong to the version of DOS that you presently have loaded.

```
Invalid Drive Specification
```

You're trying to access a drive that the operating system doesn't know is available. For example, the error might appear under this situation: During booting, an error message appears indicating that BIOS can't access the hard drive. You boot from a floppy disk in drive A and get an A prompt. You then try to access drive C from the A prompt, and you get the above message. DOS or Windows 9x tells you that it can't find drive C because it failed the test during POST. As far as the operating system is concerned, the hard drive doesn't exist.

```
Not ready reading drive A: Abort, Retry, Fail?
```

This message means the floppy disk in drive A isn't readable. Maybe the disk is missing or is inserted incorrectly. The disk might have a bad boot record, errors in the FAT, or bad sectors. Try using Nuts & Bolts or Norton Utilities to examine the disk for corruption.

```
General failure reading drive A: Abort, Retry, Fail?
```

This message means the floppy disk is badly corrupted or not yet formatted. Sometimes this error means that the floppy drive is bad. Try another disk. If you determine that the problem is the disk and not the drive, the disk is probably unusable. A bad master boot record sometimes gives this message.

```
Track 0 bad, disk not usable
```

This message typically occurs when you try to format a disk by using the wrong disk type. Check your FORMAT command. Most manufacturers write the disk type on the disk. If you have a 3½-inch floppy disk, you can determine whether you're using a high-density or double-density disk by the see-through holes at the corners of the disk. The high-density disk has holes on two corners; the double-density has a hole on only one corner. Don't try to format a disk by using the wrong density.

```
Write-protect error writing drive A:
```

The disk is write-protected and the application is trying to write to it. To write to a 3½-inch floppy disk, the write-protect window must be closed, meaning that the switch must be toward the center of the disk so that you can't see through the write-protect hole. To write to a 5¼-inch floppy disk, the write-protect notch must be uncovered.

If you have a damaged floppy disk, you have many choices to recover most, if not all, of the data on the disk, especially when you understand how the data is stored and have the right tools for the job.

Replacing a floppy drive

Replacing a disk drive is easy; here is a five-step summary of how to replace a floppy drive. Each step is described in more detail below:

1 Check that the computer and other peripherals are working. Can you boot to the hard drive or another floppy drive? You should know where your starting point is.

2 Turn off the computer and remove the cover.

3 Unplug the data cable and power cable from the old drive. Unscrew and dismount the drive.

4 Slide the new drive into the bay. Reconnect the data cable and power cable.

5 Turn the computer on and check the setup. Test the drive. Turn the computer off and replace the cover.

Check that the computer and other peripherals work

Imagine yourself in the following situation. You're asked to install a floppy disk drive in a computer. You remove the cover, install the drive, and turn on the PC. Nothing happens. No power, no lights, nothing. Or perhaps the PC doesn't boot successfully, giving errors during POST that appear to have nothing to do with your newly installed floppy drive. Now you don't know whether you created the problem or if it existed before you started. That's why you check the computer before you begin and make sure you know what's working and not working. The extra time is well worth it if you face a situation like this.

Here is a suggestion for a quick system check of a PC that you should do before you start to work:

- Turn on the computer and verify that it boots to the operating system with no errors.
- In Windows 9x, open a program and perform a task from the program.
- Get a directory listing of files on a floppy disk and a CD-ROM.
- In Windows 9x, run ScanDisk.

Turn off the computer and remove the cover

Guard the computer against static electricity by using a ground bracelet, working on a hard floor (not on carpet), and grounding yourself before you touch any components inside the case. *Never* touch anything inside the case while the power is on. Remove the cover and set its screws aside in a safe place.

Next, prepare to remove the power cable. The power supply cable is a four-pronged cable that attaches to the back of the drive. The cable can be difficult to detach at times, because the connection is very secure. Be careful not to apply so much pressure that you break off the corner of the logic board. Steady the board with one hand while you dislodge the power cable with the other.

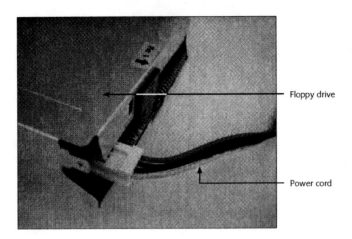

Exhibit 4-9: Power supply connection on the back of a drive

Unplug the data cable and power cable from the old drive and unscrew and dismount the drive

Before removing the cables and the drive, note carefully how they're assembled to help you in reassembling later. The data cable might go to an adapter card or directly to the system board. Before removing the cable, note that the cable has a color or stripe down one side. This edge color marks this side of the cable as Pin 1. Look on the board to which the cable is attached. Verify that Pin 1 or Pin 2 is clearly marked, and that the colored edge is aligned with Pin 1 on both the controller card and the drive. Sometimes Pin 1 on the floppy drive is marked, and sometimes the drive housing is constructed so that the cable built for the drive inserts in only one direction. Note the position of Pin 1 on the drive.

Look at the cable connecting drive A to the floppy drive controller card on the system board. There is a twist in the cable. This twist reverses the leads in the cable, causing the addresses for this cable to be different from the addresses for the cable that doesn't have the twist. The cable with the twist determines which drive will be drive A. This drive is always the one that the startup BIOS looks to first for a bootable disk, unless a change is made in CMOS Setup, instructing startup BIOS to look to a different drive. By switching the cable with the twist with the cable without the twist, you exchange drives A and B. Some computers have two drives attached to the same cable. In this case, the drive attached behind the twist is drive A, and the one attached before the twist is drive B. After you're familiar with the cable orientation and connection, remove the cable from the floppy drive.

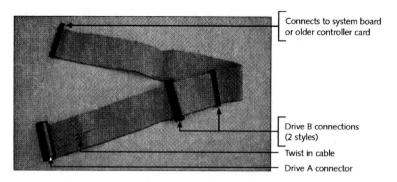

Exhibit 4-10: Twist in cable determines which drive will be drive A

Now that the cables are detached, you can remove the floppy drive. Some drives have one or two screws on each side of the drive attaching the drive to the drive bay. After you remove the screws, the drive usually slides to the front and out of the case. Sometimes there is a catch underneath the drive that you must lift up as you slide the drive forward. Be careful not to remove screws that hold the circuit card on top of the drive to the drive housing; all this should stay intact.

Slide the new drive into the bay. Reconnect the data cable and power cable.

If the new drive is too narrow to fit snugly into the bay, you can buy an adapter kit with extensions for narrow drives so that they can reach the sides of the bay. Screw the drive down with the same screws used on the old drive. You might have difficulty reaching the screw hole on the back of the drive if it's against the side of the case. Make sure the drive is anchored so that it can't slide forward, backward, up, or down even if the case is turned on its side (as many users will do).

Next, you reconnect the data cable, making sure that the colored edge of the cable is connected to the Pin 1 side of the connection. Most connections on floppy drives are oriented the same way, so this one probably has the same orientation as the old drive. The power cable goes into the power connection only one way, so you can't go wrong here.

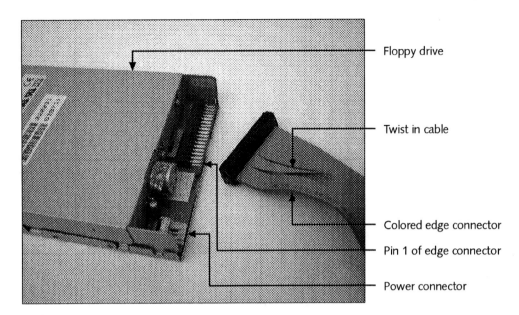

Exhibit 4-11: Connect colored edge of cable to pin 1

Turn on the computer, check the setup, and test the drive

Double-check all connections and turn on the computer. If you changed disk types, you must inform CMOS Setup by accessing setup and changing the drive type. Test the drive by formatting a disk or doing a DISKCOPY. If you determine that all is well, replace the cover and you're done.

Note that you can run the computer while the cover is off. If the drive doesn't work, it's much easier to turn off the computer, check connections, and try again with the cover off. Just make certain that you don't touch anything while the computer is on. Leaving the computer on while you disconnect a cable and connect it again is very dangerous for the PC and will probably damage something.

Do it!

B-1: Removing and reinstalling the floppy drive

Here's how
1 Power off your PC
Verify that you're properly grounded
Unplug the power cord from the system unit
2 Remove the top of the case
3 Unplug the data cable connected to the 3½-inch floppy drive
4 Unplug the power connector for the 3½-inch floppy drive
5 Dismount the 3½-inch floppy drive and remove it
6 Stand clear of the case and plug in the power cord
7 Power on your lab workstation and enter the CMOS Setup program
Remove the 3½-inch floppy drive from the Setup program
8 Save your changes and reboot your lab workstation into Windows 9x
9 Double-click **My Computer**
Verify that Windows 9x doesn't recognize any floppy drives
10 If an icon for the 3½-inch floppy drive exists, remove it (Display the System properties and on the Device Manager tab, double-click Floppy disk controllers, select the 3½ floppy drive, and press Delete.)
11 Reboot your lab workstation
Double-click **My Computer** to verify that Windows doesn't recognize any floppy drives
12 Reinstall the floppy drive and verify that it works

Removable drives

Explanation

Removable drives provide several advantages. They increase the overall storage capacity of a system, make it easy to move large files from one computer to another, serve as a convenient medium for making backups of hard drive data, and make it easy to secure important files. (To keep important files secure, keep the removable drive in a safe when it's not used.) A removable drive can be either an external or internal drive.

When purchasing a removable drive consider how susceptible the drive is when dropped. The *drop height* is the height from which the manufacturer says you can drop the drive without making the drive unusable. Also consider how long the data will last on the drive. The *half-life* (sometimes called life expectancy or shelf life) of the disk is the time it takes for the magnetic strength of the medium to weaken by half. Magnetic media, including traditional hard drives and floppy disks, have a half-life of five to seven years, but optical media such as CD-ROMs have a half-life of 30 years.

An internal removable drive should also be Plug and Play compliant meaning that the drive can interface with Plug and Play BIOS and with Windows 9x and Windows 2000 installations without having to set switches and jumpers manually.

High-capacity disk drives

The Iomega 3½-inch Zip drive stores 100 MB or 250 MB of data on each of its disks and has a drop height of eight feet. An internal 100 MB Zip drive costs less than $100 and uses an IDE interface. An IDE interface is a way for a storage device to connect to a computer system and is covered in detail later. The external Zip drive plugs into the parallel port, a USB port, or a SCSI port. The drive and disk look like a traditional 3½-inch floppy disk drive and disk, but the disk is slightly larger. If you include a Zip drive on a new PC, consider it an add-on, not a replacement for the standard 3½-inch disk drive.

Exhibit 4-12: An internal Zip drive kit includes the IDE Zip drive, documentation, drivers on floppy disk, and one Zip disk

Another removable drive technology is SuperDisk LS-120 (laser servo 120 MB), developed by Imation. The disk holds 120 MB of data and is backward compatible with double-density (720K) and high-density (1.44 MB) floppy disks. The SuperDisk is really two disk drives in one. It can use the old technology to read from and write to regular floppy disks, and it can use laser technology to read/write 120 MB. A SuperDisk is about five times faster than a regular floppy drive. One advantage SuperDisk has over Zip drives is its backward compatibility with regular floppy disks. SuperDisk drives can be purchased as external (parallel port and USB) or internal drives for about $150.

Hard disk removable drives

The Iomega Jaz drive is one example of a magnetic media removable drive that stores 1 GB or 2 GB of data on each removable disk. Both the internal and external models use a SCSI connection. Iomega advertises that you can back up 1 GB of data from your fixed hard drive to the Jaz drive in as little as five minutes. The drop height is three feet.

Installing a removable drive

Installing an internal removable drive is similar to installing a hard drive. If the external or internal drive is a SCSI drive, the SCSI host adapter must already be installed and configured. Do the following to install an external removable drive:

1   Identify the connectors. Many removable drives use the parallel port, a USB port, or a SCSI port for connection. A parallel drive has a 25-pin connector for the cable to the 25-pin parallel port on the back of the PC and another 25-pin connector for the printer cable. A SCSI drive has a 25-pin, 50-pin, or 68-pin connector on the drive for the cable to the PC and another connector for the next SCSI device on the external SCSI bus. For USB, there might be a second USB connection on the device for pass-through to another USB device.

2 For a parallel device, turn off your PC and connect the parallel cable from the drive to the parallel port on the PC. If you have a printer, connect the printer cable to the printer port on the drive. Go to Step 6.

3 For a USB device, connect the USB cable to the USB port. Go to Step 6.

4 For a SCSI device, with the SCSI host adapter installed, connect the SCSI cable to the drive and to the SCSI port on the host adapter.

5 For a SCSI drive, set the drive's SCSI ID. You might also need to set the host adapter to recognize an external device. See the documentation for the host adapter.

6 Check all your connections and plug the AC power cord for the drive into a wall socket.

7 Turn on your PC and install the software. See the installation procedures in the documentation that came with the removable drive. Most often, the software is on an accompanying disk.

8 If you have problems, turn everything off and check all connections. Power up and try again.

Do it!

B-2: Discussing removable drives

Question	Answer
1 List the advantages of using removable drives.	
2 How do external removable drives interface with the CPU?	
3 What is the drop height?	
4 Name three removable drives.	

Unit summary: Floppy drives

Topic A

You learned that **floppy disks** are popular because they're cheap and convenient, and are considered a standard device. Data is stored on floppy disks in concentric circles called **tracks** or **cylinders**. Each track is divided into **sectors**. When a disk is formatted for use, the formatting process creates tracks and sectors and places an **MBR**, **FAT**, and **root directory** on the disk.

Topic B

Installing a floppy disk drive in a PC involves firmly anchoring the drive in the bay, connecting the data cable and power cable, and informing CMOS Setup of the new drive. The computer distinguishes drive A from drive B by a twist in the data cable. The drive that gets the twist is drive A. **Removable drives** increase the overall storage capacity of a system, provide a backup medium, and make it easier to move large files and secure important ones.

Review questions

1 John's computer attempts to boot from his CD-ROM drive before the floppy drive. How can he change the boot priority of his CD-ROM drive?

2 What must you do after physically installing a floppy drive?

3 Stacey just installed a floppy drive into her PC, but the floppy drive icon doesn't show up when she boots into Windows. Assuming the drive was installed correctly, what would you recommend Stacey do to make Windows recognize it?

4 Dave recently removed one of his floppy drives from his PC. He now receives an error message every time he reboots his computer. What would you recommend Dave do to eliminate this error message?

Unit 5

Hard drives

Unit time: 150 minutes

Complete this unit, and you'll know how to:

A Identify the various types of hard drives and understand the underlying technology and advantages of each.

B Describe how data is stored on a hard drive.

C Install a hard drive.

D Troubleshoot hard drive problems and recover lost data.

Topic A: Overview of hard drives

Explanation

Hard drives used in today's microcomputers have their origin in the hard drives of early mainframe computers of the 1970s. These drives consisted of large platters or disks that were much larger and thicker than phonograph records. Several platters were stacked together with enough room so that read/write heads could move back and forth between the platters. All heads moved in unison while the platters spun at a fast speed. Applications programmers of the 1970s were responsible for how and where data was written to the platters. They wrote their programs so that data was spaced evenly over the disks so that the heads moved as little as possible while reading or writing a file. They could judge their success by standing over the clear cover of the hard drive and watching the heads. If they had programmed well, the heads moved smoothly over the platters; if not, they thrashed back and forth as data was processed. In today's systems, things are much more complicated. There are several layers of software between data stored on a hard drive or floppy disk and the applications that might be reading data from or writing data to the disk. Learning about these layers, how they relate to one another, and how they manage the hard drive is the focus of this chapter.

Hard drive technology

Modern hard drives have two or more stacked platters and spin in unison. Read/write heads are controlled by an actuator and move in unison back and forth across the disk surfaces as the disks rotate on a spindle. There are several types of hard drives for PCs, all using a magnetic medium; the data on all these drives is stored in tracks and sectors, and data files are addressed in clusters made up of one or more sectors.

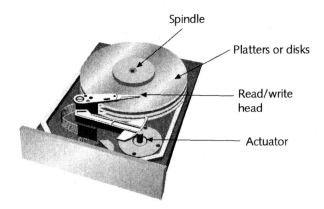

Exhibit 5-1: Inside a hard drive case

Some hard drives have four platters. All eight sides of these four platters are used to store data, although on some hard drives the top side of the first platter just holds information used to track the data and manage the disk. As with floppy drives, each side or surface of one hard drive platter is called a head. (Not to be confused with the read/write mechanism that moves across a platter, which is called a read/write head.) Also as with floppy drives, each head is divided into tracks and sectors. The eight tracks, all of which are the same distance from the center of the platters, together make up one cylinder. If a disk has 300 tracks per head, then it also has that same number of cylinders.

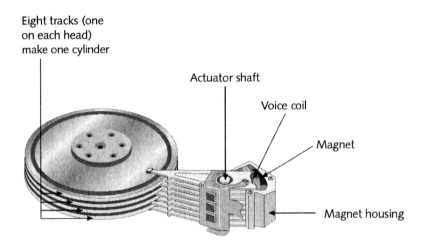

Exhibit 5-2: A hard drive with four platters

Just as with floppy disks, data is written to a hard drive beginning at the outermost track. The entire first cylinder is filled before the read/write heads move inward and begin filling the second cylinder. The tracks closer to the center of a platter are smaller, but have to store the same amount of data as the larger tracks toward the outside of a platter. At some point as the heads move toward the center of the drive and the tracks get smaller and smaller, the read/write heads have to adjust the way they write data so that sectors store a consistent number of bytes, even if they're different physical sizes. Two methods can be used to adjust for the smaller tracks: write precompensation and reduced write current.

Write precompensation speeds up the writing of data to the drive as the tracks become smaller near the center of the platters. If a hard drive uses write precompensation, it indicates at what track or cylinder the precompensation begins. Appendix B shows that some drives don't use this method. Some tables list the write precompensation as the total number of cylinders for the drive type. Interpret this to mean that precompensation isn't used.

Reduced write current means just what it says. At some cylinder near the center of the platter, the read/write heads reduce the current used to place magnetized spots on a disk, because the spots are getting closer and closer together. Reduced write current isn't as common as write precompensation.

IDE technology

Almost all hard drives on the market today use *IDE (Integrated Device Electronics* formerly Integrated Drive Electronics) standards, but it wasn't always so. Older hard drive technologies, a few of which are still in use, include MFM, RLL, and ESDI. A variation of IDE technology is Enhanced IDE (EIDE) and SCSI, which contains an IDE drive with an especially fast I/O bus with its own bus controller.

In addition to a hard drive in a PC, removable drives are becoming more and more popular. The following sections discuss how IDE, SCSI, and removable drives work; MFM and RLL drives are covered for historical reasons only, to help you understand the basics behind today's drive technology.

As described earlier, a hard drive consists of two or more platters spinning inside an airtight housing with read/write heads that move back and forth across the platters. The drive fits into a bay inside the computer case and is securely attached to the bay with supports or braces and screws. This helps prevent the drive from being jarred while the disk is spinning and the heads are very close to the disk surfaces.

A hard drive requires a controller board filled with ROM programming to instruct the read/write heads how, where, and when to move across the platters and how to write and read data. In IDE and SCSI drives, a controller is mounted on a circuit board on the drive housing and is an integral part of it. (Hence the term Integrated Device Electronics, or IDE.) Older RLL and MFM drives had the controller board as a separate, large expansion car connected to the drive with two cables. Today, the controller of an IDE drive connects to the system board by way of a data cable from the drive to an IDE connection directly on the system board. Older system boards didn't have an IDE connection on the board, so a small *adapter card* served as a simple pass-through from the drive to the system board. The data cable attached to the drive and the adapter card, which was inserted in an ISA slot on the system board. Sometimes an adapter card connects a hard drive to a system board to compensate for the system board BIOS not supporting a large-capacity drive. The adapter card contains the necessary BIOS to support the drive in the place of the system BIOS.

The following exhibit shows a hardware subsystem including an IDE hard drive and its connection to a system board. In addition to the connection for the 40-pin data cable, the hard drive has a connection for the power cord from the power supply.

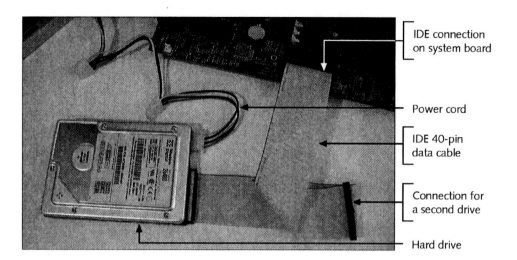

IDE connection
on system board

Power cord

IDE 40-pin
data cable

Connection for
a second drive

Hard drive

Exhibit 5-3: A PC's hard drive subsystem

Almost all drives on the market today are IDE technology. Although IDE technology is
an innovative improvement over MFM and RLL type hard drives, it also introduces
some new limitations. To understand how IDE technology differs from other drive
technologies, the details of how drives are low-level formatted must be examined.

Tracks and sectors on an IDE drive

The MFM and RLL technologies use either 17 or 26 sectors per track over the entire
drive platter. The larger tracks near the outside of the platter contain the same number of
bytes as the smaller tracks near the center of the platter. This arrangement made the
formatting of a drive and later accessing data simpler, but it wastes drive space. The
number of bytes that a track can hold is determined by the centermost track, and all
other tracks are forced to follow this restriction.

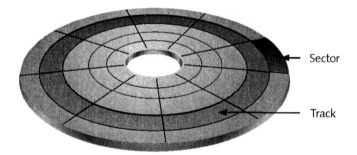

Sector

Track

*Exhibit 5-4: Floppy drives and older hard drives use a constant number of sectors per
track*

One major improvement with IDE technology is that the formatting of IDE drives eliminates this restriction. The number of sectors per track on an IDE drive isn't the same throughout the platter. In this new formatting system, called *zone bit recording*, tracks near the center have the smallest number of sectors per track, and the number of sectors increases as the tracks get larger. In other words, each track on an IDE drive is designed to have the optimum number of sectors appropriate to the size of the track. There are still 512 bytes per sector for every sector on the drive; this consistency makes it simpler for the operating system to communicate with the drive.

Because different tracks have different numbers of sectors, when the operating system communicates with an IDE drive, it can't interface with the BIOS hard drive controller by using sector and track coordinates, as it does with floppy disks and older hard drives. Newer, more sophisticated methods must be used that are discussed later in this unit.

Formatting a hard drive

When DOS formats a floppy disk, it writes sector and track markings on the disk. With IDE drives, since the track and sector markings no longer follow a simple pattern, they are written on the hard drive at the factory. This process is called *low-level formatting*. The operating system still executes the remainder of the format process (creating a boot sector, FAT, and root directory), which is called the *high-level format* or *OS format*.

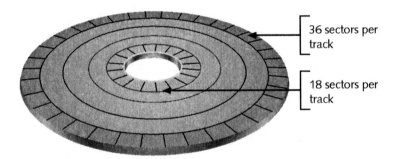

36 sectors per track

18 sectors per track

Exhibit 5-5: Zone bit recording can have more sectors per track

With older RLL and MFM technology, the system BIOS, operating system, or utility software could perform the low-level format; even now there is still a low-level format routine that is part of standard system BIOS. For an IDE drive, however, using system BIOS or standard utility software to low-level format a drive would probably ruin the drive.

Because of the unique way that an IDE drive is formatted and data is accessed, you must use a controller specific to the IDE drive. IDE drives thus have their controller built directly on top or on the bottom of the drive housing. The controller and the drive are permanently attached to one another.

Because IDE drives are low-level formatted by the manufacturer, they can't be low-level formatted as part of preventive maintenance, as older drives can be. The track and sector markings on the drive created at the factory are normally expected to last for the life of the drive. For this reason IDE drives are often referred to as disposable drives. When the track and sector markings fade, as they eventually do, you just throw the drive away and buy a new one.

However, improvements for formatting the IDE drive are becoming more commonplace. Some IDE drive manufacturers offer a low-level format program specific to their drives. If an IDE drive continues to give "Bad Sector or Sector Not Found" errors, or even becomes totally unusable, ask the manufacturer for a program to perform a low-level format of the drive. Sometimes these programs are only distributed by the manufacturer to dealers, resellers, or certified service centers.

IDE drives last several years without a refresher low-level format. By that time, you're probably ready to upgrade to a larger drive anyway.

System-based support for IDE drives

When IDE drives first entered the marketplace, an adapter card in an expansion slot connected the drive to the system board. Today, most system boards support IDE by providing one or two IDE connections directly on the system board. To alert a user when a hard disk is accessed, a system board has a two-pin connection that connects to an LED on the front of the computer case. A lit LED means a hard drive is being accessed.

Setup for IDE drives is very simple; the most important fact that setup and the OS need to know is how many sectors there are on the drive. It's important not to overestimate the number of sectors. You don't want the OS requesting use of a sector that doesn't exist. However, you can tell setup that you have fewer sectors than are present. If you do, some sectors will remain unused.

Enhanced IDE (EIDE) drives

Early IDE drives followed the IDE/ATA (Integrated Device Electronics AT Attachment) standard 1 developed by ANSI. This standard is sometimes referred to as the IDE standard or the ATA standard. It involves how the drive interfaces with BIOS and software more than it does the actual drive technology. By using this ATA standard interface, drives were limited to 528 MB and could have no more than 1,024 cylinders. There could be no more than two hard drives on the same interface. This standard applied only to hard drives and didn't include CD-ROM drives, tape drives, and so on. It has been improved several times as drive technology and methods of interface have improved.

Enhanced IDE (EIDE) drives support these newer, faster standards. The first standard supported by EIDE was ATA-2. With this new standard, you could have up to four IDE devices on the same PC. These IDE devices could be hard drives, CD-ROM drives, or tape drives as well as other IDE devices. CD-ROM drives use the ATAPI standard. As standards were developed, different hard drive manufacturers adopted different names for them, which was confusing. Standards today specify data transfer speed more than any other single factor. When selecting a hard drive standard, select the fastest standard you can, but keep in mind that the operating system, BIOS on the system board, and the hard drive must all support this standard. If one of three doesn't support the standard, the other two will probably revert to using a slower standard that all three can use.

SCSI technology

SCSI (pronounced "scuzzy"), *Small Computer Systems Interface,* is a standard for communication between a subsystem of peripheral devices and the system bus. SCSI is somewhat like a small LAN inside a computer. More accurately, SCSI is a kind of bus. The SCSI bus is a closed system that can contain, and be used by, up to 7 or 15 devices, depending on the SCSI standard used. The gateway from this bus to the system bus is an adapter card inserted into an expansion slot on the system board. The adapter card, called the *host adapter,* is responsible for managing all the devices on the SCSI bus. When one of these devices must communicate with the system bus, the data passes through the host adapter.

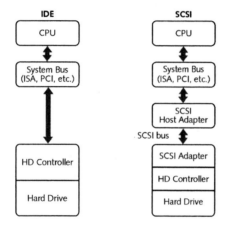

Exhibit 5-6: How SCSI and IDE hard drives communicate with the CPU

The host adapter is responsible for keeping up with the interchange between the devices on the SCSI bus and the system bus. SCSI technology has the added advantage that two devices on the SCSI bus can pass data back and forth between them across the SCSI bus without ever having to go through the CPU. This method of data transmission provides a convenient way to back up a SCSI hard drive on a tape drive on the same host adapter without involving the CPU in the activity.

The maximum number of devices the SCSI bus can support depends on the type of SCSI being used. Some SCSI buses can link up to seven, others up to 15 devices. Each device on the bus is assigned a number from zero to seven called the *SCSI ID* or the *LUN (logical unit number)*, by using DIP switches, dials on the device, or software settings. The host adapter is assigned a number larger than all other devices, either 7 or 15. Cables connect the devices physically in a straight chain. The devices can be internal or external, and the host adapter can be at end of the chain or somewhere in the middle.

A SCSI device such as a hard drive, tape drive, or CD-ROM drive interfaces with the host adapter rather than directly with the CPU. The technology of a SCSI device can be the same as the technology of a similar device that isn't SCSI, with the added functionality of being able to use the SCSI bus and communicate with the host adapter. A device is a SCSI device not because of the technology of the device but because of the bus it uses.

Just as with IDE drives, a SCSI hard drive has its controller mounted directly on the drive and can have a variable number of sectors per track, and therefore shouldn't be low-level formatted after leaving the factory. In fact, most SCSI drives are IDE drives. Technically, a SCSI drive can simply be an IDE drive with one more chip on the controller card on top of the drive and a different kind of data connection designed to fit the SCSI standard. The SCSI chip, called the *SCSI bus adapter chip (SBAC)*, controls the transfer of data over the SCSI bus.

On the left side, the CPU communicates with the hard drive controller, which is contained in the hard drive case, through the system bus. On the right side, the CPU communicates over the system bus to the SCSI host adapter, which communicates over the SCSI bus to the SCSI adapter in the hard drive case. The SCSI adapter communicates with the hard drive controller, which, in turn, communicates with the hard drive.

Some SCSI devices, including hard drives, have the SCSI host adapter built directly into the device itself. SCSI hard drives require a simple adapter card to communicate with the system bus, much as regular IDE drives do. These devices are called *embedded SCSI* devices and, because the host adapter technology resides on the drive logic board, they can have only the one device on the SCSI bus. Other SCSI devices on this computer would be altogether separate from this SCSI bus system. Embedded SCSI devices often don't conform to standard SCSI specifications, because they don't accommodate any other SCSI device.

In order to reduce the amount of electrical "noise," or interference, on a SCSI cable, each end of the SCSI chain has a *terminating resistor*. The terminating resistor can be a hardware device plugged into the last device on each end of the chain, or the chain can have software-terminated resistance, which makes installation simpler.

Differing SCSI standards

SCSI standards have improved over the years and different names are used for each standard. The two general categories of all SCSI standards used on PCs have to do with the number of bits that travel on the SCSI bus, either 8 bits (narrow SCSI) or 16 bits (wide SCSI). In almost every case, if the SCSI standard is 16 bits, then the word "wide" will be in the name for the standard. In most cases, the word "narrow" isn't mentioned in names for 8-bit standards. Narrow SCSI uses a 50-pin cable, and wide SCSI uses a 68-pin cable.

There also are two different ways that a SCSI cable can be built, depending on the method by which the electrical signal travels on the cable: single-ended and differential. A single-ended cable is less expensive than a differential cable, but the maximum cable length can't be as long because data integrity isn't as great. Cables for both narrow SCSI and wide SCSI can be either single-ended or differential. Single-ended cables and differential cables look the same, so you must make sure that you're using the correct cable. Single-ended cable is more popular than differential because it's less expensive.

The following table summarizes the different SCSI standards. There are three major standards: SCSI-1, SCSI-2, and SCSI-3, which are more commonly known as Regular SCSI, Fast SCSI, and Ultra SCSI, respectively. Other names used in the industry for these standards are also listed in the table. Both Fast SCSI and Ultra SCSI have narrow and wide versions.

Because there are several variations of SCSI, when you buy a new SCSI device, you must be sure that it's compatible with the SCSI bus you already have. All SCSI standards aren't backward compatible with earlier SCSI standards. If the new SCSI device isn't compatible, you can't use the same SCSI bus, and you must also buy a new host adapter to build a second SCSI bus system, increasing the overall cost of adding the new device.

Name(s)	Bus width	Transfer rate	Max length, single-ended cable	Max length, differential cable	Max devices
SCSI-1 (Regular SCSI)	Narrow (8 bits)	5 MB/sec	6 m	25 m	8
SCSI-2 (Fast SCSI or Fast Narrow)	Narrow (8 bits)	10 MB/sec	3 m	25 m	8
Fast Wide SCSI (Wide SCSI)	Wide (16 bits)	20 MB/sec	3 m	25 m	16
SCSI-3 (Ultra SCSI, Ultra Narrow, or Fast-20 SCSI)	Narrow (8 bits)	20 MB/sec	1.5 m	25 m	8
Wide Ultra SCSI (Fast Wide 20)	Wide (16 bits)	40 MB/sec	1.5 m	25 m	16

Name(s)	Bus width	Transfer rate	Max length, single-ended cable	Max length, differential cable	Max devices
Ultra2 SCSI	Narrow (8 bits)	40 MB/sec		12 m LVD	8
Wide Ultra2 SCSI	Wide (16 bits)	80 MB/sec			16
Ultra3 SCSI	Narrow (8 bits)	80 MB/sec		12 m LVD	8
Wide Ultra3 SCSI	Wide (16 bits)	160 MB/sec		12 m LVD	16

Note: LVD represents low voltage differential cable with lengths up to 12 meters.

The wide SCSI specification allows for a data path of 32 bits, although this hasn't been implemented in PCs. When you see a SCSI device referred to as wide, you can assume that it's 16 bits.

The faster SCSI transfer rates are gained by using *burst transfer,* a method whereby multiple packets of data can be transferred across the bus without waiting for additional clock beats and addressing information. Burst transfer can, in effect, saturate the bus with data, making for more efficient use of the bus, and, therefore, faster transfer of data.

Beginning with Ultra SCSI (SCSI-3), the SCSI standard supports *SCSI configuration automatically (SCAM)*, which follows the Plug and Play standard. SCAM makes installing SCSI devices easier, provided that the device is SCAM compatible.

Because Ultra SCSI is backward compatible with SCSI-1 and SCSI-2, all three can coexist on the same SCSI bus. Note that the only connection this subsystem has to the overall computer system and the CPU is through the host adapter. You can see from the diagram why some people compare a SCSI system to a miniature LAN inside a computer, and why SCSI can be described as outsourcing for the CPU.

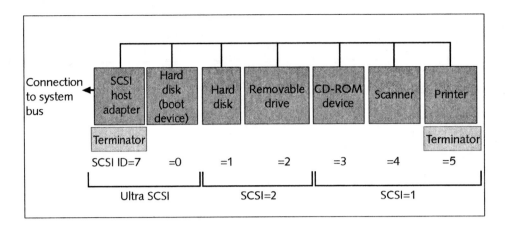

Exhibit 5-7: A sample SCSI subsystem configuration

Other variations of SCSI hardware and software

In addition to the differences in SCSI standards, there are other components of SCSI that vary. Besides the cables already discussed above, there also are variations in termination, device drivers, and host adapters.

Termination

Termination prevents an echo effect from electrical noise and reflected data at the end of the SCSI daisy chain, which can cause interference with the data transmission. There are several ways to terminate power:

- The host adapter can have a switch setting that activates or deactivates a terminating resistor on the card, depending on whether the adapter is at one end of the chain.

- A device can have either a single SCSI connection requiring that the device be placed at the end of the chain, or the device can have two connections. When a device has two connections, the second connection can be used to connect another device or can be used to terminate the chain by placing an external terminator on the connection. This external terminator serves as the terminating resistor.

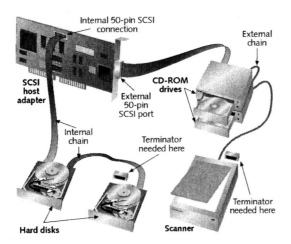

Exhibit 5-8: SCSI subsystem showing terminators at each end of the SCSI chain

- The device at the end of the chain also can be terminated by a resistor that's physically mounted on the device in a specially designated socket.
- Some devices have built-in terminators that you can turn on or off with a jumper setting on the device.
- Termination can be controlled by software.

There are several types of terminators: passive terminators, active terminators, and forced perfect terminators. Forced perfect terminators are more expensive and more reliable than the other two.

When buying terminating resistor hardware and cables for a SCSI bus, get high-quality products even if they cost a little more. The added reliability and enhanced data integrity are worth the extra money.

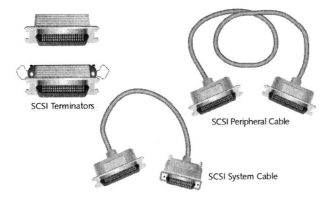

Exhibit 5-9: SCSI cables and terminators

SCSI device drivers

SCSI device drivers are needed to enable DOS or another operating system to communicate with a host adapter. Although many drivers are available, it's best to use the drivers recommended by or provided by the host adapter vendor. Two popular drivers are the *Advanced SCSI Programming Interface (ASPI)* and *Common Access Method (CAM)*. ASPI is probably the more popular of the two.

No SCSI device drivers are included with Window 3.1 or DOS. SCSI hardware manufacturers write their own drivers and include them with their devices. A SCSI driver is loaded in the CONFIG.SYS file just as other drivers are. Its DEVICE= command must appear in the CONFIG.SYS file before any device drivers for a SCSI device. For example, if you have a SCSI CD-ROM drive whose device driver must be installed in CONFIG.SYS, you must place the command for this driver after the one that installs the host adapter driver. There are similar instructions for installing the CD-ROM drive, including the specific command. Windows 9x has built-in support for SCSI devices.

Many computers have some SCSI interface software already present in their system BIOS. They have enough, in fact, so that a SCSI hard drive can be the boot device of the system. The system BIOS can access the SCSI drive, execute the load program in the drive's master boot record, and load the SCSI device drivers stored on the hard drive into memory. If there are two hard drives in a system, one being an IDE and one a SCSI, the IDE drive must be the boot device unless system BIOS can support booting from a SCSI drive even when an IDE drive is present. This is because the system board BIOS takes precedence over the BIOS on the SCSI host adapter.

Host adapter issues

An important issue when you install a SCSI bus system for the first time is the sophistication of the host adapter. More expensive host adapters are often easier to install because the installation software does more of the work for the installer and offers more help than does less expensive adapter software. When buying a host adapter, compare the installation procedures for different adapters, and also look for options, such as a built-in disk drive controller, software-controlled termination (eliminating the need for hardware terminating resistors), and configuration BIOS built into the adapter's ROM.

A SCSI host adapter controller has BIOS that loads into memory addresses on the PC and controls the operation of the SCSI bus. This SCSI controller uses a DMA channel, IRQ, and I/O addresses. You must install a SCSI device carefully to avoid resource conflicts with devices that aren't on the SCSI subsystem.

Although the installation of a SCSI system might sound complicated and requires many decisions about what components to buy, the installation instructions for SCSI devices and host adapters are usually very thorough and well written. If you carefully follow all instructions, SCSI installations can be smooth and problem-free.

Comparing SCSI hard drives and EIDE hard drives

Consider the following issues when choosing between using an EIDE hard drive and a SCSI hard drive:

- A SCSI hard drive with its supporting host adapter and cable costs more than an EIDE hard drive with its supporting adapter card.

- A SCSI subsystem provides faster data transfer than an EIDE drive, although the SCSI bus is the source of the performance rather than the hard drive technology.

- A SCSI bus supports multitasking so that the CPU can request data from more than one SCSI device at the same time, whereas when the CPU requests data from an EIDE drive on an ISA bus, it can only process data from one I/O device at a time. The CPU must wait until the ISA bus and EIDE drive complete the request before it can tackle another task. With SCSI, the CPU can perform another I/O task while waiting for the SCSI bus to complete the first request.

- A good SCSI host adapter enables you to connect other non-SCSI devices to it, such as a printer, scanner, or tape drive.

- Without SCSI technology, if you have two IDE drives on the same adapter, only one of them can be busy at any one time. For example, without SCSI, if one of your IDE devices is a CD-ROM, the hard drive must wait for the CD-ROM to complete a task before it can work again. With SCSI, two or more devices can operate simultaneously. If you plan to transfer a lot of data from CD-ROM to the hard drive, this is a good reason to choose SCSI.

Do it!

A-1: Discussing IDE and SCSI technologies

Question	Answer
1 If a hard drive has three platters, how many heads does it have?	
2 What is the purpose of the master boot record on the hard drive?	
3 Define IDE.	
4 Define SCSI.	
5 What is the difference between narrow SCSI and wide SCSI?	

Other types of hard drive interfaces

Explanation

In addition to the IDE and SCSI interface to the system bus, a hard drive also can interface with the system bus using IEEE 1394 and Fibre Channel. IEEE 1394 is also known as FireWire and i.Link (named by Sony Corporation). It uses serial transmission of data and is popular with multimedia and home entertainment applications. For example, Quantum Corporation, a large hard drive manufacturer, makes a hard drive designed for home entertainment electronics that uses 1394 for the hard drive interface (Quantum, in cooperation with Sony Corporation, calls it i.Link in the hard drive documentation). Another example of 1394 providing the interface for a hard drive is fireLINE External HotDrive by Evergreen Technologies. This external hard drive is intended for general-purpose storage and connects to a PC through a 1394 port provided either directly on the system board or by way of a 1394 expansion card. System board manufacturers have been slow to provide 1394 support on their system boards, mostly favoring support for USB instead. Generally, IDE is the lowest, SCSI is the mid-range, and 1394 is the fastest, with some overlaps in these speeds. For a system to use 1394, the operating system must support it. Windows 98 and Windows 2000 support 1394, but Windows 95 and Windows NT don't.

Fibre Channel is another type of interface that can support hard drives. Fibre Channel is designed for use in high-end systems that have multiple hard drives. It competes with SCSI for these high-end solutions. As many as 126 devices can be connected to a single Fibre Channel bus as compared to 16 SCSI devices. Fibre Channel is faster than SCSI when more than five hard drives are strung together to provide massive secondary storage but is too expensive and has too much overhead to be a good solution for the desktop PC or workstation.

Do it!

A-2: Discussing IEEE 1394 and Fibre Channel

Question	Answer
1 IEEE 1394 also is referred to by what names?	
2 Define IEEE 1394.	
3 Which Windows operating systems support 1394 technology?	
4 What is Fibre Channel?	
5 How does a Fibre Channel bus compare to a SCSI bus?	

Topic B: How a hard drive is logically organized

Explanation   Today's hard drives come from the factory already low-level formatted (that is, having track and sector markings already in place). During installation, after the hard drive is physically installed, the next step is to partition the drive into manageable areas. The high-level divisions are called *partitions*, and within the partitions, the drive is further divided into logical drives, or volumes. This section discusses the different types of division and how they are organized and used by the operating system.

Preparing a hard drive to hold data requires three steps.

1 **Low-level format.** This physically formats the hard drive and creates the tracks and sectors. For hard drives today, this is already done by the time you buy the drive, and doesn't involve an operating system.

2 **Partitioning the hard drive.** Even if only one partition is used, this step is still required. The FDISK program of Windows 9x or DOS sets up a partition table at the beginning of the hard drive. This table lists how many partitions are on the drive and their locations, and which partition is the boot partition. Within each partition, FDISK also creates logical drives, assigning letters to these drives.

3 **High-level format.** This is done by DOS, Windows 9x, or some other operating system for each logical drive on the hard drive. As each logical drive is formatted, the operating system creates a DOS boot record, a root directory, and the copies of the FAT for the logical drive. (With floppy disks, the high-level format also creates the tracks and sectors, but with hard drives this is already done by the low-level format.)

Hard drive partitions

You might have a 4 GB hard drive that you recognize as only a single physical drive. But an operating system can divide this single physical drive into more than one logical drive, which is called *partitioning the drive.* Two kinds of divisions take place. First the physical drive is divided into one or more partitions, and then each partition is further divided into logical drives, or volumes. (A logical drive is sometimes called a logical partition; don't let the two uses of the term "partition" confuse you; partitions and logical partitions are divisions at different levels.) In a typical example, the hard drive is divided into two partitions. The first partition contains one logical drive (drive C) and the second partition is divided into two logical drives (D and E). The *partition table* at the very beginning of the drive keeps a record of all these divisions contained in the master boot sector (located in the very first sector at the beginning of the hard drive, on head 0, track 0, sector 1). The following table lists the contents of a partition table. Don't confuse the first physical sector of the hard drive with sector 1 as in DOS or Windows 9x. The operating system's sector 1 comes after the physical sector 1.

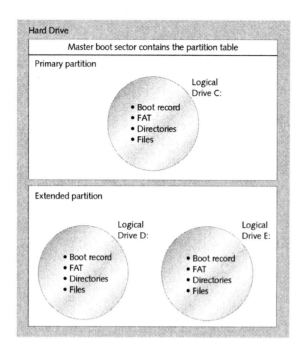

Exhibit 5-10: A hard drive is divided into one partition that contains logical drives

The partition table is exactly 512 bytes long. During POST, the partition table program, sometimes called the *master boot record*, executes and checks the integrity of the partition table itself. If it finds any corruption, it refuses to continue execution, and the disk is unusable. If the table entries are valid, this program looks in the table to determine which partition is the active partition, and it executes the boot program in the boot record of that partition.

Item	Bytes used	Description
1	446 bytes	Program that calls the boot program on the operating system boot record
2	16 byte total	Description of first partition
	1 byte	Defines the bootable partition (Yes=90h, No=00h)
	3 bytes	Beginning location of the partition
	1 byte	System indicator; possible values are: 0 = Not a DOS partition 1 = DOS with a 12-bit FAT 4 = DOS with a 16-bit FAT 5 = Not the first partition 6 = Partition larger than 32 MB
	3 bytes	Ending location of partition

Item	Bytes used	Description
	4 bytes	First sector of the partition table relative to the beginning of the disk
	4 bytes	Number of sectors in the partition
3	16 bytes	Describes second partition by using the same format as the first partition
4	16 bytes	Describes third partition by using the same format as the first partition
5	16 bytes	Describes fourth partition by using the same format as the first partition
6	2 bytes	Signature of the partition table, always AA55

A hard drive that uses DOS or Windows 9x can have only one primary partition and one extended partition, even though there's room in the partition table for four partitions. Also, the primary partition can have only a single logical drive in it. In this case, the one logical drive in the primary partition is the only logical drive on the hard drive that can boot the operating system. The extended partition can have several logical drives in it.

The partition table must be created when the drive is first installed. This is done with the DOS or Windows 9x FDISK command or third-party software such as Partition Magic. When the drive is partitioned, FDISK assigns a drive letter to each logical drive. If there is only one logical drive assigned, and this is the first hard drive installed in the system, this one drive is called drive C. FDISK first creates a partition and then creates logical drives within the partition. You designate how many logical drives you want and how large they will be.

Do it!

B-1: Creating partitions

Here's how

1 Power off your lab workstation

 Insert the DOS boot disk into drive A

 Power on your lab workstation and boot from the floppy disk

2 At the A prompt, enter **FDISK**

 From the FDISK menu, enter **4**

 Observe your current hard drive configuration

3 Press Esc to return to the FDISK Main menu

4 Select option **1** and press Enter

5 Enter **1**

6 When the FDISK utility asks if you want to use all of the available space for the primary partition and set it active, enter **Y**

7 When FDISK prompts you to enter the amount of drive space you want to use, enter **500**

8 If prompted for a volume label, enter **DRIVE 1**

9 Press **Esc** to return to the FDISK main menu

10 Press **Esc** to exit FDISK and press any key

 Your workstation restarts

Logical drives

Explanation

Both DOS and Windows 9x store data in files. Each operating system is allocated a group of whole clusters and can't share a cluster with another file. The operating system knows only the cluster numbers that it assigns to a file; it has no idea where on the drive these clusters are physically located. The operating system keeps information about files and the clusters assigned to them in its file system. This arrangement is similar to a library in which the readers are not allowed in the book stacks but must depend on a librarian to fetch the books for them. When the operating system requests BIOS to retrieve a file from the hard drive, BIOS, either on the system board or on the hard drive controller, determines where on the drive these sectors are located.

Exhibit 5-11: Software needs BIOS just as a reader requires a librarian

A *logical drive* is a portion of a hard drive that an operating system views and manages as an individual drive, much as it manages a floppy disk. In the example, the hard drive is divided into three logical drives: drive C, drive D, and drive E. For a 3 GB drive, drive C might contain 2 GB, drive D might be allocated 300 MB, and drive E might be allocated 700 MB, to account for the entire physical drive capacity.

For the configuration in Exhibit 5-10, the three commands used to format these three logical drives are:

```
Format C:/S
Format D:
Format E:
```

The /S after the first Format command transfers the system files, making the drive bootable. The operating system format for each logical drive creates these file system items at the beginning of each logical drive:

- Boot record
- FAT
- Root directory

The boot record

A boot record is used during the boot process to inform the operating system how a logical drive is organized. If the logical drive is the boot device, the boot program at the end of the boot record loads the hidden files (IO.SYS and MSDOS.SYS for DOS, and MSDOS.SYS for Windows 9x) during booting. The following table shows the complete record layout for the boot record. The medium descriptor byte tells the operating system what type of disk this is.

Description	Number of bytes
Machine code	11
Bytes per sector	2
Sectors per cluster	1
Reserved	2
Number of FATs	1
Number of root directory entries	2
Number of logical sectors	2
Medium descriptor byte	1
Sectors per FAT	2
Sectors per track	2
Heads	2
Number of hidden sectors	2
Total sectors in logical volume	4
Physical drive number	1
Reserved	1
Extended boot signature record	1
32-bit binary volume ID	4
Volume label	11

Description	Number of bytes
Type of file system (FAT12, FAT16, or FAT32)	8
Program to load operating system (boot strap loader)	Remainder of the sector

Disk type	Descriptor byte
3½-inch double-density floppy disk, 720 KB	F9
3½-inch high-density floppy disk, 1.44 MB	F0
Hard disk	F8

The FAT and the root directory

The operating system uses two tables (the FAT and a directory) to keep track of which clusters are being used for a particular file, together with other information about the file, such as the file name, the length of the file, and whether the file is read-only or hidden. This high-level view of a file is all the operating system needs to know. The physical location of the file is tracked by the BIOS or device driver managing the hard drive. The FAT and a directory are the vehicles of exchange between the operating system and the hard drive BIOS. The operating system uses only one FAT for an entire logical drive but may have more than one directory on the drive. The main or root directory on a drive can have directories within it, called subdirectories in DOS or folders in Windows 9x.

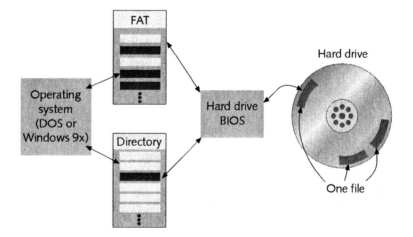

Exhibit 5-12: How the operating system views the hard drive when managing a file

To the operating system, each logical drive looks and is treated like a single floppy disk in this respect: as far as DOS or Windows 9x is concerned, a physical drive divided into three logical drives, C, D, and E, is equivalent to three separate physical drives. The reason for this is that the operating system manages a logical drive from the same high-level view whether it's a floppy drive, a part of a physical drive, or an entire physical drive—each includes a FAT, one or more directories, and files that the operating system tracks by using these tables.

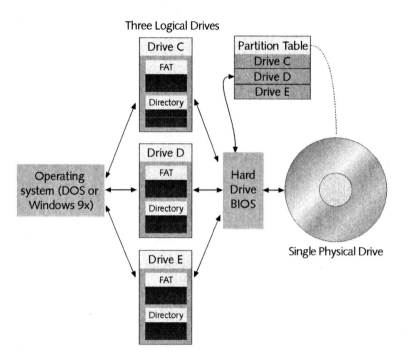

Exhibit 5-13: A single physical drive can be viewed by the operating system as one or more logical drives

For DOS and Windows 3.1, and sometimes in Windows 9x, each entry in a FAT for most hard drives is 16 bits, or a convenient 2 bytes, and the FAT is called FAT16. Besides FAT16, Windows 98 offers a FAT with 32-bit entries, and Windows NT offers an entirely different method of managing clusters called NTFS (new technology file system). Windows 95 offers a version of FAT16 that can use long file names, called virtual FAT or VFAT.

As with floppy disks, each entry in a hard drive FAT tracks the use of one cluster. The number of sectors per cluster varies from one logical drive to another. Use the CHKDSK command to display the size of one cluster. There's another way to determine the size of a cluster with a simple test. First, use the DIR command and note how much space is available on your hard drive. Then, create a text file containing only a single character. By using the DIR command again, note how much disk space is available and compare the two values, before and after a single one-character file is written to the disk. The difference in the two values is the size of one cluster, which is the smallest amount that can be allocated to a file. In the FAT entries discussed below, a hard drive is used that has one cluster equal to four sectors. A cluster is, therefore, 512 bytes/sector × 4 sectors/cluster, or 2,048 bytes.

Virtual File Allocation Table (VFAT)

Windows 95 and Windows for Workgroups feature some improved methods of hard drive access, called *VFAT*, or *virtual file allocation*. These enable Windows to use 32-bit protected-mode device drivers for hard drive access. In Windows for Workgroups, VFAT is called 32-bit file access. Windows 95 supports file names up to 256 characters. The file name and extension are stored in the root directory or in a subdirectory list. Each entry in the directory is 32 bytes long, and each 32-byte entry is called a block. Long file names require more than one block in the directory. The FAT isn't affected, but still uses 16 bits per cluster entry.

Some DOS-based disk utility programs can damage the entries in a directory in these additional blocks because they're not programmed to manage the extra blocks used to hold long file names. Even a simple DEL command under OS/2 can leave the extra blocks in the directory used to hold the long file name unavailable for later use. The Windows 9x ScanDisk utility can recover these unreleased blocks.

FAT32

Beginning with Windows 95, Service Release 2 (sometimes called Windows 95b or Windows 95 OSR2), Microsoft offered a FAT that contains 32 bits per FAT entry instead of the older 12-bit or 16-bit FAT entries. Actually, only 28 of the bits are used to hold a cluster number; the remaining four bits are reserved.

The 32-bit FAT provides better management of very large hard drives, because the number of clusters per logical volume can increase: The largest cluster number a 16-bit FAT entry can hold is 65,535. The value of a 16-bit number when all 16 bits are 1s, that is, 1111 1111 1111 1111, is 65,535, which is then the largest number of clusters that the operating system can support on a single logical drive. The largest logical drive capacity depends on the size of a single cluster and the number of clusters that can be accessed through the FAT. For FAT16, logical drives can range in size from 16 MB to 2,048 MB. But in order to get the larger sizes, the cluster size must be very large, sometimes as large as 32 KB, which can result in a lot of wasted space for a hard drive that holds many small files. This wasted space is called *slack*. FAT32 makes it possible for cluster sizes to be smaller and still have very large logical drives, because there can be many more clusters to the drive. FAT32 is recommended for hard drives larger than 1.2 GB and is efficient for drives up to 8 GB. In this range, the cluster size is 4 KB. After that, the cluster size increases to about 8 KB for drives in the 8 GB to 16 GB range. You are then reaching a hard drive size that warrants a more powerful file management system than FAT32, such as NTFS supported by Windows NT.

If you currently use FAT16 and are considering switching to FAT32, you can use Partition Magic to scan your hard drive and tell you how much of the drive is used for slack space. Knowing this can help you decide whether the change will yield you more usable drive space.

The root directory

The layout of the root directory is the same for hard drives as for floppy disks. The total number of bytes for each file entry in a directory is 32.

The maximum number of entries in the root directory for DOS and Windows 95 is fixed. The number of entries in a subdirectory, however, isn't limited. The fixed reserved length of the root directory for current versions of DOS and Windows is 512 entries; early versions of DOS didn't provide as many entries in the root directory. Note, however, that the operating system manuals recommend that you keep about only 150 entries in any one directory. Having any more entries slows access to the directory. The number of entries in the root directory is stored in the boot record of the hard drive. Using long file names reduces the number of files that can be stored in this fixed number of entries in the root directory, because the long file names require more than one entry in the directory. Windows 98 doesn't limit the size of the root directory.

Do it!

B-2: Reviewing hard drive organization

Question	Answer
1 List three functions of the FDISK utility.	
2 What will happen if an active partition isn't set?	
3 You are the desktop PC support technician for the Good Job Corporation. John, one of your customers, suspects that his hard drive isn't partitioned to use its full capacity. Describe how you would use the FDISK utility to show John his current hard drive configuration.	

Communicating with a BIOS hard drive

Explanation

Beginning with IDE hard drives, the number of sectors per track varied from one track to another. Therefore, the OS and system BIOS couldn't count on using actual hard drive cylinder, head, and sector coordinates when making requests for data through the hard drive BIOS (which is how requests were made with early hard drives). Instead, sophisticated methods were developed so that system BIOS and the OS could communicate with the BIOS hard drive controller in familiar terms, but only the BIOS controller knew where the data was physically located on the drive.

In the following exhibit, you can see the different stages in communication with these older hard drives. The OS and other software communicated the cylinder, head, and sector coordinates to system BIOS, which communicated them to the BIOS hard drive controller, which used these coordinates to locate data on the hard drive. All levels communicated the same cylinder, head, and sector information to locate data on the hard drive. With this straightforward communication, drive capacity could easily be calculated and drive access was simple, when drives were small and all tracks on the drive had the same number of sectors. Subsequently, methods used to communicate among the different levels were altered to accommodate larger drives and new drive technology.

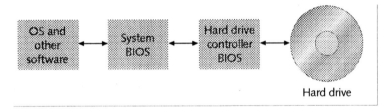

Hard drive

Exhibit 5-14: With older hard drives, cylinder, track, and sector information was communicated at each level

Calculating drive capacity

When hard drives used a constant number of sectors per track, measuring drive capacity was straightforward. The OS viewed the data as groups of sectors of 512 bytes each. The number of sectors present on the drive determined the drive capacity. Each surface or platter on a hard drive was divided into tracks and sectors. All sectors in a track held 512 bytes regardless of the radius of the track. If you knew the number of tracks, heads, and sectors per track, you could calculate the storage capacity of a drive, because all tracks had the same number of sectors. Software and operating systems were written to interface with BIOS, which managed a hard drive by this method of assuming that for each hard drive there was a fixed relationship among the number of sectors, tracks, heads, and cylinders.

Earlier, smaller drives have 17 sectors per track. Now, some drives have 26 sectors per track. Most system BIOS programs permit a user-defined hard drive type. When you choose a user-defined drive type, you must tell the setup the number of heads, tracks, and sectors that the drive has, along with other information, so that system BIOS knows how to address the drive. These drive types might seem like ancient history with respect to hard drive capacity today, but the concepts and calculations apply to today's modern drives in a similar fashion.

Tip: When installing a hard drive, it was once necessary to tell CMOS setup the drive capacity. Today, most system BIOS offers autodetection, a method whereby the BIOS detects the new drive and automatically selects the correct drive capacity and configuration for you.

You calculate the capacity of the drive as follows. First, you determine the number of total bytes on one surface, or head of the drive by using the following formula.

```
# of tracks × # sectors/track × bytes/sector = total bytes
```

Then, to calculate the total number capacity:

```
total bytes × # heads = total capacity
```

To convert bytes to kilobytes (KB) and megabytes (MB), use the following.

```
1 KB = 1,024 bytes (or 1,000 bytes)
1 MB = 1,024 KB (or 1,000 KB)
```

Adjusting for more complex hard drive organization

As hard drive size and technology improved, the OS and other software required new methods to relate to the BIOS hard drive because of two situations that arose:

- Beginning with IDE technology, the number of tracks per sector varied depending on the location of the track, which made it impossible for the OS and software to address the data on the hard drive using actual cylinder, head, and sector parameters.

- When hard drives were small, the maximum size of the parameters that the OS and software sent to the BIOS hard drive was established. These maximum values placed self-imposed limitations on the size hard drive that software could address by using actual cylinder, head, and sector parameters.

However, it was important for the industry to retain backward compatibility so that legacy operating systems and other software could work. As is common in the evolution of computers, clever methods were devised to "trick" older technology so that it could work in newer environments. The older, legacy technology (in this case, software) still sees its world unchanged because the newer technology (in this case, BIOS) shelters it from the new methodology. These "deceptions" can happen at several stages of communication, in the following ways:

- The hard drive can use a complex cylinder, head, and sector organization that only the BIOS controller knows. However, the BIOS controller communicates to system BIOS in terms of the older methodology. When this method is used, the actual organization of the hard drive is called the physical geometry of the drive, and the organization communicated to system BIOS is called the logical geometry of the drive. This method is called the CHS mode (cylinder, head, sector), or normal mode.

- The BIOS hard drive controller sends the logical geometry to system BIOS, but system BIOS communicates a different set of parameters to the OS and other software. This method is called translation, and system BIOS is said to be in large mode, or ECHS mode (extended CHS).

- The BIOS hard drive controller and system BIOS communicate by using a method entirely different from cylinder, head, and sector information. System BIOS sends cylinder, head, and sector information to the software, which is neither logical nor physical geometry. This method of translation is referred to as LBA mode (logical block addressing).

- The OS and software can bypass the system BIOS altogether and communicate directly with the BIOS controller by using device drivers. This is the method used by Windows NT and Windows 2000. True to its compromising nature, Windows 9x has its own 32-bit protected mode device drivers to access hard drives, bypassing system BIOS. However, in order to support DOS and other older software, Windows 9x also supports using system BIOS to access drives.

Physical geometry and logical geometry

Although today's hard drives no longer organize data on the drive in a straightforward manner, but rather use zone bit recording, drive capacity is calculated in the same way, as if the number of sectors per track were constant. The BIOS controller masks the actual organization of the drive, and calls its physical geometry from system BIOS and software. It communicates to system BIOS and software a number of cylinders, heads, and sectors, which, when used in calculations, yields the actual capacity of the drive, although the physical geometry might be quite different. These bogus values for cylinders, heads, and sectors are called the logical geometry of the drive.

Translation methods

With hard drives larger than 504 MB (called large-capacity drives), translation is used to bypass these limitations in our standards and maintain backward compatibility with older software. System BIOS that supports translation methods and, therefore, provides access to drives larger than 504 MB is called enhanced BIOS. Look at the CMOS settings of your computer to determine the modes your system BIOS supports.

Remember that system BIOS supports a hard drive in one of three ways:

- CHS (cylinders, heads, and sectors) mode: The traditional method by which BIOS reads from and writes to hard drives by addressing the correct cylinder, head, and sector. Also called normal mode, this method is for drives less than 504 MB.

- ECHS (extended CHS) mode: A mode of addressing information on hard drives that range from 504 MB to 8.4 GB, addressing information on a hard drive by translating cylinder, head, and sector information in order to break the 528 MB hard drive barrier. Also called large mode.

- LBA (logical block addressing) mode: A mode of addressing information on hard drives in which the BIOS and operating system view the drive as one long linear list of addressable sectors, permitting drives to be larger than 8.4 GB.

Do it!

B-3: Discussing hard drive capacity

Question	Answer
1 Given that there are 512 bytes per sector, calculate the hard drive storage for the following: Heads: 32 Tracks (cylinders): 1024 Sectors/track: 63	
2 Why does the logical geometry sometimes differ from the physical geometry of a hard drive?	
3 How does an OS or other software communicate to the CPU that it wants to access data on a hard drive?	
4 In using large mode to access a hard drive, how is the 504 or 528-MB barrier broken?	
5 How can you determine whether a PC supports large mode?	

Topic C: Installing hard drives

Explanation
Hard drive installation is much easier than it was a few years ago. Drives today come already low-level formatted with optimum interleave already established. *Interleave* is a method of reorganizing sectors in a track to speed up data access. A few years ago, when older technologies such as MFM and RLL drives were popular, to install a hard drive, you had to purchase a controller that conformed to the type of drive you had. You then low-level formatted the drive by using either a format program stored in the BIOS controller or some other utility software such as SpinRite. As you did the low-level format, the software would examine your drive and recommend the optimum interleave, and if necessary, the software would automatically change the interleave to the optimum value. Today, IDE and SCSI drives are low-level formatted at the factory. Now you should low-level format a hard drive as only a last resort by using a specific low-level format program recommended by the manufacturer to refurbish a failing drive.

Installing a hard drive

Installation of IDE and SCSI hard drives includes:

- Installing the hardware and setting jumpers and DIP switches on the drive
- Informing CMOS setup of the new drive
- Creating one or more partitions on the drive
- High-level formatting the drive partitions
- Installing the operating system and other software

Physical installation of IDE or SCSI hard drives

To install an IDE drive, you need the drive, a 40-pin data cable, and perhaps a kit to make the drive fit into a much larger bay. If the system board doesn't provide an IDE connection, you also will need an adapter card.

To install a SCSI drive, you need the drive, a cable compatible with the host adapter you are using, possibly an external terminator if the drive is on the end of the daisy chain, a host adapter if you don't already have one, and perhaps a kit to make the drive fit the bay.

Installing an IDE hard drive

IDE hard drives used today follow the EIDE standard that supports up to four IDE devices on the same system. These devices can be hard drives, CD-ROM drives, tape drives, Zip drives, or other drives that follow the EIDE standards of communication. There are four possible setups for each device:

- Primary IDE channel, master device
- Primary IDE channel, slave device
- Secondary IDE channel, master device
- Secondary IDE channel, slave device

When planning your system configuration, place the fastest devices on the primary channel and the slower devices on the secondary channel. If possible, enable the fastest hard drive as your boot device and the only device on the primary channel.

The first step in any installation is to take some precautions. First, make sure that you have a good bootable disk or Windows 9x rescue disk; test it to make sure it works. As always, just in case you lose setup information in the process, make sure you have a record of your CMOS setup on a disk. The next step requires some self-discipline. Before you take anything apart, carefully read all the documentation for the drive and the adapter card, as well as any part of your PC documentation that covers hard drive installation. Look for problems you haven't considered, such as IRQ or DMA conflicts if this is a second hard drive for your system, or an older, limited version of system BIOS. Also, check the setup of your computer to be sure it accommodates the size and type of hard drive you want to install. If you plan to use a user-defined drive type in the setup (where you must enter the drive specifications), make sure your PC accepts the values you want. You should be able to determine this from your PC documentation, or you can check setup on the PC. If you discover that your PC doesn't accommodate the large-capacity drive you have, consider changing your ROM BIOS before changing the drive. Or, you could opt to keep the large-capacity drive and not use all of it. To do so, you would define it as a smaller drive type in setup.

Make sure that you can envision the entire installation. If you have any questions, find answers to them before you begin. Either keep reading until you locate the answer, call technical support, or ask a knowledgeable friend. It's better to discover that what you are installing will not work on your computer before you begin. This avoids hours of frustration and a disabled computer. You can't always anticipate every problem, but at least you can know that you made your best effort to understand everything in advance. What you learn in thorough preparation pays off every time.

Having read the documentation for the hard drive, you should understand the meaning of each DIP switch or jumper on the drive. It's now time to set the jumpers and DIP switches. For an IDE drive, note that the default settings are usually for the drive to be a single drive on the system. Before you change any settings, write down the original ones. Then, if things go wrong, you can always revert to the original settings and begin again.

Although the settings on the drive can be configured by DIP switches, most settings use jumpers. Each drive type can have a different jumper configuration. Often a description of the jumper settings is printed on the top of the hard drive housing. If they're not written there, see the documentation or go to the Web site of the drive manufacturer. The three choices for jumper settings for this drive are listed in the following table. Note that your hard drive can have the first configuration as an option, but it should have a way of indicating if the drive can be the master device.

Some hard drives have a cable select configuration option. If you choose this configuration, you must use a cable-select data cable. When you use one of these cables, the drive nearest the system board is the master and the drive farthest from the system board is the slave. You can recognize a cable-select cable by a small hole somewhere in the data cable.

Tip: The decision as to which logical drive startup BIOS looks to first for the operating system is made in CMOS setup. The master IDE drive, the slave IDE drive, or a SCSI device can be a system's boot device. In fact, some systems have a SCSI drive as the boot device even when an IDE drive is present.

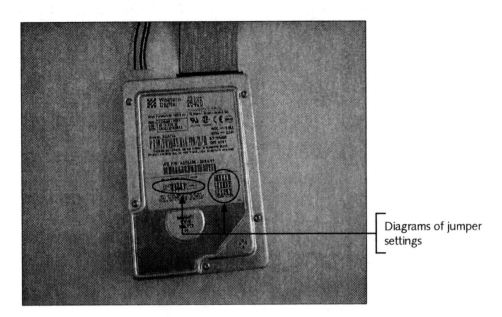

Exhibit 5-15: A typical jumper arrangement

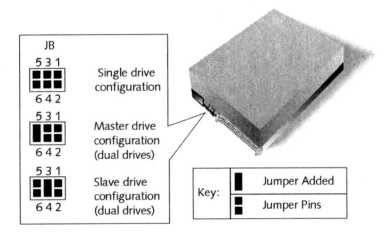

Exhibit 5-16: Jumper settings and their meanings

Configuration	Description
Single-drive configuration	This is the only hard drive on this IDE channel.
Master-drive configuration	This is the first of two drives; it most likely is the boot device.
Slave-drive configuration	This is the second drive using this channel or data cable.
Cable-select configuration	The cable-select data cable determines which of the two drives is the master and which is the slave.

The next step is to prepare a large, well-lit place to work. Set out your tools, the documentation, the new hardware, and your notebook. Remember the basic rules concerning static electricity. Ground yourself and the computer. It's a good idea not to work on carpet in the winter when there's a lot of static electricity. Some added precautions for working with hard drives are:

- Handle the drive carefully.
- Don't touch any exposed circuitry or chips.
- Prevent other people from touching any exposed microchips on the drive.
- When you first take the drive out of the static-protective package, touch the package containing the drive to a screw holding an expansion card or cover, or to a metal part of the computer case, for at least two seconds. This will drain the static electricity from the package and from your body.
- If you must set the drive down outside the static-protective package, place it component-side-up on top of the static-protective package on a flat surface.
- Don't place the drive on the computer case cover or on a metal table.

Verify the state of the computer before you turn it off. Know where your starting point is. Does everything work as it should?

Tip: Be sure to verify which of your system's devices are working before installing a new one. Later, if a resource conflict occurs causing a device not to function, the information will help you isolate the problem.

Turn the computer off and unplug it. Unplug the monitor and move it to one side. Remove the computer case cover. Check that you have an available power cord from the power supply.

If you are using an adapter card, decide which expansion slot you will use for the adapter card. Don't use the one nearest to the power supply unless it's your only choice; heat can shorten the life of any card. Check that the cable you are using reaches from the drive to the adapter card. If it doesn't, you might need to use a different expansion slot. Next, check that the wire that controls the drive light on the front of the computer case reaches from the adapter card to the front of the case or to wherever the connection for the wire is on the system board. In many situations, this wire will not reach as far as it should. Either get a new wire or just don't use the drive light.

For most installations, instead of using an adapter card, you use an IDE connection on the system board. If you use an IDE connection on the system board, use the primary IDE connection (sometimes labeled IDE1) before you use the secondary IDE connection (sometimes labeled IDE2). Locate the connection and make certain the data cable reaches from the drive bay to the connection. Most computer cases have a wire for the hard drive light on the front of the case. Identify the wire (either look for a label on the wire or trace it back to the connection on the case) and locate where the pins are on the system board for the wire. Use your system board manual to help you locate these pins.

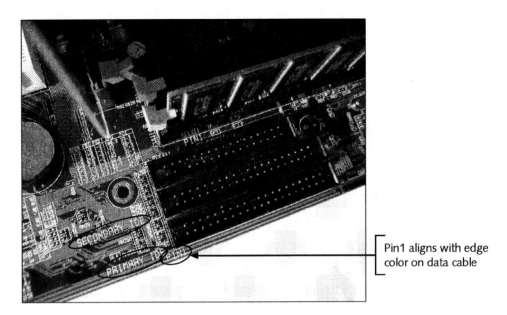

Exhibit 5-17: The primary and secondary IDE connections on a system board

Next, look at the drive bay that you will use for the drive. You must be able to securely mount the drive in the bay; there should be no free movement of the drive once it's screwed down. Line up the drive and bay screw holes and make sure everything will fit. If the bay is too large for the drive, a universal bay kit will enable you to securely fit the drive into the bay. These kits are inexpensive and should create a tailor-made fit. You can see how the universal bay kit adapter works. The adapter spans the distance between the sides of the drive and the bay.

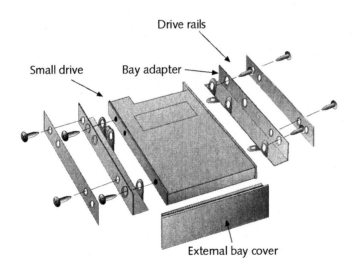

Exhibit 5-18: Use a universal bay kit to make the drive fit the bay

You don't want the drive to be stressed with any torque. For example, you don't want to force a drive into a space that's too small for it. Also, placing two screws in diagonal positions across the drive can place pressure diagonally on the drive.

For tower cases, the drive can be positioned either horizontally or vertically. There can be external bays that require a bay cover in the front of the tower or internal bays that don't involve the front of the tower.

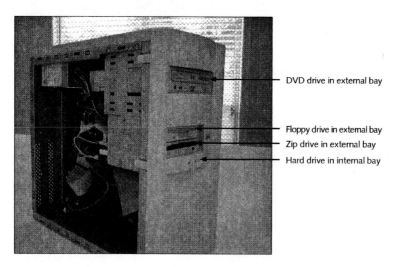

DVD drive in external bay

Floppy drive in external bay
Zip drive in external bay
Hard drive in internal bay

Exhibit 5-19: A lower case may have internal or external bays

Be sure the screws aren't too long. If they are, you can screw too far into the drive housing and damage the drive itself. After checking the position of the drive and determining how screws are placed, mount the drive in the bay. Decide whether to connect the data cable and power cord to the drive before or after you screw it down, depending on how accessible the connections are.

Once the drive is in place, if you are using an adapter card, insert the adapter card in the expansion slot, being careful not to touch the gold contact fingers on the edge connectors. Use one screw to secure the card to the case at the expansion slot. Don't eliminate this screw—without it, cards can work themselves loose over time. Be certain to place the card securely in the slot. The most common error beginners make is not seating the card properly.

Next, connect the data cable, making certain Pin 1 and the edge color on the cable are aligned correctly at both ends of the cable. Connect the power cord to the drive. The cord goes into the connection only one way, so you can't go wrong here.

When using an adapter card, connect the wire from the adapter card to the front of the case. This wire controls the hard drive activity light on the front of the case. When using a system-board connection, connect the wire from the computer case to the system board. If you reverse the polarity of the LED wire to the drive light at the front of the case, the light will not work. Unless the screw holes in the drive don't align with the screw holes in the bay, or there is some other unusual situation, physical installations go rather quickly.

Tip: If the drive light doesn't work after installing a new drive, try reversing the LED wire on the system board pins.

Before you replace the computer case, plug in the monitor and turn on the computer. Verify that your system BIOS can find the drive before you replace the cover. If you have a problem, it will most likely involve a loose cable or adapter card. Here are some things to do in this situation:

- Turn off the computer and monitor before you do anything inside the case.
- Remove and reattach all drive cables. Check for correct Pin 1 orientation.
- Remove and reseat the adapter card.
- Place the adapter card in a different slot.
- Check the jumper or DIP switch settings.
- Inspect the drive for damage such as bent pins on the connection for the cable.
- To determine if the hard drive is spinning, listen to the hard drive or lightly touch the metal drive (with power on).
- Check the cable for frayed edges or other damage.
- Check the installation manual for things you might have overlooked. Look for a section about system setup and carefully follow all directions that apply.

Do it!

C-1: Researching jumper settings

Here's how

1 You plan to install a Quantum Fireball CR 4.3 GB hard drive as a second drive on a PC. You want the drive to be the slave drive and know that you must change the current jumper settings. There are four jumpers on the drive, labeled DS, CS, PK, and Rsvd. From the description of the jumpers, you don't know how to set the jumpers so the drive is the slave.

2 To access the drive manufacturer's Web site for information, go to www.quantum.com.

Informing setup of the new hard drive

Explanation

The newly installed drive isn't available for booting until the installation is complete. So, if this drive is the boot device on your computer, you need to boot the computer from a floppy disk. You're now ready to use setup to tell CMOS the hard drive type you are installing. The text below first discusses setup for drives less than 528 MB, then setup for large-capacity drives, and finally setup when your BIOS doesn't support your large-capacity drive.

Today, BIOS offers a setup program that makes configuring hard drives easy. You can choose IDE Auto Detection and let the BIOS do the work for you. Recall that for this to work, both the BIOS and the hard drive must be built to communicate this information. Exhibit 5-20 shows the four setup screens that are typical of modern-day setup programs in which you can change hard drive parameters. You can see the choice for IDE HDD Auto Detection in the third item in the second column. You can make this selection, then save and exit setup and continue with the installation. Later, after you have rebooted with the new drive detected, you can return to setup, view the selections that it made, and make changes where appropriate.

a) CMOS setup utility opening menu

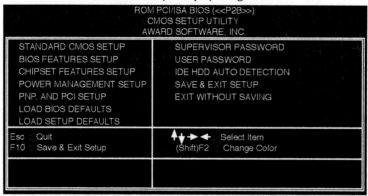

b) Standard CMOS setup

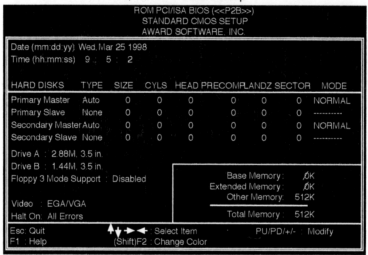

Exhibit 5-20: CMOS setup screens

c) CMOS setup for chipset features

```
                    ROM PCI/ISA BIOS (<<P2B>>)
                         CHIPSET FEATURES
                       AWARD SOFTWARE, INC.

  SDRAM Configuration     : By SPD   Onboard FDC Controller    : Enabled
  SDRAM CAS Latency       : 2T       Onboard FDC Swap A & B     : No Swap
  SDRAM RAS to CAS Delay  : 3T       Onboard Serial Port 1      : 3F8H/IRQ4
  SDRAM RAS Precharge Time  3T       Onboard Serial Port 2      : 2F8H/IRQ3
  DRAM Idle Timer         : 16T      Onboard Parallel Port      : 378H/IRQ7
  SDRAM MA Wait State     : Normal   Parallel Port Mode         : ECP+EPP
  Snoop Ahead             : Enabled  ECP DMA Select             : 3
  Host Bus Fast Data Ready  Enabled  VART2 Use Infrared         : Disabled
  16-bit I/O Recovery Time : 1BUSCLK Onboard PCI IDE Enable     : Both
  8-bit I/O Recovery Time : 1BUSCLK  IDE Ultra DMA Mode         : Auto
  Graphics Aperture Size  : 64MB     IDE0 Master PIO/DMA Mode   : Auto
  Video Memory Cache Mode : UC       IDE0 Slave   PIO/DMA Mode  : Auto
  PCI 2.1 Support         : Enabled  IDE1 Master  PIO/DMA Mode  : Auto
  Memory Hole At 15M-16M  : Disabled IDE1 Slave   PIO/DMA Mode  : Auto
  DRAM are 64 (Not 72) bits wide
  Data Integrity Mode     : Non-ECC  Esc  : Quit          ↑↓→←      : Select Item
                                     F1   : Help          PU/PD/+/- : Modify
                                     F5   : Old Values     (Shift)F2 : Color
                                     F6   : Load BIOS  Defaults
                                     F7   : Load Setup Defaults
```

d) CMOS setup for BIOS features

```
                    ROM PCI/ISA BIOS (<<P2B>>)
                        BIOS FEATURES SETUP
                       AWARD SOFTWARE, INC.

  CPU Internal Core Speed  : 350Mhz  Video   ROM BIOS Shadow  : Enabled
                                     C8000  - CBFFF  Shadow   : Disabled
  Boot Virus Detection    : Enabled  CC000  - CFFFF  Shadow   : Disabled
  CPU Level 1 Cache       : Enabled  D0000  - D3FFF  Shadow   : Disabled
  CPU Level 2 Cache       : Enabled  D4000  - D7FFF  Shadow   : Disabled
  CPU Level 2 Cache ECC Check Disabled  D8000 - DBFFF Shadow  : Disabled
  BIOS Update             : Enabled  DC000  - DFFFF  Shadow   : Disabled
  Quick Power On Self Test : Enabled
  HDD Sequence SCSI/IDE First IDE    Boot Up NumLock Status    : On
  Boot Sequence           : A,C      Typematic Rate Setting
  Boot Up Floppy Seek     : Disabled Typematic Rate (Chars/Sec) : 6
  Floppy Disk Access Control : R/W   Typematic Delay (Msec)     : 250
  IDE HDD Block Mode Sectors HDD MAX
  Security Option         : System
  PS/2 Mouse Function Control Auto   Esc  : Quit          ↑↓→←      : Select Item
  PCI/VGA Palette Snoop   : Disabled F1   : Help          PU/PD/+/- : Modify
  OS/2 Onboard Memory > 64M Disabled F5   : Old Values     (Shift)F2 : Color
                                     F6   : Load BIOS  Defaults
                                     F7   : Load Setup Defaults
```

Exhibit 5-21: CMOS setup screens (continued)

Do it!

C-2:   Removing and installing the IDE hard drive

Here's how

1   Power off the lab workstation and unplug the power cord. (It's not necessary to unplug all other cords.)

2   Remove the case from the lab workstation and locate the hard drive.

3   Unplug the IDE cable and the power connector from the hard drive. Note the position of the data and power connector.

4   Use the Torx bit driver or a screwdriver to dismount the hard drive.

5   Stand clear of the workstation and plug in the power cord.

6   With the hard drive removed, power on the lab workstation and wait for the BIOS error message.

7   Enter the setup program, if necessary, and follow the menu instructions for the workstation's BIOS to validate the hard drive changes.

8   Save the changes and reboot the workstation.

9   Power off the lab workstation and unplug the power cord.

10 By using the hard drive taken from Student 1's CPU, mount the hard drive in its original position.

11 Connect the IDE data cable and the power connector. (Be sure that you connect the cables in the same manner they were previously connected. The red stripe on the data cable should be aligned with the Pin 1 setting on the hard drive.)

12 Stand clear of the workstation and plug in the power cord.

13 When the workstation boots, enter the setup program.

14 Verify that the BIOS automatically detected the hard drive.

15 Save the BIOS changes and exit the setup program.

16 Reboot the workstation and test the installation by booting into the operating system.

17 Shut down the workstation and power it off.

18 Unplug the power cable and secure the case.

19 Plug the workstation back in and power it on.

Partitioning the hard drive

Explanation

After the hard drive is physically installed, and setup knows about the drive, the next step is to partition the drive. The *partition table* is written at the very beginning of the drive and contains information about the size of each partition on the drive and which partition contains the operating system from which the PC boots. Partitions are created by the DOS and Windows 9x FDISK setup programs.

Before you can use the Windows 9x CD for Windows 9x upgrades, you must first install DOS on the hard drive and boot from it. (You also will need the first Window 3.x setup disk because Window 9x setup asks for it during Window 9x installation.) Insert DOS disk 1 in drive A and boot the computer. FDISK automatically executes by the install procedure on this disk. Or you can boot from any bootable disk and run FDISK from the disk. In either case, you see the FDISK opening menu. Select option 1 first to create the DOS partition. Use option 1 to create the primary DOS partition. If you plan to install Windows 9x later, be sure this partition is at least 150 MB, preferably more. Make this first partition the active partition. In DOS terms, the active partition is the partition that is used to boot DOS. The active partition will be drive C.

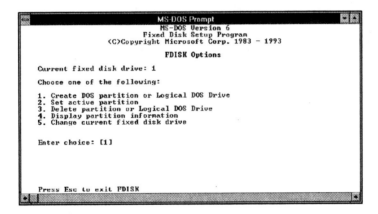

Exhibit 5-22: Fixed disk setup program menu

Next, you can use option 2 on the menu to create an extended DOS partition by using the remainder of the hard drive. Then, you use option 3 on the menu to create logical drives in the extended partition. They will be drive D, drive E, and so on.

The non-upgrade version of Windows 9x begins with DOS. The software comes with a DOS-bootable disk. Boot from the disk, which prompts you to partition the drive, format it, and provide the necessary DOS files on the hard drive to install Windows 9x.

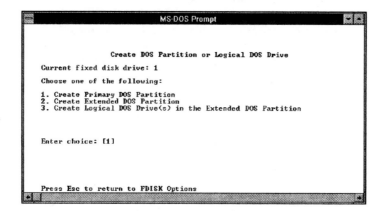

Exhibit 5-23: FDISK menu to create partitions and logical drives

When FDISK is completed, the hard drive has a partition table, an active and extended partition, and logical drives within these partitions. You can choose option 4 of FDISK to display partition information.

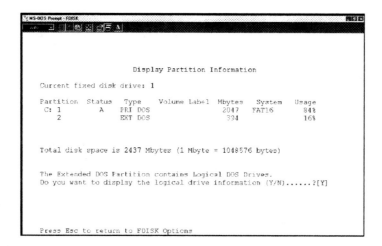

Exhibit 5-24: FDISK displays partition information

Using more than one logical drive

The primary partition can hold only one logical drive, the boot device. If you want to have more than one logical drive or volume, create an extended partition and put the other logical drives in it.

Some people prefer to use more than one logical drive to organize their hard drives, especially if they plan to have more than one operating system on the same drive. However, the main reason you need multiple logical drives is to optimize space and access time to the drive. The larger the logical drive, the larger the cluster size, and the more slack or wasted space occurs. When deciding how to allocate space to logical drives, the goal is to use as few logical drives as possible and still keep cluster size to a minimum. You also can use FAT32 for very large drives, which results in an even smaller cluster size for the logical drive size. The following table gives the information you need to decide how to slice your drive. The largest logical drive possible using FAT16 is 2 GB (this limitation is rooted in the largest cluster number that can be stored in a 16-bit FAT entry). However, you can see from the table that, in order to make a drive that big, the cluster size must be huge. Also, the largest hard drive that FAT16 can support is 8.4 GB; if the drive is larger than that, you must use FAT32.

Type	Size of logical drive	Size of cluster
FAT 16	Up to 128 MB	4 sectors per cluster
	128 to 256 MB	8 sectors per cluster
	256 MB to 512 MB	16 sectors per cluster
	512 MB to 1 GB	32 sectors per cluster
	1 GB to 2 GB	64 sectors per cluster
FAT32	512 MB to 8 GB	4 sectors per cluster
	8 GB to 16 GB	8 sectors per cluster
	16 GB to 32 GB	16 sectors per cluster
	More than 32 GB	32 sectors per cluster
NTFS	Up to 512 MB	1 sector per cluster
	512 MB to 1 GB	2 sectors per cluster
	More than 1 GB	4 sectors per cluster

Notice that the smallest logical drive that FAT32 supports is 512 MB. If you want to create a FAT32 volume by using the FDISK program that comes with Windows 9x, when it asks you whether you want to "enable large disk support," answer yes.

Operating system or high-level format

After the hard drive is partitioned, an operating system must individually format each volume or logical drive within a partition. This is called the *high-level format* or the *operating system format*. The Windows 9x or DOS format writes the *boot record* in the first sector of each volume. Recall that this boot record is sometimes called the DOS boot record (DBR) or volume boot record. DOS or Windows 9x identifies this sector as sector 0 for each volume. Following the boot record, the operating system creates two copies of the FAT as well as the root directory, just as it does on floppy disks. When the operating system creates the FAT, the Format program scans the track and sector markings that were created by the low-level format of the drive performed by the manufacturer. If the low-level format encounters bad or unusable sectors, it marks these sectors so that the FORMAT program can recognize them as bad. FORMAT marks them in the FAT as bad sectors. The FFF7 entry in the FAT marks an entire cluster as bad so that the drive will not use that area.

For DOS, use this command: FORMAT C:/S. If you include the /S option in the FORMAT command, the program also writes the two hidden files and COMMAND.COM to the drive. The hard drive is now bootable. Use the FORMAT command for each logical drive. For example, for drive D, enter the command FORMAT D.

For Windows 9x, the Windows 9x CD-ROM contains the real-mode drivers necessary to access the CD-ROM without having Windows installed. Place the Windows 9x Startup disk in the floppy drive and reboot. When you see the message, "Start computer with CD-ROM support," press Enter. The prompt indicates the CD-ROM letter. Insert the Windows 9x CD in the drive and type "setup" after the CD-ROM drive letter. If the setup process begins, follow the instructions on screen to install Windows 9x.

If you can't access the Windows 9x CD, then the generic CD-ROM drivers on the Startup disk don't work with your CD-ROM drive. In this case, you must install the CD-ROM drivers before you can install Windows 9x from CD.

To install the drivers for your CD-ROM drive, see the instructions that came with your CD-ROM drive. The drive also comes with a floppy disk that has the drivers on it. Follow the instructions to install these drivers on the hard drive.

Installing software

You are now ready to install Windows 9x. If you are using the non-upgrade version of Windows 9x, the DOS bootable disk has put the necessary DOS files on the hard drive so that you can boot from the drive.

As you prepare a hard drive for Windows 9x, it's clear that Windows 9x still uses the DOS core. DOS 7.0 (part of Windows 95) or DOS 7.1 (part of Windows 98) creates the partition, the FAT, and the root directory in preparation for Windows. And DOS 7.1 utilities such as FDISK and FORMAT are revised to provide the FAT32 support for Windows 98.

If you are installing Windows 9x from a CD-ROM, the CD-ROM driver needs to be installed next. You can generally load the CD-ROM drivers onto the hard drive by using the disk that comes with the CD-ROM drive.

After your new hard drive is bootable and you installed Windows 9x, you're ready to load the applications software. Once your drive has software completely loaded and working, there's no better time to make a complete backup of the entire drive—to tape or removable drive—with utility software designed for that purpose. Also, for Windows 3.x and DOS, make a bootable disk that contains all the files in the root directory of the drive. This disk will be your emergency disk if you have trouble with the drive later.

Saving the partition table to disk

If you have Nuts & Bolts, Norton Utilities, or other similar software, create a rescue disk to recover from a corrupted partition table. How to save the partition table by using Nuts & Bolts and Norton Utilities is covered when each software program is introduced in the next section. To use DOS to make a copy of the partition table, follow these directions:

Use the DOS 5 MIRROR command to save the partition table. The command line is:

```
C:\> MIRROR /PARTN
```

When things go wrong

Sometimes you might run into trouble during the installation process. Keeping a cool head, thinking things through carefully a second, third, and fourth time, and using all available resources will most likely get you out of any mess. Installing a hard drive isn't difficult unless you have an unusually complex situation.

For example, your first hard drive installation shouldn't involve installing a second SCSI drive into a system that has two SCSI host adapters. Nor should you install a second drive into a system that uses an IDE connection for one drive on the system board and an adapter card in an expansion slot for the other. If a complicated installation is necessary and you have never installed a hard drive, consider asking for some expert help. Know your limitations. Start with the simple and build your way up. You should be able to install a single IDE drive in a PC, or install a second slave drive by using the same adapter card and cable as the master drive. After mastering that, tackle something more complicated.

Here are some errors that might occur during a hard drive installation, their causes, and what to do about them.

1 The IDE adapter card and IDE hard drive are physically installed. The machine is turned on and the setup is told what drive is present. When the machine reboots from a disk, the following error message is displayed:

```
Hard drive not found.
```

Even though the hard drive isn't yet bootable, POST should be able to find it. Check all cables; the data cable or power cable might not be tightly connected.

2 You replace the cover on the computer case. When you reboot from a disk, POST beeps three times and stops.

Recall that diagnostics during POST are often communicated by beeps if the tests take place before POST has checked video and made it available to display the messages. Three beeps on most computers signal a memory error. Turn the computer off and check and reset the memory SIMMs on the system board.

3 The card and drive are physically installed and the computer is turned back on. The following error is displayed:

```
No boot device available.
```

You forgot to insert a bootable disk. Put the disk in the drive and reboot the machine.

4 You physically installed the drive, inserted a floppy disk in the disk drive, and rebooted. The following error message is displayed:

```
Configuration/CMOS error. Run setup.
```

This error message is normal. POST found a hard drive it wasn't expecting. The next step is to run setup.

5 You installed the drive and tried to reboot from a floppy disk. The error message 601 appeared on the screen. Any error message in the 600 range refers to the floppy disk. Look at the data and power connections the floppy disk drive—you may have knocked them off while installing the hard drive.

6 The hard drive doesn't physically fit into the bay. The screw holes don't line up. We get a bay kit, but it doesn't seem to work. Ask others to help who view the brackets, holes, and screws from a fresh perspective.

7 You physically install a drive after changing DIP switch settings on the drive. You boot up, change setup, and reboot. The following error message is displayed:

```
Hard drive not present.
```

You recheck all physical connections. If everything is OK, check the jumper settings. In most cases, the jumpers were set at the factory to be correct when the drive is the only drive.

When things aren't going well, you can tense up and make mistakes more easily. But there's one very costly error that you want to be certain to avoid. Be sure to turn off the machine before doing anything inside. Failing to unplug the machine puts you and the equipment in danger.

Calling technical support

To make calls to technical support more effective, have as much of the following information as you can available before you call:

- Drive model and description
- Manufacturer and model of your computer
- Exact wording of error message, if you have one
- Description of the problem
- Hardware and software configuration for your system

Installing a SCSI hard drive

A SCSI hard drive installation is a little more complicated than an ordinary IDE installation, but having a *SCSI bus* on your system enables you to add other SCSI devices to this bus, such as a CD-ROM drive or a cassette tape for backups.

When you install a SCSI hard drive, make sure that your host adapter and the cables you're using are compatible with the SCSI drive. The vendor can help you here. Read the documentation for both the SCSI host adapter and the hard drive before beginning. Most SCSI documentation is well written and thorough. In addition to the procedure already discussed for IDE hard drives, a SCSI installation requires that you configure the SCSI host adapter and the SCSI hard drive so that they can communicate with each other. This is done as follows:

1 **Set SCSI IDs.** Set the ID for each device on the SCSI bus. The host adapter documentation will probably explain that the host adapter must be set to ID 7. If the hard drive will be the boot device for the system, its ID must be 0. The second hard drive ID is usually 1. These ID settings might be set by jumpers or DIP switches on the drive.

   Tip: Sometimes jumpers on a SCSI device used to set the SCSI ID represent the binary value of the ID. For example, an ID of 6, which is 110 in binary, requires three jumpers set to on, on, and off.

2 **Disable or enable disk drive and hard drive controllers.** If the host adapter has a built-in disk drive controller that you're not using, the controller must be disabled with jumpers or DIP switches, or from the SCSI software setup program. The host adapter documentation will explain how to do this. Incidentally, if you're not using a hard drive or disk drive controller on your system board, you must disable these controllers by setting jumpers or DIP switches on the system board. See the documentation for your system board. Sometimes CMOS setup gives you the option of booting from the SCSI hard drive even if there is an IDE hard drive installed.

3 **Terminating resistors.** Devices on both ends of the bus must have terminating resistors enabled so that the voltages to these devices don't spike due to reflected signals at the end of the SCSI bus. The documentation will advise you to use terminating resistors that plug into a socket on the board or device, or to use terminating resistor connections where the cable plugs into the device. Some host adapters have jumper or DIP switches that enable or disable resistors on the card. Again, the documentation will be specific.

4 **CMOS setup for a SCSI system.** After you have physically installed the SCSI host and drive, you must tell setup that the SCSI system is present. Remember that for SCSI devices, the computer doesn't communicate with the hard drive directly but interfaces with the SCSI host adapter. To use a SCSI hard drive, some computers require that you tell setup that no hard drive is present. The SCSI host provides that information to the computer by way of a device driver. Sometimes, the computer setup will have the choice of a SCSI hard drive type. That's all it needs to know, and the SCSI host adapter takes over from there. To recognize a SCSI drive, some computers require that the drive type be set to 1 in setup.

5 **SCSI device drivers.** A SCSI bus system on a computer using DOS requires a SCSI device driver to be loaded in the CONFIG.SYS file of the bootable drive. Windows 9x offers its own SCSI driver. However, if the host adapter documentation recommends that you use the adapter's driver instead, then do so. The two better-known device drivers for SCSI systems are ASPI and CAM. After the physical installation and changing CMOS setup, the next step in any hard drive installation is to boot from a floppy disk. The hard drive package will include a bootable disk that loads the device driver to access the SCSI system. In addition to the files necessary to boot to a DOS prompt, for a SCSI installation the disk has a CONFIG.SYS file that contains the DEVICE= line to load the SCSI driver. In addition to the CONFIG.SYS file, the file containing the driver program must also be on the disk. (It's a good idea to have more than one bootable disk available. If you have problems, you can boot from the one that doesn't have the SCSI driver on it.) After you have partitioned and DOS-formatted the drive, the installation disk will put this same device driver on your hard drive.

The procedure has more steps if the SCSI drive is installed on the same computer with an IDE drive. For this installation, the IDE drive must be the boot drive and the SCSI drive must be the secondary drive unless your system BIOS supports SCSI hard drives. Because the SCSI bus doesn't contain the boot device, you must communicate the location of the boot drive to the SCSI host adapter. Again, the documentation for the host adapter will explain how to do this. It might tell you to disable the SCSI host adapter BIOS and run the SCSI bus with a device driver loaded in the CONFIG.SYS file of the bootable non-SCSI hard drive.

If you have a CD-ROM drive or other device on the SCSI bus, its device drivers might need to be installed in CONFIG.SYS for the device to operate. Place the DEVICE= command for any SCSI device after the DEVICE= command that loads the SCSI host device driver.

Multiple operating systems

Sometimes it's desirable for a PC to have more than one operating system on a hard drive. This is called dual booting. During the boot process, you decide which operating system will load and complete the boot. The operating system that controls the logical drive C (or whichever logical drive is specified in CMOS setup) always begins the boot process, because it's the one that BIOS turns to when searching for a boot device. During the boot, it's up to this operating system on that boot partition to offer the user the option of using another operating system on the drive. Each operating system manages a certain portion of the hard drive, which is accomplished by each operating system formatting it own logical drive.

For example, you can install Windows 9x and Windows 2000 on the same hard drive so that you can use software made for each operating environment within its native operating system.

When you install Windows 9x on a DOS machine, DOS will still be available; when you halt the Windows 9x boot and reboot to the previous version of MS-DOS, Windows 9x renames the DOS files back to the names that DOS expects.

Name when Windows 9x is active	Name when DOS is active	This file belongs to
Autoexec.bat	Autoexec.w40	Windows 9x
AUTOEXEC.DOS	AUTOEXEC.BAT	DOS
Command.com	Command.w40	Windows 9x
COMMAND.DOS	COMMAND.COM	DOS
Config.sys	Config.w40	Windows 9x
CONFIG.DOS	CONFIG.SYS	DOS
IO.sys	Winboot.sys	Windows 9x
IO.DOS	IO.SYS	DOS
Msdos.sys	Msdos.w40	Windows 9x
MSDOS.DOS	MSDOS.SYS	DOS

Do it!

C-3: Reviewing hard drive installation

Question	Answer
1 You can identify the location of Pin 1 on a power connector by the red wire. True or false?	
2 The BIOS must be modified when the hard drive configuration has been changed. True or false?	
3 You should always unplug the hard drive cables while the PC is powered on. True or false?	
4 Hard drives aren't ESD sensitive. True or false?	
5 Are all IDE hard drive controllers integrated on the system board? True or false?	

6 Donna wants to install a second hard drive in her PC. She currently has only one IDE controller, which has both a hard drive and CD-ROM drive attached to it. Without upgrading the system board, describe how Donna can add a second hard drive to her system and list the hardware she needs to purchase.

7 Before you call the manufacturer's technical support for a hard drive during installation, what should you have in hand?

8 When you install a SCSI drive and an IDE drive on the same system, under what circumstances can the SCSI drive be the boot device?

9 In a dual boot situation between Windows 98 and DOS 6, when Windows 98 boots, what does it do with the DOS 6 system files?

Topic D: Troubleshooting hard drives

Explanation

The remainder of this unit focuses on solving problems with hard drives and recovering corrupted data. We will examine in detail what can go wrong with a hard drive and what to do about it. Special attention is given to recovering data lost through hard drive problems. Also, a section on general troubleshooting guidelines summarizes the material in this topic.

An ounce of prevention

Taking good care of your hard drive isn't difficult, but it does require a little time. Before we begin a discussion of hard drive troubleshooting and data recovery, here are some precautions you can take to protect your data and software as well as the drive itself.

- **Make backups and keep them current.** It's worth saying again: keep backups. Never trust a computer; it'll let you down. Make a backup of your hard drive partition table, boot record, and CMOS setup. Whenever you install a new software package, back it up to disks or tape. Keep data files in directories separate from the software, to make backing up data easier. Back up the data as often as every four hours of data entry. Rotate the backup disks or tapes by keeping the last two or three most recent backups.

- **Defragment files and scan the hard drive occasionally.** A fragmented hard drive increases access time, and reading and writing files wears out the drive. If you're trying to salvage a damaged file, it's much more difficult to recover a fragmented file than one stored in contiguous clusters. Regularly scan your hard drive for lost or cross-linked clusters.

- **Don't smoke around your hard drive.** To a read/write head, a particle of smoke on a hard drive platter is like a boulder with a 10-foot circumference on the highway. Hard drives aren't airtight. One study showed that smoking near a computer reduced the average life span of a hard drive by 25%.

- **Don't leave the PC turned off for weeks or months at a time.** Once my daughter left her PC turned off for an entire summer. At the beginning of the new school term, the PC wouldn't boot. We discovered that the master boot record had become corrupted. PCs are like cars in this respect: long spans of inactivity can cause problems.

- **High humidity can be dangerous for hard drives.** High humidity isn't good for hard drives. I once worked in a basement with PCs, and hard drives failed much too often. After we installed dehumidifiers, the hard drives became more reliable.

- **Be gentle with a hard drive.** Don't bump the PC or move it when the drive is spinning.

Utility software

There are many disk utilities, such as Partition Magic, Gibson SpinRite, and Norton Utilities to help with the installation, maintenance, and repair of hard disk drives. A good disk utility can make your job a lot easier.

Categorizing hard drive problems

Both hardware and software can cause problems with hard drives. Problems also can be categorized as those that prevent the hard drive from booting and those that prevent the data from being accessed. Hardware and software causes of hard drive problems can be summarized as follows:

- Hardware problems:
  - Problems with the hard drive controller, power supply, data cable, BIOS, or setup—that is, with the supporting firmware and hardware needed to access the drive
  - Damage to the drive mechanism or physical damage to the disk surface where the partition table, boot record, directories, FAT, and/or the data itself are stored
- Software problems:
  - Corrupted operating system files
  - Corrupted partition table, boot record, or root directory, making all data on the hard drive inaccessible
  - Corruption of the FAT area that points to the data, the data's directory table, or the sector markings where the data is located
  - Corruption of the data itself
  - Data or access to it destroyed by a virus

Resolving hard drive problems

Hardware problems usually show up at POST, unless there is physical damage to an area of the hard drive that isn't accessed during POST. Hardware problems often make the hard drive totally inaccessible.

Sometimes older drives refuse to spin at POST. Drives that are having trouble spinning often whine at startup for several months before they finally refuse to spin altogether. If your drive whines loudly when you first turn on the computer, never turn the computer off. One of the worst things you can do for a drive that's having difficulty starting up is to leave the computer turned off for an extended period of time. Some drives, just like old cars, will refuse to start if they are left unused for a long time.

Don't trust valuable data to a drive that's having this kind of trouble. Plan to replace the drive soon. In the meantime, make frequent backups and leave the power on.

Data on a hard drive sometimes "fades" off the hard drive over time. Also, the read/write heads at the ends of the read/write arms on a hard drive get extremely close to the platters but don't actually touch them. This minute clearance between the heads and platters makes hard drives susceptible to destruction. Should a computer be bumped or moved while the hard drive is in operation, a head can easily bump against the platter and scratch the surface. Such an accident causes a "hard drive crash," often making the hard drive unusable.

If the head mechanism is damaged, the drive and its data are probably a total loss. If the first tracks that contain the partition table, boot record, FAT, or root directory are damaged, the drive could be inaccessible even though the data might be unharmed.

Here's a trick that might work for a hard drive whose head mechanism is intact but whose first few tracks are damaged. Find a working hard drive that has the same partition table information as the bad drive. With the computer case off, place the good drive on top of the bad drive housing, and connect a spare power cord and the data cable from the adapter to the good drive. Leave a power cord connected to the bad drive. Boot from a disk. No error message should show at POST. Access the good drive by entering C: at the A prompt. The C prompt should show on the monitor screen.

Without turning off the power, gently remove the data cable from the good drive and place it on the bad drive. Don't disturb the power cords on either drive or touch chips on the drive logic boards. Immediately copy the data you need from the bad drive to floppy disks by using the DOS COPY command. If the area of the drive where the data is stored, the FAT, and the directory aren't damaged, this method should work. If the FAT is damaged, you might need to read sectors instead of files to retrieve the data by using either DEBUG (repeating the LOAD and WRITE commands for all sectors) or utility software.

Here's another trick for an older hard drive that's having trouble spinning when first turned on. Remove the drive from the case and, holding it firmly in both hands, give the drive a quick and sudden twist in such a way that the platters are forced to turn inside the drive housing. Reinstall the drive. It might take several tries to get the drive spinning. Once the drive is working, immediately make a backup and replace the drive.

For a hard drive to be accessible by DOS or Windows 9x, these items, listed in the order they're accessed, must be intact:

- The partition table
- The boot record
- The FAT
- The root directory

In order for the hard drive to be bootable, in addition to the preceding items the following must be intact:

- For DOS:
  - The two DOS hidden files, IO.SYS and MSDOS.SYS (or IBMBIO.COM and IBMDOS.COM)
  - COMMAND.COM
  - CONFIG.SYS and AUTOEXEC.BAT (these are optional)

- For Windows 9x:
    - The two Windows 9x hidden files, Io.sys and Msdos.sys
    - Command.com
    - Config.sys and Autoexec.bat (these are optional)
    - Vmm32.vxd and several files that it uses to load the desktop

Windows 9x can be loaded to a command prompt, rather than a desktop. You can load just enough of the operating system to attain a command prompt. If you press F8 during the process of loading Windows 9x, you can then choose the command prompt. Doing this gives you the C prompt provided by Command.com and prevents Vmm32.vxd from loading.

The hard drive doesn't have to be bootable to access the data. You can always boot from a floppy disk and then access drive C. After Windows 9x or DOS accesses the drive, in order for the operating system to access the data these items must be intact:

- The directory in which the files are located
- In the FAT, the sector information where the files are located
- The beginning of the file, sometimes called the header information, and the end of the file, called the end-of-file marker
- The data itself

Looking back at the preceding three lists, you can see that there are several opportunities for failure. To recover lost data due to a software problem, you must first determine which item in the three lists is corrupted. Then you must either repair the item or bypass it to recover the data.

Damaged partition table

If the hard drive and its supporting hardware pass the POST tests performed by startup BIOS, then BIOS will try to load an operating system from the hard drive provided no floppy disk is in drive A. If the operating system loads from a floppy disk, the partition table and the boot record must be intact for the operating system to access the hard drive. The FAT and root directory must be readable for the operating system to read data stored on the drive.

The BIOS first reads the master boot program at the beginning of the partition table information on the hard drive. If the partition table is damaged, the error message is as follows:

```
Invalid drive or drive specification.
```

In this case, you should still be able to boot from a floppy disk. When you get to the A prompt and try to access the hard drive by entering C:, you'll get the same error.

If you suspect that the partition table is corrupted, use the FDISK command to display the partition table information. The FDISK command will give an error when trying to display the information if the table is corrupted.

Restoring the partition table is impossible if the track is physically damaged. However, if you have saved the partition table previously and there is no physical damage, the process is simple. You can save the partition table to a disk by using Norton Utilities, Nuts & Bolts, or the DOS 5 MIRROR command. If you haven't saved this information, but you have another hard drive with a matching partition table, try saving the table from the good drive and writing it to the bad drive. Sometimes the UNFORMAT command will do this, and sometimes not.

Command	Description
UNFORMAT /PARTN	Restores the partition table if you have saved the information by using the DOS MIRROR command.
	The command prompts you for the disk containing the file PARTNSAV.FIL, and it restores the partition table and boot records for all partitions on the drive.
UNFORMAT /U	This variation of the UNFORMAT command might recover the FAT, directories, and files.

Nuts & Bolts Disk Minder and Norton Disk Doctor also can repair a damaged partition table. You must have the utility software on floppy disks and execute the program from the disks. If you made a set of rescue disks with Nuts & Bolts or Norton Utilities, use these disks to restore the partition table. If you haven't made a set of rescue disks, try the emergency disks, which can sometimes correct the problem. If SpinRite instructs you to make a bootable disk on another PC, install SpinRite on the disk, and then use the disk to repair the hard drive.

Don't use FDISK to make a new partition table, because it will also overwrite the first few sectors on the hard drive that contain the FAT. You can recover part of the partition information by using FDISK with the /MBR parameter. When the following error message is displayed, first boot from a floppy disk.

```
Invalid drive or drive specification.
```

Then to restore the boot program in the partition table (called the master boot record), which is at the very beginning of the partition table information, try this command:

```
A> FDISK /MBR
```

Often, this command solves the problem. Note that the /MBR option isn't documented in the DOS or Windows 9x manuals. The FDISK program must be stored on the floppy disk in drive A; keep a copy of it on an emergency bootable disk for just this purpose.

You can, however, start all over by repartitioning and reformatting the drive. Even though the first few tracks are damaged, you might still be able to recover part of the storage space on the drive. The partition table is written on the very first sector of the hard drive, and this sector must be accessible. After that, you can skip as many sectors as you need to by making a non-DOS or non-Windows 9x partition at the beginning of the drive. This partition will never be used. Make the second partition, which will be the first DOS or Windows 9x partition, the bootable partition. All this is done by using the FDISK command available in either DOS or Windows 9x, or you can use Partition Magic.

Don't perform a low-level format on an IDE or SCSI drive unless the drive is otherwise unusable. Use the low-level format program recommended by the manufacturer, and follow its instructions. Call the drive manufacturer's technical support to find out how to get this program, or check the manufacturer's Web site for details.

Damaged boot record

If the boot record on a hard drive is damaged, you will not be able to boot from the hard drive. After you boot from a floppy disk and try to access the hard drive, you might get an error message such as "Invalid media type," "Non-DOS disk," or "Unable to read from Drive C."

If the boot record is damaged, the best solution is to recover it from the backup copy you made when you first became responsible for the PC. If you didn't make the backup, try something like Norton Utilities Disk Doctor. A floppy disk has only one boot record, but a hard drive has one master boot record in the partition table area and a boot record at the beginning of each logical drive or volume on the drive. Norton Disk Doctor will test and repair the damaged boot record if it can.

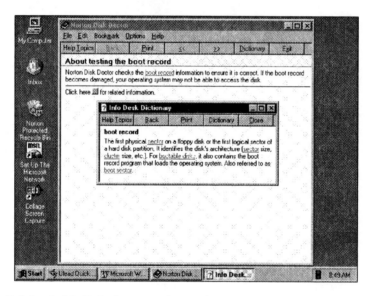

Exhibit 5-25: Help from Norton Utilities about testing the boot record

Damaged FAT or root directory

The partition table and boot record are easily backed up to disk; they will not change unless the drive is repartitioned or reformatted. Always back them up as soon as you can after you buy a new computer or become responsible for a working one.

Unlike the partition table and boot record, the FAT and the root directory change often and are more difficult to back up. Hard disk utilities provide tools to repair a damaged FAT or root directory. Their degree of success depends on the degree of damage to the tables.

One message generated by a hard drive with a damaged FAT is:

```
Sector not found reading drive A, Abort, Retry, Ignore, Fail?
```

Sometimes, however, there is no error message; files or directories are simply missing. Disk utilities can be used to recover from a corrupted FAT.

If the physical areas of the FAT and root directory are damaged and you can't repair them, you can still read data from the hard drive by reading sectors instead of files. Some disk utilities and recovery software can recover data if your FAT has been corrupted or even if the drive has been repartitioned.

Corrupted system files

If the two operating system hidden files are missing or corrupted, you should see the following error message in DOS:

```
Non-system disk or disk error...
```

The Windows 9x error message will be as follows:

```
Invalid system disk...
```

When this happens, first boot from a floppy disk, then access drive C and begin looking for the problem. Use the ATTRIB command to unhide all files in the root directory, as follows:

```
C:\> ATTRIB -H *.*
```

You should see the two exposed hidden files if they're there. If they're missing or corrupted, you can use the COPY command to copy them from a disk to the hard drive root directory. (Unhide them on the disk first, so COPY can find them.) Once they're on the hard drive, hide them again with these commands:

```
C:\> ATTRIB +H IO.SYS
C:\> ATTRIB +H MSDOS.SYS
```

Substitute another file name as necessary. You also can use this command:

```
A:\> SYS C:
```

The SYS command copies the two hidden files and COMMAND.COM from the disk to the hard drive.

COMMAND.COM must be in the root directory. If COMMAND.COM is missing, you should get an error message similar to the following:

```
Command file not found
```

You will probably find a spare copy in the \DOS directory or \Windows\command, or you can copy it from your bootable disk.

CONFIG.SYS and AUTOEXEC.BAT sometimes give error messages when changes are made to them or when they're accidentally erased. Keep a backup of these files so that you will not have to remember all the commands listed in them if you have to rebuild.

To prevent a user from accidentally erasing COMMAND.COM, CONFIG.SYS, and AUTOEXEC.BAT, you might want to hide these files, using the ATTRIB command in DOS or the Properties sheet in Windows 9x. You also can make them read-only files by using this version of ATTRIB for each file. For example, in COMMAND.COM you can use:

```
ATTRIB +R COMMAND.COM
```

Corrupted sector and track markings

The first few bits of each sector are labels that the hard drive BIOS must read before it reads any data in that sector. The data might be perfectly fine, but if the sector markings are faded, BIOS will not read the sector. DOS will give you the following error message:

```
Bad Sector or Sector Not Found.
```

A disk utility might be able to read the sector. Try that first. If one of them can read the data, copy the data to a disk and have the utility mark the cluster as bad in the FAT so that it will not be used again. If the drive continues to report bad sectors, it needs to be low-level formatted. Only the low-level format will refresh these sector bits.

There are two kinds of *low-level formats*: a nondestructive and a destructive format. The *nondestructive format* doesn't destroy the data. It copies the data on one track to another area of the drive, rewrites the sector bits on that track, and then copies the data back to the track.

A *destructive low-level format* completely ignores old format information and starts all over again, writing track and sector markings to the drive and overwriting all data. The advantages of using a destructive format are that it's faster and does a better job of determining bad sectors and marking them than a nondestructive format. If you have a choice, choose the destructive format.

Warning: It's dangerous to perform a low-level format on an IDE drive because the track and sector locations can be specific to this drive. Use only a low-level format program recommended by the drive manufacturer.

Corrupted data and program files

Data and program files can become corrupted for many reasons, ranging from power spikes to user error. If the corrupted file is a program file, the simplest solution might be to reinstall the software or recover the file from a previous backup.

To restore a data file that isn't backed up, you have three basic options:

- Use operating system tools and commands to recover the file.
- Use a disk utility or recovery software to recover the file.
- If neither of these approaches works, you can turn to a professional data recovery service. These services can be expensive, but, depending on how valuable the data is, the cost might be justified.

Hard drive troubleshooting guidelines

This section summarizes the steps you can follow when troubleshooting a hard drive problem. It lists several problems, their causes, and possible solutions. These and other troubleshooting guidelines are collectively listed in Appendix E, as a quick reference while on the job, to help give you ideas as to how to proceed when problem solving.

Begin troubleshooting by interviewing the user, being sure to include the following questions:

- Was the computer recently moved?
- Was any new hardware recently installed?
- Was any new software recently installed?
- Was any software recently reconfigured or upgraded?
- Does the computer have a history of similar problems?

There are a number of ways that hard drives can malfunction, including the ones discussed below.

Hard drive doesn't boot

If the hard drive doesn't boot, proceed as follows:

- Confirm that both the monitor and computer switches are turned on.
- Sometimes the startup BIOS displays numeric error codes during POST. Errors in the 1700s or 10400s generally mean fixed disk problems. Check the Web site of the BIOS manufacturer for explanations of these numeric codes.
- For SCSI drives, numeric error codes 096xxxx, 112xxxx, 113xxxx, 206xxxx, 208xxxx, 210xxxx, or 1999xxxx generally mean problems with the host adapter.
- For SCSI drives, reseat the host adapter card and check terminators.
- Disconnect and clean the edge connectors on the adapter card, if present.
- Check CMOS setup for errors in the hard drive configuration.
- Try using a bootable disk, then log on to drive C. If you have a Windows 9x rescue disk, you can use SCANDISK, CHKDSK, or FDISK to examine the system.
- If the PC will not boot from the boot disk, verify that the boot disk is good. Try using it in a different computer. To protect against viruses, write-protect the boot disk first.
- Check to be sure the power cable and disk controller cable connections are good.

If the drive still doesn't boot, exchange the three field-replaceable units for a hard drive subsystem (the data cable, the adapter card, and the hard drive itself). Perform the following procedures in order.

- Reconnect or swap the drive data cable.
- Reseat or exchange the drive adapter card, if one is present.
- Exchange the hard drive for one you know is good (in computer jargon, this is called a known-good unit).

A bad power supply or a bad system board might also cause a disk boot failure. If the problem is solved by exchanging one of the above field-replaceable units, you still must reinstall the old unit to verify that the problem wasn't caused by a bad connection.

Damaged, missing, or mismatched system files (COMMAND.COM, IO.SYS, MSDOS.SYS) can keep a hard disk from booting. You can see whether they're of the same version by typing DIR/AH. This will show the hidden system files and their dates. If COMMAND.COM and the hidden files have different dates, then they're usually mixed and incompatible versions. You can replace the three system files by using the following steps:

- Boot a rescue or system DOS disk from drive A (make sure you're using the same DOS version).
- Restore hidden system files on drive C (A:\>SYS C:).
- Older versions of DOS require you to copy COMMAND.COM separately. You can restore COMMAND.COM by typing:

  ```
  A:\>COPY COMMAND.COM C:
  ```
- Run SCANDISK.
- Run a current version of an antivirus program.

Drive retrieves and saves data slowly

If the drive retrieves and saves data slowly, proceed as follows:

- This might be caused by fragmented files that have been updated, modified, and spread over different portions of the disk. Run DEFRAG to rewrite fragmented files to contiguous sectors.
- Verify that the hard disk drivers are properly installed.

Computer will not recognize a newly installed hard drive

If the computer will not recognize a newly installed hard drive, proceed as follows:

- Does the manual state that you must first do a low-level format or run a Disk Manager? IDE drives are already low-level formatted. Older drives require the user to perform this routine.
- Has the FDISK utility been run successfully? Choose Display Partition Information from the FDISK menu to verify the status.
- FORMAT C:/S is the last required "format" step. Has this been done?
- Has the CMOS setup been configured correctly?
- Are there any drivers to install?
- Are there any DIP switches or jumpers that must be set?
- Has the data cable been connected properly? Verify that the cable stripes are connected to Pin 1 on the edge connectors of both the card and cable.
- Call the drive manufacturer if the above steps aren't productive.

Do it!

D-1: Troubleshooting review

Question	Answer
1 List three components to check or examine if a hard drive doesn't boot.	
2 What is the one most important thing you can do to protect your data on a hard drive?	
3 How can you unerase a file in Windows 98?	
4 What is one way that you can make a backup of partition information on a hard drive?	
5 Name two third-party utility software applications that can be used to manage and maintain hard drives.	

Unit summary: Hard drives

Topic A   You learned that most hard drives today use **IDE technology**, which has a complex method of organizing **tracks** and **sectors** on the disks. The term **SCSI** refers more to the bus used by the drive than to the technology of the drive. There are several types of SCSI, including SCSI-1, SCSI-2, Wide SCSI, Ultra SCSI, and Ultra Wide SCSI.

Topic B   You learned that a hard drive is **partitioned** into logical drives, or volumes. A master boot record at the beginning of the hard drive contains a table of partition information. Each logical drive contains a boot record, FAT, and root directory. **Hard drive capacity** is determined by the number of heads, tracks, and sectors on the disk, each sector holding 512 bytes of data.

Topic C   You learned that **installing a hard drive** includes setting jumpers or DIP switches on the drive; physically installing the adapter card, cable, and drive; changing CMOS setup; and partitioning, formatting, and installing software on the drive.

Topic D   You learned how to resolve **hard drive installation problems**. You also learned how to identify a problem and use **basic troubleshooting methods** to solve it.

Independent practice activity

In this activity, you will install a slave drive by using the master/slave configuration.

1 Power off the lab workstation and unplug the power cord. (It isn't necessary to unplug all other cords.)

2 Remove the case from the lab workstation.

3 Locate the hard drive.

4 Unplug the IDE cable and the power connector from the hard drive.

5 Use the Torx bit driver or a screwdriver to dismount the hard drive, if necessary, to view the hard drive jumper configuration.

6 Verify that the installed hard drive is set to Master. (Note: Refer to hard drive documentation or the label on the hard drive for a description of jumper settings. Some drives have separate settings for single master and master with slave.)

7 Set the jumper on the second hard drive to the Slave position.

8 Locate an available bay to mount the second hard drive.

9 Mount the second hard drive.

10 Plug in the power connectors to each hard drive.

11 Plug in the IDE data cable to each hard drive.

12 Plug in the power cord and stand clear of the case.

13 Power on the lab workstation and wait for the BIOS error message.

14 In the setup program, follow the menu instructions for the BIOS to validate the hard drive changes. The BIOS should now recognize two hard drives.

15 Save the changes and reboot the workstation.

16 Boot into the operating system to verify that it recognizes the additional drive.

Unit 6

Troubleshooting fundamentals

Unit time: 90 minutes

Complete this unit, and you'll know how to:

A Identify the available troubleshooting tools.

B Isolate problems and design a course of action.

C Troubleshoot problems that happen after a successful boot as well as problems with add-on devices.

D Develop a preventive maintenance plan.

Topic A: Introduction to troubleshooting

Explanation
When you try to solve a computer problem, you should avoid making the situation worse by damaging hardware, software, or valuable data, or harming yourself. This unit discusses the troubleshooting tools that are essential and describes some "nice-to-have" tools.

Troubleshooting perspectives

There are several perspectives a person might have as a PC troubleshooter. You might have a problem to solve on your own PC, or you might be solving a problem for someone else, such as a friend, a coworker, or a PC technician. As a PC technician, there are four different job functions you might fulfill:

- A PC support technician working on-site who closely interacts with users and is responsible on an ongoing basis for the PCs he or she maintains
- A PC service technician who goes to a customer site in response to a service call and, if possible, repairs a PC on-site
- A bench technician working in a lab environment, who might interact with the person who actually uses the PC being repaired, and isn't permanently responsible for this PC
- A help-desk technician providing telephone support

A PC support technician is the only one of the four listed above who is responsible for the PC before trouble occurs and, therefore, has the opportunity to prepare for a problem by keeping good records and maintaining backups (or teaching the user how to do so).

PC service technicians are usually not responsible for the ongoing maintenance of a PC, but usually have the opportunity to interact with the user of the computer.

Bench technicians are probably not working at the same site where the PC is kept. They might have the benefit of interviewing the user to get information about the problem, or they might simply be presented with a PC to repair without the ability to call the user to ask a question.

Help-desk technicians, who don't have physical access to the PC, are at the greatest disadvantage of the four. They're limited to interacting with the user over the phone and must obviously use different tools and approaches than the technician at the PC.

In this unit, the primary emphasis is on the first job function listed, that of an on-site PC support technician who is free to interact with the user and has overall responsibility for the PCs he or she maintains and repairs. However, the special needs and perspectives of the service technician, the bench technician, and the help-desk technician also will be addressed.

Protect yourself, the hardware, and the software

Please remember that every time you work on a PC, you run the risk of hurting yourself, the hardware, and the software. However, there are precautions you can take to protect all three, and they're extremely important to remember. You can compound a problem, causing even more damage, by carelessly neglecting these safety precautions.

The most common threat to hardware is *electrostatic discharge (ESD),* commonly known as *static electricity.* Damage by ESD can cause a catastrophic failure, which can destroy components, or can cause an upset failure that produces unpredictable malfunctions of components, which are often difficult to detect or diagnose.

The three best protections against ESD as you work on a computer are a ground strap, a ground mat, and static shielding bags. A *ground bracelet,* sometimes called a ground strap or a static strap, is worn on your wrist and is grounded to a ground mat, computer case, or a ground prong of a wall outlet. A *ground mat* often comes equipped with a cord to plug into the ground prong of the wall outlet and a snap on the mat to which you can attach the end of your ground strap. New components come shipped in static shielding bags. Save the bags to store other devices not currently installed on your PC.

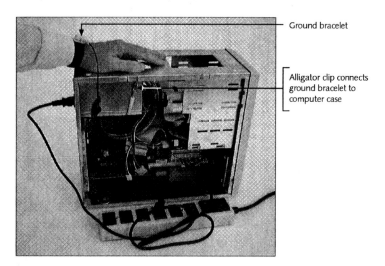

Exhibit 6-1: A ground bracelet

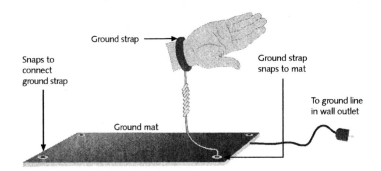

Snaps to
connect
ground strap

Ground strap

Ground strap
snaps to mat

To ground line
in wall outlet

Ground mat

Exhibit 6-2: A ground mat

Here are some tips on how to further protect disks and other hardware as you work:

- Don't touch chips or edge connectors on boards unless absolutely necessary.
- Don't stack boards.
- Don't touch chips with a magnetized screwdriver.
- Don't use a graphite pencil to change DIP switch settings.
- Don't put cards on top of or next to the monitor.
- When laying down components, lay them on a grounded mat or static shielding bag.
- Always turn off the PC before moving it (even a few inches) to protect the hard drive.
- When working inside a monitor, be careful *not* to ground yourself.
- When unpacking hardware or software, remove the packing tape from the work area as soon as possible
- Don't place a PC on the floor where it might get kicked.
- Keep disks away from magnetic fields, heat, and extreme cold.
- Don't open a disk's shuttle window or touch the surface of a disk.
- Always verify that the ground plug in an outlet is physically grounded by using a circuit tester.

Troubleshooting tools

Before we turn our attention on how to troubleshoot a PC problem, we will first look at the hardware and software tools needed, and describe some of them in detail. There are many tools to help you diagnose and repair computer problems. Your choice depends on the amount of money you can spend and the level of support you provide for PCs. Below is a list of essential and convenient tools.

Tools that are essential for PC troubleshooting are as follows. All but the bootable rescue disk can be purchased easily in one handy PC tool kit:

- Bootable rescue disk
- Flat-head screwdriver
- Phillips-head screwdriver
- Torx screwdriver
- Tweezers for picking pieces of paper out of printers or dropped screws from tight places
- Chip extractor to remove chips (To pry up the chip a simple screwdriver is usually more effective, however.)
- Extractor, a spring-loaded device that looks like a hypodermic needle (When you push down on the top, three wire prongs come out that can be used to pick up a fallen screw where hands and fingers can't reach.)

The following tools might not be considered essential, but they're very convenient:

- Multimeter to check the power supply output
- Needle-nose pliers for holding things in place while you screw (especially nuts on cable connectors)
- Flashlight to see inside dark places in the PC case
- Ground bracelet or ground mat
- Small cups or bags to help keep screws organized as you work
- Antistatic bags to store unused parts
- Pen and paper for taking notes
- Bootable rescue disks
- Diagnostic cards and diagnostic software — Examples include POSTcard V3 by Unicore Software, Inc., Post Code Master by MSD, Inc., POSTmortem Diagnostic Card by System Optimization, Inc., and PC-Technician and PC-Diagnosys by Windsor Technologies, Inc. For more information on these diagnostic cards and software, check out the manufacturer's Web sites.
- Utility software — Examples include First Aid 2000 by McAfee, Nuts & Bolts by Network Associates, Norton Utilities by Symantec, and Partition Magic and Drive Image Pro by PowerQuest. For more information on these utilities and others, check out the manufacturer's Web sites.
- Virus detection software on disks

Keep your tools in a toolbox designated for this purpose. If you put disks and hardware tools in the same box, don't include a magnetized screwdriver, and be sure to keep the disks inside a plastic case. Make sure the diagnostic and utility software you use is recommended for the hardware and software you are working with.

Do it!

A-1: Discussing troubleshooting safety

Question	Answer
1 When working with hardware, when is it important to *not* ground yourself?	
2 What is ESD and how can you protect against it?	
3 Why are magnetized screwdrivers dangerous around computer equipment?	

Bootable rescue disk

Explanation

An essential tool for PC troubleshooting is a bootable rescue disk. Not only can a *bootable disk* enable you to boot the PC even when the hard drive fails, but, by booting from the rescue disk, you're assured that the cleanest boot possible is attained. A "clean boot" doesn't load any extraneous software, drivers, or other TSRs, which might be loaded from startup routines on the hard drive.

Bootable disk for DOS

For DOS, make a bootable disk by using the same version of DOS that is on the PC's hard drive. Use this command:

```
C:\> FORMAT A:/S
```

The /S option tells DOS to copy to disk the necessary files in order to load DOS. On the disk will be a small boot record that identifies the layout of the disk and the names of the two DOS hidden files. This command also puts the two hidden files and COMMAND.COM on the disk.

It's important that the boot disk has the same version of DOS that is on the hard drive. If you're consistent with versions, then once the computer boots you can use some of the DOS loaded from the disk and some DOS program files on the hard drive without DOS displaying error messages about using different versions of DOS. Use the VER command at the DOS prompt to display the current version of DOS.

You also can add some DOS utility commands to the disk so that it can serve as a rescue disk if necessary. In addition to the boot files, copy these files to the disk:

- ATTRIB.EXE
- CHKDSK.EXE
- EDIT.COM (which might also require QBASIC.EXE if you're using an older version of DOS)
- EMM386.EXE
- FDISK.EXE
- FORMAT.COM
- MSCDEX.EXE
- SCANDISK.EXE
- SYS.COM
- DEFRAG.EXE
- HIMEM.SYS
- UNDELETE.EXE

Rescue disk for Windows 9x

For a Windows 9x rescue disk, also include the necessary files to access the CD-ROM without depending on the hard drive. You'll learn how to do this later. Windows 98 places these real-mode driver files on the disk automatically.

Do it!

A-2: Discussing troubleshooting tools

Question	Answer
1 Name some essential troubleshooting tools.	
2 Why is a bootable rescue disk necessary even if you have diagnostic software?	
3 In addition to starting a failed hard drive, what advantage does a bootable rescue disk provide?	
4 Why should you run a virus scan on the bootable disk that you use for troubleshooting?	

Topic B: Isolating problems and designing action plans

Explanation

When a computer doesn't work and you're responsible for fixing it, you should generally approach the problem first as an investigator and discoverer, always being very careful not to compound the problem through your own actions. If the problem seems difficult to you, see it as an opportunity to learn something new. Ask questions until you understand the source of the problem. Once you understand it, you're almost done, because most likely the solution will then be evident. Take the attitude that you can understand the problem and solve it, no matter how deeply you have to dig, and you probably will. In this section we discuss how to approach a troubleshooting problem, including how to interact with the user and how to handle an emergency.

Fundamental rules

Here are a few fundamental rules for PC troubleshooting.

- **Approach the problem systematically.** Start at the beginning and walk your way through the situation in a thorough, careful way. This one rule is worth its weight in gold. Remember it and apply it every time. If you don't find the explanation to the problem after one systematic, logical walk-through, then repeat the entire process. Check and double-check to find the step you overlooked the first time. Most problems with computers are simple, such as a loose cable or circuit board. Computers are logical, and so the problem will be logical.

- **Divide and conquer.** This rule is the most powerful. Isolate the problem. In the overall system of hardware and software, remove one hardware or software component after another, until the problem is isolated to a small subsystem of the whole system. You'll learn many methods of applying this rule in this book. For starters, here are a few:

  - Remove any memory-resident programs (TSRs) to eliminate them as the problem.

  - Boot from a disk to eliminate the operating system and startup files on the hard drive as the problem.

  - Remove any unnecessary hardware devices, such as a scanner card, internal modem, and even the hard drive.

  Once down to only the essentials, start exchanging components you know are good for those you suspect might be bad, until the problem goes away.

- **Don't overlook the obvious.** Ask simple questions. Is the computer plugged in? Is it turned on? Is the monitor plugged in? Most problems are so simple that we overlook them because we expect the problem to be difficult. Don't let the complexity of computers fool you. Most problems are simple and easy to fix.

- **Check the simple things first.** It's more effective to first check the components that are easiest to replace. For example, if the video doesn't work, the problem might be with the monitor or the video card. When faced with the decision of which one to exchange first, choose the easy route: exchange the monitor before you exchange the video card.

- **Make no assumptions.** This rule is the hardest one to follow, because there is a tendency to trust anything in writing and assume that people tell you exactly what happened. But documentation is sometimes wrong, and people don't always describe events exactly as they occurred—so do your own investigating. For example, if the user tells you that the system boots up with no error messages, but his or her software still doesn't work, boot for yourself. You never know what that user might have overlooked.

- **Become a researcher.** Following this rule is the most fun. When a computer problem arises that you can't easily solve, be as tenacious as a bulldog. Read, make phone calls, ask questions, then read, make more phone calls, and ask more questions. Take advantage of every available resource, including online help, the Internet, documentation, technical support, and books such as this one. What you learn will be yours to take to the next problem. This is the real joy of computer troubleshooting. If you're good at it, you're always learning something new.

- **Write things down.** Keep good notes as you're working. They'll help you think more clearly. Draw diagrams. Make lists. Write down clearly and precisely what you're learning. Later, when the entire problem gets "cold," these notes will be invaluable.

- **Reboot and start over.** This is an important rule. Fresh starts are good for us and uncover events or steps that might have been overlooked. Take a break; get away from the problem. Begin again.

- **Establish your priorities.** This rule can help make for a satisfied customer. Decide what your first priority is. For example, the first priority might be to recover data that's lost, or it might be to get the PC back up and running as soon as possible. Consult the user or customer for his or her advice when practical.

- **Keep your cool.** In an emergency, protect the data and software by carefully considering your options before acting, by not assuming data is lost even when hard drive and floppy drive errors occur, and by taking practical precautions to protect software and operating system files. When a computer stops working, if there is data still in memory that hasn't been saved, or if there is data or software on the hard drive that isn't backed up, look and think carefully before you act. A wrong move can be costly. The very best advice is: don't hurry. Carefully plan your moves. Read the documentation if you're not sure what to do, and don't hesitate to ask for help. Don't simply try something, hoping it will work—unless you've run out of more intelligent alternatives.

- **Don't assume the worst.** When it's an emergency and your only copy of data is on a hard drive that isn't working, don't assume that the data is lost. Much can be done to recover data, but one important point is worth repeating. If you want to recover lost data on a hard drive, don't write anything to that hard drive; you might write on top of lost data, eliminating all chances of recovery.

- **Know your starting point.** Before trying to solve a computer problem, know for certain that the problem is what the user says it is. If the computer doesn't boot, carefully note where in the boot process it fails. If the computer does boot to an operating system, before changing anything or taking anything apart, verify what does and doesn't work, preferably in the presence of the user.

Devising a course of action

When solving a computer problem, the above rules prepare you to effectively apply a successful course of action. This course of action is threefold:

1. Interact with the user. Gather as much information up front as you can before you try to solve the problem. Have the user describe the problem to you in detail, and ask questions. Don't settle for secondhand information unless that is your only choice. Later, as you work, consult the user before taking drastic action, such as formatting the hard drive.

2. Isolate the problem by eliminating the unnecessary and trading good for suspected bad.

3. Follow established guidelines toward a solution.

Interacting with the user

Ask the user to explain to you in detail exactly what happened when the computer stopped working. What procedure was taking place at the time? What had just happened? What recent changes did the user make? When did the computer last work? What has happened in the meantime? What error messages did the user see? Recreate the circumstances that existed when the computer stopped, as best you can, and in as much detail as you can. Make no assumptions. All users make simple mistakes and then overlook what they did. If you realize that the problem was caused by the user's mistake, take the time to explain the proper procedures, so that the user understands what went wrong and what to do next time.

Use diplomacy and good manners when you work with a user to solve a problem. For example, if you suspect that the user dropped the PC, don't ask, "Did you drop the PC?" Rather, put the question in a less accusatory manner: "Could the PC have been dropped?" If the user who asked for your help is sitting in front of the PC, don't assume you can take over the keyboard or mouse without permission. Also, if the user is present, ask permission before you make a software or hardware change, even if the user has just given you permission to interact with the PC.

When working at the user's desk, consider yourself a "guest" and follow these general guidelines:

- Don't "talk down" to or patronize the user.
- Don't take over the mouse or keyboard from the user without permission.
- Don't use the phone without permission.
- Don't pile your belongings and tools on top of the user's papers, books, etc.
- Accept personal inconvenience to accommodate the user's urgent business needs. For example, if the user gets an important call while you are working, step out of the way so he or she can handle it.

If you're at the user's desk, you should generally follow these guidelines when working with the user:

- Don't take drastic action such as formatting the hard drive before you ask the user about important data on the hard drive that might not be backed up.
- Provide the user with alternatives when appropriate before you make decisions affecting him or her.
- Protect the confidentiality of data on the PC, such as business financial information.
- Don't disparage the user's choice of computer hardware or software.
- If you make a mistake or must pass the problem on to someone with more expertise, be honest.

In some PC support situations, it's appropriate to consider yourself as a support to the user, as well as a support to the PC. Your goals might include educating the user as well as repairing his or her computer. In this kind of situation, if you want the user to learn something from a problem he or she caused, don't fix the problem yourself unless the user asks you to. Explain how to fix the problem and walk him or her through the process, if necessary. It takes a little longer this way, but is more productive in the end because the user learns more and is less likely to repeat the mistake.

Here are some helpful questions to ask the user when you're first trying to identify the problem:

- When did the problem start?
- Were there any error messages or unusual displays on the screen?
- What programs or software were you using?
- Did you move your computer system recently?
- Has there been a recent thunderstorm or electrical problem?
- Have you made any hardware changes?
- Did you recently install any new software?
- Did you recently change any software configuration setups?
- Has someone else been using your computer recently?

The goal is to gain as much information from the user as you can before you begin investigating the hardware and the software.

Isolate the problem

After gathering as much information from the user as possible, set about isolating the computer problem. The two approaches that are the most effective are to eliminate the unnecessary and to trade good for suspected bad.

Eliminate the unnecessary

This rule can be applied in many ways. For example, when the PC will not boot successfully, it's often unclear if the problem is a hardware problem or a software problem. When using Windows 9x, you can boot into Safe Mode (press F5 at startup) and eliminate much of the operating system's customized configuration. But if you still have problems, it might be possible to boot from your bootable rescue disk.

Boot from a disk that you know is good and that has a minimal operating system configuration (that is, no CONFIG.SYS or AUTOEXEC.BAT files). By doing so, you eliminate all the applications software that load at startup on the PC, all the TSRs that load at startup, and much of the operating system, especially in Windows 9x. If the problem goes away, you can deduce that the problem is with (1) the software on the PC or (2) the hard drive and/or its subsystem that's used as the boot device.

If you suspect the problem is caused by faulty hardware, eliminate any unnecessary hardware devices. If the PC still boots with errors, disconnect the network card, the CD-ROM drive, the mouse, and maybe even the hard drive. You don't need to remove the CD-ROM or hard drive from the bays inside the case. Simply disconnect the data cable and the power cable. For the network card, remove the card from its expansion slot. Remember to place it on an antistatic bag or grounded mat—not on top of the power supply or case. If the problem goes away, you know that one or more of these devices is causing the problem. Replace them one at a time until the problem returns. Remember that the problem might be a resource conflict. If the network card worked well until the CD-ROM drive was reconnected, and now neither works, try the CD-ROM drive without the network card. If the CD-ROM drive now works, you most likely have a resource conflict.

Trade good for suspected bad

When diagnosing hardware problems, this method serves you well if you can draw from a group of parts that you know work correctly. Suppose the monitor doesn't work; it appears dead. The parts of the video subsystem are the video card, the power cord to the monitor, the cord from the monitor to the PC case, and the monitor itself. Also, don't forget that the video card is inserted into an expansion slot on the system board, and the monitor depends on electrical power. Suspect each of these five components to be bad. Try these things one at a time. Trade the monitor for a monitor that you know works. Trade the power cord, trade the cord to the PC video port, move the video card to a new slot, and trade the video card. When you're trading a good component for a suspected bad one, work methodically by eliminating one component at a time. Don't trade the video card and the monitor and then turn on the PC to determine if they work. It's possible that both the card and the monitor are bad, but first assume that only one component is bad before you consider whether multiple components need trading.

In this situation, suppose you keep trading components in the video subsystem until you have no more variations. Next, take the entire subsystem—video card, cords, and monitor—to a PC that you know works, and plug each of them in to see if they work. If they do, you have isolated the problem to the PC, and not the video. Now turn your attention back to the PC—the system board, the software settings within the operating system, the video driver, and so on. Knowing that the video subsystem works on the good PC gives you a valuable tool to work with. Compare the video driver on the good PC to the one on the bad PC. Make certain the CMOS settings, software settings, and such are the same.

An alternate approach to trading good for suspected bad

There's an alternate approach to trading good for suspected bad that works very well in certain situations. If you have a working PC that's configured similarly to the one you're troubleshooting (a common situation in many corporate or educational environments), rather than trading good for suspected bad, you can trade suspected bad for good. Take each component that you suspect is bad and install it in the working PC. If the suspected bad component works on the good PC, then you have eliminated it as the suspect. If the working PC breaks down, then you have probably identified the bad component.

Do it!

B-1:   Developing good troubleshooting habits

Question	Answer
1 What are two fundamentals rule of troubleshooting?	
2 Give five possible questions that should be asked of a user who is experiencing computer problems.	
3 When isolating a problem, what does "eliminate the unnecessary" mean?	
4 By using the "trade good for suspected bad" rule, describe how to easily troubleshoot a video problem.	
5 Describe the alternate approach to the trade good for suspected bad method.	

Topic C: Problems after a successful boot

Explanation

Troubleshooting a PC problem begins with isolating the problem into one of two categories: problems that prevent the PC from booting and problems that occur after a successful boot. Begin by asking the user questions to learn as much as you can from the user. Next, ask yourself the question, "Does the PC boot properly?" If the screen is blank and the entire system is "dead"—no lights, spinning drive, or fan, then proceed to troubleshooting the power system.

Determining what needs to be fixed

When POST completes successfully, it sounds a single beep indicating that all is well, regardless of whether the monitor works or is even present. If you hear that single beep, then the problem is with the video, and the next step is to troubleshoot it. If you don't hear the single beep or you hear more than one beep, then POST encountered an error. In this case, proceed to troubleshooting the system board.

If there's an error message on the screen, then the obvious next step is to respond to the message. An example of such an error is, "Keyboard not present." If the error message occurs as the operating system loads, and you don't understand the message or know what to do about it, begin by troubleshooting the operating system.

If video works, but the boot message is confusing or unreadable, then begin to eliminate the unnecessary. Perform a clean boot. For Windows 9x, the simplest way to do this is to boot to Safe Mode. If this doesn't work, use your bootable rescue disk.

If the PC boots up properly, turn your attention to the system that isn't working and begin troubleshooting there.

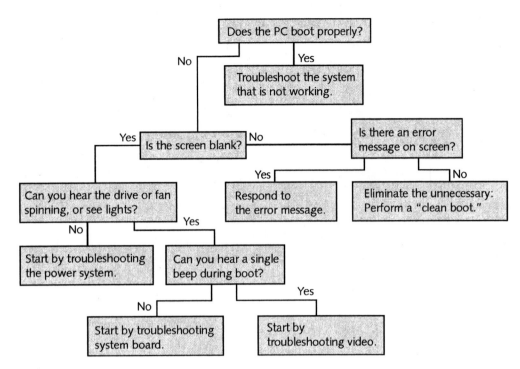

Exhibit 6-3: Begin problem solving with the question, "Does the PC boot properly?"

Troubleshooting the power system

If the PC appears "dead," ask these questions:

- Are there any burnt parts or odors? (Definitely not a good sign!)
- Is everything connected and turned on? Are there any loose cable connections? Is the computer plugged in?
- Are all the switches turned on? Computer? Monitor? Surge protector? Uninterruptible power supply? Separate circuit breaker? Is the wall outlet (or surge protector) good?
- If the fan isn't running, turn off the computer, open the case, and check the connections to the power supply. Are they secure? Are all cards securely seated?

Once you answer these questions and you still haven't isolated and fixed the problem, proceed this way:

- For the newer ATX power supplies, there's a wire that runs from the power switch on the front of the ATX case to the system board. This wire must be connected to the pins on the system board and the switch turned on before power comes up. Check that the wire is connected correctly to the system board. Exhibit 6-4 shows the wire, which is labeled "REMOTE SW," connected to pins on the system board labeled "PWR.SW." If you aren't sure of the correct connection on the system board, see the system board documentation. Next, check the voltage output from the power supply.

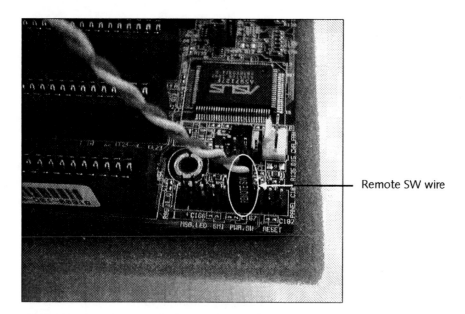

Remote SW wire

Exhibit 6-4: Verify that the remote SW wire is connected to the system board

- Remove all nonessential expansion cards (modem, sound card, mouse) one at a time. This verifies that they're not drawing too much power and pulling the system down. It's possible that the expansion cards are all good, but that the power supply isn't capable of supplying enough current for all the add-on boards. It could be that there are too many cards, and the computer is overheating. The temperature inside the case shouldn't exceed 113° F.

- Vacuum the entire unit, especially the power supply's fan vent, or use compressed air to blow out the dust. Excessive dust insulates components and causes them to overheat.

- Trade the power supply for another one that you know is good. For an AT system board, be certain to follow the black-to-black rule when attaching the power cords to the system board.

- Is there strong magnetic or electrical interference? Sometimes an old monitor emits too much static and EMF (electromagnetic force), and brings a whole system down.

Troubleshooting the system board

When troubleshooting the system board, use whatever clues POST can give you. Before video is checked out, POST reports any error messages as beep codes. When a PC boots, one beep indicates that all is well after POST. Error messages on the screen indicate that video works. Look up the error message if the message on the screen isn't clear. You also can try the Web site of the ROM BIOS manufacturer for information.

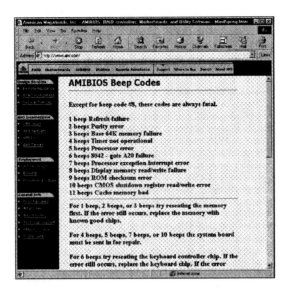

Exhibit 6-5: The manufacturer's Web site can provide information about beep codes

Remember that you can try substituting good hardware components for suspected bad ones. Be cautious here. A friend once had a computer that wouldn't boot. He replaced the hard drive, with no change. He replaced the system board next. The computer booted up with no problem; he was delighted, until it failed again. Later he discovered that a faulty power supply had damaged his original system board. When he traded the bad one for a good one, the new system board also got zapped! Check the voltage coming from the power supply before putting in a new system board!

If the problem doesn't improve, ask yourself, "Is the system in a Doze or Sleep Mode?" Many "green" systems can be programmed through CMOS to suspend the monitor or even the drive if the keyboard and/or CPU have been inactive for a few minutes. Pressing any key usually causes operations to resume exactly where the user left off. If this doesn't resolve the problem, try these things:

- If the fan is running, reseat or replace the CPU, BIOS, or RAM. Try installing RAM in a different slot. A POST code diagnostic card is a great help at this point.

- Sometimes a dead computer can be fixed by simply disassembling it and reseating cables, adapter cards, socketed chips, and SIMMs and DIMMs. Bad connections and corrosion are common problems.

- Check jumpers, DIP switches, and CMOS settings. Look for physical damage on the system board.

- If the battery is dead, or dying, it might cause problems. Sometimes, after a long holiday, a weak battery causes the CMOS to forget its configuration.

- Reduce the system to essentials. Remove any unnecessary hardware, such as expansion cards, and then try to boot again.

- Exchange the system board, but before you do this, measure the voltage output of the power supply in case it's producing too much power and has damaged the board.

The computer doesn't recognize all installed RAM or SIMMs

When the computer doesn't recognize all installed RAM or SIMMs, answer the questions below:

- Are CMOS settings correct?
- Run diagnostic software such as PC-Technician to test memory.
- Are SIMM or DIMM modules properly seated? Remove and reinstall each one. For a DIMM module, try a different memory slot.
- Look for bent pins or chips installed the wrong way on cache memory.
- Place your fingers on the individual chips. Sometimes a bad chip might be noticeably hotter than the other chips.
- Make sure the SIMMs have correct or consistent part numbers. For example, if there are four installed SIMMs, they usually must be the same size (in megabytes) and same speed (in nanoseconds).
- Replace memory modules one at a time. For example, if the system recognizes only 6 out of 8 MB of RAM, swap the last two SIMM modules. Did the amount of recognized RAM change? You might be able to solve the problem just by reseating the modules. Use SIMM modules with the same part number.
- Sometimes a problem can result from a bad socket or a broken trace (a fine printed wire or circuit) on the system board. If this is the case, you might have to replace the entire system board.

Do it!

C-1: Troubleshooting the boot process

Here's how

Breaking the machine (create only one problem):

1 Power off the lab workstation and unplug the power cord. (It isn't necessary to unplug all other cords.)

2 Remove the case from the lab workstation.

3 Problem 1: Unplug the P8 and P9 connectors from the system board.

Problem 2: Locate the hard drive and move the jumper of the hard drive to the Slave position.

4 Replace the case and plug in the power cord.

Troubleshooting:

5 Power on the workstation.

6 Are there any error messages? If so, write them down.

7 What is the specific problem?

8 List possible solutions.

9 Test your solution and record the results.

10 How did you discover the problem?

Troubleshooting the operating system and hard drive

Explanation

To troubleshoot the operating system and hard drive, proceed as follows:

- Try a hard boot. A soft boot might not do the trick, because TSRs aren't always "kicked out" of RAM with a soft boot.

- Learn to use the Windows 9x Startup menu. Option 4 is displayed if the PC is configured for a network, and Option 8 is displayed if an earlier version of DOS is installed. Try Safe Mode first. If that doesn't work, use the step-by-step confirmation to identify the command causing the problem. Use the Logged option and examine the BOOTLOG.TXT file created. Try booting to just the command prompt. If none of these steps work, boot from the Windows 9x rescue disk or try booting from a rescue disk created by utility software such as Nuts & Bolts or Norton Utilities.

1.	Normal
2.	Logged (\BOOTLOG.TXT)
3.	Safe Mode
4.	Safe Mode with network support
5.	Step-by-step confirmation
6.	Command prompt only
7.	Safe Mode command prompt only
8.	Previous version of MS-DOS
	Enter a Choice: 1

Exhibit 6-6: Windows 9x Startup menu when F8 is pressed during startup

When you boot from a floppy disk, you should boot to an A prompt. If you're successful, the problem is in the hard drive subsystem and/or the software on the drive.

If you can get a C prompt, then the problem is in the software that's used on the hard drive to boot, including the partition table, master boot record, operating system hidden files, and command interface files. If necessary, run diagnostic software to test for hard drive hardware problems.

Problems after the computer boots

Either hardware or software can cause problems that occur after the computer boots.

If you suspect the software, try diagnostic software such as Nuts & Bolts, ScanDisk, or Norton Utilities before reloading the software package.

If you suspect the hardware, first isolate the problem by removing devices and substituting good components for suspected bad ones. Be aware that the problem might be a resource conflict.

- Check the voltage output from the power supply with a multimeter.
- Check jumpers, DIP switches, and CMOS settings for the devices.
- Suspect a corrupted device driver. Reinstall the driver.
- Suspect the applications software that uses the device. Try another application or reinstall the software.

Do it!

C-2: Troubleshooting the hard and floppy drives

Here's how

Breaking the machine (create only one problem):

1 Power off the lab workstation and unplug the power cord. (It isn't necessary to unplug all other cords.)

2 Remove the case from the lab workstation.

3 Problem 1: Locate the hard drive and unplug the IDE cable and the power connector from the hard drive.

Problem 2: Locate the floppy drive and unplug the floppy drive data cable. By using the incorrect connector on the data cable, plug the floppy drive into the data cable.

4 Replace the case and plug in the power cord.

Troubleshooting:

5 Power on the workstation.

6 Are there any error messages? If so, write them down.

7 What is the specific problem?

8 List possible solutions.

9 Test your solution and record the results.

10 How did you discover the problem?

Problems with the software

Explanation

Suppose the computer boots with no errors, and all but one software package on the computer work correctly. When you try to load the problem software package, however, you get an error message and the software terminates. If this is the case, you can probably conclude that the software caused the error. Ask yourself these questions: Has this software ever worked? If it hasn't, then try installing it again. Maybe wrong information was given during the installation. Be sure you check the requirements for the software. Maybe you don't have enough memory or space on your hard drive to create the necessary working files.

When was the last time the software worked? What happened differently then? Did you get an error message that didn't seem significant at the time? What has happened to your computer since the software last worked? Have you added more software or changed the hardware configuration?

Problems caused by other software

Software problems might be caused by other software. Windows 9x uses files stored in the \Windows\System directory to support software files for many software applications as well as Windows. These files can have extensions of .dll, .ocx, .oca, .vbx, and so on. The most common are the DLL (dynamic-link library) files. The following exhibit shows the results of a search for these files on a hard drive: 938 DLL files were located. These files perform tasks for many software packages, such as displaying and managing a dialog box on screen. When you install an application, the installation program might write a DLL to the \Windows\System directory and overwrite an earlier version of the DLL used by another application. The original application may have problems because it can't use the new DLL. If the software being investigated started to have problems after you installed another software program, the problem may well be the DLL it's unsuccessfully trying to use.

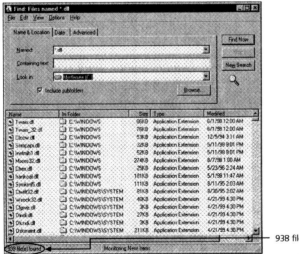

938 files found

Exhibit 6-7: DLL files shared by several applications can cause problems

Intermittent problems

Intermittent problems can make troubleshooting challenging. The trick in diagnosing problems that come and go is to look for the patterns or clues as to when the problems appear. If the problem is such that you or the user can't reproduce the problem at will, ask the user to keep a log of when the problems occur and exactly what messages appear on the screen. Show the user how to get a printed screen of the error messages when they appear. Here's the method:

- For simple DOS systems, the PrintScreen key directs the displayed screen to the printer.

- In Windows, the PrintScreen key copies the displayed screen to the Clipboard.

- Launch the Paint software accessory program and paste the contents of the Clipboard into the document. You might need to use the Zoom Out command on the document first. You can then print the document with the displayed screen by using Paint. You also can paste the contents of the Clipboard into a document created by a word-processing application such as Word.

Do it!

C-3: Troubleshooting software problems

Question	Answer
1 What is the best way to document intermittent problems?	
2 What are DLL files and why could they cause problems?	
3 List the steps to get a printed screen of an error message by using Windows.	

Problems with the keyboard and monitor

Explanation

If the peripheral devices, such as the keyboard or monitor, don't work, ask questions like these: Does the device work in situations other than the current one? Perhaps the problem is with the applications software interfacing with the device, rather than with the device itself. Has the device ever worked? Will another device work in this same situation? Exchange the keyboard or monitor for one you know works. If the good device now fails to work, you can then eliminate the original device as the source of the problem. The problem must be the software, the cable, the computer, or the user. Check all connections and exchange cables.

Troubleshooting keyboard problems

Often dirt, food, or drink in the keyboard causes one or more keys to stick or not work properly. These and other keyboard problems and what you can do about them are described next.

Because of the low cost of keyboards, if a keyboard doesn't work, the solution is most often to replace it. However, there are a few simple things you can do to repair one that is not working.

A few keys don't work: If a few keys don't work, remove the caps on the bad keys with a chip extractor. Spray contact cleaner into the key well. Repeatedly depress the contact in order to clear it out. Don't use rubbing alcohol to clean the key well, because it can leave a residue on the contact. If this method of cleaning solves the problem, then clean the adjacent keys as well.

Turning the keyboard upside down and lightly bumping multiple keys with your flat palm will help loosen and remove debris.

The keyboard doesn't work at all — If the keyboard doesn't work at all, first determine that the cable is plugged in. PC keyboard cables might become loose or disconnected.

If the cable connection is good and the keyboard still doesn't work, swap the keyboard with another keyboard of the same type that you know is in good condition, to verify that the problem is in the keyboard and not in the computer.

If the problem is in the keyboard, check the cable. If possible, swap the cable with a known good one, perhaps from an old discarded keyboard. Sometimes a wire in a PC keyboard cable becomes pinched or broken. Most cables can be easily detached from the keyboard by removing the few screws that hold the keyboard case together, then simply unplugging the cable. Be careful as you work; don't allow the key caps to fall out!

On the system board, the two chips that affect the keyboard functions are the keyboard chip and the ROM BIOS chip. You might choose to replace each of these chips on the system board. Otherwise, the entire system board might have to be replaced.

Key continues to repeat after being released — This problem can be caused by a dirty contact. Some debris might have conductive properties, short the gap between the contacts, and therefore cause the key to repeat. Try cleaning the key switch with contact cleaner. Very high humidity and excess moisture sometimes short key switch contacts and cause keys to repeat because water is an electrical conductor. The problem usually resolves itself once the humidity level returns to normal. You can hasten the drying process by using a fan (not a hot hair dryer) to blow air at the keyboard.

Keys produce the wrong characters — This problem is usually caused by a bad chip. PC keyboards actually have a processor mounted on the logic board inside the keyboard. Try swapping the keyboard for one you know is good. If the problem goes away, replace the keyboard.

Major spills on the keyboard — When coffee or other drinks with sugar in them spill on the keyboard, you can be left with a sticky mess. The best way to deal with this is to thoroughly rinse the keyboard in running water. A shower works great. It's most important that the keyboard be completely dry before you use it. Give it about two days to dry. It will dry faster if you set it out in the sun or in front of a fan.

Troubleshooting monitor problems

For monitors, as well as other devices, do the easy things first. There are hardware and software adjustments you can easily make. Also, remember the "trade good for suspected bad" method. Many monitor problems are caused by poor cable connections or bad contrast/brightness adjustments. Also, check whether the monitor is still under warranty. Remember that many warranties are voided if an unauthorized individual works inside the monitor.

Power light (LED) doesn't go on, no picture

- Verify that the wall outlet works by plugging in a lamp, radio, etc.
- If the monitor power cord is plugged into a power strip or surge protector, verify that the power strip is turned on and working and that the monitor also is turned on.
- If the monitor power cord is plugged into the back of the computer, verify that the connection is tight and the computer is turned on.
- A blown fuse could be the problem. Some monitors have a fuse that is visible from the back of the monitor. It looks like a black knob that you can remove (no need to go inside the monitor cover). Remove the fuse and look for the broken wire indicating a bad fuse.
- The monitor may have a switch on the back for choosing between 110 volts and 220 volts. Check that the switch is in the right position.
- If none of these solutions solves the problem, the next step is to take the monitor to a service center.

Power LED light is on, no picture on power-up

- Check the contrast adjustment. If there's no change, then leave it at a middle setting.
- Check the brightness adjustment. If there's no change, then leave it at a middle setting.
- Is the cable connected securely to the computer?
- If the monitor-to-computer cable detaches from the monitor, exchange it for a cable you know is good or check the cable for continuity.
- If this solves the problem, reattach the old cable to verify that the problem wasn't simply a bad connection.
- Confirm that the proper system configuration has been set up. Some older system boards have a jumper or DIP switch that can be used to select the monitor type.
- Test a monitor you know is good on the computer you suspect to be bad. It's very important to do both this and the previous step, to cover all your bases. If you think the monitor is bad, make sure that it also fails to work on a good computer.
- Check the CMOS settings or software configuration on the computer. When using Windows 9x, boot into Safe Mode (press F5 during the boot) so that the operating system selects a generic display driver and low resolution. If this works, then you can try changing the driver and resolution.
- Reseat the video card. Move the card to a different expansion slot. Clean the card's edge connectors by using a contact cleaner or a white eraser. Be certain not to allow crumbs from the eraser to fall into the expansion slot.
- If there are socketed chips on the video card, remove the card from the expansion slot and, by using a screwdriver, press down very firmly on each corner of each socketed chip on the card, in case a chip has worked its way loose.
- Trade a good video card for the video card you suspect is bad. Test the video card you think is bad on a computer that works. Test a video card you know is good on the computer that you suspect might be bad. Whenever possible, try to do both.
- If the video card has some socketed chips that appear dirty or corroded, consider removing them and trying to clean the pins. You can use a clean pencil eraser to do this. Normally, however, if the problem is a bad video card, the most cost-effective measure is to replace the card.
- Go into setup and disable the shadowing of video ROM.
- Test the RAM on the system board with diagnostic software.
- For an older system board that supports both VESA and PCI, and if you're using a VESA video card, try using a PCI card.
- Trade the system board for one you know is good. Sometimes, though rarely, a peripheral chip on the system board of the computer can cause the problem.

Power on, but monitor displays the wrong characters

- Wrong characters are usually not the result of a bad monitor but of a problem with the video card. Trade the video card for one you know is good.
- Exchange the system board. Sometimes a bad chip, ROM or RAM, on the system board displays the wrong characters on the monitor.

Monitor flickers and/or has wavy lines

- Monitor flicker can be caused by poor cable connections. Check that the cable connections are snug.
- Does the monitor have a degauss button to eliminate accumulated or stray magnetic fields? If so, press it.
- Check if something in the office is causing a high amount of electrical noise. For example, you might be able to stop a flicker by moving the office fan to a different outlet. Bad fluorescent lights or large speakers have also been known to produce interference. Two monitors placed very close together also can cause problems.
- If the vertical scan frequency (the refresh rate at which the screen is drawn) is below 60 Hz, a screen flicker might appear.
- Try using a different refresh rate. In Windows 9x, right-click on the desktop and select Properties from the menu.
- For older monitors that don't support a high enough refresh rate, your only solution might be to purchase a new monitor.
- Before making a purchase, verify that the new monitor will solve the problem.
- Check Control Panel, Display, Settings to see if a high resolution (greater than 800 × 600 with more than 256 colors) is selected. Consider these issues:
  - The video card might not support this resolution/color setting.
  - There might not be enough video RAM; 2 MB or more might be required.
  - The added (socketed) video RAM might be of a different speed than the soldered memory.

No graphics display or the screen goes blank when loading certain programs

- A special graphics or video accelerator card isn't present, or is defective.
- Software isn't configured to do graphics, or the software doesn't recognize the installed graphics card.
- The video card doesn't support the resolution and/or color setting.
- There might not be enough video RAM; 2 MB or more might be required.
- The added (socketed) video RAM might be of a different speed than the soldered memory.
- The wrong adapter/display type is selected. Start Windows 9x from Safe Mode to reset display.

Screen goes blank 30 seconds or one minute after the keyboard is left untouched

- A "green" system board (green system boards follow energy-saving standards) used with an Energy Saver monitor can be configured to go into a Standby or Doze mode after a period of inactivity. This might be the case if the monitor resumes after you tap a key or move the mouse. Doze times can be set for periods from as short as 20 seconds to as long as one hour. The power LED light normally changes color from green to orange to indicate Doze Mode.

- You might be able to change the Doze features by entering the CMOS menu and looking for an option such as Power Management, or in Windows 9x by going to the Control Panel and selecting Display, Screen Saver.

- Some monitors have a Power Save switch on the back of the system. This might not be switched to your desired setting.

Poor quality color display

- Read the documentation for the monitor to learn how to use the color-adjusting buttons on the outside of the monitor to fine-tune the color.

- Exchange video cards.

- Add more video RAM; 2 MB or 4 MB might be required for higher resolutions.

- Check whether there is a fan or large speaker (speakers have large magnets) or another monitor nearby that could be causing interference.

Picture out of focus or out of adjustment

- Check the adjustment knobs on the control panel on the outside of the monitor.

- Change the refresh rate. Sometimes this can make the picture appear more in focus.

- There also are adjustments inside the monitor that might solve the problem. If you aren't trained to work inside the monitor, take the monitor to a service center for adjustments.

Crackling sound

An accumulation of dirt or dust inside the unit might be the cause. Someone trained to work on the inside of the monitor can vacuum the inside.

Configuring monitor settings and drivers in Windows 9x

If the video card is supported by Windows 9x, the driver and settings can be changed through the Display icon of the Control Panel. For drivers not supported by Windows 9x, you can reinstall the drivers by using the CD or floppy disks that came with the video card. The settings for this type of driver can most likely be changed through the Control Panel's Display icon.

Changing the video driver configuration

1   Select the Display icon from the Control Panel.

2   Select the Settings tab to change the color palette, resolution (for example, from 800 × 600 to 1024 × 768), or change the driver for the video card or monitor type.

3   Click on Advanced from the Settings tab to show the Change Display Type window. From this window, you can change the video card or the monitor type. If you increase the resolution, the Windows icons and desktop text become smaller. Consequently you might want to select Large Fonts under the Settings tab and increase the Desktop Icon size found under the Appearance tab.

Returning to standard VGA settings

When the display settings don't work, you should return to standard VGA settings. For Windows 9x, reboot the system and tap the F8 function key after the first beep. When the Microsoft Windows 9x Startup menu appears, select Safe Mode to boot up with minimal configurations and standard VGA display mode. Select the Display icon from the Control Panel and reset to the correct video configuration.

Troubleshooting printer problems

When troubleshooting printer problems, first determine that the problem is truly with the printer. The problem might be the computer hardware communicating with the printer, the applications software using the printer, the printer driver, the printer cable, or the printer.

Ask these questions and try these things:

- Is the printer turned on, and is the printer online?
- Is the correct printer selected as the default printer?
- Can an applications software program other than the program currently running use the printer?
- Is the printer using the correct driver? Does the driver need updating? Is the driver installed correctly?
- Can on you move the printer to another computer and print from it? Will another printer work on this computer?

Once you're convinced that the problem isn't with the computer hardware or software but is indeed a problem with the printer itself, you're ready for the following troubleshooting information.

Laser printer problems

The printer documentation can be very helpful and most often contains a phone number to technical support for the printer manufacturer. A good test for a printer is to print the manufacturer's test page from the PC, not just directly from the printer. If you're using Windows 98, for an HP LaserJet 5L, access the Control Panel and double-click Printers. The printer control appears. Right-click the printer you want to test to display the drop-down menu. Choose Properties to display the Properties box. Click on Print Test Page to send a test page to the printer.

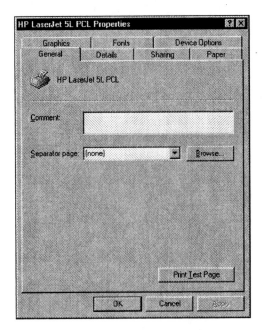

Exhibit 6-8: A printer Properties box

Printer never leaves warm-up mode

The warming up message should disappear as soon as the printer establishes communication with the PC. If this doesn't happen, try the following:

- Turn the printer off and disconnect the cable to the computer.
- Turn on the printer. If it now displays a Ready message, the problem is communication.
- Verify that the cable is connected to the correct printer port, and not to a serial port.
- Verify that data to the installed printer is being sent to the parallel port. For example, access the Properties box of the installed printer and verify that the print job is being sent to LPT1.

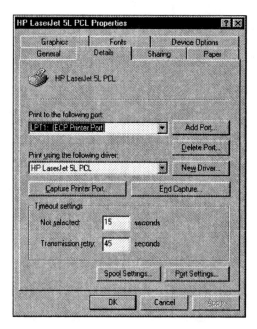

Exhibit 6-9: The printer port setting in the Properties box

- Check that the parallel port is enabled in CMOS setup and is set to the correct mode.
- Replace the cable.

A Paper Out message is displayed

- Remove the paper tray. Be sure there is paper in the tray. Carefully replace the tray, being certain the tray is fully inserted in the slot.
- Check the lever mechanism that falls into a slot on the tray when no paper is present. Is it jammed or bent?

A Toner Low message is displayed, or print is irregular or light

Remove the toner cartridge from the printer, tap the cartridge to redistribute the toner supply, and replace it in the printer. Don't shake the cartridge too hard, to avoid flying toner. This is really just a temporary fix for a cartridge low on toner. Eventually the user must put a new toner cartridge in the printer. Extreme humidity might cause the toner to clump in the cartridge and give the same error message.

A Paper Jam message is displayed

- If paper is jammed inside the printer, follow the directions in the printer documentation to remove the paper. Don't jerk the paper from the printer mechanism, but pull evenly on the paper, with care.
- If there's no jammed paper, then remove the tray and check the metal plate at the bottom of the tray. Can it move up and down freely? If not, replace the tray.
- When you insert the tray in the printer, does the printer lift the plate as the tray is inserted? If not, the lift mechanism might need repairing.

One or more white streaks appear in the print

Remove the toner cartridge, tap it to redistribute the toner supply, and replace the cartridge. Check the printer manual for specific directions as to what part might need replacing if this problem occurs.

Print appears speckled

Try replacing the toner cartridge. If the problem continues, the power supply assembly might be damaged.

Printed images are distorted

- Check for debris that might be interfering with the printer operation.
- Replace the toner cartridge.

Dot matrix printer problems

Problem	Suggestions
Print quality is poor	Begin with the ribbon. Does it advance normally while the carriage moves back and forth? Replace the ribbon.
	If the new ribbon still doesn't advance properly, check the printer's advance mechanism.
	Adjust the print head spacing. There's usually a lever adjustment that can alter the distance between the print head and plate.
	Check the print head for dirt. Make sure it's not hot before you touch it. If there is a debris buildup, wipe off each wire with a cotton swab dipped in alcohol or contact cleaner.
Printer self-test works, but printing from a computer application doesn't work	To perform a printer self-test, see the printer documentation. This test ensures that the printer itself is functioning correctly, and that the problem is communication from the PC.
	Check cable connections. Is the printer online?
Print head moves back and forth, but nothing prints	Check the ribbon. Is it installed correctly between the plate and print head?
	Does the ribbon advance properly?

Ink-jet printer problems

Problem	Suggestions
Print quality is poor	Is the correct paper for ink-jet printers being used?
	Is the ink supply low, or is there a partially clogged nozzle?
	Remove and reinstall the cartridge.
	Follow the printer's documentation to clean each nozzle.
	In the Printer Setup dialog box, click the Media/Quality tab, and then change the Print Quality selection. Try different settings with sample prints.
	Is the print head too close to or too far from the paper?
	If you're printing on transparencies, try changing the fill pattern in your application.
Printing is intermittent or absent	Is the ink supply low?
	Are nozzles clogged?
	Replace the ink cartridges or replenish the ink supply.

Do it!

C-4: Troubleshooting the keyboard, monitor, and printer

Question	Answer
1 Describe what to do if you've just spilled soda pop on your keyboard.	
2 Starting with the easiest procedures, list five things to check if a monitor doesn't display a picture.	
3 Name three things that might cause monitor flicker.	
4 What is the value of installing additional video RAM?	
5 Starting with the easiest procedures, list five things to check if your printer doesn't print.	
6 What can you do to temporarily solve streaking or light printing on a laser printer?	

Topic D: Preventive maintenance

Explanation

The other side of the troubleshooting coin is anticipating and preventing problems. PC hardware failures are caused by many different environmental and human factors, including heat, dust, magnetism, power supply problems, static electricity, human error (such as spilled liquids or an accidental change of setup and software configurations).

The goals of preventive maintenance are to reduce the likelihood that the events that cause PC failures will occur, and to lessen the damage if and when they do occur. When designing a preventive maintenance plan, consider what you can do to help prevent each cause, and incorporate preventive actions into your plan.

A preventive maintenance plan

If your company has established written guidelines for PC preventive maintenance, read them and put in place the necessary procedures to make them work. If your company doesn't have an established plan, make your own. A preventive maintenance plan tends to evolve from a history or pattern of malfunctions within the organization. For example, dusty environments might mean more maintenance, whereas a clean environment might mean less maintenance. The following table lists some guidelines for developing a preventive maintenance plan that might work for you.

Component	Maintenance	How often?
Inside the case	Make sure air vents are clear.	Yearly
	Use compressed air to blow the dust out of the case, or use a vacuum to clean the vents, power supply, and fan.	
	Ensure that chips and expansion cards are firmly seated.	
	Clean the contacts on expansion cards.	
CMOS setup	Keep a backup record of setup (for example, use a Nuts & Bolts rescue disk).	Whenever changes are made
Floppy drive	Clean the floppy drive head only when the drive doesn't work.	When the drive fails
Hard drive	Perform regular backups.	At least weekly
	Automatically execute a virus scan program at startup.	At least daily
	Defragment the drive and recover lost clusters regularly.	Monthly

Component	Maintenance	How often?
	Don't allow smoking around the PCs.	Always
	Place the PC where it will not be jarred, kicked, or bumped.	Always
Keyboard	Keep the keyboard clean.	Monthly
	Keep the keyboard away from liquids.	Always
Mouse	Clean the mouse rollers and ball.	Monthly
Monitor	Clean the screen with a soft cloth.	At least monthly
Printers	Clean out the dust and bits of paper by using compressed air or a vacuum. Small pieces of paper can be removed with tweezers.	At least monthly
	Clean the paper and ribbon paths with a soft lint-free cloth.	
	Don't re-ink ribbons or use recharged toner cartridges.	
Software	If directed by your employer, check that only authorized software is present.	At least monthly
	Regularly delete files from the Recycle Bin and \Temp directories.	
	Delete any temporary files in the \DOS directory.	
Written record	Keep a record of all software, including version numbers and the OS installed on the PCs.	Whenever changes are made
	Keep a record of all hardware components installed, including hardware settings.	
	Record when and what preventive maintenance is performed.	
	Record any repairs done to the PCs.	

The general idea of preventive maintenance is to do what you can to make a PC last longer and give as little trouble as possible. You might also be responsible for ensuring that data is secure and backed up, that software copyrights aren't violated, and that users are supported. As with any plan, when designing your preventive maintenance plan, first define your overall goal or goals, and then design the plan accordingly.

Keeping records

Record keeping and maintaining documentation are often overlooked when discussing preventive maintenance. A record of what's done to a PC is valuable when problems arise or when upgrading is under consideration. Secure all manufacturer hardware documentation. Users who aren't responsible for hardware might not realize the significance of a user manual for a hardware device, such as a sound card or modem, and might not be careful to protect these documents over time. You might want to file these documents together in an envelope with a log of everything you've done to the PC for regular maintenance, installations, and repairs and a boot disk that contains a copy of CMOS setup for a particular PC. Consider taping the envelope to the inside of the computer case. This works especially well when you're responsible for PCs at off-site locations where you might not have assigned filing cabinet space. This information might also be kept in a notebook along with other similar notebooks at your workstation. Label each notebook to identify the PC that it tracks. You also can keep records on a separate PC.

Moving equipment

When shipping a PC, there's always the possibility that damage will be caused by rough handling, or by exposure to water, heat, and cold. Also, the PC is sometimes misplaced, lost, or stolen. When you prepare a PC for shipping, take extra precautions to protect the PC and the data. Here are some general guidelines to follow when preparing to ship a PC:

- Back up the hard drive onto a tape cartridge. If you don't have access to a tape cartridge, back up important system and configuration files to a floppy disk. Whatever you do, don't ship a PC that has the only copy of important data on the hard drive or data that should be secured from unauthorized access.

- Remove any floppy disks, tape cartridges, or CDs from the drives. Make sure that the tapes or disks holding the backup data are secured and protected during transit. Consider shipping them separately.

- Turn off power to the PC and all other devices.

- Disconnect the power cords from the electrical outlet and from the devices. Disconnect all external devices from the computer.

- If you think there might be a problem with later identifying which cord or cable belongs to which device or connection, label the cable connections with white tape or white labels.

- Coil up all cords and secure them with plastic ties or rubber bands.

- Pack the computer, monitor, and all devices in their original shipping cartons or similar boxes with enough packing material to protect them.

Disposing of used equipment

As a PC technician, it will often be your responsibility to dispose of used equipment and consumables, including batteries, printer toner cartridges, and monitors. The following table lists items and how to dispose of them. Manufacturer documentation and local environmental regulators also can provide disposal instructions or guidance. Monitors and power supplies can contain a charge even after the devices are unplugged. To discharge the capacitors in either device, place a screwdriver across a hot prong and the ground prong of the electrical connections. To discharge the actual CRT in a monitor, the monitor must be opened. Ask a technician trained to fix monitors to do this for you.

A *material safety data sheet* (*MSDS*) provides information about how to properly handle substances such as chemical solvents. An MSDS includes information such as physical data, toxicity, health effects, first aid, storage, disposal, and spill procedures. MSDSs come packaged with the chemical, or you can order them from the manufacturer, or find them on the Internet (go to www.ilpi.com/msds).

Parts	How to dispose of them
Alkaline batteries, including AAA, AA, A, C, D, and 9 volt	Normal trash
Button batteries used in digital cameras, Flash Path, and other small equipment Battery packs used in notebooks	These batteries can contain silver oxide, mercury, lithium, or cadmium and are considered hazardous waste. Dispose of these either by returning them to the original dealer or by taking them to a recycling center. To recycle them, pack them separately from other items. If you don't have a recycling center nearby, contact your county for local regulations for disposal.
Laser printer toner cartridges	Return to the manufacturer or dealer to be recycled.
Ink-jet printer ink cartridges Computers Monitors Chemical solvents and cans	Check with local county or environmental officials for laws and regulations in your area for proper disposal of these items. The county might provide a recycling center that will receive them. Before disposing of a monitor, first discharge the monitor.

Do it!

D-1:   Developing a preventive maintenance plan

Exercise

You're the network administrator for a 75-user network. Your employer asks you to create a preventive maintenance plan for all of the hardware components connected to the network. Start this project by creating a list of tasks that can be done for each of the following components:

1 System unit

2 CMOS setup

3 Floppy drive

4 Hard drive

5 Keyboard and mouse

6 Monitors

7 10 laser printers

8 7 ink-jet printers

Unit summary: Troubleshooting fundamentals

Topic A   In this topic, you learned that while you work on a computer, you need to **protect** the computer and its components **against ESD**. Tools for solving computer problems include a **repair kit, bootable disk,** and **diagnostic hardware and software**.

Topic B   You learned that two important rules when troubleshooting are to **eliminate unnecessary hardware** and software and to **trade components** you know are good for those you suspect might be bad. Learn to ask the user questions (by exhibiting good manners and diplomacy) that help you understand the history behind the problem.

Topic C   This topic introduced **guidelines for solving specific problems**. Problems with computers can be divided into two groups: the computer boots or it doesn't boot. Guidelines for troubleshooting keyboards, monitors, and printers were covered in this topic.

Topic D   In this topic, you learned how to develop a **preventive maintenance plan** to protect your computer system and components from damage. You also learned about the correct way to **dispose of hazardous waste** that results from old computer parts.

Review questions

1 What could you do differently in the future to improve your troubleshooting process?

2 What are the six steps of the troubleshooting process?

3 What is troubleshooting documentation?

4 List three things that should be done before moving or shipping a computer.

5 How do you properly dispose of a battery pack from a notebook computer?

Unit 7

Supporting I/O devices

Unit time: 90 minutes

Complete this unit, and you'll know how to:

A Use standard resources when installing add-on devices.

B Use ports and expansion slots for add-on devices and resolve resource conflicts.

C Install a SCSI device to support other devices.

D Define how a keyboard, mouse, and monitor work.

Topic A: Overview of peripheral devices

Explanation

This unit introduces procedures and guidelines that are common to most I/O installations, including how to use serial, parallel, and USB ports and expansion slots. We then turn our attention to the I/O devices common to every computer—a keyboard, pointing device, and monitor.

Basic principles of peripheral installations

When you add new a peripheral to a computer, the device needs a device driver or BIOS, system resources (which might include an IRQ, a DMA channel, some I/O addresses, and some upper memory addresses), and applications software. Consider these fundamental principles:

- The peripheral is a hardware device that's controlled by software. You must install both the hardware and the software.

- The software might exist at different levels. For example, a device could require driver software that interfaces directly with the hardware device and an applications software package that interfaces with the driver. You must install all levels of software.

- More than one peripheral device might attempt to use the same computer resources. This conflict could disable a device or cause it to hang up. Possible conflicts arise when more than one device attempts to use any of the following four system resources:

  - The same IRQ
  - The same DMA channel
  - The same I/O addresses
  - The same upper memory addresses (for 16-bit drivers)

Do it!

A-1: Reviewing system resources

Question	Answer
1 What's an IRQ?	
2 What are I/O addresses?	
3 What's a DMA channel?	
4 How are upper memory addresses used by devices?	

Installation overview

Explanation

There are three basic steps to install an add-on device:

- Install the device
- Install the device driver
- Install the applications software

The device can be an internal (installed inside the computer case) or external (installed outside the case) device. Devices installed inside the case are drives (hard drives, floppy drives, CD-ROM drives, DVD drives, Zip drives, etc.) or devices that are inserted in expansion slots on the system board (a modem card, video capture card, etc.). An external device can be installed by using an existing port (serial, parallel, or USB port), or an interface card installed in an expansion slot can provide a port.

An example of this last situation is a scanner, which is an external device. It uses an expansion card installed inside the case to interface with the system board. When you buy a scanner, you usually get physical scanner, the expansion card that interfaces with the computer (optional), the cable to connect the scanner to its expansion card or the USB port, the device driver on disk, some applications software for using the scanner, and, very importantly, the documentation. Installing the hardware includes installing the expansion card in one of the expansion slots on the system board and then plugging in the scanner.

After the physical installation of the device, install the device driver. In Windows 9x, the setup program is executed from the Start, Run command and installs the device driver automatically, or you can use the Control Panel, Add New Hardware option.

The driver and the scanner expansion card are specific for each brand and model of scanner; however, the applications software doesn't have as narrow an application. Any application package that uses a scanner should work with most scanners. In fact, you might have several applications that use the same hardware device.

Hardware devices

Consider a hardware device such as a modem. You know that a modem provides a way to connect one computer to another, forming a network. There are many kinds of modems and networks. Some modems use normal telephone lines for communication, whereas others use dedicated circuits. Internal modems are expansion cards that are installed inside the computer case; they provide one or (usually) two, telephone-line ports that connect a telephone line directly into the back of the computer. External modems are contained in their own case with their own power supply. The external modem is connected to the computer by a cable that plugs into the back of the computer case, usually to a serial port. The telephone line then plugs into the back of the modem. In either case, the modem converts the computer's bits to a form that can be communicated over telephone lines and other circuits.

Most often internal devices are less expensive than external devices, because external devices have the additional expense of the power supply and case. Internal devices also offer the added advantage of not taking up desk space, and they have all cables and cords neatly tucked away. An advantage of external devices is that they can be moved easily from one computer to another. In the case of a modem, the external device provides added security.

If you've ever shopped for a peripheral device, such as a modem or a sound card, you know what a large variety of features and prices today's market offers. Research pays. First, know your own computer system. Know which CPU, system bus, and local bus you have, and how much memory and what size hard drive your system currently has. Know which operating system you have and what version it is. Determine how much space is available on your hard drive, and how many expansion slots and what kinds of slots are free in your computer.

In addition to a basic knowledge of your system, you might need some technical information. For example, most computers have a power supply that well exceeds the requirements of the standard system, making it possible to add internal devices without exceeding the total available wattage. However, if your computer is old (computers over five years old), and you're adding more than one internal device, the power supply could limit your choices. If you install more internal devices than the power supply can handle, you might need to upgrade it as well.

Unless you're using Plug-and-Play-compliant devices and a Plug-and-Play operating system, it might be important to know what IRQs, I/O addresses, DMA channels, and upper memory addresses your present devices use. It's recommended that you keep a notebook to record each device and its current settings.

Generally, if you buy a device and other accompanying hardware (such as the interface board and cables) from the same source, they're more likely to be compatible.

Embedded BIOS on devices

A peripheral device might require several levels of software to make it work. The most fundamental software needed is stored on ROM chips inside the device or on the interface board, and is called BIOS, or firmware. Some devices also contain some memory or RAM to temporarily store data moving through the device. Sometimes it's necessary to interface with the BIOS to set a parameter, such as the IRQ number. If the device and your system are Plug and Play, you don't need to change the resource parameters of the device. If you're not using Plug and Play, you can set a parameter of the BIOS by changing a DIP switch or jumper setting. However, for some sophisticated devices, you can interface with the BIOS by using programs provided by the manufacturer, which present a chip setup screen similar to the system board CMOS setup screen. The documentation for the device should tell you what parameters can be changed and how to communicate those changes to the BIOS. SCSI devices quite often use this method for setup.

The DIP switches and jumpers are normally set by the manufacturer with the most commonly used default settings. Don't change a DIP switch or jumper on a device without writing down the original settings and carefully reading the documentation.

Why change a BIOS parameter? The most common reason is to prevent a conflict in the assignment of computer resources. If you buy a second modem to install on your computer, and both modems use the same IRQ by default, you might be able to instruct the new modem to use an alternate IRQ by changing DIP switches or jumpers on the modem. Making this change tells BIOS on the modem to use the alternate IRQ.

The example in the following exhibit is a modem that has a bank of DIP switches on the back of the card and a bank of jumpers on the card itself. By using combinations of these DIP switches and jumpers, you can configure this modem either to be Plug and Play-compliant or to use a specific set of IRQ and I/O addresses.

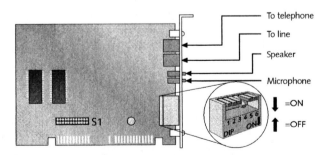

Exhibit 7-1: Diagram of a modem card

In addition to BIOS on the device, system BIOS might also be involved. A good example of this is a hard drive. BIOS on the hard drive housing manages direct access to the drive, but system BIOS on the system board can manage communication between the hard drive BIOS and the OS.

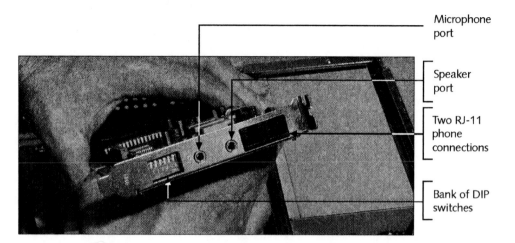

Exhibit 7-2: Ports and DIP switches on the back of an internal modem

Device drivers

The second level of software needed by a peripheral device is a device driver. There are two kinds of device drivers: 16-bit real-mode drivers and 32-bit protected-mode drivers. Windows 9x contains 32-bit drivers for hundreds of hardware devices. Windows automatically loads these drivers into extended memory (memory above 1024 KB) at startup. However, not all devices are supported by 32-bit drivers so you might need to use an older 16-bit real-mode device driver. These 16-bit drivers are loaded by entries in the CONFIG.SYS file and use upper memory addresses.

Device drivers under Windows 9x

Windows 9x provides 32-bit device drivers for a mouse. However, if you want to boot to DOS from a floppy disk and use a mouse, you need to put the mouse device driver entry in the CONFIG.SYS file on your disk together with the driver file MOUSE.SYS.

For Windows 9x, the device driver is installed at the time the hardware device is installed. Information about the driver installation is kept in the Windows 9x Registry, and then the driver is automatically executed each time Windows 9x starts.

Most often the device driver comes as part of the hardware package. For example, when you buy a video or sound card, a disk is enclosed that contains the driver. You want to use the latest 32-bit driver available. Windows 98 has added many drivers to the list of those supported by Windows 95. Select the latest driver available for that device, either provided by Windows or by the device manufacturer. Occasionally, a manufacturer will release a new, improved device driver for a device. You can most likely download these new drivers from the manufacturer's Web site.

You can view and change current device drivers from the Control Panel. For example, in Windows 98, to view the current video driver selected, choose Start, Settings, Control Panel, and double-click Display. Click the Settings tab to view the currently installed display driver.

Exhibit 7-3: Viewing the current display driver in the Display Properties box

To change the driver:

1 Click Advanced.

2 Click the Adapter tab.

3 Click the Change button. The Windows 98 Update Device Driver Wizard is displayed.

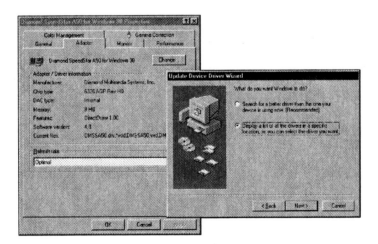

Exhibit 7-4: The Windows 98 Update Device Driver Wizard

4 Click Next. Windows 98 can search for a new driver from its list of supported drivers or you can perform the search manually.

If you have a new driver that's not supported by Windows 98 (such as one that you just downloaded from the Internet), choose to perform the search manually.

5 Select Display a list of all the drivers in a specific location, so you can select the driver you want, and then click Next. The currently selected driver is selected.

6   Click Have Disk to provide the new driver from a floppy disk, a CD-ROM, or a downloaded folder on your hard drive.

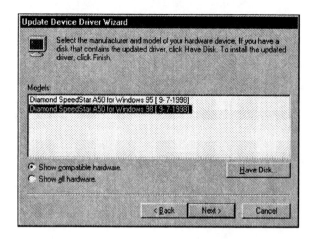

Exhibit 7-5: The currently installed device drivers

Sixteen-bit drivers under Windows 9x can cause slow performance, so you want to use 32-bit drivers when possible. To determine whether Windows 9x is using a 16-bit driver, choose Start, Settings, Control Panel, open System, and select Device Manager. Look for an exclamation point beside the device, which indicates that there is a problem with the driver.

If Windows 9x or Windows NT doesn't support a hardware device installed on your system, the solution might be to use the Internet to locate a new driver for your device.

Characteristic	16-bit device drivers	32-bit device drivers
Operating mode	Real mode	Protected mode
Use of memory	Might use upper memory addresses	Stored in extended memory
How loaded	Loaded by a DEVICE= line in CONFIG.SYS or AUTOEXEC.BAT	Automatically loaded by Windows 9x at startup or when the device is used
How changed	Edit the CONFIG.SYS or AUTOEXEC.BAT file.	From Device Manager, select the device and use Properties, Driver tab.
How to identify the type	In Device Manager, look for an exclamation point beside the device name.	Look for no exclamation point beside the device name in Device Manager. Also, typically "32" is included in the driver file name.
How to use this type	Use a 16-bit driver under Windows only when a 32-bit driver isn't available. When operating under DOS, 16-bit drivers are required.	When possible, always use 32-bit drivers because they're faster.

Do it!   **A-2: Examining the device drivers**

Here's how
1 Boot your lab workstation in Windows 9x
2 Choose **Start**, **Settings**, **Control Panel**
3 Double-click **System**
4 Click the **Device Manager** tab
5 Expand keyboard and select the listed device
6 Click **Properties**
Click the **Driver** tab
7 Observe the device driver
8 Examine the other device drivers

Topic B: Ports and expansion slots for add-on devices

Explanation

Devices may be plugged directly into a serial, parallel, or USB port, or they might use an expansion card plugged into an expansion slot. Some devices use a peripheral bus, called a SCSI bus, which interfaces with the local bus through a SCSI expansion card called the host adapter.

All computers come with one or two serial ports, one parallel port, and, on newer computers, a USB port. Newer system boards have all three kinds of ports directly on the board (called on-board ports), but, on older system boards, an *I/O controller card* in an expansion slot supplies the serial and parallel ports.

Using serial ports

Serial ports transmit data in single file, or serially. You can identify these ports on the back of a PC case by counting the pins and determining whether the port is male or female. The following exhibit shows serial ports together with a game port and a parallel port, for comparison. On the left you'll find one 9-pin serial port and one 25-pin parallel port. On the right is one 25-pin serial port and a 15-pin game port. Serial ports are sometimes called DB-9 and DB-25 connectors. DB stands for data bus and refers to the number of pins on the connector. Serial ports are almost always male ports, and parallel ports are almost always female ports.

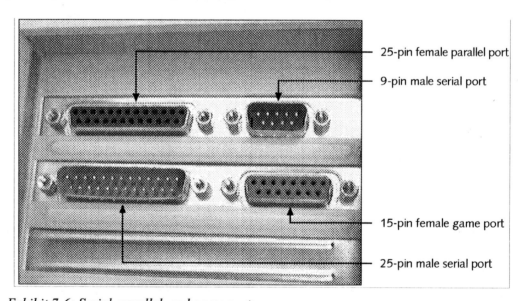

Exhibit 7-6: Serial, parallel, and game ports

To make the allocation of system resources easier, two configurations for these serial ports were designated as COM1 and COM2, and then later two more configurations were designated as COM3 and COM4. These COM assignments each represent a designated IRQ and I/O address. Think of the serial ports as physical, and of COM1 and COM2 as logical assignments to these physical ports, much as a phone number is a logical assignment to a physical telephone. In reality, COM1 is just a convenient way of saying IRQ 4 and I/O address 03F8h. The following table also shows that the two parallel port configurations are named LPT1 and LPT2 and each is assigned an IRQ and I/O address. DOS, Windows, and most applications that use serial devices know about and comply with these assignments. For example, you can tell your communications software to use COM1 to communicate with a modem, and it then knows that the modem is using IRQ 4 to signal the CPU and "listening" for instructions by way of I/O address 03F8h.

Port	IRQ	I/O Address (in Hex)	Type
COM1	IRQ 4	03F8 – 3FF	Serial
COM2	IRQ 3	02F8 – 2FF	Serial
COM3	IRQ 4	03E8 – 3EF	Serial
COM4	IRQ 3	02E8 – 2EF	Serial
LPT1	IRQ 7	0378 – 37F	Parallel
LPT2	IRQ 5	0278 – 27F	Parallel

770-555-3233

COM2

Serial port   Telephone

Exhibit 7-7: COM2 is assigned to serial ports like phone numbers to a telephone

Serial ports were originally intended for input and output devices, and parallel ports were intended for printers. Serial ports can be configured for COM1, COM2, COM3, or COM4. Parallel ports can be configured as LPT1, LPT2, or LPT3.

To configure a serial port with a COM assignment located on an I/O card, you most likely set jumper switches on the card. If they're connected directly to the system board, most often the assignments are made in CMOS setup. Sometimes the setup screen shows the COM assignments, and sometimes you see the actual IRQ and I/O address assignments, as seen in Exhibit 7-8.

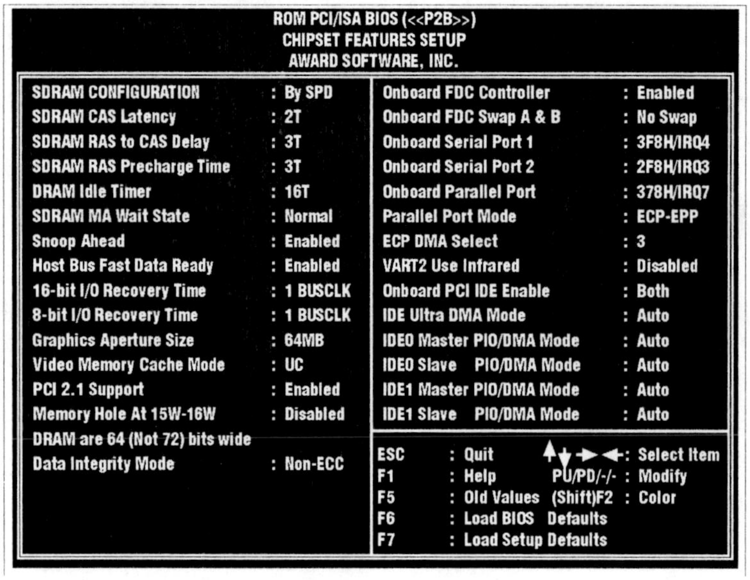

```
                    ROM PCI/ISA BIOS (<<P2B>>)
                       CHIPSET FEATURES SETUP
                        AWARD SOFTWARE, INC.
 SDRAM CONFIGURATION       : By SPD    Onboard FDC Controller    : Enabled
 SDRAM CAS Latency         : 2T        Onboard FDC Swap A & B     : No Swap
 SDRAM RAS to CAS Delay    : 3T        Onboard Serial Port 1      : 3F8H/IRQ4
 SDRAM RAS Precharge Time  : 3T        Onboard Serial Port 2      : 2F8H/IRQ3
 DRAM Idle Timer           : 16T       Onboard Parallel Port      : 378H/IRQ7
 SDRAM MA Wait State       : Normal    Parallel Port Mode         : ECP-EPP
 Snoop Ahead               : Enabled   ECP DMA Select             : 3
 Host Bus Fast Data Ready  : Enabled   VART2 Use Infrared         : Disabled
 16-bit I/O Recovery Time  : 1 BUSCLK  Onboard PCI IDE Enable     : Both
 8-bit I/O Recovery Time   : 1 BUSCLK  IDE Ultra DMA Mode         : Auto
 Graphics Aperture Size    : 64MB      IDE0 Master PIO/DMA Mode   : Auto
 Video Memory Cache Mode   : UC        IDE0 Slave   PIO/DMA Mode  : Auto
 PCI 2.1 Support           : Enabled   IDE1 Master PIO/DMA Mode   : Auto
 Memory Hole At 15W-16W    : Disabled  IDE1 Slave   PIO/DMA Mode  : Auto
 DRAM are 64 (Not 72) bits wide
 Data Integrity Mode       : Non-ECC   ESC  : Quit  ↑↓→←: Select Item
                                       F1   : Help      PU/PD/-/- : Modify
                                       F5   : Old Values  (Shift)F2 : Color
                                       F6   : Load BIOS   Defaults
                                       F7   : Load Setup Defaults
```

Exhibit 7-8: CMOS setup screen for chipset features

A serial port conforms to the standard interface called RS-232c (Reference Standard 232 revision c) and is sometimes called the RS-232 port. This interface standard originally called for 25 pins, but since microcomputers use only nine of the pins, a modified 9-pin port was often installed by the manufacturer. Today, some computers have a 9-pin serial port, and some have a 25-pin serial port, or both. Both ports work the same way. The 25-pin port uses only 9 pins; the other pins are unused. Serial 25-pin ports are often found on modems. You can buy adapters that convert 9-pin ports to 25-pin ports, and vice versa, to accommodate a cable you already have.

One of the 9 pins on a serial port transmits data in a sequence of bits, and a second pin receives data sequentially. The other 7 pins are used to establish the communications protocol. A protocol is a set of agreed-upon rules for communication that's established before data is actually passed from one device to another. The following table describes the functions of the pins of a serial port connection to a modem that's connected to another remote modem and computer. External modems sometimes use lights on the front panel to indicate the state of these pins. The labels on these modem lights are listed in the last column.

The following table is included to show that more than just data is included in a serial communication session. Also, when the system uses serial ports, one of the devices is called the DTE (Data Terminal Equipment), and the other device is called the DCE (Data Communications Equipment). For example, when using a modem, the modem is called the DCE and the computer on which it is installed is called the DTE.

Pin number for 9-pin	Pin number for 25-pin	Pin use	Description	LED light
1	8	Carrier detect	Connection with remote is made	CD or DCD
2	3	Receive data	Receiving data	RD or TXD
3	2	Transmit data	Sending data	SD or TXD
4	20	Data terminal ready	Modem hears the computer	TR or DTR
5	7	Signal ground	Not used with PCs	
6	6	Data set ready	Modem is able to talk	MR or DSR
7	4	Request to send	Computer wants to talk	RTS
8	5	Clear to send	Modem is ready to talk	CTS
9	22	Ring indicator	Someone is calling	RI

Serial ports are controlled by a chip called the *UART chip (universal asynchronous receiver/transmitter chip)*. This chip controls all 9 pins of a serial port, establishes the communications protocol to be used, and converts parallel data bits coming to it from the system bus into serial bits for transmission. It also converts incoming serial data bits it receives into the parallel form needed by the system bus.

You can view I/O addresses by using the DOS or Windows MSD command or from Device Manager of Windows 9x.

In summary, serial ports are used for various input/output data transfers, including data transferred over a modem, to a mouse, to a printer, and to other computers. Serial port s follow the RS-232c industry standard for communication. Each port is assigned a unique IRQ and a unique I/O address. The UART chip controlling the port is partially responsible for the speed of the port.

Do it!

B-1:   Resolving serial port conflicts

Question	Answer
1 The Device Manager can be found by opening the Control Panel and then clicking the Network icon. True or false?	
2 A red "X" in the Device Manager means that the device is disabled. True or false?	
3 All serial ports can be configured by using the BIOS Setup program. True or false?	
4 Serial ports can conflict with only modems. True or false?	
5 To what IRQ does COM4 default?	
6 List two ways to resolve a serial conflict.	

Using parallel ports

Explanation

Parallel ports, commonly used by printers, transmit data in parallel, 8 bits at a time. If the data is transmitted in parallel over a very long cable, the integrity of the data is sometimes lost because bits might separate from the byte they belong to. Most parallel cables are only six feet long, and there are no established standards as to maximum cable length; however, try to avoid using a parallel cable longer than 15 feet, to ensure data integrity.

Parallel ports were originally intended for printers only. However, some parallel ports are now used for input devices. These parallel ports, called bi-directional parallel ports, are often used for fast transmission of data over short distances. One common use is to download and upload data from a PC to a laptop. Some external CD-ROM drives use a bi-directional parallel port to transmit and receive data. If an existing parallel port can be used to install a peripheral device, installation is very simple. Just plug the device into the port and load the software. To accommodate a second parallel port, configure the port as LPT2. The uses of the pin connections for a 25-pin parallel port are listed in the following table.

Pin	Input or output from PC	Description
1	Output	Strobe
2	Output	Data bit 0
3	Output	Data bit 1
4	Output	Data bit 2
5	Output	Data bit 3
6	Output	Data bit 4
7	Output	Data bit 5
8	Output	Data bit 6
9	Output	Data bit 7
10	Input	Acknowledge
11	Input	Busy
12	Input	Out of paper
13	Input	Select
14	Output	Auto feed
15	Input	Printer error
16	Output	Initialize paper
17	Output	Select input
18	Input	Ground for bit 0
19	Input	Ground for bit 1
20	Input	Ground for bit 2
21	Input	Ground for bit 3
22	Input	Ground for bit 4
23	Input	Ground for bit 5
24	Input	Ground for bit 6
25	Input	Ground for bit 7

Types of parallel ports

There are presently three different categories of parallel ports: standard, *enhanced parallel port (EPP)*, and *extended capabilities port (ECP)*. The standard parallel port (SPP) is sometimes called a normal parallel port or a Centronics port, named after the 36-pin Centronics connection used by printers. A standard port allows data to flow in only one direction and is the slowest of the three types of parallel ports. EPP and ECP are both bi-directional. ECP was designed to increase speed over EPP by using a DMA channel; therefore, when using ECP mode you're using a DMA channel. Over the years there have been several implementations of parallel port designs created by manufacturers of both hardware and software, all attempting to increase speed and performance. To help establish industry standards, a committee was formed in the early '90s supported by the Institute of Electrical and Electronics Engineers (IEEE), which created the IEEE 1284 standards for parallel ports. These standards require backward compatibility with previous parallel port technology. Both EPP and ECP are covered under the IEEE 1284 specifications.

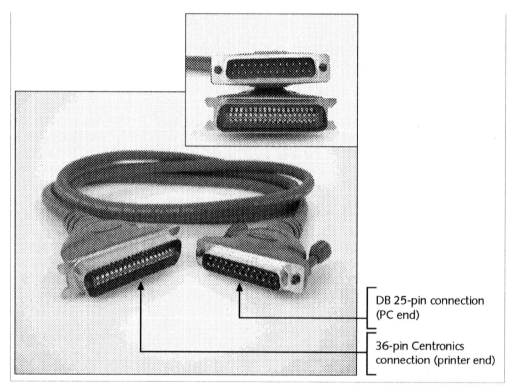

DB 25-pin connection (PC end)

36-pin Centronics connection (printer end)

Exhibit 7-9: A parallel cable with one DB-25 and one 36-pin Centronics connection

Configuring parallel ports

When configuring a parallel port, if the port is on an I/O card, then look to the documentation for the card to know how to assign system resources to the port. If the parallel port is coming directly off the system board, then look to CMOS setup to configure the port. In setup, there can be up to three different settings for parallel ports. For the BIOS in this exhibit, choices for parallel port mode are Normal, EPP, ECP, and EPP 2 ECP. If you select ECP or EPP + ECP, you must also make an ECP DMA selection. Choices are DMA Channel 1 or 3. If you have problems with resource conflicts, try disabling ECP mode for the parallel port. EPP mode gives good results and doesn't tie up a DMA channel.

Do it!

B-2: Creating and resolving parallel port conflicts

Here's how

Creating a conflict:

1 Power off the lab workstation and unplug the power cord

Remove the case

2 Locate the sound card

Change the sound card jumper settings from IRQ 5 to IRQ 7

3 Replace the case and plug in the power cord

4 Power on your lab workstation and boot to Windows 9x. Note that depending on the type of system, you might receive an error message during the POST. Observe any error messages and continue to boot the system by following the instructions on the screen.

5 Choose **Start**, **Settings**, **Control Panel**

Double-click **System** and click the **Device Manager** tab

6 Look for yellow exclamation points located on top of LPT1 and the sound card icon. If you see the yellow exclamation points, you have successfully created a resource conflict between the two devices.

Resolving the conflict:

7 Reboot your lab workstation

8 Enter the BIOS setup program

9 Locate the parallel configuration section

Change your parallel port resources settings to IRQ 5 (Be sure to use a different I/O address.)

Save the changes and reboot the workstation in Windows 9x.

10 Choose **Start**, **Settings**, **Control Panel** and double-click **System**

11 On the Device Manager tab, double-click **Ports** and double-click **LPT1**

12 On the Resources tab, verify that the IRQ and I/O settings now read what you previously chose in the BIOS setup program

USB ports

Explanation

Using USB ports is easier than using parallel or serial ports because the USB controller together with support from the operating system manages the USB port resources for you. Newer system boards have one or two USB ports. For older system boards, you can purchase a PCI expansion card to provide a USB port.

All the USB ports and USB devices connected to them use a single IRQ, I/O address, and DMA channel, which is similar to the way a SCSI bus works. The operating system must support the USB host controller. Windows 95 OSR 2.1 was the first Microsoft operating system to support USB, although Windows 98 offers much improved USB support. Windows NT and Windows 95a don't support USB. The current version of the USB standard is version 1.1, which supports speeds up to 12 Mbps. An improved standard, USB 2.0, is expected soon and will support speeds between 120 and 240 Mbps. USB transfers data in packets and can partly improve the speeds of serial and parallel ports because it uses higher quality cabling. A USB cable has four wires; two are used for data, one is ground, and one provides up to 5 volts of power to the device. You don't need to manually assign system resources to a USB device, because the operating system and the USB host controller automatically assign resources at startup.

To install a USB device, you need:

- A system board or expansion card that provides a USB port and USB firmware
- An operating system that supports USB
- A USB device
- A USB device driver

Windows 98 provides many USB device drivers. If you install a USB device, don't use a device driver from the manufacturer that claims to work only for Windows 95. Windows 98 made several improvements in USB support that you will want to take advantage of. Sometimes setup on a system board allows you to disable USB support. When installing a USB device, be sure that USB support is enabled in setup.

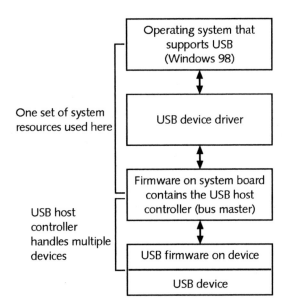

Exhibit 7-10: Only one IRQ, I/O address, and DMA channel are needed for a USB host controller to manage multiple devices

Follow these steps to install a USB device:

1 By using Device Manager, verify that the USB host controller driver is installed under Windows 9x. Note in the exhibit the symbol for USB. If the controller isn't installed, install it from the Control Panel by double-clicking the Add New Hardware icon. If you have a problem installing the controller, verify that support for USB is enabled in setup.

2 Plug in the USB device and install its device driver. For example, for a scanner, insert the CD that came with the scanner in the CD-ROM drive and enter Setup.exe in the Run dialog box. After the drivers are installed, you should see the device listed in Device Manager. Verify that Windows sees the device with no conflicts and without errors.

3 Install the applications software to use the device. Most scanners come with some scaled-down version of software to scan and edit images. After you install the software, use it to scan an image.

Using IEEE 1394 Ports

IEEE 1394 ports are sometimes found on newer high-end system boards and are expected to become standard ports on all new system boards, as commonplace as USB ports are now. These ports have two types of connectors: a 4-pin port that doesn't provide voltage to a device and a 6-pin port that does. The two extra pins in the 6-pin port are used for voltage and ground. The cable for a 6-pin port is fatter than the 4-pin cable.

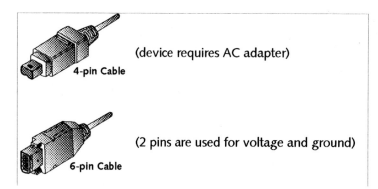

Exhibit 7-11: Two types of IEEE 1394 cable connectors. The 6-pin cable provides voltage to the device from the PC

The four wires used for data in a 1394 cable are two pairs of shielded twisted pair cable wrapped in a common cord. Shielding refers to how wires are enclosed in a protective covering to reduce interference, and twisted pair refers to the fact that two wires are twisted to reduce interference. Some network cabling also is shielded and uses twisted pair wires. In fact, IEEE 1394 uses a design similar to Ethernet, the most popular network design. Just as with Ethernet, data is broken into small packets before it's sent over 1394 cable. Each device on the IEEE 1394 network can communicate with any other device on the network without involving the computer's CPU.

IEEE 1394 uses isochronous data transfer meaning that data is transferred continuously without breaks. This works well when transferring real-time data such as that received by television transmission. Because of the real-time data transfer and the fact that data can be transferred from one device to another without involving the CPU, IEEE 1394 is an ideal medium for data transfers between consumer electronics products such as camcorders, VCRs, TVs, and digital cameras.

The current standard for IEEE 1394 is IEEE 1394.A, which supports speeds of 100, 200, or 400 Mbps, allows for cable lengths up to 4.5 meters and is hot-pluggable. Hot-pluggable means that you can plug in a 1394 device without rebooting your PC and remove the device without receiving an error message. A new standard under development, IEEE 1394.B will support speeds up to 1.6 Gbps (gigabits per second) and extend the maximum cable length to 100 meters.

Windows 98 and Windows 2000 support IEEE 1394. Windows 98 Second Edition supports storage devices, but IEEE 1394 printers and scanners aren't supported. Windows 2000 supports all these devices. For Windows 98 Second Edition, you can download an update from the Microsoft Web site (windowsupdate.microsoft.com). The update solves previous problems when devices are removed while the PC is still running.

To use a 1394 port, follow these steps:

1 Verify that Windows 98 recognizes that an IEEE 1394 controller is present on the system board. Just as with the USB controller, by using Device Manager, look for the 1394 Bus Controller listed as an installed device. Click the + sign beside the controller in Device Manager to see the specific brand of 1394 controller that the board contains. If the controller isn't installed or isn't working, then reinstall the driver. In the Control Panel, double-click the Add New Hardware icon. If you have problems installing the driver, verify that 1394 support is enabled in setup.

2 Plug the device into the 1394 port. Install the device drivers for the 1394-compliant device. For example, for a Sony camcorder, insert the CD that contains supporting software in the CD-ROM drive and execute Setup.exe from the Run dialog box. When the device is plugged in and the drivers are installed, you should see the device listed in Device Manager under Sound, video and game controllers. If you don't see the device listed, turn the camcorder off and back on.

3 Install the applications software to use the device. A 1394-compliant camcorder is likely to come bundled with video editing software. Run the software to use the device.

For system boards that don't support IEEE 1394, you can install an IEEE 1394 host adapter to provide the support. For example, FireBoard by Unibrain, Inc. uses a PCI expansion slot and follows the IEEE 1394.A standard. See www.unibrain.com.

PCI expansion slots

The PCI bus is a local bus that can support up to four PCI expansion slots on the system board. The PCI slots are often white, which easily distinguishes them from the black ISA slots on the board. Because the PCI bus is faster than the ISA bus, PCI slots are often used for fast I/O devices such as a video card or network card. The PCI bus master, that's part of the system board chip set, manages the PCI bus and the expansion slots. The PCI bus master assigns IRQ and I/O addresses to PCI expansion cards, which is why you don't see jumpers or DIP switches on these cards. To be more accurate, the PCI bus assigns resources to a PCI slot; move the card to a different slot, and you'll get a new set of resources assigned to it.

PCI bus IRQ steering

PCI 2.1 specifications support *PCI bus IRQ steering*, a feature making it possible for PCI devices to share an IRQ, which can help solve the problem of not having enough IRQs to support all devices in a system. In order for the system to use the feature, both the system board BIOS and Windows must support it. During booting, startup BIOS records the IRQs used by ISA devices and the PCI bus in a table that Windows can read later when reassigning IRQs. Windows 95, release 2, (OSR2) and Windows 98 support PCI bus IRQ steering.

ISA expansion slots

Using legacy ISA bus devices is a little more difficult than using either USB or PCI, because the configuration isn't as automated. The ISA bus doesn't manage the system resources, as do the USB and PCI bus masters. It's up to the ISA device to request system resources at startup. If the ISA device doesn't support Windows 9x Plug and Play, then you select the I/O address, DMA channel, and IRQ by setting jumpers or DIP switches on the card. If the ISA device is Plug-and-Play-compliant, then at startup Windows 9x Plug and Play allocates the required resources to the device. To know whether a device is Plug-and-Play-compliant, look for "Ready for Windows 95" or "Ready for Windows 98" on the box, or read the documentation.

Do it!

B-3:   Observing the resources used by your system

Here's how	Here's why
1 Choose **Start**, **Settings**, **Control Panel**	
Double-click **System**	
Click the **Device Manager** tab	
2 Select **Computer**	
Click **Properties**	
3 Click the **View Resources** tab	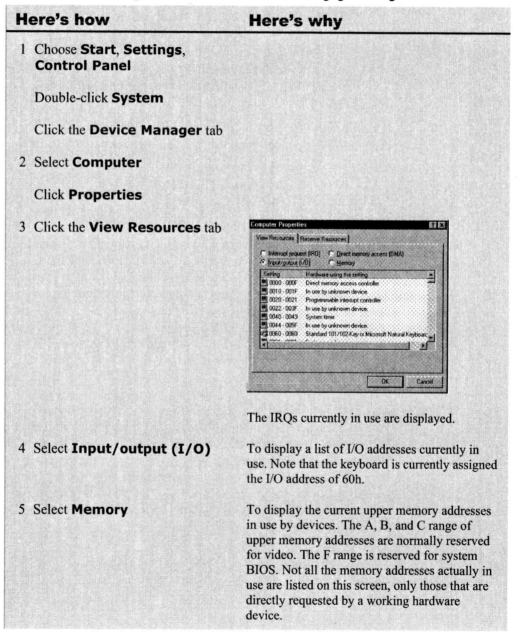
	The IRQs currently in use are displayed.
4 Select **Input/output (I/O)**	To display a list of I/O addresses currently in use. Note that the keyboard is currently assigned the I/O address of 60h.
5 Select **Memory**	To display the current upper memory addresses in use by devices. The A, B, and C range of upper memory addresses are normally reserved for video. The F range is reserved for system BIOS. Not all the memory addresses actually in use are listed on this screen, only those that are directly requested by a working hardware device.

Topic C: SCSI devices

Explanation

This topic looks at SCSI as a bus that can support other devices. Installing a SCSI device is normally accomplished in one of two ways:

- Install the SCSI device by using a simplified version of a SCSI host adapter designed to accommodate one or two devices. These adapters often come bundled in the SCSI device package.

- Install the SCSI device on an existing or new host adapter designed to handle several devices.

Matching the host adapter to the SCSI devices it supports

When selecting a SCSI host adapter or when determining whether an existing host adapter will work with a new SCSI device, consider the issues described below.

SCSI standard. SCSI-1, SCSI-2, and Fast SCSI use a 50-pin connection. All wide SCSIs use a 68-pin connection. Your device should match the host adapter according to the number of pins on the connections. Also, your device and host adapter should have compatible standards.

The host adapter must be made for the correct expansion slot. The host adapter must fit the expansion slot you plan to use. SCSI host adapters are made for 8-bit ISA, 16-bit ISA, 16-bit MCA, 32-bit MCA, 32-bit EISA, VL-Bus, and PCI buses. For a Pentium system board, you probably can choose either a 16-bit ISA host adapter or a PCI host adapter. Choose the 32-bit PCI bus for a faster data transfer rate, instead of the 16-bit ISA bus.

Bus mastering. Choose a host adapter that uses bus mastering, if your system bus supports it. For PCI buses that do support bus mastering, you have the added advantage that the SCSI host adapter doesn't require a DMA channel.

A host adapter that supports several SCSI standards. With a host adapter that supports both 50-pin connections, 68-pin connections, and several standards, you can choose a variety of devices without having to purchase a second host adapter.

Device driver standard. Select a host adapter that supports one of the two leading driver standards for SCSI, either the ASPI or the CAM standard. ASPI, a standard developed by Adaptec, a leading SCSI manufacturer, is probably the better known of the two. ASPI (Advanced SCSI Programming Interface) or CAM (Common Access Method) describes the standard for the way the host adapter communicates with the SCSI device driver. The ASPI or CAM standard has nothing to do with the SCSI-1, SCSI-2, or SCSI-3 types, but rather with the way the drivers are written. Be sure that the host adapter and all the device drivers meet the same standard. The ASPI or CAM standard also affects the way the host adapter relates to the operating system. For Windows 9x, the SCSI driver is built-in, but many host adapters provide their own host adapter drivers. The manufacturer of the host adapter usually provides the SCSI driver on floppy disk or CD-ROM.

Single-ended and differential SCSI. Select a host adapter that matches the devices according to electronic signaling method. The two choices are single-ended SCSI devices and differential SCSI devices. Single-ended devices use only half the number of wires in the cable that differential devices do, but the total length of the cable has limitations. Don't mix the two types of devices on the same SCSI system or use a host adapter that doesn't match. You can damage the devices if you do.

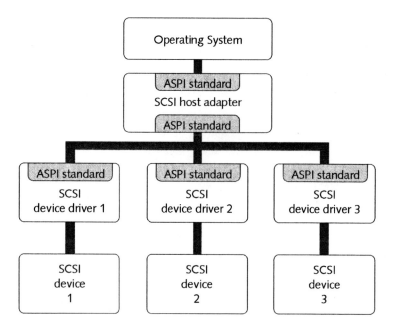

Exhibit 7-12: A SCSI device driver standard affects the interaction of the host adapter with the device drivers and the operating system

SCAM-compliant. SCAM (SCSI Configuration AutoMatically) is a method by which SCSI devices and the host adapter can be Plug-and-Play-compliant. SCAM-compliant host adapters and devices can assign SCSI IDs dynamically at startup. Most SCSI devices currently in use aren't SCAM-compliant, and you will need to set the unique ID on the device, by using jumpers, rotary dials, or other methods. Newer SCSI host adapters use software that comes with the card to configure the SCSI BIOS. With the software, you can set the SCSI IDs, SCSI parity checking, and termination.

There are two levels of SCAM. Level 1 requires that the devices, but not the host adapter, be assigned an ID at startup by software. Level 2 requires that the host adapter, as well as the devices, be assigned an ID at startup by software. SCSI-2 devices must be SCAM-compliant to carry the logo "Designed for Windows 95" or "Designed for Windows 98."

Installing a host adapter for a single device

This example looks at installing a typical host adapter designed to be used by a single external device and one or more internal devices. In this case, you are installing the Adaptec 1505 ISA-to-SCSI host adapter that is Plug-and-Play compliant. It has one external 25-pin SCSI connection and one internal 50-pin connection. The card comes with software to control its BIOS that is run from a bootable floppy disk included with the card. A single jumper on the card can be used to control the I/O addresses assigned to the card if system BIOS isn't Plug-and-Play compliant.

The card only supports one external device, hence the 25-pin connection; it uses only 25 of the 50 pins of the SCSI cable. The card comes with one 50-pin internal cable that has connections for the host adapter and two devices. The package also includes a 25-pin external cable for external devices.

Termination is achieved by three sets of sockets on the card that must be filled by three terminating resistors. One resistor is removed from a socket and is shown beneath the card. If you install both internal and external devices, remove all three resistors from the sockets and store them in a safe place. If you install only an external device or an internal device, but not both, then the host adapter is at the end of the SCSI chain and the three resistors should be in place.

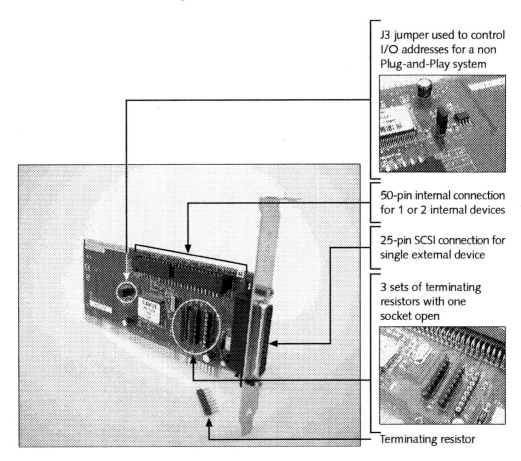

J3 jumper used to control I/O addresses for a non Plug-and-Play system

50-pin internal connection for 1 or 2 internal devices

25-pin SCSI connection for single external device

3 sets of terminating resistors with one socket open

Terminating resistor

Exhibit 7-13: SCSI host adapter for a single external and multiple internal devices

For a Plug-and-Play system using Windows 98, follow these general steps to install this host adapter:

- Install the card in an ISA expansion slot.

- In most cases, the default settings for the host adapter are the correct ones, but you can change or verify these settings using the setup program on floppy disk. To use the setup program, boot the PC from the floppy disk included with the card. The disk boots the system (using DOS) and automatically executes the SCSI setup program. The two options on the opening menu are SCSI Disk Utilities (for installing a SCSI hard drive) and Configure the Host Adapter. Select Configure the Host Adapter. You see the host adapter configuration screen.

- Verify the settings. Under the Advanced Configuration Options, you see two settings: enable or disable Plug and Play and enable or disable SCAM support. Both are normally set to enable. After verifying settings, exit the setup program, remove the floppy disk, and reboot.

- When Windows 9x loads, it senses a new hardware device and automatically launches the Add New Hardware Wizard. Because Windows supports the host adapter, it loads the device drivers automatically and installs the host adapter.

To verify that the host adapter is installed correctly, choose Start, Settings, Control Panel, and double-click System. Select Device Manager. Double-click SCSI controllers. The Adaptec host adapter should be displayed. Notice in the exhibit the broken diamond icon that stands for SCSI. Select the host adapter and click Properties to display the host adapter Properties dialog box. Click the Resources tab to note the resources assigned to the card by Plug and Play.

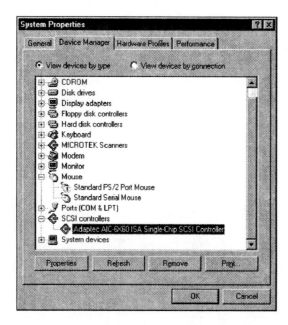

Exhibit 7-14: Device Manager displays the newly installed host adapter

After you install the host adapter, you're ready to install the external SCSI device. If the device is a SCSI scanner, for example, follow these directions:

1 Install the software to run the scanner, which will include the scanner driver.
2 Plug the SCSI cable into the host adapter port.
3 Plug the other end of the cable into the scanner.
4 Set the SCSI ID on the scanner.
5 Connect the scanner's power cord to a wall outlet, and turn on the scanner.
6 Restart your PC and test the scanner.

Do it!

C-1: Installing a SCSI device

Here's how

1 Power off the lab workstation and unplug the power cord

2 Remove the case

3 Locate the available expansion slot for your SCSI host adapter

4 Verify that your SCSI card is configured to your instructor's resource specifications

5 Insert the SCSI card into the appropriate slot and secure it by using a screw

6 Replace the case and plug in the power cord

7 Power on your lab workstation and boot to Windows 9x

   As the system boots, observe whether the new SCSI card is automatically detected

8 If prompted for the drivers, insert the driver disk (provided by your instructor)

9 Select **Drivers provided by the hardware manufacturer**

   Follow the prompts to install the drivers

10 If the SCSI card isn't detected, double-click **Add New Hardware** on the Control Panel

11 Follow the prompts to install the driver from the disk

12 Verify that the SCSI host adapter driver is installed without any errors (There shouldn't be any yellow exclamation points. On the Control Panel, double-click System, activate the Device Manager tab, and double-click SCSI Controllers.)

Topic D: Keyboard, mouse, and monitor devices

Explanation

The remainder of the unit addresses the essential I/O devices for a PC: the keyboard, a pointing device, and video display.

Keyboard

Keyboards have either a traditional straight design or a newer ergonomic design. The word *ergonomic* means designed for safe and comfortable interaction between human beings and machines. The ergonomically safer keyboard is designed to keep your wrists high and straight. Some users find it comfortable, and others don't. The following exhibit demonstrates the correct position of hands and arms at the keyboard. Keyboards also differ in the feel of the keys as you type. Some people prefer more resistance than others, and some like more sound as the keys make contact. A keyboard might have a raised bar or circle on the F and J keys to help your fingers find the home keys as you type. Another feature is the depth of the ledge at the top of the keyboard that holds pencils and other writing tools. Some keyboards have a mouse port on the back of the keyboard, and there are specialized keyboards with trackballs or magnetic scanners for scanning credit cards in retail stores.

Exhibit 7-15: Keep wrists level, straight, and supported while at the keyboard

Users who work with computer keyboards for hours at a time are at risk of developing a type of *repetitive stress injury* (RSI) known as *carpal tunnel syndrome* (CTS). CTS results from keeping the wrists in an unnatural position and having to execute the same motions (such as pressing keys on a keyboard) over prolonged periods of time.

Keyboard manufacturers use one of two common technologies in the way the keys make contact: foil contact or metal contact. With a foil-contact keyboard, when you press a key, two layers of foil make contact and close a circuit. A small spring just under the keycap raises the key again after it's released.

Metal-contact keyboards are more expensive and heavier, and generally provide a different touch to the fingers than foil keyboards. Made by IBM and AT&T, as well as other companies, the metal-contact keyboards add an extra feel of quality that is noticeable to most users, giving the keystroke a clear, definitive contact. When a key is pressed, two metal plates make contact, and a spring is again used to raise the key when it's released.

Keyboard connectors

Keyboards connect to a PC by one of three methods: a PS/2 connector (sometimes called a mini-DIN), a DIN connector, or, more recently, a USB port. The DIN connector (DIN is an acronym of the German words meaning German industry standard) is round and has five pins. The smaller round PS/2 connector has six pins. The following table shows the pinouts (position and meaning of each pin) for both connector types. If the keyboard you're using has a different connector than the keyboard port of your computer, use a keyboard connector adapter to convert DIN to PS/2 or PS/2 to DIN. Also, some keyboards are cordless, using radio transmission to communicate with a sensor connected to the keyboard port. An example of a cordless keyboard is by Logitech that uses a sensor that plugs into a normal keyboard port.

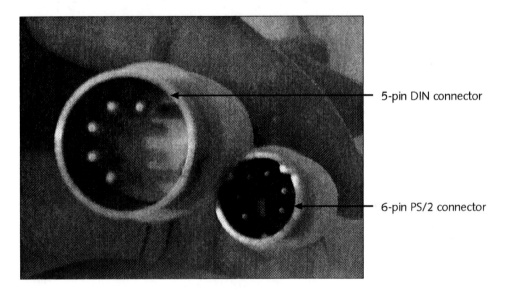

5-pin DIN connector

6-pin PS/2 connector

Exhibit 7-16: Two common keyboard connectors

Description	6-pin connector (PS/2)	5-pin connector (DIN)
Keyboard data	1	2
Not used	2	3
Ground	3	4
Current (+5 volts)	4	5
Keyboard clock	5	1
Not used	6	--

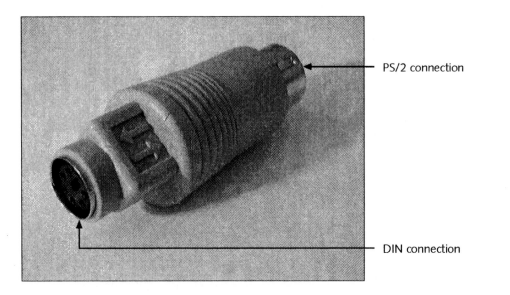

— PS/2 connection

— DIN connection

Exhibit 7-17: A keyboard adapter

Regardless of the type of connection or the construction of the keyboard, when a key is pressed, the same logical progression occurs. First, a code is produced called the *make code*. Releasing the key produces the *break code*. A chip in the keyboard processes these codes to produce a scan code that's sent to the CPU. The chip determines the location of the key pressed and sends that location together with the IRQ to the CPU. The scan code is temporarily stored in memory. The keyboard driver, which is most often stored in the system BIOS, converts the scan code to the character assigned to that code, according to the keyboard driver selected. The different drivers available to interpret scan codes vary by language.

Pointing devices

A device that you use to move a pointer around on the screen and perform functions such as clicking on a command button in applications software is called a pointing device. Common pointing devices are the mouse, the trackball, and touch pads.

Exhibit 7-18: A mouse, trackball, and touch pad

Mouse

Inside a mouse is a ball that moves freely as you drag the mouse around on a surface. Two or more rollers on the sides of the ball housing turn as the ball rolls against them. Each roller turns a wheel. The turning of the wheel is sensed by a small light beam as the wheel "chops" the light beam when it turns. The chops in the light beams are interpreted as mouse movement and are sent to the CPU. One of two rollers tracks the x-axis (horizontal) movement of the mouse, and a second roller tracks the y-axis (vertical) movement.

An optical mouse replaces the ball in a standard mouse with a microchip, miniature red light, and camera. The light illuminates the work surface, the camera takes 1,500 snapshots every second, and the microchip reports the tiniest changes to the PC. An optical mouse works on most surfaces and doesn't require a mouse pad. The bottom of an optical mouse has a tiny hole for the camera rather than a ball and the light glows as you work. An example of an optical mouse is Intelli-Eye by Microsoft.

A mouse can have two or three buttons. Software must be programmed to use these buttons; few software packages use the third or center button. Almost all applications use the left button. Windows 9x makes great use of the right button.

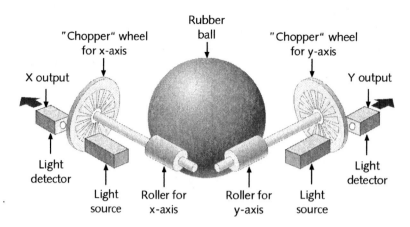

Exhibit 7-19: How a mouse works

A mouse can connect to the computer by several methods:

- By using the serial port (the mouse is then called a *serial mouse*)
- By using a dedicated round mouse port coming directly from the system board (*system-board mouse* or *PS/2-compatible mouse*)
- By using a mouse bus card that provides the same round mouse port (*bus mouse*)
- By using the USB port
- By using a Y-connection with the keyboard so that both the keyboard and the mouse can share the same port

Because all these produce the same results (that is, the mouse port type is "transparent to the user"), the advantages and disadvantages of each connection type are based mainly on the resources they require. The system-board mouse is the first choice for most users because the port on the system board doesn't take up any resources that other devices might need. If you're buying a new mouse that you plan to plug into the system-board port, don't buy a bus mouse unless the system-board documentation states that you can use a bus mouse. The system-board port and the bus port are identical, but a bus mouse might not work on the system-board port.

If you have a system-board port, use it. If it becomes damaged, then you can switch to a serial port or bus port. The system-board mouse port will most likely use IRQ 12. If you're not using a mouse on this port, the system board might release IRQ 12 so that other devices can use it. Check the documentation for your system board to determine how the unused IRQ is managed.

The serial mouse requires a serial port and an IRQ for that port. Most people prefer a bus mouse rather than a serial port mouse because they can assign the serial ports to other peripheral devices. A bus mouse can use a bus card if the system board doesn't have a mouse port.

The rollers inside the mouse housing collect dirt and dust and occasionally need cleaning. Remove the cover to the mouse ball from the bottom of the mouse. The cover usually comes off with a simple press and shift or turn motion. Clean the rollers with a cotton swab dipped in a very small amount of liquid soap.

Trackballs and touch pads

Another pointing device is a *trackball*, which is really an upside-down mouse. You move the ball on top to turn rollers that turn a wheel that is sensed by a light beam. *Touch pads* duplicate the mouse function. You can move the pointer by applying light pressure with one finger somewhere on a pad that senses the x, y movement. Some touch pads enable you to double-click by tapping the touch pad's surface. Buttons on the touch pad serve the same function as mouse buttons. Use touch pads or trackballs where surface space is limited, because they remain stationary when you use them. Trackballs are commonly found on notebook computers.

Do it!

D-1: Discussing keyboards and pointing devices

Question	Answer
1 Describe the size and pins on a DIN connectors and a PS/2 connector for a keyboard.	
2 What makes a device an ergonomic device?	
3 Name three types of pointing devices.	
4 If a mouse begins to be difficult to operate, what simple thing can you do to help?	

Monitors

Explanation

The primary output device of a computer is the monitor. The two necessary components for video output are the video controller and the monitor itself. The common types of monitors today are rated by screen size, resolution, refresh rate, and interlace features. There are still many older VGA (Video Graphics Adapter) monitors in use, but most sold today meet the standards for Super VGA. Monitors use either the older CRT (cathode-ray tube) technology used in television sets or the new LCD (liquid crystal display) technology used in notebook PCs and available for desktop use.

How a CRT monitor works

Most monitors use CRT technology, in which the filaments at the back of the cathode tube shoot a beam of electrons to the screen at the front of the tube. Plates on the top, bottom, and sides of the tube control the direction of the beam. The beam is directed by these plates to start at the top of the screen, move from left to right to make one line, and then move down to the next line, again moving from left to right. As the beam moves vertically down the screen, it builds the displayed image. By turning the beam on and off and selecting the correct combination of colors, the control grid in front of the filaments controls what goes on the screen when the beam hits that portion of the line or a single dot on the screen. Special phosphors placed on the back of the monitor screen light up when hit and produce colors. The grid controls which one of three electron guns is fired, each gun targeting a different color (red, green, or blue) positioned on the back of the screen.

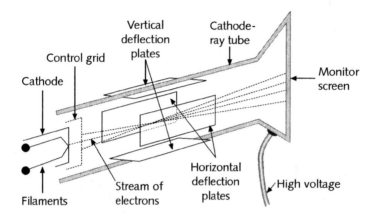

Exhibit 7-20: How a CRT monitor works

Monitor features

Screen size

The screen size of a monitor is the one feature that affects price the most. Common sizes of monitor screens are 14-inch, 15-inch, 17-inch, and 21-inch. The 15-inch monitor is the most popular. The small screen, 14-inch monitor is losing popularity.

When you match a monitor to a video card, a good rule of thumb is to match a low-end video card to a small monitor (14-inch), a midrange video card to a 15-inch monitor, and a high-end video card to a large monitor (17-inch) to get the best performance from both devices. However, you might prefer to compare the different features of the video card to those of the monitor, such as the resolutions supported, the refresh rate, and the bandwidth. *Bandwidth* is the difference between the highest and lowest frequencies that an analog communications device such as a video cable can carry.

Macintosh computers can use special monitors designed for page layouts on legal-sized paper. The larger the screen size, the more expensive the monitor. The monitor I'm now using is advertised as having a 17-inch screen. The actual dimensions of the lighted screen are 9 1/2 inches by 11 1/2 inches. The diagonal measurement of the lighted area is 15 inches, and the diagonal measurement of the screen surface is 17 inches.

Refresh rate

The refresh rate, or vertical scan rate, is the number of times in one second an electronic beam can fill the screen with lines from top to bottom. Refresh rates differ among monitors. The Video Electronics Standards Association (VESA) has set a minimum refresh rate standard of 70 Hz, or 70 complete vertical refreshes per second, as one requirement of Super VGA monitors. Slow refresh rates make the image appear to flicker while faster refresh rates make the image appear solid and stable.

Interlaced or noninterlaced

Interlaced monitors draw a screen by making two passes. On the first pass, the electronic beam strikes only the even lines, and on the second pass the beam strikes only the odd lines. The result is that a monitor can have a slow refresh rate with a less noticeable overall effect than there would be if the beam hit all lines for each pass. Interlaced monitors generally have slightly more flicker than *noninterlaced monitors*, which always draw the entire screen on each pass. Buy a noninterlaced monitor if you plan to spend long hours staring at the monitor. Your eyes will benefit.

Dot pitch

The *dot pitch* is the distance between the spots, or dots on the screen that the electronic beam hits. Remember that there are three beams building the screen, one for each of three colors (red, green, and blue). Each composite location on the screen is made up of three dots and is called a triad. The distance between these triads is the dot pitch. The smaller the pitch, the sharper the image. A dot pitch of .28 mm or .25 mm gives the best results and costs more, although less expensive monitors can have a dot pitch of .35 mm or .38 mm. These less expensive monitors with dot pitches of .35 mm or .38 mm can still give a "muddy" image even with the best video cards.

Resolution

Resolution is a measure of how many spots on the screen are addressable by software. Each addressable location is called a *pixel* (for picture element), which is composed of several triads. Because resolution depends on software, the resolution must be supported by the video controller card, and the software you're using must use the resolution capabilities of the monitor. The standard for most software packages is 800 by 600 pixels, although many monitors offer a resolution of 1024 by 768 pixels or higher. The resolution is set in Windows from the Control Panel and requires a driver specific for that resolution. Higher resolution usually requires more video RAM.

Multiscan monitor

Multiscan monitors offer a variety of vertical and horizontal refresh rates so they can support a variety of video cards. They cost more but are much more versatile than other monitors.

Green monitor

A *green monitor* is a monitor that saves electricity, thus making its contribution to conserving our natural resources. A green monitor meets the requirements of the EPA Energy Star program and uses 100 to 150 watts of electricity. When the screen saver is on, the monitor should use no more than 30 watts of electricity.

Monitors and ELF emissions

There is some debate about the danger of monitors giving off ELF (extremely low frequency) emissions of magnetic fields. Standards to control ELF emissions are Sweden's MPR II standard and the TCO '95 standards. The TCO '95 standards also include guidelines for energy consumption, screen flicker, and luminance. Most monitors manufactured today comply with the MPR II standard, and very few comply with the more stringent TCO '95 standards.

Flat panel monitors

Increasing in popularity, even though their cost is still three times that of comparable CRT monitors, are flat panel monitors (also called flat panel display) that use LCD screens. *Flat panel monitors* take up much less desk space than CRT monitors, are lighter, require less electricity to operate, and provide a clearer, more precise image. An LCD panel produces an image by using a liquid crystal material that's made of large, easily polarized molecules. The LCD panel consists of multiple layers that create the image. At the center of the layers is the liquid crystal material. Next to it is the layer responsible for providing the color to the image. These two layers are sandwiched between two grids of electrodes. One grid of electrodes is aligned in columns, and the other electrodes are aligned in rows. The two layers of electrodes make up the electrode matrix. Each intersection of a row electrode and a column electrode forms one pixel on the LCD panel. Software can manipulate each pixel by activating the electrodes that form it. The image is formed by scanning the column and the row electrodes, much as the electronic beam scans a CRT monitor screen.

The polarizer layers outside the glass layers are responsible for preventing light from passing through the pixels when the electrodes aren't activated. When the electrodes are activated, light on the back side of the LCD panel can pass through one pixel on the screen, picking up color from the color layer as it passes through.

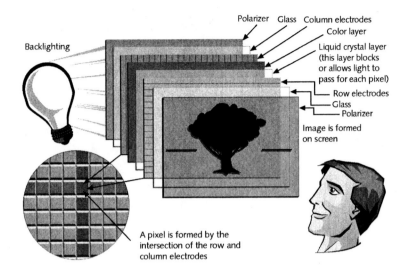

Exhibit 7-21: Layers of the LCD panel

There are two kinds of LCD panels on the market today, active-matrix and dual-scan passive matrix displays. A dual-scan display is less expensive than an active-matrix display and doesn't provide as high-quality an image. With dual-scan display, two columns of electrodes are activated at the same time. With active-matrix display, a transistor that amplifies the signal is placed at the intersection of each electrode in the grid, which further enhances the pixel quality.

Flat panel monitors are built to receive either an analog signal or a digital signal from the video card. If the signal is analog, it must be converted to digital before the monitor can process it. Flat panel monitors are designed to receive an analog signal so that you can use a regular video card that works with a CRT monitor, thus reducing the price of upgrading from a CRT monitor to an LCD monitor. As you will see in the upcoming discussion of video cards, video cards convert digital data from the CPU to analog before sending it on to the monitor. Therefore, with analog LCD monitors, the data is converted from digital to analog and back to digital before being used by the flat panel monitor. These conversions reduce the quality of the resulting image. To get the best output, use a digital flat panel monitor along with a digital video card designed to support the monitor.

Do it!

D-2: Examining monitor settings

Here's how	Here's why
1 At the Windows 9x computer, display the Control Panel	Choose Start, Settings, Control Panel.
2 Double-click **Display**	There are six tabs that you can use to control the screen display.
3 Experiment with changing the background, screen saver, and appearance	Use the Background, Screen Saver and Appearance tabs.
Select the same foreground and background colors	This makes your screen unreadable.
4 Boot into Safe Mode	To start fixing the problem.
Fix the problem and reboot	

Video cards

Explanation

The video controller card is the interface between the monitor and the computer. These cards are sometimes called graphic adapters, video boards, graphics cards, or display cards. Sometimes the video controller is integrated into the system board. If you're buying a system board with this integrated video controller, check that you can disable the controller on the system board if it needs replacement or gives you trouble. You can then install a video card and bypass the controller on the system board.

The quality of a video subsystem of a computer system is rated according to how it affects overall system performance, video quality (including resolution and color), power-saving features, and ease of use and installation. Because the video controller is separated from the core system functions, manufacturers can use a variety of techniques to improve performance without being overly concerned with compatibility with functions on the system board. An example of this flexibility is seen in the many different ways memory is managed on a video controller. This section looks at the features available on video cards, especially video memory. The two main features to look for in a video card are the bus it uses and the amount of video RAM it has or can support.

How a video card works

Four basic steps happen on the video card. The RAM DAC (digital-to-analog converter) technology might be housed on a single RAM DAC chip on the video card or might be embedded in the video chip set. RAM DAC actually includes three digital-to-analog converters, one for each of the monitor's three color guns: red, green, and blue (RGB).

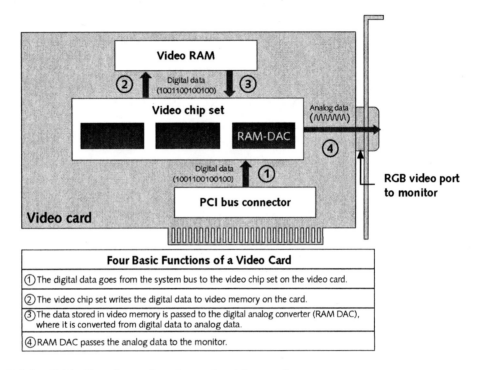

Four Basic Functions of a Video Card
① The digital data goes from the system bus to the video chip set on the video card.
② The video chip set writes the digital data to video memory on the card.
③ The data stored in video memory is passed to the digital analog converter (RAM DAC), where it is converted from digital data to analog data.
④ RAM DAC passes the analog data to the monitor.

Exhibit 7-22: Four basic functions of a video card

The bus used by the video card

The speed and performance of a video card are partly a function of the bus that the card uses. Since 1995, video cards have been designed to use only the PCI bus and more recently to use the AGP slot. Older video cards were made to run on VESA local buses (VL-bus), a proprietary local bus, ISA buses, and EISA buses.

The fastest bus for video on a system board today is AGP with a 32-bit-wide data bus, running at up to 1 GB/sec, depending on the AGP standard used. The regular AGP slot has 132 pins and AGP Pro has 188 pins. The added pins used by the AGP Pro standard provide voltage for high-end graphic accelerator cards discussed in the next section. After AGP, the PCI bus is next in throughput, providing either 132 or 264 MB/sec. If you play computer games or use extensive graphics software, such as that for CAD or desktop publishing, invest in a fast video card that uses a fast bus.

A proprietary device is a device made by a manufacturer specifically to interact with its other devices and generally isn't easily interchanged with devices made by other manufacturers. Many older 486 PCs had proprietary 32-bit video buses that accommodated video cards made specifically for that brand of system board.

On the video card itself, performance is affected by the chip set, memory, and the RAM DAC, as well as by the bus speed and size. One method to improve performance is to allow both the video chip set and the RAM DAC (both the input and the output processes) to access video memory at the same time. This method, called *dual-porting*, requires a special kind of video RAM discussed later in this section. Another method of increasing performance is to place a processor on the video card, making the card a *graphics accelerator*.

The bus external to the video card is the PCI bus or the AGP bus, but there also is an internal video bus on the card itself. The volume of data that can travel on the bus is called bandwidth. Current video buses use a data path that may be 32 bits, 64 bits, 128 bits, or even 256 bits wide. The effective bandwidth of the bus is partly determined by the width of the data path and by how much memory is on the card.

Graphics accelerators

One of the more important advances made in video cards in recent years has been the introduction of graphics accelerators. A graphics accelerator is a type of video card that has its own processor to boost performance. With the demands that graphics applications make in the multimedia environment, graphics accelerators have become not just an enhancement but also a common necessity.

The processor on a graphics accelerator card is similar to a CPU, but specifically designed to manage video and graphics. Some features included on a graphics accelerator are MPEG decoding, 3-D graphics, dual porting, color space conversion, interpolated scaling, EPA green PC support, and applications support for popular high-intensity graphics software such as AutoCAD, Ventura Publisher, Windows 9x, and Windows NT. All these features are designed, in some way, to reduce the burden on the system board CPU and perform the function much faster than the system-board CPU.

For more information about graphics accelerator cards, see these manufacturers at their Web sites: ATI Technologies at www.ati.com, Matrox Graphics, Inc, at www.matrox.com, and 3-Dfx Interactive, Inc. at www.3-Dfx.com (makers of the popular Voodoo graphics card).

Video memory

Older video cards don't have memory, but today video memory is a necessity in order to handle the large volume of data generated by increased resolution and color. Video memory is stored on video cards as memory chips. The first video cards to have memory all used DRAM chips, but now there are several technologies for video memory chips. This section discusses how much video memory is needed and what kinds of video memory chips can be used on a card to obtain the best possible performance.

How much video memory is needed?

The amount of data received by a video card from the CPU for each frame (or screen) of data is determined by the screen resolution (measured in pixels) and the number of colors, which is called the *color depth* (measured in bits). The more data required to generate a single screen of data, the more memory is required to hold that data. Recall that this memory is called the frame buffer. There are other needs for memory on the video card, besides the frame buffer, including the memory used by some cards to store font or other graphical information. Aside from these other uses of memory, the following table shows the amount of memory needed to hold the frame buffer, which is determined by the screen resolution and number of colors.

Video resolution	4-bit, 16 colors	8-bit, 256 colors	16-bit, 65,000 colors	24-bit, true color, 16.7 million colors	32-bit (24-bit, true color w/ 8-bit Alpha Channel)
640 × 480	256 KB	512 KB	1 MB	1 MB	2 MB
800 × 600	512 KB	512 KB	1 MB	2 MB	2 MB
1,024 × 768	1 MB	1 MB	2 MB	4 MB	4 MB
1,152 × 1,024	1 MB	2 MB	2 MB	4 MB	4 MB
1,280 × 1,024	1 MB	2 MB	4 MB	4 MB	6 MB
1,600 × 1,200	2 MB	2 MB	4 MB	6 MB	8 MB

Color depth is directly related to the number of bits used to compose one pixel and can be 4, 8, 16, or 24 bits per pixel. The larger the number of bits allocated to storing each piece of data, the more accurate the value can be; similarly, the greater the number of bits allocated to store the value of pixel color, the greater the number of color shades you can use and color depth you can have.

To determine the number of colors that can be represented by these numbers of bits, use the number of bits as the power (exponent) of the number 2. For example, to calculate the number of colors represented by 4 bits per pixel, raise 2 to the fourth power, which equals 16 colors. (Note that the largest 4-bit number is 1111, which equals 15 in decimal. If you include 0, then the number of values that can be stored in a 4-bit number is 16.) A color depth of 24 bits per pixel equals 2 to the twenty-fourth power, or 16.7 million colors.

To determine the amount of RAM needed for one frame buffer, multiply the number of bits per pixel times the number of pixels on the screen, giving the total number of bits per screen. Divide the number of bits by 8 to determine the number of bytes of RAM needed for the buffer.

For example, for a screen resolution of 1,024 by 768 and 256 colors, the table above shows that the amount of RAM required is 1 MB. The way that number is derived is illustrated below:

- The number of pixels for one frame buffer: $1,024 \times 768 = 786,432$ pixels

- For 256 colors, you need an 8-bit color depth, or 8 bits per pixel. (Remember that 1111 1111 in binary equals 255 in decimal, which, along with the value zero, provides 256 options.)

- Number of bits for one frame buffer: 786,432 pixels $\times$ 8 bits/pixel = 6,291,456 bits

- Number of bytes of memory needed: 6,291,456 bits/8 bits per byte = 786,432 bytes

- Since RAM comes in 512 KB, 1 MB, 2 MB, or 4 MB increments, you must have 1 MB of video RAM to accommodate the frame buffer of 786,432 bytes.

In building a pixel on screen, each pixel uses three channels for color: red, green, and blue. However, when building 3-D graphics, a fourth channel is sometimes added called the alpha channel. The alpha channel controls the way the three colors are displayed and can add transparency or opacity to the image. The term for adding these effects is alpha blending which can create the effect of shading or making one color partly visible behind another color, such as when you are looking through colored glass at a different color behind the glass. The alpha channel adds another 8 bits to the information kept for each pixel. When using 24-bit true color with an 8-bit alpha channel, 32 bits per pixel is needed, resulting in 32-bit graphics used by high-end video cards.

Another factor that determines how much video memory is required is the bus width on the card. Just as with system boards, the RAM configuration on the card must conform to the bus width so that data can move from the bus to the card. A normal 1 MB memory chip on a video card has a bus width of 32 bits. Because each 1 MB video RAM chip is 32 bits wide, you can see why 2 MB of memory are needed if the video bus is 64 bits wide. In fact, this bit width of the video chip is the reason that a video card that has a 64-bit bus width and only 1 MB of installed memory is so slow. If your video card uses a 64-bit bus, be sure to install at least 2 MB of RAM.

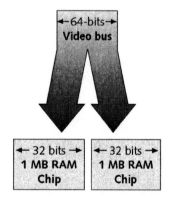

Exhibit 7-23: Video bus with 64-bit width addressing two 1 MB memory chips with 32-bit widths

In the following exhibit, 4 MB of RAM are required to make the most efficient use of the 128-bit video bus width. Some manufacturers of video chip sets have developed a method to use a 128-bit bus with less than 4 MB of memory. For example, the Tseng Labs ET6000 chip set uses a special kind of video RAM called *Multibank DRAM (MDRAM)* that's able to use the full 128-bit bus path without requiring the full 4 MB of RAM.

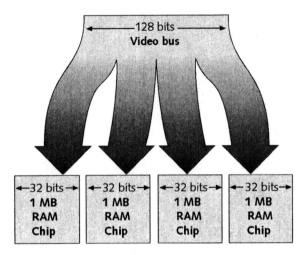

Exhibit 7-24: 128-bit video bus addressing 4 MB of video memory

All these factors affect how much memory is required to build a single frame buffer. The most memory needed to build a single frame buffer is 8 MB. However, in addition to needing memory to hold each frame buffer, a graphics accelerator card might also need memory for other purposes. Software that builds 3-D graphics on screen often uses textures, and sometimes a graphics card holds these textures in memory to build future screens. Large amounts of video RAM keep the card from having to retrieve these textures from the hard drive or system RAM multiple times. In addition, the graphics card might use double or triple buffering to improve performance where the card holds not just the frame being built, but the next one or two frames. Because of texturing and triple buffering, a card might need as much as 32 MB of RAM.

Types of video memory

You have already been introduced to several different versions of video memory: Dual-ported memory, one type of which is sometimes called *video RAM* or *VRAM*, is designed so that video memory can be accessed by both the input and output processes at the same time. MDRAM memory chips are designed so that the full width of the video bus can be used with fewer memory chips than needed to provide the full bus width access to RAM. Three other types of memory chips designed to improve performance of video cards are: WRAM, SGRAM, and 3D RAM.

SGRAM (synchronous graphics RAM) is similar to SDRAM, but designed specifically for video card processing. SGRAM, like SDRAM, can synchronize itself with the CPU bus clock, which makes the memory faster. SGRAM also uses other methods to increase overall performance for graphics-intensive processing.

WRAM (Window RAM) is another type of dual-ported RAM, but is faster and less expensive than VRAM. WRAM was named more for its ability to manage full-motion video than for its ability to speed up Microsoft Windows video processing. WRAM's increase in speed is primarily due to its own internal bus on the chip, which has a data path that is 256 bits wide.

Some video processing involves simulating 3-D graphics; *3D RAM* was designed specifically to improve this performance. Much of the logic of 3-D processing is embedded on the chip itself. A graphics card chip set normally calculates which pixel of a 3-D graphic is to be displayed, depending on whether the pixel is behind other pixels and, therefore, out of sight in a 3-D graphic. After the pixel is drawn and a calculation is made as to whether the pixel is seen, if the pixel isn't to be displayed, the chip set writes it back to memory to be used later. With 3D RAM, the chip set simply passes the data to the 3D RAM chip that draws the pixel and decides whether to display it without involving the chip set.

Do it!

D-3: Discussing monitors and video cards

Question	Answer
1 How much video RAM is required to produce a resolution of 800 by 600 with 65,000 colors?	
2 Which provides better quality, an interlaced monitor or a noninterlaced monitor? Why?	
3 What type of monitor can offer a variety of refresh rate?	
4 What size frame buffer is needed on a video card to hold the data for 1,280 by 1,024 screen resolution and 65,000 colors?	
5 What three colors are used to build all colors on a color monitor screen?	
6 Which provides better image quality, a .25-mm dot pitch monitor or a .28-mm dot pitch monitor? Why?	

Unit summary: Supporting I/O devices

Topic A   **Adding new devices** to a computer requires installing both hardware and software, and resolving possible resource conflicts. Most hardware devices require similar resources from a computer, including an **IRQ, DMA channel, I/O addresses**, and some **upper memory addresses** to contain their device drivers. Use **MSD** under DOS and **Device Manager** under Windows 9x to determine the resources the currently installed devices are using.

Topic B   You learned that most computers provide two **serial ports** and one **parallel port** to be used for a variety of devices. Newer system boards also provide one or two USB ports.

Topic C   When selecting a **SCSI host adapter**, consider the bus slot the adapter will use, the device driver standard used by the host adapter, single-ended versus differential SCSI, SCAM compliance, and whether the host offers bus mastering.

Topic D   In this topic, you learned how a **keyboard, a mouse, and a monitor works**. Because users are offered a choice of different I/O devices, it's important for you to know how to support each device.

Review questions

1 You're the desktop PC support technician for the Good Job Corporation. Janet, one of your customers, suspects that she has a resource conflict between her newly installed modem and one of her serial ports on her laptop. Describe how you could use Device Manager to confirm or deny her suspicions

2 Steve, one of your customers, just installed an I/O card into his PC because he needed more than 2 COM ports. He is now receiving an error message every time he starts his system. Steve asks you to troubleshoot. Describe the steps you would take to resolve Steve's conflict.

3 You're working on a PC that has the parallel port built into the system board. You are about to install a new sound card that will use IRQ 7. Describe the steps you need to take to avoid an IRQ conflict with the sound card.

4 When a PC is configured to use both SCSI and IDE, which drive must be drive C, and why?

5 How is SCAM helpful?

Unit 8

Multimedia technology

Unit time: 90 minutes

Complete this unit, and you'll know how to:

A Describe the fundamental workings of multimedia technology.

B Install and support CD-ROM drives.

C Install and support sound cards.

D Install and support digital multimedia, such as digital cameras and DVD players.

Topic A: Overview of multimedia

Explanation

The ability of PCs to create output in a vast array of media—audio, video, and animation, as well as text and graphics—has turned PCs into multimedia machines. The multimedia computer offers much to take advantage of, from video conferencing for executives to teaching the alphabet to four year-olds.

Introduction to multimedia

The goal of *multimedia* technology is to create or reproduce lifelike representations for audio, video, and animation. Computers store data digitally, and ultimately as a stream of only two numbers: 0 and 1. In contrast, sights and sounds have an infinite number of variations. The challenge of multimedia technology is to bridge these two worlds. The key to doing this is twofold: reduce the infinite number of variations to a finite few, and record as many as needed to reproduce an approximation of the original sight or sound, without overloading the capacity of the computer to hold data. These tasks require (1) a lot of storage capacity and (2) the ability to process large quantities of data at high speed and at the lowest cost possible. This unit focuses on how the industry is attempting to meet the challenge.

The right tools for the job

Desktop computer systems are designed for three major purposes: low-end systems designed as e-machines and thin clients, mid-range systems designed for desktop publishing, home computing, and general business needs, and high-end systems designed for computer-intensive engineering applications. E-machines simply access the Internet and use its applications, and thin clients use the data and applications served to them by network application servers. Generally these machines aren't intended for upgrade and might include a system board that has many proprietary components with no room for expansion. High-end systems meant for engineering applications focus on powerful and sometimes multiple CPUs, large amounts of memory and hard drive space, and use powerful operating systems such as Windows 2000 or UNIX.

This unit focuses on the mid-range computer system designed for desktop publishing, graphics design, home entertainment, multimedia presentations, and entertainment from the Internet. These systems benefit from a CPU designed with multimedia in mind and from powerful graphics accelerator cards and sound cards. In addition, most of these systems can interface with multimedia devices such as camcorders, digital cameras, and scanners. Applications for these systems include Web-authoring software, desktop publishing, multimedia presentations, and games.

Technicians who help make purchasing decisions about multimedia hardware and software need to stay abreast of the latest innovations in the marketplace as the technology changes rapidly and choices and price ranges abound. Before you purchase or make a recommendation about the purchase of a new computer system or a peripheral, research the purchase. Some of your best resources are:

- Other satisfied users, retailers, books, the Internet, and computer service centers.

- Trade magazines, such as *PC Computing, PC World, Home PC, Computer Shopper, PCNovice, PC Magazine*, and *PC Today*. Look for reviews describing hardware and software, how they work and popular features.

- Special interest Web sites such as www.imaging-resource.com, which focuses on digital imaging, or Tom's Hardware Guide at www.tomshardware.com, which focuses on hardware.

- Magazine Web sites, including:
    - www.zdnet.com — several technical magazines
    - www.cshopper.com — Computer Shopper
    - www.pcmag.com — PC Magazine
    - www.pcworld.com — PC World
    - www.pccomputing.com — PC Computing
    - www.pcguide.com — PC Guide

Do it!

A-1:   Discussing multimedia

Question	Answer
1 Describe multimedia.	
2 What challenges does multimedia present to the industry?	
3 Comparing low-, mid-, and high-end systems, which is most likely used for multimedia?	
4 What considerations are there when purchasing a system for multimedia purposes?	
5 What types of resources are available for multimedia information?	

Software requirements

Explanation

Typically, the minimum software and hardware requirements for an adequate desktop publishing, Web-authoring, entertainment, or multimedia presentations system include:

- A Pentium II-compatible computer or higher with a hard drive and a minimum of 64 MB of RAM, a mouse, and a high-resolution color monitor and video card
- A word-processing software package
- A scanner and related software
- A laser printer or ink-jet photo-quality printer
- A graphics software package to create and/or edit graphics
- Optional equipment for Web authoring and multimedia presentations such as a video-capturing card and a digital camera
- For desktop publishing, a page composition software package, such as Adobe PageMaker, to bring together all the individual elements of text, graphics, and scanned images into an easy-to-read and visually appealing finished document

Exhibit 8-1: An example of a page composition software package

- For Web authoring, an authoring tool such as Microsoft FrontPage or Netscape Publisher, which brings together individual elements of text, graphics, video, scanned images, and sound into one or more Web pages
- For multimedia presentations, a presentation package such as Microsoft PowerPoint, which ties individual elements of text, graphics, video, and sound into a sight and sound presentation
- For entertainment, access to the Internet with a fast enough connection to play streaming audio and video data and, for game playing, a fast graphics accelerator card

If your budget is limited, spend money on the computer itself rather than the peripherals. A computer system is no faster than the CPU, no matter how sophisticated the peripherals. A laser printer is an expensive item; you can use an ink-jet or dot matrix printer for rough drafts and then take your work on disk to another system with a photo-quality laser printer. By postponing the purchase of a laser printer, you might be able to afford a faster Pentium processor or more memory on the system board. The speed and reliability of the computer are invaluable.

Bits are still bits

Just as with every other component of a microcomputer, multimedia devices represent data as a series of 0s and 1s. For example, a black-and-white scanner sends a light beam across an image and reads that image as a series of black and white dots. Each dot is represented as a 1 or 0, and is stored in a file called a *bit map file*. A sound card captures sound, converts each segment of the sound into a series of 0s and 1s, and stores these in a MIDI file that can later be interpreted once again as sound. A video-capturing card captures a segment of video and converts it to a series of 1s and 0s, when it's stored in a file.

Another uniform quality of multimedia devices is that each device transfers its data over the same bus to the CPU; the CPU processes the data in the same way and sends it as output to a multimedia device, just as it does with other devices. Each device might require an IRQ, a DMA channel, an I/O address, and room in memory for its BIOS or drivers. When working with these devices, don't be intimidated by their complexity. All their basic computing needs are the same.

Multimedia on a PC

Multimedia has traditionally targeted the home market, with games and more games at the top of the list of multimedia software. Until recently, the trend in the business market has been to acquire more powerful PCs for computing, networking, and remote management.

Now, however, business use of multimedia PCs is the norm. Video conferencing, computer-based training (CBT), and multimedia presentations are now common on the corporate scene. This trend affects the development of hardware and software, as both attempt to satisfy market demands.

Another important fact that helps to understand development trends is that, in the evolution of computers, hardware must improve in advance of the software designed to use it. A good example of this is the MMX (multimedia extensions) technology used with the Intel MMX Pentium CPU. When the hardware technology arrived, more software became available to use the technology. In the future, you can expect continuing improvements in multimedia hardware, which will continue to lead to the development of new software.

Evidence of the inroads multimedia technology is making into the business market is the introduction of the Pentium III CPU, which is marketed as a high-end CPU for servers, yet includes SSE, which is technology designed to improve on MMX multimedia processing.

Do it!

A-2:   Discussing multimedia requirements

Question	Answer
1 What are the minimum requirements for a computer to run multimedia?	
2 What type of software is required for multimedia?	
3 If working with a limited budget, what should you definitely purchase?	
4 What must be true before MMX and SSE technology can improve multimedia performance on a PC?	

Multimedia fundamentals

Explanation

Before you study multimedia technology, examine the special challenge confronting multimedia technology: reproducing something that is continuously changing such as sights and sounds, on a PC, which is incapable of making continuous changes because it is digital. A PC has only two states and can change from only one state to another, with no gradations in between.

All computer communication must be expressed in binary digits (or bits). And because a computer is binary, it's also digital. Thus, to be produced on a computer, sound and images must be converted into bits so that the computer can cross the bridge from analog to digital.

Understanding the distinction between analog and digital signals is essential to grasping the challenges facing multimedia technology. Exhibit 8-2 illustrates the difference between using digital communication to describe the shape of a loading ramp and a staircase. A loading ramp is essentially analog because the changes in height of the ramp are gradual, continuous, with smooth transition, making the number of different heights of the loading ramp infinite. A staircase is essentially digital because changes in height move abruptly from one state to another, with no transition in between, similar to counting. You can easily recreate the shape of the staircase because it's easy to measure the exact height of every part of the staircase, and there are a finite number of these heights. However, it's not so easy to recreate the shape of the loading ramp, because its height continuously changes gradually over the entire ramp. Measuring the heights at a series of representative points on the ramp in order to approximately reproduce the shape of the ramp is called *sampling*.

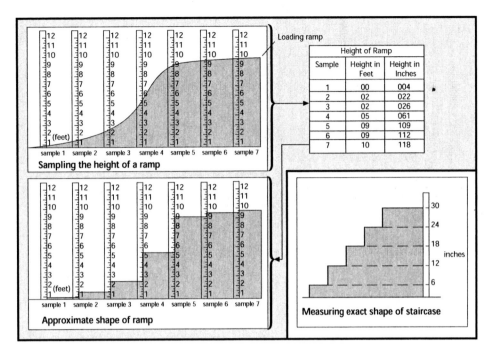

Exhibit 8-2: Expressing analog phenomena in digital terms is a challenge of multimedia

Tip: When analog data is converted to digital data for a PC, the data is sampled, meaning that samples are taken at discrete intervals and stored individually as digital data. This process is called *digitizing the data*, and the resulting data is an approximation of the original data.

To record and store a sound wave in a PC and reproduce it as closely to its original analog nature as possible, you must first record the sound wave as numbers—that is, digitize the analog wave—because your PC can only store data in this way. To digitize the wave, first select how many samples you want to take (how frequently you'll take a sample), how accurate your measurements will be, and how you will store these numbers. Later, you must follow the reverse process to retrieve these numbers and use them to reproduce a sound wave as close to the original as possible.

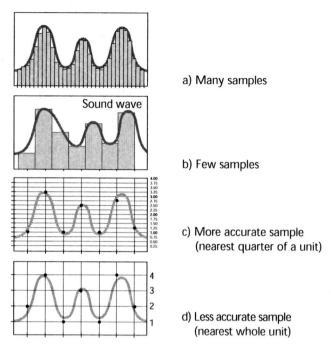

a) Many samples

b) Few samples

c) More accurate sample
(nearest quarter of a unit)

d) Less accurate sample
(nearest whole unit)

Exhibit 8-3: Sampling a sound wave

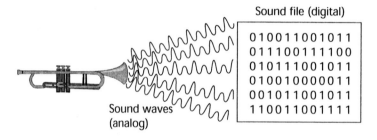

Exhibit 8-4: Sound has analog properties, but sound files store sound digitally

When digitizing a sound wave to produce the best possible reproduction, the more samples taken over a period of time and the more accurate each measurement, the more accurate the representation of the sound. However, there is a trade-off between the quality of a reproduction and the cost of the resources needed to create that reproduced sound. In other words, you need more resources both to store more samples and to store more accurate measurements of these samples, both of which lead to creating better sound. This trade-off is important in the multimedia world and drives many purchasing decisions.

The number of samples and the accuracy of each sample determine the amount of storage needed to hold the values. The amount of storage needed to hold each measurement is called the *sample size*. However, you can use techniques to compress the data. You need a compression method that doesn't lose too much information, and another method to decompress the values when you're ready to use them.

The impact of increasing measurement accuracy can be even greater in the binary world of the computer. Increasing the accuracy of the ramp measurement from feet to inches increases the storage space needed by 50 percent (from 2 digits for feet to 3 digits for inches). But remember that computers use bits instead of digits. So, 10 (feet) in binary is stored as 1010 (in 4 bits), but 120 inches is stored as 1111000 (7 bits) in binary. Since bits are stored in most multimedia files in even numbers of bits and not odd, measurements in feet require 4-bit values, but measurements in inches require 8-bit values, which creates a 100 percent increase in the storage requirement to gain added accuracy. In this unit, look for the size in bits of the numeric values being stored as an indication of the accuracy of the data and the storage requirements.

There are basically two types of data processing: repetitive looping with high input/output volume used by multimedia technology, and computer-intensive data processing, which involves many and/or complex calculations and a relatively low volume of data. A CPU is designed to best support one type of data processing or the other.

Standardizing multimedia

Early on, the multimedia industry tried to standardize hardware and software. In the early 90s the Multimedia Marketing Council established the MPC (Multimedia Personal Computer) guidelines. Sponsored by the Software Publishers Association (SPA), three levels of standards were developed, the last one being MPC3 released in 1996. Today, no standards organization has attained enough prominence in the marketplace to have an impact, resulting in many methods for capturing, compressing, storing and processing multimedia data. Also, the technology is improving at such a fast pace that a standard today is likely to be outdated tomorrow. For these reasons, look for new and different technologies immerging in the industry.

How CPU technologies affect multimedia

Two enhancements by Intel to CPU technology designed with multimedia applications in mind are MMX, which is used by the Pentium MMX, Pentium Pro, and Pentium II, and SSE, which is used by the Pentium III. Multimedia software tends to use input/output operations more than it performs complex computations. Both MMX and SSE were designed to speed up the repetitive looping of multimedia software and manage the high-volume input/output of graphics, motion video, animation, and sound. MMX technology added three new architectural enhancements to the Pentium, all designed to speed up the repetitive looping of multimedia.

- New instructions. Intel added 57 new instructions to the CPU logic, all designed to handle the parallel, repetitive processing found in multimedia operations.

- SIMD process. A process called single-instruction, multiple-data (SIMD) was added so that the CPU can execute a single instruction on multiple pieces of data rather than repetitively looping back to the previous instruction many times.

- Increased cache. Intel increased the size of the internal cache to 32K on the processor, reducing the number of times the CPU must access slower, off-chip memory for information.

The Pentium III introduced *streaming SIMD extension (SSE)*, which is designed to improve the performance of high-end multimedia software. SSE can improve 3-D graphics, speech recognition, MPEG, and some scientific and engineering applications.

To compete with SSE, AMD introduced 3DNow!, a CPU instruction set that helps AMD processors perform better in 3D graphics and other multimedia data processing. 3Dfx, the manufacturer of the Voodoo graphics accelerator card, was the first hardware manufacturer to use the 3DNow! instruction set, although it's now being used by many hardware and software manufacturers.

To know that software or hardware is taking advantage of a CPU enhancement, look on the product package for the Intel MMX, Intel SSE, or 3DNow! symbols.

Do it!

A-3: Examining multimedia technology

Question	Answer
1 Describe the methodology used to convert analog data into digital data.	
2 What two factors determine how accurately digital data represents analog data?	
3 Compare a DAC to an ADC. Where would you expect to find either of these components?	
4 What does MPC represent?	
5 Why are there no multimedia standards?	
6 What three architectural enhancements were introduced by MMX?	

Topic B: CD-ROM drives

Explanation

Now that you have an understanding of the fundamentals of multimedia technology and insight into some of the early decisions made concerning hardware and software, you're ready to learn about several multimedia devices. This topic covers the popular multimedia device called CD-ROM drives.

CD-ROM drives: the basics

The most popular multimedia device is the CD-ROM drive. The technology of a CD-ROM drive is different from that of a hard drive, even though both are designed to hold data. By using technology that enables them to hold much larger volumes of data, CD-ROMs can accommodate the large space requirements of video and sound files. CD-ROM drives are read-only devices. Read/writeable CD drives are discussed later.

During the manufacturing process, data can be written to a CD-ROM disc only once, because the surface of the disc is actually embedded with the data. Exhibit 8-5 shows a CD-ROM surface that is laid out as one continuous spiral of sectors of equal length that hold equal amounts of data. The surface of a CD-ROM stores data as pits and lands. Lands are raised areas, and pits are recessed areas on the surface, each representing either a 1 or a 0, respectively. The bits are read by the drive with a laser beam that distinguishes between a pit and a land by the amount of deflection or scattering that occurs when the light beam hits the surface.

Exhibit 8-5: The spiral layout of sectors on a CD-ROM surface

A small motor with an actuator arm moves the laser beam to the sector on the track it needs to read. If the disc were spinning at a constant speed, the speed near the center of the disc would be greater than the speed at the outer edge. To create the effect of constant linear velocity (CLV), the CD-ROM drive uses a mechanism that speeds up the disc when the laser beam is near the center of the disc, and slows it down when the laser beam is near the outer edge so that the beam is over a sector for the same amount of time no matter where the sector is. (Since the outer edge has more sectors than the inner edge, the light beam needs more time to read near the outer edge than it does near the inner edge.) The transfer rate of the first CD-ROM drives was about 150K per second of data, with the rpm (revolutions per minute) set to 200 when the laser was near the center of the disc. This transfer rate was fine for audio CDs. To show video and motion without a choppy effect, the speed of the drives was increased to double speed (150K per sec 3 2), quad speed (150K per sec 3 4), and so on. It's not uncommon now to see CD-ROM drives with speeds at 40 times the audio speed. Audio CDs must still drop the speed to the original speed of 200 rpm and a transfer rate of 150K per second.

Because of the problems of changing speeds by using CLV, newer, faster CD-ROM drives use a combination of CLV and constant angular velocity (CAV), the same technology used by hard drives, whereby the disc rotates at a constant speed.

When you choose a CD-ROM drive, look for the multisession feature, in which the drive that reads a disc has been created in multisessions. To say a disc was created in multisessions means that data was written to the disc at different times rather than in a single long, continuous session.

Some CD-ROM drives have power-saving features controlled by the device driver. For example, when the drive waits for a command for more than five minutes, it enters Power Save Mode, causing the spindle motor to stop. The restart is automatic when the drive receives a command.

Caring for CD-ROM drives and discs

Most problems with CD-ROMs are caused by dust, fingerprints, scratches, defects on the surface of the CD, or random electrical noise. Don't use a CD-ROM drive if it's standing vertically, such as when someone turns a desktop PC case on its side to save desktop space. Use these precautions when handling CDs:

- Hold the CD by the edge; don't touch the bright side of the disc where data is stored.
- To remove dust or fingerprints, use a clean, soft, dry cloth.
- Don't write on, or paste paper to, the surface of the CD. Don't paste any labels to the top of the CD, because this can imbalance the CD and cause the drive to vibrate.
- Don't subject the CD to heat or leave it in direct sunlight.
- Don't use cleaners, such as alcohol, on the CD.
- Don't make the center hole larger.
- Don't bend the CD.
- Don't drop the CD or subject it to shock.
- If a CD gets stuck in the drive, use the emergency eject hole to remove it. Turn off the power to the PC first. Then insert an instrument such as a straightened paper clip into the hole to manually eject the tray.

How CD-ROM drives interface with system board

CD-ROM drives can interface with the system board in one of several ways. The drive can:

- Use an IDE interface; it can share an IDE connection and/or cable with a hard drive
- Use a SCSI interface with a SCSI host adapter
- Use a proprietary expansion card that works with only CD-ROMs from a particular manufacturer
- Use a proprietary connection on a sound card
- Use external port on your PC and function as a portable drive

Most CD-ROM drives are Plug-and-Play-compliant so that a system can avoid resource conflicts. Boxes marked "Ready for Windows 95" or "Ready for Windows 98" indicate Plug-and-Play CD-ROM drives.

CD-R drives

A CD-ROM is a read-only medium meaning that CD-ROM drives can only read, not write. In the past, writing to a CD required expensive equipment and wasn't practical for personal computer use. Now, *CD-Recordable (CD-R)* drives cost around $300, and the CD-R disc costs less than $5, making "burning" your own CD a viable option. These CD-R discs can be read by regular CD-ROM drives and are excellent ways to distribute software or large amounts of data. Besides having a lot of data storage space on a relatively inexpensive medium, another advantage of distributing software and/or data on a CD-R disc is that you can be assured that no one will edit or overwrite what's written on the disc.

A regular CD-ROM is created by physically etching pits into the surface of the disc, but a CD-R disc is created differently. Heat is applied to special chemicals on the disc and causes these chemicals to reflect less light than the areas that aren't burned, thus creating the same effect as a pit does on a regular CD. Referring to writing data to a CD-R as burning the CD-R is actually fairly accurate. When you purchase and install a CD-R drive, good software to manage the writing process is an important part of the purchase, because some less robust software can make burning a disc a difficult process. Also, some CD-R drives are multisession drives and some aren't.

CD-RW drives

Also available at a higher cost is a *rewritable CD (CD-RW)*, where you can overwrite old data with new data. The process of creating a CD-RW disc is similar to that used by CD-R discs. The chemicals on the surface of the CD-RW disc are different. The process of writing a less-reflective spot to the surface of the disc is reversed so that data can be erased. One drawback to these CD-RW discs is that the medium can't always be read successfully by older CD-ROM drives.

CD-RW discs are useful in the process of developing CDs for distribution. A developer can create a disc, test for errors, and rewrite to the disc without having to waste many discs during the development process. Once the disc is fully tested, then CD-R discs can be burned for distribution. The advantages of distributing on CD-R discs rather than CD-RW discs are that CD-R discs are less expensive and can be read by all CD-ROM drives.

Do it!

B-1: Discussing CD-ROM drives

Question	Answer
1 Compare the speed of a hard drive platter turning on a spindle to the speed of a CD-ROM.	
2 Name three ways a CD-ROM drive can interface with a system board.	
3 Which side of a CD contains data?	
4 Define constant linear velocity (CLV) technology.	
5 Define constant angular velocity (CAV) technology.	
6 What is the difference between a CD-R drive and a CD-RW drive?	

Installing a CD-ROM drive

Explanation

Installing a CD-ROM drive is easy, especially when the adapter is already present. If you're using a SCSI CD-ROM drive, install the host adapter or sound card first, and then install the drive. If you're using a proprietary adapter, install both at the same time. If you're using an existing IDE adapter card or connection on the system board, simply install the CD-ROM drive by using an existing connection on the board or an extra connection on the hard drive data cable.

Exhibit 8-6 shows the front of a typical CD-ROM drive, and Exhibit 8-7 shows the rear view, where the power cord, data cable, sound cord, and ground connector attach. Also note that there is an "audio out" connection that supports a direct connection to a sound card. The jumper pins on a SCSI CD-ROM drive can:

- Control the SCSI ID for the drive
- Enable or disable SCSI parity checking
- Enable or disable the built-in SCSI terminator on the drive

The example shown is a SCSI CD-ROM drive. However, for IDE CD-ROM drives, expect to find jumpers that can set the drive as either the single drive, a slave drive, or the master drive in the IDE subsystem.

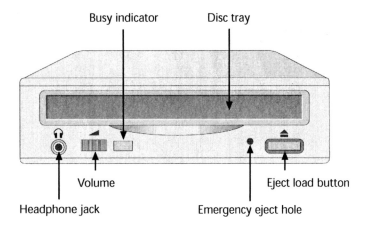

Exhibit 8-6: Front view of a typical CD-ROM drive

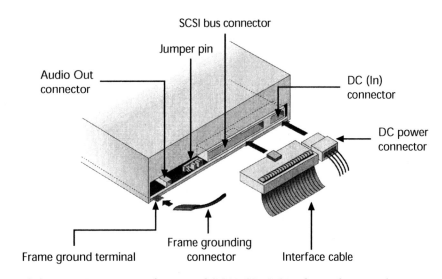

Exhibit 8-7: Rear view of a typical SCSI CD-ROM drive showing drive connections

The CD-ROM drive documentation is your best installation guide, but here are a few general guidelines. The CD-ROM drive becomes another drive on your system, such as drive D or E. After it's installed, you access it just like any other drive by typing D: or E: at the DOS prompt, or by accessing the drive through Explorer in Windows 9x. The major differences are (1) the CD-ROM drive is read-only—you can't write to it, (2) a CD-ROM holds a lot more data than a hard drive, and (3) a CD-ROM is a little slower to access than a hard drive.

Configuring an IDE CD-ROM drive

An IDE CD-ROM drive uses the ATAPI (Advanced Technology Attachment Packet Interface) standard, an extension of the IDE/ATA standard that enables tape drives and CD-ROM drives to be treated just like other hard drives on the system. With hard drives, IDE refers to the integrated drive electronics, but IDE as applied to a CD-ROM drive refers to the interface protocol between the drive and the CPU that requires software at the OS level to complete the interface. Windows 9x supports this protocol internally.

Exhibit 8-8 shows the rear of an IDE CD-ROM drive. Note the jumper bank that can be set to cable select, slave, or master. For enhanced IDE, there are four choices for drive installations: primary master, primary slave, secondary master, and secondary slave. If the drive will be the second drive installed on the cable, then set the drive to slave. If the drive is the only drive on the cable, since single isn't a choice, choose master.

When given the choice of putting a CD-ROM drive on the same cable with a hard drive or on its own cable, choose to use its own cable. If the CD-ROM drive shares a cable with a hard drive, it can slow down the hard drive's performance. Most systems today have two IDE connections on the system board, so most likely you'll be able to use IDE2 for the CD-ROM drive.

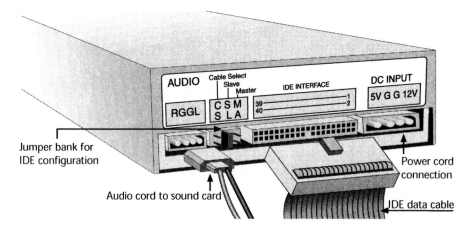

Exhibit 8-8: Rear view of an IDE CD-ROM drive

Inserting the CD-ROM drive

Some systems use rails on a CD-ROM drive to slide it into the bay. If you have them (the rails should come with your computer), screw the rails in place and slide the drive into the bay. If you don't have rails, then put two screws on each side of the drive, tighten the screws so the drive can't shift, but avoid overtightening them. Use the screws that come with the drive; screws too long can damage the drive. If necessary, buy a mounting kit to extend the sides of the drive so that it will fit into the bay and be securely attached.

Connect the cables and cords

Find an unused four-prong power cord from the power supply and plug it into the drive. For IDE drives, connect the 40-pin cable to the IDE adapter and the drive, being careful to follow the Pin 1 rule: match the edge color on the cable to Pin 1 on both the adapter card and the drive.

Some CD-ROM drives come with an audio cord that attaches the interface card to a sound card, which then receives sound input directly from the CD-ROM. Attach the audio cord if you have a sound card. Don't make the mistake of attaching a miniature power cord designed for a 3½-inch disk drive coming from the power supply to the audio input connector on the sound card. The connections appear to fit, but you'll probably destroy the drive by doing this.

Some drives have a ground connection, with one end of the ground cable attaching to the computer case. Follow the directions included with the drive.

Verify power to the drive

Check all connections, and turn on the power. Press the eject button on the front of the drive. If it works, then you know power is getting to the drive.

Do it!

B-2:   Installing a CD-ROM drive in Windows 9x

Here's how	Here's why
1 Remove the case from the lab workstation	You'll need to power off the machine and unplug the power cord first.
2 Locate an available 5½-inch drive bay	
From the front of the case, remove any blank disk	To provide an opening from the front of the computer.
3 Verify that the hard drive is set to master	
4 Change the CD jumper to slave	
5 Slide the CD-ROM drive into the bay	Use screws to secure the drive and mount it to the inside of the case.
6 Connect the IDE data cable	Be sure that the red, or blue, stripe is aligned with Pin 1.
7 Plug in the four-pronged power cord	

8	Connect the audio cable to the back of the CD-ROM drive	If there's a sound card present.
9	Verify that the workstation boots properly	
10	Double-click **My Computer**	Verify that Windows recognizes the CD-ROM drive.
11	Insert a CD-ROM into the drive	To verify that you can view the contents of the disc.

Install the device driver

Explanation   To operate in a DOS environment, a CD-ROM drive needs a device driver that is loaded from the CONFIG.SYS file. The driver interfaces with the drive and a real-mode program called the Microsoft CD-ROM extension for DOS (MSCDEX.EXE), which must be loaded from AUTOEXEC.BAT. Both of these programs come on floppy disk with the CD-ROM drive. Run the installation program that also is on the disk. It copies the files to the hard drive and edits both the CONFIG.SYS and the AUTOEXEC.BAT files. Restart the computer so that the changes take effect.

Install the device driver for Windows 9x

Windows 9x supports CD-ROM drives without add-on drivers. Click Start, Settings, Control Panel, and double-click Add New Hardware. When prompted, click Next to begin installing the software for the new device. Complete the installation by following the directions on the Add New Hardware sheet.

When Windows 9x starts up, it assigns the next available drive letter to the drive. To dictate what the drive letter should be, use Device Manager. Click Start, Settings, Control Panel, and select System. Click the Device Manager tab. Select the CD-ROM drive and click Properties, then the Settings tab, where the drive is designated as E. Select a range of letters to be used by the drive and click OK.

Tip: When you update or install additional features on applications software, some software expects the same drive letter for the CD-ROM drive that was used when it was first installed. Permanently setting the CD-ROM drive letter satisfies the requirements of this software.

Test the drive

The drive is now ready to use. Press the eject button to open the drive shelf, and place a CD in the drive. Since data on CDs is written only on the bottom, be careful to protect it. Now access the CD by using Explorer (use the assigned drive letter).

If you have a problem reading the CD, verify that the CD is placed in the tray label-side-up, and that the format is compatible with your drive. If one CD doesn't work, try another—the first CD might be defective or scratched.

Do it!

B-3: Installing a CD-ROM driver

Here's how	Here's why
1 Choose **Start, Settings, Control Panel** Double-click **Add New Hardware**	Windows 9x normally detects a CD-ROM drive installation. However, you can manually install the CD-ROM driver.
2 Click **Next** three times	To allow Windows to detect the new hardware.
3 Install the proper device driver	
4 Reboot the machine	
5 Test the CD-ROM drive again	Verify that Windows recognizes the CD-ROM drive and insert a CD-ROM to verify that you can see its contents.

Update your Windows 95 rescue disk to include access to the CD-ROM drive

Explanation

The Windows 9x emergency startup disks used to start a system in the event of a hard drive failure need to include access to the CD-ROM drive, because Windows 9x is normally loaded from a CD-ROM. Windows 98 automatically adds the real-mode CD-ROM device drivers to this rescue disk, but Windows 95 doesn't.

Windows 9x has its own built-in 32-bit protected-mode drivers for CD-ROM drives, but when booting from a rescue disk, you're using older 16-bit real-mode drivers. Two files are required, the 16-bit device driver provided by the manufacturer of the CD-ROM drive (or a generic real-mode driver that works with the drive) and the 16-bit real-mode OS interface to the driver, MSCDEX.EXE. The device driver loads from CONFIG.SYS, and MSCDEX.EXE loads from AUTOEXEC.BAT.

If you've run the DOS installation program that came with the CD-ROM drive, then your AUTOEXEC.BAT and CONFIG.SYS files should already have the correct entries in them. You can add these lines to these same files on your rescue disk, correcting paths to the two files as needed. Copy the two files to your rescue disk so you can access the CD-ROM drive when you boot from this disk, even when the hard drive isn't accessible.

For example, on a rescue or boot disk designed to access the CD-ROM drive without depending on any files or commands on the hard drive, the CONFIG.SYS file might contain this command (the parameters in the command lines are explained below):

```
DEVICE = SLCD.SYS /D:MSCD001
```

The AUTOEXEC.BAT file might contain this command line:

```
MSCDEX.EXE /D:MSCD001 /L:E /M:8
```

The explanations of these command lines are as follows:

- Two files needed to manage the drive are MSCDEX.EXE and SLCD.SYS, which must be copied to this disk.

- When the program MSCDEX.EXE executes, it uses the MSCD001 entry as a tag back to the CONFIG.SYS file to learn which device driver is being used to interface with the drive—in this case, SLCD.SYS.

- To MSCDEX.EXE, the drive is named MSCD001 and is being managed by the driver SLCD.

- MSCDEX.EXE will use SLCD as its "go-between" to access the drive.

- MSCDEX.EXE also assigns a drive letter to the drive. If you want to specify a certain drive letter, use the /L: option in the command line. In our example, the CD-ROM drive will be drive E. If you don't use the /L: option, then the next available drive letter is used.

- The /M: option controls the number of memory buffers.

- If the files referenced in these two commands are stored on the floppy disk in a different directory from the root directory, then include the path to the file in front of the file name.

If your hard drive fails and you start up from your rescue disk, once the CD-ROM drivers are loaded and the CD-ROM drive is recognized, you can install or reinstall Windows 9x from CD. To do this, insert the Windows 9x CD into the CD-ROM drive, and from the CD-ROM drive prompt (either D, E, or some other letter), type Setup and then press Enter. Once Windows 9x is installed, it will often ignore existing CONFIG.SYS lines (turning them into comment lines by adding REM to the beginning of the line) and handle the CD-ROM drivers through its own protected-mode drivers.

Optimizing CD-ROM cache

For Windows 9x, VCACHE replaced SmartDrive in Windows 3.x as the disk-caching software. For removable drives, VCACHE caches when reading data but not when writing. VCACHE decides how much memory to use when caching data, based on the speed of the CD-ROM drive and how much memory is installed in the system. You can affect this decision using the Performance tab in System Properties. Click Start, Settings, Control Panel, and select System. In the Properties dialog box, click the Performance tab and then click File System. Click CD-ROM on the File System Properties box, as seen in Exhibit 8-9. By changing the CD-ROM speed in this box, you're changing the amount of memory allotted to the cache. The amount is displayed in the last sentence on this box.

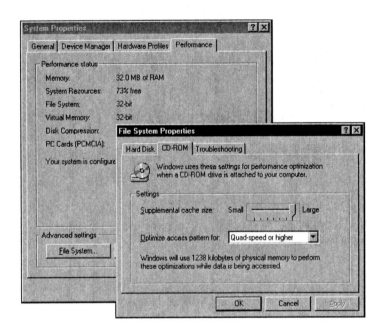

Exhibit 8-9: By changing the CD-ROM speed in the File System Properties box, you can change the amount of memory Vcache uses

Problems with a CD-ROM installation

The following are general guidelines to use when a CD-ROM drive installation under DOS presents the indicated problems.

Error message "invalid drive specification" appears while system is starting up

1 Check that the CONFIG.SYS or AUTOEXEC.BAT file command lines have no errors according to the documentation that came with the CD-ROM. Did you get an error message during startup, such as "Bad Command" or "File Not Found"?

2 Turn off the computer, reseat the adapter card, and check cable connections.

3 The MSCDEX.EXE program might not be loaded because it's placed too late in the AUTOEXEC.BAT file. Sometimes when an installation program edits the CONFIG.SYS or AUTOEXEC.BAT files, the command is added too late in the file. If AUTOEXEC.BAT has the command to load the CD-ROM program after the command to execute Windows, the CD-ROM command will not execute. If this is the case, move the command up near the beginning of the AUTOEXEC.BAT file.

4 You might be using a version of the MSCDEX.EXE program that's different from the version that comes with DOS. If you have DOS 6+, use the version of MSCDEX.EXE that is in the \DOS directory. Change the path to the command in AUTOEXEC.BAT so it accesses the DOS MSCDEX.EXE. For example, let's say the command line looks like this:

```
C:\CDROM\MSCDEX /D:MSCD001 /M:10
```

In this case, you should change it to read:

```
C:\DOS\MSCDEX /D:MSCD001 /M:10
```

Install process is terminated with the message "MSCDEX.EXE Not Found"

MSCDEX.EXE must be copied onto the hard drive. Put it in the \DOS directory, and then restart the install process. Sometimes MSCDEX is placed in the Windows directory, and sometimes a copy is put in the newly created CD-ROM directory.

The Error Message "Not Enough Drive Letters" Appears During the Startup Process

By default, DOS only accepts five logical drive letters (A through E). If you have used all of these, then you must tell DOS to accept more drive letters, with the LASTDRIVE line in CONFIG.SYS. The line can look like this:

```
LASTDRIVE=Z
```

Conflict errors exist

These errors appear during startup as error messages, or they can cause some other device to fail to operate. The IRQ and I/O address of your CD-ROM should be in the documentation. If not, call the manufacturer's technical support for this information or check the manufacturer's Web site.

Computer doesn't recognize the CD-ROM drive

In these cases, there is no D: prompt in DOS, or no drive D is listed in Windows 9x Explorer. Here's what you do:

1   Check the data cable and power cord connections to the CD-ROM drive. Is the stripe on the data cable correctly aligned to Pin 1? (Look for an arrow or small 1 printed on the drive. Usually Pin 1 is next to the power connector.)

2   For an IDE drive, is the correct master/slave jumper set? For example, if both the hard drive and the CD-ROM drive are hooked up to the same ribbon cable, one must be set to master and the other to slave. If the CD-ROM drive is the only drive connected to the cable, then it must be set to single or master.

3   For an IDE drive, is the IDE connection on the system board disabled in CMOS setup?

4   If you're using a SCSI drive, are the proper IDs set, and is the device terminated if it's the last item in the SCSI chain?

5   If you're using DOS, check the driver entries in CONFIG.SYS and AUTOEXEC.BAT, and verify that MSCDEX.EXE is in the correct directory.

6   Is another device using the same port settings or IRQ number? For Windows 9x, see Control Panel, System, Device Manager.

7   Suspect a boot virus. Run a virus scan program.

Do it!

B-4:   Troubleshooting CD-ROM problems

Question	Answer
1 When you install a CD-ROM drive, what is the solution when the DOS error message at startup reads, "Not enough drive letters"?	
2 Which Windows 9x version automatically adds the real-mode CD-ROM device drivers to the rescue disk?	
3 Laura has just installed a CD-ROM drive into her computer. Now when she powers on the system it doesn't boot properly. What is most likely the problem? Explain your answer.	

Topic C: Sound cards

Explanation

A *sound card* is an expansion card that records sound, saves it to a file on your hard drive, and plays it back. Some cards give you the ability to mix and edit sound, and even to edit the sound using standard music score notation. Sound cards have ports for external stereo speakers and microphone input. Also, sound cards may be Sound Blaster compatible, which means that they can understand the commands sent to them that have been written for a Sound Blaster card, which is generally considered the standard for PC sound cards. Some play CD audio by way of a cable connecting the CD to the sound card. For good quality sound you definitely need external speakers and perhaps an amplifier.

Sampling and digitizing the sound

Sound passes through three stages when it is computerized: (1) digitize or input the sound, that is, convert it from analog to digital, (2) store the digital data in a compressed data file, and later (3) reproduce or synthesize the sound (digital to analog).

Converting sound from analog to digital storage is done by first sampling the sound and then digitizing it. Sampling and digitizing the sound are done by a method called *pulse code modulation* (PCM) and involves a component called an *analog-to-digital converter* (A/D or ADC). It follows that the opposite technology, which converts digital to analog, also is needed, and that conversion is done by a *digital-to-analog converter* or DAC. The DAC technology on a sound card converts digital sound files back into analog sound just before output to the speakers.

When recording sound, the analog sound is converted to analog voltage by a microphone and is passed to the sound card, where it's digitized. As explained earlier in the unit, the critical factor in the performance of a sound card is the accuracy of the samples (determined by the number of bits used to hold each sample value, which can be either 8 or 16 bits). This number of bits is called the sample size. The sampling rate of a sound card (the number of samples taken of the analog signal over a period of time) is usually expressed as samples (cycles) per second, or hertz. One thousand hertz (one kilohertz) is written as kHz. A low sampling rate provides a less accurate representation of the sound than does a high sampling rate. Our ears detect up to about 22,000 samples per second or hertz. The sampling rate of music CDs is 44,100 Hz, or 44.1 kHz. When recording sound on a PC, the sampling rate is controlled by the software.

As explained above, sample size is the amount of space used to store a single sample measurement. The larger the sample size, the more accurate the sampling. The number of values used to measure sound is determined by the number of bits allocated to hold each number. If 8 bits are used to hold one number, then the sample range can be from -128 to +128. This is because 1111 1111 in binary equals 255 in decimal, which, together with zero, equals 256 values. Samples of sound are considered to be both positive and negative numbers, so the range is -128 to +127 rather than 0 to 255. However, if 16 bits are used to hold the range of numbers, then the sample range increases dramatically because 1111 1111 1111 1111 in binary is 65,535 in decimal, meaning that the sample size can be -32,768 to +32,767, or a total of 65,536 values.

An 8-bit sound card uses 8 bits to store a sample value, or uses a 256 sample size. A 16-bit sound card has a sample size of 65,536. Sound cards typically use 8- or 16-bit sample sizes, with a sampling rate from 4,000 to 44,000 samples per second. For high-quality sound, use a 16-bit sound card. Samples might also be recorded on a single channel (mono) or on two channels (stereo).

Don't confuse the sample size of 8 bits or 16 bits with the ISA bus size that the sound card uses to attach to the system board. A sound card may use an 8-bit sample size but a 16-bit ISA bus. When you hear people talk about an 8-bit sound card, they're speaking of the sample size, not the bus size.

Storing sound in files

Sound cards store sound in files in two ways: MIDI and WAV files. MIDI (*musical instrument digital interface*, pronounced "middy") technology, a standard for digitizing sound, dictates a specific number of sound samples and the quality of those samples. MIDI files have a .mid file extensions. Nearly all sound cards support MIDI. The MIDI standard is supported by most synthesizers, so sounds created on one synthesizer can be played by another. Computers with a MIDI interface can receive sound created by a MIDI synthesizer and then manipulate the data in MIDI files to produce new sounds. The MIDI standards include storing sound data, such as a note's pitch, length, and volume, and can include attack and delay times. Data compression is used because sound files can be quite large.

Sampled files, which Microsoft calls WAV files (pronounced "wave"), have a .wav file extension. When Windows records sound by using a sound card, the sound is stored in a .wav file. Most game music is stored in MIDI files, but most multimedia sound is stored in WAV files.

Sound files are often large. For example, CD-quality sound is recorded using a 16-bit sample size and 44.1 kHz sampling rate with stereo. The calculations of data size are:

$$16 \text{ bits} \times 44{,}100 \text{ samples/sec} \times 2 = 1{,}411{,}200 \text{ bits/sec or } 176{,}400 \text{ bytes/sec}$$

This yields more than 30 MB of disk space for a three-minute song. Because of these large file sizes, methods of compressing data have evolved.

Compressing data

You can compress data using several standards. Some apply to just audio and others to audio and video. To see the standards currently installed under Windows, double-click the Multimedia icon in Control Panel, and then click the Devices tab. Click the plus sign next to Audio Compression Codecs. Compressing and later decompressing data is called CODEC (Compressor/Decompressor). A CODEC method that doesn't drop any data is called lossless compression, and a method that works by dropping unnecessary data is called lossy compression. The term CODEC also can refer to hardware that converts audio or video signals from analog to digital or from digital to analog. When the term is used this way, it stands for coder/decoder.

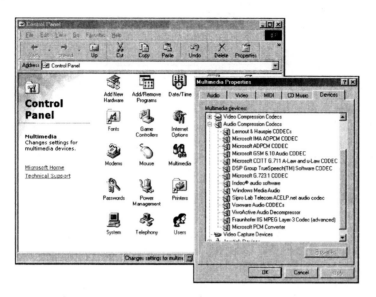

Exhibit 8-10: Use the Multimedia icon in Control Panel to see the codecs supported by Windows

One of the better-known data compression standards is MPEG, an international standard for data compression for motion pictures. Developed by the Moving Pictures Experts Group (MPEG), it tracks movement from one frame to the next, and only stores what changes, rather than compressing individual frames. MPEG is a type of lossy compression. MPEG compression can yield a compression ratio of 100:1 for full-motion video (30 frames per second, or 30 fps).

There are currently several MPEG standards, MPEG-1, MPEG-2, MPEG-3, and MPEG-4. MPEG-1 is used in business and home applications to compress images. MPEG-2 is used to compress video films on DVD-ROM. MPEG-3 is best known for audio compression. MPEG-4 is used for video transmissions over the Internet.

MPEG level 3 audio compression, better known as MP3, is a way to compress sound files to a compression ratio of 1:12 and even as low as 1:24 for stereo sound without losing sound quality. This compression is possible because the data is compressed in such a way that sound that's not normally heard or noticed by the human ear is cut out or drastically reduced. Sound files downloaded from the Internet are most often MP3 files. MP3 files have an .mp3 file extension. For more information about MPEG and MP3, see www.mpeg.org.

Digital-to-Analog conversion

Sound cards use two methods to convert digitally stored sound into real analog sound: FM (frequency modulation) synthesis and wavetable synthesis. The difference between the two is that FM synthesis creates a sound by artificially creating a wave similar to the sound wave produced by the instrument. With FM synthesis, sound is reproduced by making a mathematical approximation of the musical sound wave. For example, the sound of a trumpet would be produced by imitating the sound wave produced by the trumpet, through a series of mathematical calculations. Wavetable synthesis produces the sound by using a sample recording of the real instrument. This table of stored sample sounds is called the wave table, and a group of samples for each instrument is called a voice. Wavetable synthesis produces better sound than does FM synthesis, but also is more expensive.

With Sound PlaybackOnce, the sound is converted back into an analog signal, so you need speakers to play back the sound by using a sound card. Unlike speakers used for other sound equipment, speakers made for computers have built-in amplifiers and extra shielding to protect the monitor from the magnetic fields around regular speakers.

Tip: If you plan to put speakers close to a monitor, be certain they are shielded. Speakers that aren't shielded cause the monitor to display strange colors, and can eventually do permanent damage to the monitor. Also, setting floppy disks on top of unshielded speakers can damage the data on the disks.

Do it!

C-1: Discussing sound card technology

Question	Answer
1 How do you access the volume control under Windows 9x for sound?	
2 What field replaceable unit hardware device converts sound from analog to digital?	
3 When sound is digitized, what's the number of bits to hold each sample called?	
4 What is the purpose of a microphone?	

5 What unit of measure is used to express the sampling rate of a sound card?

6 What are the two most common file extensions for sound files?

7 What does CODEC represent?

Installing a sound card and software

Explanation

Most sound cards come with a device driver as well as all the software needed for normal use, such as applications software to play music CDs. The installation of a sample sound card is described below. The sample card used is the Creative Lab's Sound Blaster PCI128, shown in Exhibit 8-11. It's Plug and Play compliant, uses a PCI slot, and supports a 128-voice wavetable. It will work under DOS 6+, Windows 9x, Windows NT, or Windows 2000. The card comes with drivers and software on a CD-ROM and a user's guide.

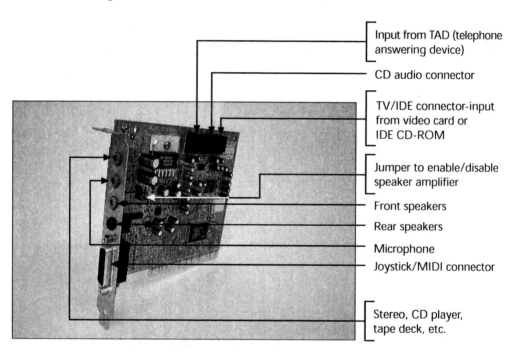

Exhibit 8-11: A Sound Blaster sound card

The three main steps in this example of a sound card installation are to install the card itself in an empty PCI slot on the system board, install the driver under Windows 98, and then install the applications stored on the sound card's CD.

To install a sound card, use the following steps:

1 Turn the PC off, remove the cover, and locate an empty expansion slot for the card. Since this installation uses the connecting wire from the sound card to the CD-ROM drive (the wire comes with the sound card), place the sound card near enough to the CD-ROM drive so that the wire can reach between them.

2 Attach the wire to the sound card (see Exhibit 8-12) and to the CD-ROM drive.

3 Remove the cover from the slot opening at the rear of the PC case and place the card into the slot, making sure that the card is seated firmly. Use the screw taken from the slot cover to secure the card to the back of the PC case.

4 Check again that both ends of the wire are still securely connected, and replace the case cover.

5 Plug in the speakers to the ports at the back of the sound card and turn on the PC. The speakers might require their own power source.

Exhibit 8-12: Connect the wire to the sound card to make the direct audio connection from the CD

Installing the sound card driver

Once the card is installed, the device drivers must be installed. When Windows 98 starts, it detects that new hardware is present. The New Hardware Found dialog box opens, indicating that it has discovered the Sound Blaster PIC128.

1 The New Hardware Wizard gives you this option: Search for the Best Driver for Your Device (Recommended). Select this option and click the Next button.

2 Clear all check boxes and check only the Specify a Location check box.

3 Click the Browse button and point to the driver path:

```
D:\Audio\English\Win95drv
```

In this example, the CD-ROM drive is drive D, and the sound card's user guide lists the location of the driver on the CD. Substitute your CD-ROM drive letter and, for other sound card installations, see the documentation for the location of the driver on the CD-ROM.

4 Click Next to continue the driver installation.

5 Click Finish when the installation is complete and reboot your PC.

With most sound cards, on the CD containing the sound card driver, you can find some special applications software to use the special features offered by the card. Sometimes, as is the case with this Sound Blaster card, the software is installed at the same time as the drivers so you can use the software at this point in the installation. With other sound cards, after the driver installation is complete and the sound card is working under Windows 9x, you can then install the additional software. See the documentation that comes with the sound card to learn if applications software is present and how and when to install it.

Do it!

C-2:   Verifying sound card installation

Here's how	Here's why
1 Choose **Start**, **Settings**, **Control Panel**	
Double-click **System**	After you install the driver, reboot, and enter Windows, so that you can use Device Manager to verify that the device and driver are correctly installed.
2 Click the **Device Manager** tab	
Expand the sound devices	

System Properties

General   Device Manager   Hardware Profiles   Performan

○ View devices by type   ○ View devices by conn

- ⊞ 🖴 Disk drives
- ⊞ 🖵 Display adapters
- ⊞ 🖴 Floppy disk controllers
- ⊞ 🖴 Hard disk controllers
- ⊞ 🖉 HCFMODEM
- ⊞ ⌨ Keyboard
- ⊞ 🖉 Modem
- ⊞ 🖵 Monitors
- ⊞ 🖱 Mouse
- ⊞ 🖳 Network adapters
- ⊞ 🖉 Ports (COM & LPT)
- ⊟ 🎮 Sound, video and game controllers
  - 🎮 YAMAHA DS-XG GamePort
  - 🎮 YAMAHA DS-XG Legacy Sound System
  - 🎮 YAMAHA DS-XG PCI Audio CODEC

3 Select the card	
Click **Properties**	
Click **Resources**	

YAMAHA DS-XG PCI Audio CODEC Properties   ❓

General   Driver   Resources

🎮   YAMAHA DS-XG PCI Audio CODEC

☑ Use automatic settings

Setting based on: Basic configuration 0000

Resource type	Setting
Interrupt Request	09
Memory Range	F0010000 - F0017FFF

To see the resources used by the card.

4 Click **Cancel** twice	To close the open windows.
5 Close the Control Panel	

Using sound with Windows 9x

Explanation

Windows 9x offers some support for sound, such as playing a music CD or a WAV file or providing sound when performing certain Windows functions (such as starting an application or exiting Windows). This section will look at these features.

To configure the Windows 9x sound system to use the new sound card, first determine that sound control is installed under the Windows 9x Multimedia section, and then test the sound by using Windows 9x:

1 Click Start, Settings, Control Panel, and then double-click Add/Remove Programs.

2 Click the Windows Setup tab. From this tab, you can install components of Windows 9x that were not installed at the original installation.

3 Click Multimedia, and then click Details to see the components of Windows 9x multimedia support. Installed components are checked.

4 If CD Player, Volume Control, and Sound Recorder aren't installed, then install them now. Select the files by clicking the check boxes.

5 Click Apply to install these components. You might be asked to insert the Windows 9x CD or floppy disks.

To test the sound, access the Multimedia group of Windows 95 or the Entertainment group of Windows 98. Note that the controls and windows displayed might be slightly different depending on the Windows 9x components, sound card drivers, and other audio software installed:

1 In Windows 95, choose Start, Program, Accessories, Multimedia. In Windows 98, choose Start, Program, Accessories, Entertainment.

2 To play a music CD, click CD Player. The CD Player window is displayed.

3 Insert a music CD in the CD-ROM drive and click the play button, which is a forward arrow.

4 To adjust the volume of the sound card, click Start, point to Programs, Accessories, Entertainment, and click Volume Control. The Volume Control window in Exhibit 8-13 appears. Adjust the volume and close the dialog box when finished.

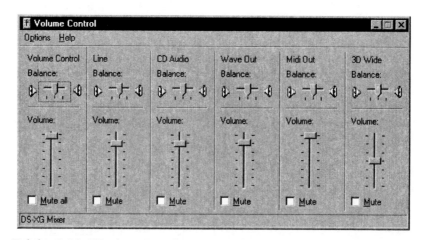

Exhibit 8-13: Windows 9x volume control

You can easily adjust the volume in Windows by keeping the volume control on the taskbar. To do this, use the Multimedia control in Control Panel: Click Start, Settings, Control Panel, double-click Multimedia, and then click the Audio tab of the Multimedia window. Check Show volume control on the taskbar.

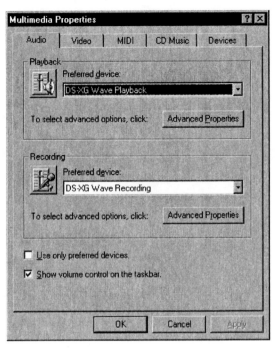

Exhibit 8-14: Windows 98 multimedia audio selection includes the option to put volume control on the taskbar

Do it!

C-3: Testing the sound in Windows 9x

Here's how	Here's why
1 Choose **Start**, **Settings**, **Control Panel** Double-click **Add/Remove Programs** Click the **Windows Setup** tab	
2 Click **Multimedia** Click **Details**	

Components:	
☑ 🎵 Audio Compression	0.2 MB
☑ 💿 CD Player	0.2 MB
☑ 🎬 Macromedia Shockwave	3.1 MB
☑ 🎬 Macromedia Shockwave Flash	0.2 MB
☑ 💿 Multimedia Sound Schemes	6.5 MB

	To see the multimedia components that Windows 9x supports. The check mark indicates that the component is installed.
3 Verify that CD Player, Volume Control, and Sound Recorder are installed Close the open Control Panel windows	You can install them now if they're not already installed. You will need access to the Windows 9x CD.
4 Choose **Start**, **Programs**, **Accessories** If you're using Windows 95, choose **Multimedia**	If you're using Windows 98, choose Entertainment.
5 Choose **CD Player**	To play music. If you have a music CD, insert it now and test the sound. You can control the volume in the Volume Control windows, as shown in Exhibit 8-13.
6 Close the CD Player	

Recording sound

Explanation

In addition to being able to play sound, a multimedia system must be able to record it, for which you need a microphone. You can attach a microphone to the MIC port on the back of the sound card. Windows 9x saves sound files in the WAV file format.

Controlling Windows 9x sounds

When certain events occur, Windows 9x plays sounds that are controlled by the Sounds control of the Windows 9x Control Panel. To customize these sounds and the times at which they occur, access Control Panel (click Start, Settings, Control Panel), and then double-click the Sounds icon. The items listed that have a horn icon beside them cause a sound. The sound for this item is defined in the Name list. For example, in Exhibit 8-15, for the event Exit Windows, the sound is The Microsoft Sound.wav. To preview the sound, click the Play button to the right of the file name. You can develop your own customized choices of sounds for chosen events by using this box. Save the scheme as a file by using the Save As option at the bottom of the box, and use it to create a multimedia sound experience when working with Windows 9x.

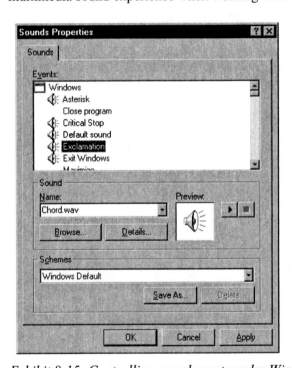

Exhibit 8-15: Controlling sound events under Windows 9x

Troubleshooting sound problems

When there is no sound, you can use the following suggestions to fix the problem.

- Is the sound cable attached between the CD-ROM and the analog audio connector on the sound card?
- Are the speakers turned on?
- Is the speaker volume turned down?
- Are the speakers plugged into the "Out" line or the "Spkr" port of the sound card?
- Is the transformer for the speaker plugged into an electrical outlet on one end and into the speakers on the other end?
- Is the volume control for Windows turned down? (To check this, choose Start, Programs, Accessories, Multimedia, Volume Control.)
- Does the sound card have a "diagnose" file on the install disk?
- Reinstall the sound card drivers.
- Is another device using the same I/O addresses or IRQ number?
- To check for a bad connection, turn off the computer, remove, and reinstall the sound card.
- Replace the sound card with one you know is good.

Do it!

C-4: Recording sound in Windows 9x

Here's how	Here's why
1 Start the Sound Recorder	Choose Start, Programs, Accessories, Multimedia (or Entertainment), Sound Recorder.
2 Click the Record button	

(The red dot on the right side of the dialog box.) The sound enters the microphone and moves as an analog signal to the sound card, which samples and digitizes it before passing it on to the CPU via the system bus.

3 Click the Stop button	To finish recording.
4 Choose **File**, **Save As**	To save the sound file for later use.
5 Open the Sound Properties dialog box	Double-click the Sound icon on the Control Panel. You can use this dialog box to choose the sounds that are used when different actions are performed.
Close the Sound Properties dialog box	

Topic D: Digital cameras and DVD

Explanation

A recent introduction to multimedia, with markets in both business and home computing, is the digital camera, which is becoming more popular as quality improves and prices decrease. *Digital camera* technology works much like scanner technology, except that it's much faster. It essentially scans the field of images set by the photographer, and translates the light signals into digital values, which can be stored as a file and viewed with software that interprets the stored values appropriately.

Digital cameras

TWAIN (technology without an interesting name) format is a standard format used by both digital cameras and PCs for transferring an image. Transfer the image to your computer's hard drive by using a serial cable supplied with the camera, a parallel cable, or some external disk medium such as a flash RAM card, which is faster and more convenient than other methods. Exhibit 8-16 shows a SmartMedia card from a digital camera inserted into a FlashPath card that can then be inserted into a floppy disk drive to upload images to the PC.

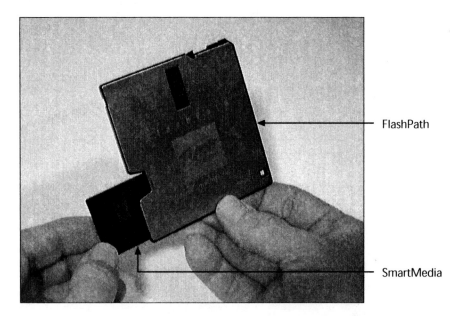

Exhibit 8-16: The small SmartMedia card holds the digital images from a digital camera. FlashPath enables a PC to read SmartMedia via a floppy disk drive

Once the images are on the PC, use the camera's image-editing software or another program such as Adobe PhotoShop to view, touch up, and print the picture. The picture file, which is usually in JPEG (Joint Photographic Experts Group) format, can then be imported into documents. JPEG is a common lossy compression standard for storing photos.

Most digital cameras also have a video-out port so that you can attach the camera to any TV by using a serial cable. You can then display pictures on the TV or copy them to videotape.

The image sensing can be done by two kinds of technology: infrared sensor or charge-coupled device (CCD). The image sensor captures light reflected off the subject and converts that light to a serial stream of small DC voltages. The image sensor is made up of three sensors, each filtering a different color (red, green, or blue). Exhibit 8-17 shows the process a digital camera uses to create a picture. The exhibit shows only one channel of the three channels used (one channel for each color). The image sensor captures the light and converts it into voltage signals that will become pixels. These signals move through the DC restore or DC clamping stage and then on to the gain stage, where the signals are amplified and buffered. Next, the signals enter the ADC (analog-to-digital converter), where they're digitized. The digital pixels are then processed by the image processor and sent on to storage through the I/O process. The controller in the diagram controls all processing of the digital signals.

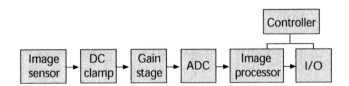

Exhibit 8-17: The signal chain used by a digital camera

MP3 player

A popular audio compression codec is *MP3*, an advanced method of MPEG-3, that can reduce the size of a sound file as much as 1:17 without a noticeable loss in quality. An MP3 player is a device or software that plays these MP3 files. Portable MP3 players store the MP3 files on a compact storage device such as a SmartMedia card by Toshiba. When using a digital camera, data is transferred or uploaded from a camera to a PC, but when using a portable MP3 player, data is downloaded from a PC to the player.

You can purchase MP3 music files on the storage media suitable for your MP3 player, from regular CDs, or from Web sites on the Internet such as eMusic at www.emusic.com. Download them from the Internet to your PC, and then play them by using MP3 player software such as Windows Media Player or MusicMatch Jukebox (see www.musicmatch.com). You also can play the MP3 files directly from the Internet without first downloading them, which is called streaming audio.

Traditional music CDs store music files in CD format. You can use software that copies a music file from a CD and converts it to a WAV file, which isn't compressed. This software is called a ripper because you're "ripping off" the CD. Once the file is in WAV format on your hard drive, use encoder software to compress the file into MP3 format. Next, copy the MP3 file to a SmartMedia card or other type of flash storage device. For example, I-Jam portable MP3 players use a flash card smaller than SmartMedia called SanDisk. Data is downloaded to the card by way of a serial port interface. For more information about I-Jam MP3 players, see www.ijamworld.com and for information about the SanDisk flash card, see www.sandisk.com. CD rippers, MP3 encoders, and MP3 player software can be downloaded from the Internet. For example, see the MusicMatch site at www.musicmatch.com.

Video-capturing card

An NTSC (National Television Standards Committee) *video-capturing card* is another multimedia option. With this card, you can capture input from a camcorder or directly from a TV. Video can be saved as motion clips or stills, edited, and, with the right card, copied back to videotape for viewing by a VCR and television. Look for these features on a video capture card: an IEEE 1394 port to interface with a digital camcorder, data transfer rates (which affect the price of the card), capture resolution and color-depth capabilities of the card, ability to transfer data back to the digital camcorder or VCR, stereo audio jacks, and the video editing software bundled with the card. Other options include a TV tuner, which makes it possible to turn your PC into a television complete with instant replay and program scheduling. Ports on a video-capturing card might include an antenna or cable TV port for input and a TV or VCR port for output. Other ports are a PC monitor video port and possibly an IEEE 1394 port for a camcorder. Expect the card to fit into an AGP slot and take the place of your regular video card. For an excellent example of a video-capturing card, see the All-in-Wonder card from ATI Technologies at www.ati.com.

Digital Video Disc (DVD)

With multimedia, the ability to store massive amounts of data is paramount to the technology's success. The goal of storing a full-length movie on a single unit of computerized, inexpensive storage medium has been met by more than one technology, but the technology that has clearly taken the lead in popularity is *digital video disc*, or *digital versatile disc* (DVD) technology (see Exhibit 8-18). It takes up to seven CDs to store a full-length movie, and only one DVD disc. A DVD disc can hold 8.5 GB of data, and, if both the top and bottom surfaces are used, can hold 17 GB of data, which is enough for more than eight hours of video storage.

Exhibit 8-18: A DVD device

Both DVD and CD-ROM technologies use patterns of tiny pits on the surface of a disc to represent bits, which are then readable by a laser beam. When looking at the surface of either disc, it's difficult to distinguish between the two. They both have the same 5-inch diameter and 1.2-mm thickness, and the same shiny surface. But, because DVD uses a shorter wavelength laser, it can read smaller, more densely packed pits, which increases the disc's capacity. In addition, there is a second layer added to DVD discs, an opaque layer that also holds data, which almost doubles the capacity of the disc. Also, a DVD disc can use both the top and bottom surfaces for data.

DVD uses MPEG-2 video compression and requires an MPEG-2 controller card to decode the compressed data. Audio is stored on DVD in Dolby AC-3 compression. This audio compression method also is the standard to be used by HDTV (high-definition TV), soon to be introduced into the marketplace. Dolby AC-3 compression also is known as Dolby Digital Surround or Dolby Surround Sound and supports six separate sound channels of sound information for six different speakers, each producing a different sound! These speakers are known as Front Left and Right, Front Center, Rear Left and Right, and Subwoofer. Because each channel is digital, there is no background noise on the channel, and a sound engineer can place sound on any one of these speakers.

The DVD controller card decodes both MPEG-2 video and Dolby AC-3 audio data and outputs them to a video port and speaker port, respectively. This PCI controller card can be configured to work in more than one way. Exhibit 8-19 shows one configuration demonstrating how the flow of data can come from a DVD disc through the PC to speakers and monitor. The DVD drive is attached to the system board via a SCSI controller that enables the data to bypass the CPU and to be routed directly to the MPEG-2 decoder card. The MPEG-2 decoder separates the video data from the sound data, decodes both, and sends the video data to the video controller card and on to the monitor. The DVD controller also is acting as a sound card. The sound data is sent to a DAC on the card that directs the analog sound signal to the speakers.

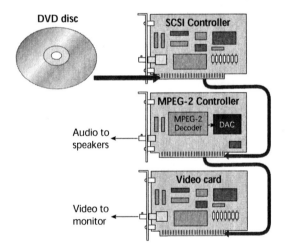

Exhibit 8-19: How a PC can use DVD data

Other DVD Devices

Besides DVD ROM, new DVD devices will be introduced that are read-writeable. Table 10-1 describes these devices.

DVD device	Description
DVD-ROM	Read-only device. A DVD-ROM drive also can read CD-ROMs.
DVD-R	DVD recordable. Uses a similar technology as that used by CD-R drives. Holds about 4.7 GB of data. Can read DVD-ROM discs.
DVD-RAM	Recordable and erasable. Multifunctional DVD device that uses phase-dual (PD) technology. Can read DVD-RAM, DVD-R, DVD-ROM, and CD-R discs.
DVD-RW or DVD-ER	Rewritable DVD device, also known as erasable, recordable device. Uses phase-dual technology. Media can be read by most DVD-ROM drives.
DVD+RW	A technology similar to and currently competing with DVD-RW. Can read DVD-ROM and CD-ROM discs, but will not be compatible with DVD-RAM discs.

The last three items in the preceding table are competing with one another. All have similar, yet different, features, and compatibility and standards are issues. It's yet to be seen which of these three media will prevail in the marketplace. When purchasing one, pay close attention to compatibility with other media, such as CD-ROM, and availability and price of discs.

Do it!

D-1: Discussing digital cameras and DVDs

Question	Answer
1 Describe the purposes of FlashPath and SmartMedia technology.	
2 What two things does a DVD controller decode?	
3 What compression methods are used for both?	

Unit summary: Multimedia technology

Topic A

In this topic, you were introduced to **multimedia** technology. You learned that multimedia PCs and devices are designed to create and reproduce lifelike presentations of sight and sound. The process of converting analog to digital is known as **digitizing** the data. Once digitized, the data can then be saved as a file and used on the computer.

Topic B

You learned that the **CD-ROM drive** is the most popular multimedia component. You explored how the CD-ROM works and how to **install** a CD-ROM drive. You also were introduced to the other types of ROMs: **CD-R** and **CD-RW** drives.

Topic C

In this topic, you learned about **sampling** and **digitizing sound** and how sound is stored in files. You learned how to **install** a **sound card** and a **sound card driver**.

Topic D

You were introduced to the technology behind **digital cameras**, **MP3**, and Digital Video Disc (**DVD**).

Independent practice activity

1 Work with a partner. Each of you should set up a problem with a PC and have the other troubleshoot the problem. Some suggestions as to what problems to set up are:

- Speaker cables disconnected
- Speaker turned off
- Speaker cable plugged into the wrong jack
- Volume turned all the way down
- Wrong/missing driver
- Wrong settings

2 As you troubleshoot the problem, write down the initial symptoms of the problem and the steps you should take towards the solution.

Unit 9

Electricity and power supplies

Unit time: 75 minutes

Complete this unit, and you'll know how to:

A Measure the voltage of a computer power supply.

B Troubleshoot and change a faulty computer power supply.

C Protect a computer from damaging changes in electrical power and power failure.

Topic A: Measuring the voltage of a power supply

Explanation

To most people, volts, ohms, watts, and amps are vague, ambiguous words that simply mean electricity. If these terms are mysterious to you, they'll become clear in this section as electricity is discussed.

A brief introduction to electricity

Electricity is energy with properties that can be measured in various ways.

Unit	Definition	As applied to a computer
Volts (measures potential difference)	Abbreviated as V (for example, 110 V). Volts are measured by finding the potential difference between the electrical charges on either side of an electrical device in an electrical system.	An AT power supply supplies four separate voltages: +12 V, -12 V, +5 V, -5 V. An ATX power supply supplies these and also 3.3 V.
Amps or Amperes (measures electrical current)	Abbreviated as A (for example, 1.5 A). Amps are measured by placing an ammeter in the flow of current and measuring that current.	A 17-inch monitor requires less than 2 A to operate. A small laser printer uses about 2 A. A CD-ROM drive uses about 1 A.
Ohms (measures resistance)	Abbreviated with the symbol □ (for example, 20 □). Devices are rated according to how much resistance they offer to electrical currents. The ohm rating of a resistor or other electrical device is often written somewhere on the device. The resistance of a device is measured when the device isn't connected to an electrical system.	Current can flow in typical computer cables and wires with a resistance of less than 20 ohms. This condition of low resistance that enables current to flow is called *continuity*.
Watts (measures power)	Abbreviated W (for example, 20 W). Watts are calculated by multiplying volts by amps.	A computer power supply is rated at 200 to 600 watts.

Common electrical components

A PC contains many electronic components. It's interesting to understand what basic electronic components make up a PC and how they work. Basic electrical components in a PC include transistors, capacitors, diodes, and resistors. Materials used to make these and other electrical components can be:

- Conductors. Material that easily conducts electricity such as gold or copper.
- Insulators. Material that resists the flow of electricity such as glass or ceramic.
- Semiconductors. Material such as silicon with an ability to conduct electricity that falls between that of conductors and insulators.

A *transistor* is an electronic device that can serve as a gate or switch for an electrical signal and can amplify the flow of electricity. Invented in 1947, the transistor is made of three layers of semiconductor material. A charge (either positive or negative, depending on how the transistor was designed) placed on the center layer can cause the two outer layers of the transistor to complete a circuit to create an "on" state. An opposite charge placed on the center layer can cause the reverse to happen, causing the transistor to create an "off" state. By manipulating these charges to the transistor, it can be used to hold a logic state, either on or off (translated to 0 or 1 in binary). When the transistor is maintaining this state, it requires almost no electrical power. Because the initial charge sent to the transistor isn't as great as the resulting current created by the transistor, sometimes a transistor is used as a small amplifier. The transistor is the basic building block of an integrated circuit (IC) that's used to build a microchip.

A *capacitor* is an electronic device that can hold an electrical charge for a period of time and is used to smooth out the uneven flow of electricity through a circuit. Capacitors inside a PC power supply create the even flow of current needed by the PC. Capacitors maintain their charge long after current is no longer present, which is why the inside of a power supply can be dangerous even when it's unplugged.

A *diode* is a semiconductor device that enables electricity to flow in only one direction. (A transistor contains two diodes.) One to four diodes used in various configurations can be used to convert the AC to DC. Singularly or collectively, depending on the configuration, these diodes are called a rectifier.

Measuring voltage

If you suspect a problem with a power supply, one thing you can do is measure the voltage output. When a power supply is working properly, voltages all fall within an acceptable range (plus or minus 5 percent). However, be aware that even if measured voltage is within the appropriate range, a power supply can still cause problems. This is because problems with power supplies often come and go. Therefore, if the voltages are correct, you should still suspect the power supply to be the problem when certain symptoms are present. To learn for certain whether the power supply is the problem, replace it with a unit you know is good.

ESD and EMI

ESD (electrostatic discharge) is a brief flow of electricity caused by two objects that have a difference in voltage potential coming in contact with one another. This discharge can damage delicate electronics, so it's important that you be grounded before you work with computer components. If both you and the component you're working with are grounded, then there will be no potential voltage difference between you and the component, and no electrical discharge will occur when you touch it.

Warning: There are exceptions to the rule of always being grounded when you work with PCs. You *don't* want to be grounded when working inside a monitor or with a power supply. These devices maintain high charges of electricity, even when the power is turned off. *Don't* wear a ground bracelet when working inside these devices, because you don't want to be the ground for these charges!

Another problem with computers that can be caused by electricity is *electromagnetic interference* (*EMI*). EMI is caused by the magnetic field that's produced as a side effect when electricity flows. EMI in the radio frequency range is called radio frequency interference (RFI), which can cause problems with radio and TV reception. Data in data cables that cross this magnetic field can become corrupted, which is called crosstalk. Crosstalk is partly controlled by using shielded data cables covered with a protective material. Power supplies also are shielded to prevent EMI from emitting from them. PCs also can emit EMI to other nearby PCs, which is one reason why a computer needs to be inside a case, and the case shouldn't have holes—so always install face plates in empty drive bays or over empty expansion slots.

If a PC persists in giving mysterious, intermittent errors, one thing to suspect is EMI. Try moving the PC to a new location. If the problem persists, try moving it to a location that uses an entirely different electric circuit. One simple way to detect the presence of EMI is to use a small inexpensive AM radio. Turn the tuning dial away from a station into a low-frequency range. With the radio on, you can hear the static produced by EMI. Try putting the radio next to several electronic devices to detect the EMI emitted.

If EMI in the electrical circuits coming to the PC is a significant problem, you can use a line conditioner that filters out the electrical noise causing the EMI. Line conditioners are discussed later in the unit.

Using a multimeter

A voltmeter measures the difference in electrical potential between two points in volts, and an ammeter measures electrical current in amps. The following exhibit shows a *multimeter*, which can be used as either a voltmeter or an ammeter, or can measure resistance or continuity (the presence of a complete circuit), depending on a dial or function switch setting. Less expensive multimeters commonly measure voltage, resistance, and continuity, but not amps. Measure voltage and amps while the electricity is on. Measure resistance and continuity while the electricity is off. For the specific details of how to use your multimeter, consult the manual, which explains what you can measure with the multimeter and how to use it.

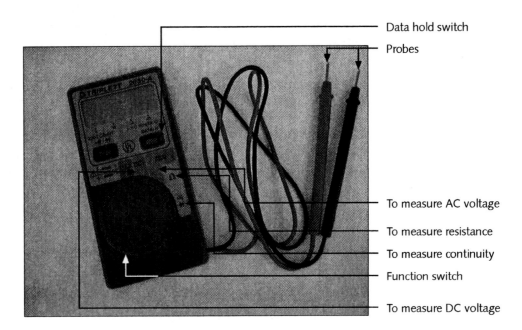

Data hold switch
Probes

To measure AC voltage

To measure resistance

To measure continuity

Function switch

To measure DC voltage

Exhibit 9-1: A digital multimeter

A multimeter can provide either a digital or an analog display. A digital display shows the readings as digits displayed on an LCD (liquid crystal display) panel. A digital multimeter is sometimes called a DMM (digital multimeter) or a DVM (digital voltage meter). An analog display shows the readings as a needle moving across a scale of values. Multimeters are sometimes small, portable, battery-powered units. Larger ones are designed to sit on a countertop and are powered by a wall outlet.

When you use a multimeter, you must set three things before you begin: (1) what you want it to measure (voltage, current, or resistance), (2) whether the current is AC or DC, and (3) what range of values it should expect. If you're measuring the voltage output from a wall outlet (110–120 V), the range should be much higher than when measuring the voltage output of a computer power supply (3-12 V). Setting the range high assures you that the meter will be able to handle a large input without pegging the needle (exceeding the highest value that the meter is designed to measure) or damaging the meter. However, if you set the range too high, you might not see the voltage register at all. Set the range low enough to ensure that the measure will be as accurate as you need, but not so low as to be less than the expected voltage.

For example, to measure the voltage of house current, if you expect the voltage to be 115 volts, set the voltage range from 0 to somewhere between 120 and 130 volts. You want the high end of the range to be slightly higher than the expected voltage. Most meters don't accept a very large voltage or current into the meter when the range is set low, in order to protect the meter. Some multimeters are *autorange meters*, which sense the quantity of input and set the range accordingly.

A meter comes with two test probes. One is usually red and the other black. Install the red probe at the positive (+) jack on the meter and the black probe at the negative (–) jack.

To measure voltage, place the other end of the black probe at the ground point and the other end of the red probe at the hot point, without disconnecting anything in the circuit and with the power on. For example, to measure voltage by using the multimeter shown in the picture, turn the function switch dial to DCV for DC voltage measurement. This meter is autoranging, so this is all that needs to be set. With the power on, place the two probes in position and read the voltage from the LCD panel. The DATA-H switch (data hold) enables you to freeze the displayed reading.

To measure current in amps, the multimeter must be part of the circuit. Disconnect the circuit at some point so that you can connect the multimeter in line to get a measure in amps. Not all multimeters can measure amps.

A multimeter also can be used to measure continuity, which indicates if there is little or no resistance (less than 20 ohms gives continuity in a PC) in a wire or a closed connection between two points. This means that the path for electricity between the two points is unhindered or "continuous." This measurement is taken with no electricity present in the circuit.

For example, if you want to know that Pin 2 on one end of a serial cable is connected to Pin 3 on the other end of the cable, set the multimeter to measure continuity, and work without the cable being connected to anything. Put one probe on Pin 2 at one end of the cable and the other probe on Pin 3 at the other end. If the two pins connect, the multimeter will indicate this with a reading on the LCD panel, or a buzzer will sound (see the multimeter documentation). In this situation, you might find that the probe is too large to extend into the pinhole of the female connection of the cable. A straightened small paper clip works well here to extend the probe. However, be very careful not to use a paper clip that is too thick and might widen the size of the pinhole, which can later prevent the pinhole from making a good connection.

To determine if a fuse is good, you actually measure continuity. With a multimeter set to measure continuity, place its probes on each end of the fuse. If the fuse has continuity, then it's good. If the multimeter doesn't have a continuity setting, set it to measure resistance. If the reading in ohms is approximately zero, there is no resistance and the fuse is good. If the reading is infinity, there is infinite resistance and the fuse is blown and shouldn't be used.

How to measure the voltage of a power supply

To determine that a power supply is working properly, measure the voltage of each circuit supported by the power supply. First, open the computer case and identify all power cords coming from the power supply. Look for the cords from the power supply to the system board and other power cords to the drives. Follow the directions described in the next section to measure the voltage of the power supply output to the system board.

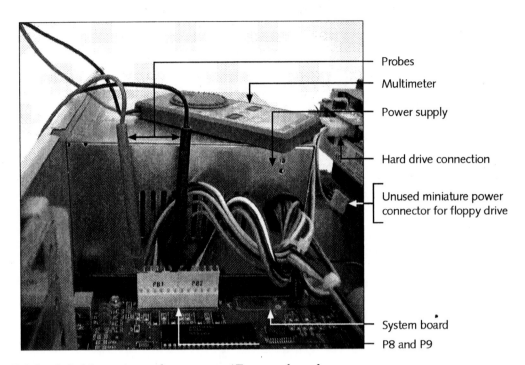

- Probes
- Multimeter
- Power supply
- Hard drive connection
- Unused miniature power connector for floppy drive
- System board
- P8 and P9

Exhibit 9-2: Measuring voltage on an AT system board

Testing the output of the power supply

The computer must be turned on to test the power supply output. Be very careful not to touch any chips or disturb any circuit boards as you work. The voltage output from the power supply is no more than 14 volts, which isn't enough to seriously hurt you if you accidentally touch a hot probe. However, you can damage the computer if you're not careful.

You can hurt yourself if you accidentally create a short circuit from the power supply to ground through the probe. If you touch the probe to the hot circuit and also to ground, the current will be diverted away from the computer circuit and through the probe to ground. This short might be enough to cause a spark or to melt the probe, which can happen if you let the two probes to touch each other while one of them is attached to the hot circuit and the other is attached to ground. Make *sure* the probes only touch one metal object, preferably only a single power pin on a connector, or you could cause a short.

Because of the danger of touching a hot probe to a ground probe, you might prefer not to put the black probe into a ground lead that's too close to the hot probe. Instead, when the directions say to place the black probe on a lead that's very close to the hot probe, you can use a black wire lead on an unused power supply connection meant for a hard drive. The idea is that the black probe should always be placed on a ground or black lead.

All ground leads are considered at ground, no matter what number is assigned that lead. Therefore, you can consider all black leads to be equal. For an AT system board, the ground leads for P8 and P9 are the four black center leads 5, 6, 7, and 8. For an ATX system board, the ground leads are seven black leads in center positions on the ATX P1 power connector. The ground leads for a hard drive power connection are the two black center leads, 2 and 3.

Measuring voltage output to an AT system board

To measure the voltage, you'll need to remove the cover of the computer. The voltage range for each connection is often written on the top of the power supply. The two power connections to the system board are often labeled P8 and P9. Each of the two connections has six leads, for a total of 12 leads. Of these 12, four are ground connections, and lead 1 is a "power good" pin, used to indicate that the system board is receiving power. A common arrangement for these 12 leads is listed in the table below.

Lead	Description	Acceptable range
P8-1	"Power Good"	
P8-2	Not Used or +5 V	+4.4 to +5.2 V
P8-3	+12 V	+10.8 to +13.2 V
P8-4	-12 V	-10.8 V to -13.2 V
P8-5	Black ground	
P8-6	Black ground	
P9-7	Black Ground	
P9-8	Black ground	
P9-9	-5 V	-4.5 V to -5.5 V
P9-10	+5 V	+4.5 V to +5.5 V
P9-11	+5 V	+4.5 V to +5.5 V
P9-12	+5 V	+4.5 V to +5.5 V

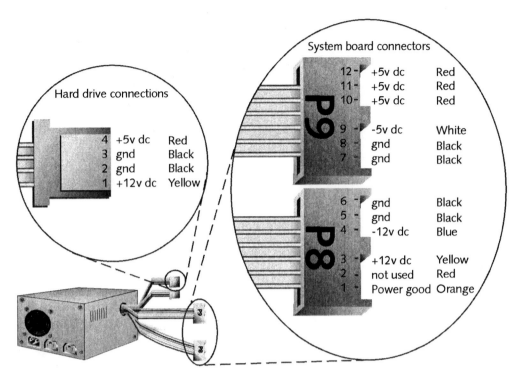

Exhibit 9-3: AT power supply connectors

Measuring voltage output to an ATX system board

To measure the output to the ATX system board, follow the same procedure as with the AT system board. Recall that the ATX board uses 3.3, 5, and 12 volts coming from the power supply. The exhibit shows the power output of each pin on the connector. You can see the distinguishing shape of each side of the connector. Notice the different hole sizes on each side of the connector, ensuring that the plug from the power supply will be oriented correctly in the connector. The next table lists the leads to the system board and their acceptable voltage ranges.

Lead (unnotched side)	Description	Acceptable range
1	+12 V	+10.8 to +13.2
2	+5 volts standby	+4.5 to +5.5
3	"Power good"	
4	Black ground	
5	+5 volts	+4.5 to +5.5
6	Black ground	
7	+5 volts	+4.5 to +5.5
8	Black ground	
9	+3.3 volts	+3.1 to +3.5
10	+3.3 volts	+3.1 to +3.5

Lead (notched side)	Description	Acceptable range
1	+5 volts	+4.5 to +5.5
2	+5 volts	+4.5 to +5.5
3	−5 volts	−4.5 to −5.5
4	Black ground	
5	Black ground	
6	Black ground	
7	Power supply on	
8	Black ground	
9	−12 volts	−10.8 to −13.2
10	+3.3 volts	+3.1 to +3.5

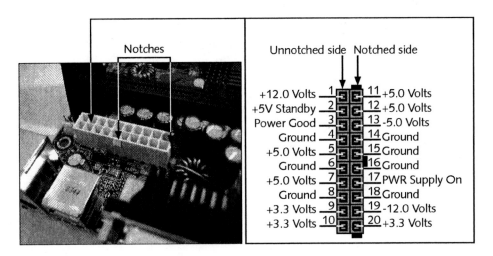

Exhibit 9-4: ATX system board power connector

Testing the power output to a floppy or hard drive

The power cords to a floppy disk drive, hard drive, and CD-ROM drive all supply the same voltage: one +5-volt circuit and one +12-volt circuit. The power connection to any drive uses four leads; the two outside connections are hot, and the two inside connections are ground. The power connection to a 3 1/2-inch floppy disk drive is usually a miniature connection. Follow these steps to measure the voltage to any drive:

1   With the drive plugged in, turn the computer on.
2   Set the multimeter to measure voltage as described above.
3   Place the red probe on lead 1 and place the black probe on the lead next to it (lead 2), which is ground. The acceptable range is +10.8 to +13.2 volts.
4   Place the red probe on lead 4, and place the black probe on the lead next to it (lead 3). The acceptable range is +4.5 to +5.5 volts.

You might choose to alter the method you use to ground the black probe. In step 4 above, the red probe and black probe are very close to each other. You might choose to keep them farther apart by placing the black probe in a ground lead of an unused hard drive connection.

Do it!

A-1: Measuring power supply voltage

Here's how

1 Configure your multimeter to measure voltages within the following range: –5V DC/+15 V DC

2 Set the multimeter to measure voltage in a range of 20 volts of DC current. Insert the black probe into the – jack and the red probe into the + jack of the meter

3 Unplug your lab workstation

4 Attach the respective multimeter leads to the ground and +12 V DC wires (Connect the multimeter to the power supply connector outside the case on a flat surface that can be easily seen and controlled.)

5 Before plugging in the PC, verify that no other metal pieces or objects are touching the system board or power supply, which could cause a short

6 Plug in the power cord

7 Stand clear of the lab workstation and power it on

8 Record the results displayed on the multimeter

9 Refer to the table above to verify that the recorded voltage falls within the acceptable range

10 Power off your lab workstation

11 Repeat steps 3 through 9 to test the other leads, adjusting step 4 appropriately: keep the black probe grounded, and move the red probe to a different lead for each iteration. Remember to power off and unplug the system before moving the probes each time. Use the P8/P9 connector exhibit above to guide you. Measure the voltage on both P8 and P9 connectors.

Topic B: Problems with the power supply

Explanation

If you assemble a PC from parts, most often you purchase a computer case with the power supply already installed in it. However, you might need to exchange the present power supply because it's damaged, or because you need to upgrade to one with more power. In this section, you'll learn how to detect a faulty power supply and how to exchange one.

Power supplies can be dangerous

The power supply has capacitors inside it, which hold their electrical charge even after the power is disconnected. Never open the case of the power supply unless you are trained in how to protect yourself from high-voltage equipment.

Warning: If you do open the case to work inside the power supply, don't wear your antistatic bracelet. Recall that the bracelet grounds you, and you don't want to be a ground for the high voltage (110 to 120 volts) of the power supply!

Power supply troubleshooting guidelines

Problems with the PC's power supply or the house current might express themselves in the following ways:

- The PC sometimes halts during booting. After several tries, it boots successfully.
- Error codes or beep codes occur during booting, but the errors come and go.
- The computer stops or hangs for no reason. Sometimes it might even reboot itself.
- Memory errors appear intermittently.
- Data is written incorrectly to the hard drive.
- The keyboard stops working at odd times.
- The system board fails or is damaged.
- The power supply overheats and becomes hot to the touch.

An overheated system can cause intermittent problems. Use compressed air to blow the dust out of the power supply and the vents over the entire computer. Dust acts like an insulator and retains heat inside the computer case. Check that the power supply fan and the fan over the CPU are both working.

The symptoms of electrical power problems might be caused by a brownout (reduced current) of the house current or by a faulty power supply. If you suspect that the house current could be low, check the other devices that are using the same circuit. A copy machine, laser printer, or other heavy equipment might be drawing too much power. Remove the other devices from the same house circuit.

A system with a standard power supply of about 250 watts that has multiple hard drives, multiple CD-ROM drives, and several expansion cards is most likely operating above the rated capacity of the power supply, which can cause the system to perform unexpected reboots or give intermittent, otherwise unexplained errors. Calculate the total wattage requirements of all devices drawing power from the power supply and compare it to the rated capacity of the power supply.

Wattage is calculated as volts 3 amps. The power supply is rated in watts, and it should run at about 60 percent of its rated capacity or less. When operating at this capacity, the power supply lasts longer, runs cooler, and provides more consistent (or cleaner) power. In most cases, the computer's power supply is more than adequate if you add only one or two new devices. A project at the end of this chapter gives you practice calculating total wattage needs of a computer system. Upgrade the power supply as needed to accommodate an overloaded power system.

If these suggestions don't correct the problem, check the power supply by measuring the voltage output or by exchanging it for one you know is good. Remember that the power supply might give correct voltages when you measure it, but still be the source of problems.

An electrical conditioner might solve the problem of intermittent errors caused by noise in the power line to the PC. Try installing an electrical conditioner to monitor and condition the voltage to the PC. Conditioners are discussed later in the chapter.

The fan on the power supply stops working

Usually just before a fan stops working, it hums or whines, especially when the PC is first turned on. If this happens, replace the fan if you're trained to service the power supply. If not, then replace the entire power supply, which is considered an FRU (field replaceable unit) for a PC support technician. If you replace the power supply or fan and the fan still doesn't work, the problem might not be the fan. The problem might be caused by a short somewhere else in the system drawing too much power. Don't operate the PC with the fan not working. Computers without cooling fans can quickly overheat and damage chips.

Turn the power off and remove all power cord connections to all components, including the connections to the system board, and all power cords to drives. Turn the power back on. If the fan comes on, the problem is with one of the systems you disconnected, not with the power supply or its fan.

Turn the power off and reconnect the power cords to the drives. If the fan comes on, you can eliminate the drives as the problem. If the fan doesn't come on, try one drive after another until you identify the drive with the short.

If the drives aren't the problem, suspect the system board subsystem. With the power off, reconnect all power cords to the drives.

Turn the power off and remove the power to the system board by disconnecting P8 and P9 or P1. Turn the power back on.

If the fan comes back on, the problem is probably not the power supply, but a short in one of the components powered by the power cords to the system board. The power to the system board also powers interface cards.

Remove all interface cards and reconnect plugs to the system board.

If the fan still works, the problem is with one of the interface cards. If the fan doesn't work, the problem is with the system board or something still connected to it.

The system board, just as with all other components inside the computer case, should be grounded to the chassis. Look for a metal screw that grounds the board to the computer case. However, a short might be the problem with the electrical system if some component on the board is making improper contact with the chassis. This short can cause serious damage to the system board. Check for missing standoffs (small plastic or metal spacers that hold the system board a short distance away from the chassis), the problem that most often causes these improper connections.

Shorts in the circuits on the system board might also cause the problem. Look for damage on the bottom side of the system board. These circuits are coated with plastic, and quite often damage is difficult to spot.

Frayed wires on cable connections also can cause shorts. Disconnect hard drive cables connected directly to the system board. Power up with P8 and P9 or P1 connected, but with all cables disconnected from the system board. If the fan comes on, the problem is with one of the systems you disconnected.

Note: Never replace a damaged system board with a good one without first testing the power supply. You don't want to subject another good board to possible damage.

Upgrading the power supply

If you are installing a hard drive or CD-ROM drive and are concerned that the power supply might not be adequate, test it after you finish the installation. Make both the new drive and the floppy drive work at the same time by copying files from one to the other. If the new drive and the floppy drive each work independently, but data errors occur when both are working at the same time, suspect a shortage of electrical power.

If you prefer a more technical approach, you can estimate how much total wattage your system needs by calculating the watts for each circuit and adding them together as discussed earlier. In most cases, the computer's power supply is more than adequate if you add only one or two new devices.

Power supplies can be purchased separately. Power supplies for microcomputers range from 200 watts for a small desktop computer system to 600 watts for a tower floor model that uses a large amount of multimedia or other power-hungry devices.

Installing a new power supply

The easiest way to fix a power supply you suspect is faulty is to replace it. You can determine if the power supply really is the problem by turning off the PC, opening the computer case, and setting the new power supply on top of the old one. Disconnect the old power supply's cords and plug the PC devices into the new power supply. Turn on the PC and verify that the new power supply solves your problem before installing it.

If a new power supply is needed, follow these procedures:

1 Turn off the power and remove all external power cables from the power supply connections.

2 Remove the cover.

3 Disconnect all power cords from the power supply to other devices.

4 Determine which components must be removed before the power supply can be safely removed from the case. You might need to remove the hard drive, several cards, or the CD-ROM drive. In some cases, the system board might even need to be removed.

5 Remove all the components necessary to get to the power supply. Remember to protect the components from static electricity, as described in Chapter 8.

6 Unscrew the screws on the back of the computer case that hold the power supply to the case.

7 Look on the bottom of the case for slots that are holding the power supply in position. Often the power supply must be shifted in one direction to free it from the slots.

8 Remove the power supply.

9 Place the new power supply into position, sliding it into the slots used by the old power supply.

10 Replace the power supply screws.

11 Replace all other components.

12 Before replacing the case cover, connect the power cords, turn on the PC, and verify that all is working.

13 Test the voltage output of the new power supply and verify that it falls within acceptable ranges.

14 Turn off the PC and replace the cover.

Do it!

B-1:   Removing and replacing a power supply

Here's how
Student 1 removes the power supply:
1 Unplug your lab workstation
2 Unplug all of the power connectors
3 Locate the mounting screws of the power supply
4 Unscrew and dismount the power supply
Student 1 hands the power supply to student 2, who replaces it:
5 Place the power supply back into the mounting position
6 After verifying that the power supply is properly aligned, screw the screws into place
7 Attach each of the power connectors to their respective devices
8 Plug in the power cord
9 Stand clear of the lab workstation and power it on
Verify that all of the devices are functioning properly

Topic C: Surge protection and battery backup

Explanation

There is a wide range of devices on the market that filter the AC input to computers and their peripherals (this is, condition the AC input to eliminate highs and lows) and that provide backup power when the AC current fails. These devices, installed between the house current and the computer, fall into three general categories: surge suppressors, power conditioners, and uninterruptible power supplies (UPSs). All these devices should have the UL (Underwriters Laboratory) logo, which ensures that the device has been tested by this agency, a provider of product safety certification.

Surge suppressors

A *surge suppressor*, also called a *surge protector*, provides a row of power outlets and an on/off switch that protects equipment from overvoltages on AC power lines and telephone lines. Surge suppressors can come as power strips (but not all power strips have surge protection), wall-mounted units that plug into AC outlets, or consoles designed to sit on a desk top with the monitor placed on top. Some provide an RJ-11 telephone jack to protect modems and fax machines from spikes.

Note: Whenever there is a power outage, unless you have a reliable power conditioner or UPS installed, unplug all power cords to the PC, printers, monitors, etc. Sometimes when the power returns there are sudden spikes accompanied by another brief outage. You don't want to subject your equipment to these surges.

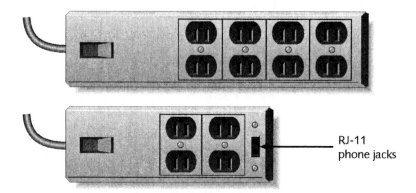

RJ-11
phone jacks

Exhibit 9-5: Power strips with surge suppression

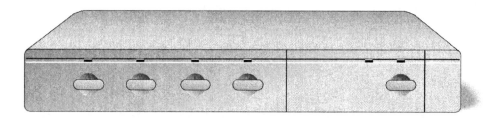

Exhibit 9-6: Some surge suppressors sit under the monitor

Surge suppressors aren't always reliable, and once the fuse inside the suppressor is blown, a surge suppressor no longer protects from a power surge. It continues to provide power without warning you that the protection is lost. The performance of a surge suppressor as protection against spikes is measured in two ways: let-through voltage and joules.

The maximum voltage that can pass through a suppressor to the device being protected is called the *let-through*. Less is better. The better units are expected to let through under 330 volts. Less expensive suppressors let through 400 volts or more.

The degree of protection of a surge suppressor can be measured in *joules*, a measure of energy that takes into account both voltage and current over a one-second interval. More is better. Look for devices that offer at least 240 joules of protection.

A surge suppressor might be a shunt type that absorbs the surge or might be a series type that blocks the surge from flowing, or it might be a combination of the two. The shunt-type suppressor is measured by *clamping voltage*, a term that describes the let-through voltage.

When buying a surge suppressor, look for those that guarantee against damage from lightning and that reimburse for equipment destroyed while the surge suppressor is in use.

Data line protectors

A *data line protector* serves the same function for your telephone line to your modem that a surge suppressor does for the electrical lines. Telephone lines carry a small current of electricity and need to be protected against spikes, just as electrical lines do. The let-through rating for a data line protector for a phone line should be no more than 260 volts.

Measuring power ranges of devices

The next two types of protective devices are power conditioners and uninterruptible power supplies, both of which condition (alter so as to provide continuous voltages) the power passing through them. They provide a degree of protection against spikes (temporary surges of voltage) and raise the voltage when it drops during brownouts (temporary reductions of voltage). Both types of devices are measured by the load they support in watts, volt-amperes (VA), or kilovolt-amperes (kVA).

To determine how much VA is required to support your system, multiply the amperage of each component by 120 volts and then add up the VA for all components. For example, a 17-inch monitor has 1.9 A written on the back of the monitor, which means 1.9 amps. Multiply that value times 120 volts and you see that 228 VA is required. A Pentium PC with a 17-inch monitor and tape backup system requires about 500 VA of support.

Power conditioners

In addition to providing protection against spikes, *power conditioners* also regulate, or condition, the power, providing continuous voltage during brownouts. These voltage regulators, sometimes called *line conditioners*, can come as small desktop units.

Low-cost line conditioners use a stepped transformer to adjust the output voltage. Higher priced models use a *ferroresonant regulator*, which contains a magnetic coil that can retain a charge of power to be used to raise the voltage during a brownout.

These electricity filters are a good investment if the AC current in your community suffers from excessive spikes and brownouts. However, if the device is rated under 1 kVA, it will probably provide only corrections for brownouts, and not spikes. Line conditioners, like surge suppressors, provide no protection against a total blackout.

Exhibit 9-7: A power conditioner

Do it!

C-1: Installing a surge protector

Here's how
1 Power off your lab workstation
2 Power off your monitor and any other peripheral devices
3 Plug the provided surge protector into the wall outlet
4 Plug each of your peripheral devices into the surge protector (this includes the system unit and monitor)
5 Power on the surge protector
6 Power on your lab workstation
7 Power on your monitor and other peripheral devices (this includes the system unit and monitor)
8 Verify that your PC functions properly

Uninterruptible Power Supply (UPS)

Explanation   Unlike a power conditioner, the *UPS* (*uninterruptible power supply*) provides a backup power supply in the event the AC current fails completely. The UPS also offers some filtering of the AC current. A UPS device is designed as either a standby device, an inline device, or a line-interactive device (which combines features of the first two). Among these three UPS devices, there are several variations on the market, whose prices vary widely.

A common UPS device is a rather heavy box that plugs into an AC outlet and provides one or more outlets for the computer and its peripherals. It has an on/off switch, requires no maintenance, and is very simple to install.

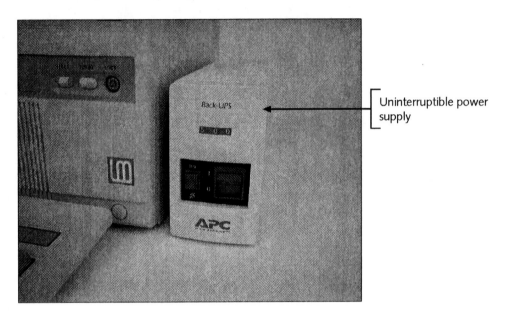

Uninterruptible power supply

Exhibit 9-8: An uninterruptible power supply (UPS)

Standby and inline UPSs differ in the circuit the devices use as the primary circuit, and in the way they function when the AC power fails. A *standby UPS* switches circuits from the AC circuit to the battery-powered circuit. In contrast, the *inline UPS* continually provides power through the battery-powered circuit and therefore requires no switching, which ensures continuous power.

UPS prices increase dramatically depending on the features offered. A UPS device is rated according to the amount of power it can provide, in VA during a complete blackout, and the length of time it can sustain that power. Most UPSs for microcomputer systems claim to provide backup power for only about 15 minutes, only enough time to save any work in progress and to do an orderly shutdown. The high cost of a UPS prohibits greater power.

The standby UPS

Exhibit 9-9 shows how UPSs work. The solid line represents the primary circuit by which electricity normally flows. The dashed line represents the secondary circuit that's used when the AC current fails. For the standby UPS, the primary circuit is the house AC current circuit with an inline surge suppressor and filter. A relatively small amount of the current flows to the secondary circuit to keep the battery charged in case it's ever needed. When the AC current fails, the UPS switches from the primary to the secondary circuit and the battery provides the power, which is converted from DC to AC before it leaves the UPS.

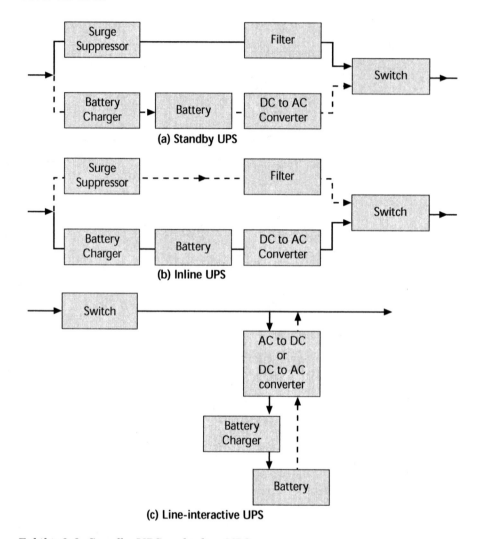

Exhibit 9-9: Standby UPS and inline UPS

The switching time (the time it takes for the UPS to switch from the AC circuit to the battery-charged circuit) caused problems for earlier computers, even causing PCs to reboot. Today, however, computer power supplies are better designed and able to keep a computer running during the fraction of a second it takes to switch the power in the UPS. One variation on a standby UPS, is that it uses a ferroresonant regulator to deliver power to the circuit during the switching time, to virtually eliminate any interruption of power.

Other variations of this type of UPS reduce costs by eliminating the filter. The purpose of the filter is to condition the AC current, reducing the effect of brownouts and spikes. These electricity filters, or line conditioners, must be purchased separately.

The inline UPS

Notice that the inline UPS uses the battery-powered circuit as the primary circuit, instead of the AC circuit. The AC circuit is used only if the battery-powered circuit registers any error conditions caused by the failure of some component in the circuit. These conditions aren't related to spikes, brownouts, or blackouts of the AC current, but rather to the performance of the components.

With inline UPSs, when the AC current fails, no switching is needed because the primary circuit continues to be the battery-powered circuit. The only thing that's lost is the battery's recharging. These UPS devices are sometimes called true UPSs, because they truly do provide uninterruptible power.

The inline UPS also provides more line conditioning than does the standby UPS, and, because of the clean, constant 120-volt current it produces, it can extend the life of computer equipment. Because the inline UPS converts the AC power to battery power in DC and then back to AC power, the inline design is sometimes referred to as *double conversion*. Because the battery is in constant use, the inline UPS battery tends to wear out sooner than does the standby UPS battery.

The inline UPS is more expensive than the standby UPS; one less-expensive variation eliminates the secondary circuit altogether, leaving the battery-charged circuit with no backup.

The line-interactive UPS

The *line-interactive UPS* is a variation of the standby UPS that shortens the switching time by always keeping the inverter working, so that there's no charging-up time for the inverter. An inverter is a device that converts DC to AC. However, during regular operation, the inverter filters electricity and charges the battery by converting AC to DC. If the power fails, the inverter switches roles and begins to convert the battery's DC to AC. The delay for the inverter to switch roles is shorter than the delay for a standby UPS that must start up the inverter.

The line-interactive UPS also offers good line conditioning because there is an automatic voltage regulator, called the *buck-boost* feature. During spikes in electrical power, the regulator decreases (in other words, bucks) the voltage, and it boosts it during brownouts. The boost feature means that the line-interactive UPS doesn't need to draw on battery power to respond to a brownout, as does the true standby UPS.

The intelligent UPS

Some UPSs can be controlled by software from a computer, for additional functionality. For example, from the front panel of some UPSs you can check for a weak battery. If the UPS is an *intelligent UPS*, you can perform the same function from the utility software installed on your computer. In order for a UPS to accommodate this feature, it must have a serial port connection to the PC and a microprocessor on board. Some of the things this utility software and an intelligent UPS can do are:

- Diagnose the UPS.
- Check for a weak battery.
- Monitor the quality of electricity received.
- Monitor the percentage of load the UPS is carrying during a blackout.
- Automatically schedule the weak-battery test or UPS diagnostic test.
- Send an alarm to workstations on a network to prepare for a shutdown.
- Close down all servers protected by the UPS during a blackout.
- Provide pager notification to a facilities manager if the power goes out during weekends.
- After a shutdown, perform startup from a remote location over phone lines.

Windows NT and Windows 2000 offer support for intelligent UPSs. You can monitor and control the devices from the Power Options dialog box accessible through Control Panel. The Windows 2000 controls were developed by Microsoft and American Power Conversion (APC), a leading manufacturer of UPSs.

Buying a UPS

The power supplies in most computers can operate over a wide range of electrical voltage input, but operating the computer under these conditions for extended periods of time can shorten the life not only of the power supply, but also of the computer as well. Power protection devices offer these benefits:

- Condition the line for both brownouts and spikes.
- Provide backup power during a blackout.
- Protect against very high spikes that could damage the equipment.

When you purchase a UPS, cost often drives the decision about how much and what kind of protection you buy. However, don't buy an inline UPS that runs at full capacity. A battery charger operating at full capacity produces heat, which can reduce the life of the battery. The UPS rating should exceed your total VA or wattage output by at least 25 percent. Also be aware of the degree of line conditioning that the UPS provides. Consider the warranty and service policies as well as the guarantee the UPS manufacturer gives for the equipment that the UPS protects.

Do it!

C-2:   Installing a UPS

Here's how

1   Power off your system unit

2   Power off any additional peripherals that you want to be protected by the UPS device

3   Unplug the system unit and the peripheral devices

4   Plug the UPS device into the wall outlet

5   Plug the system unit into the UPS device

6   Plug the additional peripheral devices into the UPS

7   Power on the UPS device

8   Power on the system unit and additionally protected peripherals

9   Verify that the system unit and each additionally protected device are functioning properly

   Observe the functionality of the UPS as follows:

10   Power on your system unit and boot into Windows 9x

11   Power on your additional peripheral devices

12   Unplug the UPS device

13   Record the results

Topic D: Energy Star (Green Star) computers

Explanation

Energy Star computers and peripherals have the U.S. Green Star, which indicates that they satisfy certain energy-conserving standards of the U.S. Environmental Protection Agency (EPA). Devices that can carry the Green Star are computers, monitors, printers, copiers, and fax machines. Such devices are designed to decrease the overall consumption of electricity in the U.S. to protect and preserve our natural resources. These standards, sometimes called the Green Standards, generally mean that the computer or the device has a standby program that switches the device to sleep mode when it's not being used. During sleep mode, the device must use no more than 30 watts of power.

Office equipment is among the fastest growing source of power consumption in industrialized nations. Much of this electricity is wasted, because computers and other equipment are often left on overnight. Because Energy Star devices go into sleep mode when they are unused, they create an overall energy savings of about 50 percent.

Energy Star PCs

Computer systems use three power management methods to conserve energy:

- Advanced Power Management (APM), championed by Intel and Microsoft
- AT Attachment (ATA) for IDE drives
- Display Power Management Signaling (DPMS) standards for monitors and video cards

These energy-saving features are designed to work in incremental steps, depending on how long the PC is idle. The features can sometimes be enabled and adjusted by using CMOS setup or using the OS. In CMOS setup, a feature might not be available, setup might include additional features, or a feature might be labeled differently from those described below.

Green Timer on the System Board

This sets the number of minutes of inactivity that must pass before the CPU goes into sleep mode. You can enable or disable the setting and select the elapse time in number of minutes.

Doze Time

Doze time is the time that elapses before the system reduces 80 percent of its power consumption. This is accomplished in different ways by different systems. For example, when one system enters Doze mode, the system BIOS slows down the bus clock speed.

Standby Time

The time before the system reduces 92 percent of its power consumption is Standby time. For example, a system might accomplish this by changing the system speed from turbo to slow and suspending the video signal.

Suspend Time

The time before the system reduces 99 percent of its power consumption is Suspend time. The way this reduction is accomplished varies. The CPU clock might be stopped and the video signal suspended. After entering suspend mode, the system needs a warm-up time so that the CPU, monitor, and other components can reach full activity.

Hard Drive Standby Time

Hard drive standby time is the amount of time before a hard drive shuts down.

Sample Power Management Setup Screen

Exhibit 9-10 shows the Power Management Setup screen of the CMOS setup for Award BIOS for an ATX Pentium II system board. Using the Video options on the left of the screen, you can enable or disable power management of the monitor. When power management is enabled, you can control Energy Star features. The PM Timers feature controls doze, standby, and suspend modes for the hard drive. The Power Up Control determines the way the system can be controlled when it's started or when power to the computer is interrupted. The features on the right side of the screen monitor the power supply fan, CPU fan, optional chassis fan, temperatures of the CPU and the motherboard (MB), and voltage output to the CPU and system board.

```
                    ROM PCI/ISA BIOS (<<P2B>>)
                    POWER MANAGEMENT SETUP
                    AWARD SOFTWARE, INC.

Power Management    : User Define    ** Fan Monitor **
Video Off Option    : Suspend -> Off  Chasis Fan Speed    :  3300RMP
Video Off Method    : DPMS OFF        CPU Fan Speed       :  3800RMP
                                      Power Fan Speed     :  Ignore
     ** PM Timers **                 ** Thermal Monitor **
HDD Power Down       : Disable        CPU Temperature     :  50C/ 112F
Suspend Mode        : Disable         MB Temperature      :  25C/  77F
                                      ** Voltage Monitor **
   ** Power Up Control **            VCORE Voltage        :  3.3V
PWR Button < 4 Secs  : Soft Off      +3.3V Voltage        :  3.3V
PWR Up On Modem Act  : Enabled       +5V  Voltage         :  5.0V
AC PWR Loss Restart  : Disabled      +12V Voltage         :  12.0V
Wake On LAN          : Enabled       -12V Voltage         :  -12.0V
Automatic Power Up   : Disabled      -5V  Voltage         :  -5.0V

                                     ESC   : Quit      ↑↓→←: Select Item
                                     F1    : Help      PU/PD/+/- : Modify
                                     F5    : Old Values (Shift)F2 : Color
                                     F6    : Load BIOS  Defaults
                                     F7    : Load Setup Defaults
```

Exhibit 9-10: A Power Management Setup screen showing power management features

Energy Star monitors

Most computers and monitors sold today are Energy-Star-compliant, displaying the green Energy Star logo onscreen when the PC is booting.

In order for a monitor's power-saving feature to function, the video card or computer must also support this function. Most monitors that follow the Energy Star standards adhere to the Display Power Management Signaling (DPMS) specifications developed by VESA, which enable the video card and monitor to go into sleep mode simultaneously.

Do it!

D-1: Examining an Energy Star monitor

Here's how	Here's why
1 At the Windows 98 computer, display the desktop	If you're using a Windows 95 machine, open the Display Properties. On the Settings tab, select Change Display Type and observe the check box.
2 Right-click and choose **Properties**	
3 Click the **Settings** tab	
4 Click the **Advanced** button	To display the Monitor Properties dialog box.
5 Click the **Monitor** tab	

Windows 9x sometimes recognizes that a monitor is an Energy Star monitor by its brand and model.

6 Click **Cancel**	To close the Monitor properties.
7 Click the **Screen Saver** tab	To use the Energy Star features of your monitor.
Click the **Settings** button	

8 Observe the Power Schemes tab

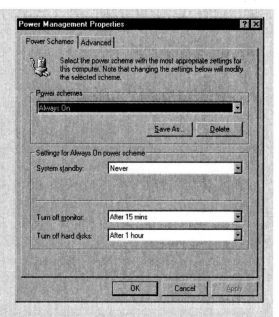

You can set system standby to activate after a specified number of minutes. Select the minutes under Turn off monitor to activate sleep mode. Read the documentation that comes with your monitor to learn about the energy-saving features.

9 Click the **Advanced** tab

10 Observe the settings

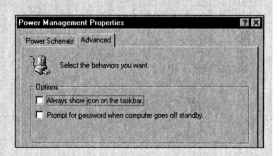

You can add the Power Management icon to the taskbar for easier access.

11 Close all open dialog boxes

Unit summary: Electricity and power supplies

Topic A   You learned how to use a **multimeter** to measure the **voltage** of a computer power supply and the **voltage output** of system boards, floppy drives, and hard drives.

Topic B   You learned how to **troubleshoot electrical problems** with a computer, determine whether the power supply is faulty, **test the power supply** for insufficient power, and **install a new power supply**.

Topic C   You learned how to protect computer equipment from **overvoltages** on AC power lines with **surge protectors**. Power conditioners do this and also maintain consistent power during brief brownouts. **UPSs** provide protection against surges and brownouts, and also provide battery backup in case of total failure of AC current.

Topic D   In this topic, you learned about **Energy Star computers** and **monitors** that can be used to conserve resources. You examined the various energy-saving features and observed the **power management options** for a Green monitor.

Review questions

1   What are the five voltages produced by an ATX power supply?

2   What are the four voltages produced by an AT power supply?

3   Why is a power supply dangerous even after the power is disconnected?

4   List some of the symptoms that indicate a faulty power supply.

5 If you measure the voltage of a power supply and find it to be within acceptable ranges, why is it still possible that the power supply may be faulty?

6 With the PC power turned on, if you have set a DVM to measure voltage and place one probe on a ground lead of a hard drive power connection and the other probe on the computer case, what will be the voltage reading?

7 What are the two main types of uninterruptible power supplies?

8 How does an intelligent UPS differ from one that's not intelligent?

9 Name two ways that a surge suppressor is measured.

Unit 10

Communicating over phone lines

Unit time: 75 minutes

Complete this unit, and you'll know how to:

A Install and configure a modem and understand its basic function.

B Troubleshoot common modem communication problems.

C Define alternative communication technologies that include ISDN, DSL, cable modems, and satellite.

Topic A: Modem basics

Explanation

Most personal computers today have modems. In fact, modems are almost considered standard equipment on new PCs that target the home market because of the popularity of e-mail, the Internet, and the World Wide Web, and also because telecommunication employees offer advantages to their companies. However, there is a speed ceiling on regular phone lines, which is resulting in an emphasis on the development of digital alternatives, such as ISDN and DSL—digital replacements for regular phone lines and cable modems.

Overview of modems

The *modem*, a device used by a PC to communicate over a phone line, is both hardware and firmware. Inside an external modem or on an internal modem card is firmware on ROM chips that contain the protocol and instructions needed to format and convert data so that it can be transported over phone lines to a receiving modem on the other end. In general, modems are considered to be hardware, but it's fundamental to an understanding of communications that they also be considered firmware.

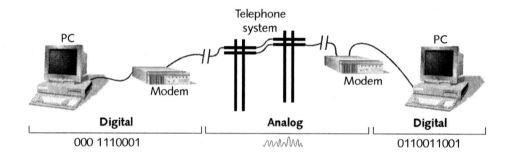

Exhibit 10-1: Modems convert data from digital to analog and back again

Computers are digital; regular phone lines are analog. Data is stored inside a PC and communicated to a modem as binary or digital data—that is, 0s and 1s. A modem converts this binary or digital data into an analog signal (this process is called *modulation*) that can travel over a phone line. The modem at the receiving end then converts the data back to digital (this process is called *demodulation*) before passing it on to the receiving PC. The two processes of MOdulation/DEModulation lead to the name of the device: modem.

Exhibit 10-2: SupraSonic external modem

Flash ROM microchip

Exhibit 10-3: 3Com U.S. Robotics 56k Winmodem modem card

To reduce total cost of a computer system, some system boards have a small expansion slot, less than half the length of a PCI slot, called an Audio/Modem Riser (AMR) slot or a Communication and Networking Riser (CNR) slot. The small slot accommodates a small, inexpensive type of modem card called a modem riser card. In addition, the AMR slot can support an audio riser card, and the CNR slot can support an audio riser card or a networking riser card. A riser card has part of the audio, modem, or networking logic on the card and part on a controller on the system board.

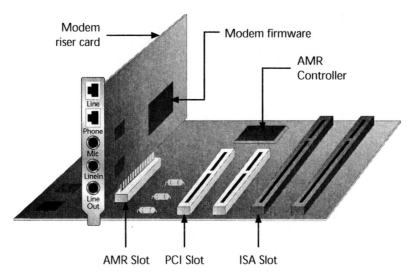

Figure 16-6   An audio/modem riser slot can accommodate an inexpensive modem riser card

Exhibit 10-4: An audio/modem riser slot can accommodate an inexpensive modem riser card

An analog signal is made up of an infinite number of possible values in its range of values, but a *digital signal* has only a finite number of values in its range of values. Remember also that phone lines were designed to transmit sound (that is, the human voice, which is analog). Sound traveling over regular phone lines is transmitted as analog signals, meaning that there are an infinite number of sound values, just as there are an infinite number of sound values in the human voice. When data is transmitted over phone lines, even though the data from a PC is inherently digital, it too must be converted to an analog signal to use telephone technology. Think of PC data as being converted from two simple states or measurements (0 and 1, or off and on) to waves (such as sound waves), which have a potentially infinite number of states or measurements. Modems use different characteristics of waves to correspond with the 0s and 1s of digital communication.

Two PCs communicate over phone lines by using either internal or external modems. Either way, the modem provides a connection for a regular phone line called an *RJ-11* connection, which is the same type of connection that you see for a regular phone wall outlet. In addition to a line-in connection from the wall outlet, a modem also has an extra RJ-11 connection for a telephone.

A modem must be able to both receive and transmit data. Communication in which there can be transmission in only one direction at a time is called *half-duplex*; an example of this type of communication is a CB radio. A modem that can communicate in only one direction at a time is called a half-duplex modem. Communication that transmits in both directions at the same time is called *full-duplex*; regular voice phone conversations are an example of full-duplex communication. If a modem can communicate in both directions at the same time, it's called a full-duplex modem.

Modem properties

When you first use a modem to make a dial-up call to another PC, you hear the modem making noises as the dial-up is completed. The two modems are establishing the rules of communication between them. What you hear are the sounds being sent over the phone lines as the two modems negotiate these rules. This process is called training or *handshaking*. Modems use one of many protocols (agreed-on methods of communication) to communicate, and, in this handshaking phase, the calling modem and the receiving modem are communicating the protocols and speeds they can support, and arriving at the best possible common solution. The decisions made about protocols include how to handle data compression and error checking, and what methods of data transfer will be used.

Modem speeds

The speed at which a modem passes data over phone lines is partly determined by the transmission standard the modem is using. Modem speed is measured either in *baud rate* (named after the inventor, J. M. E. Baudot), which is the number of times a signal changes in one second, or in bits per second (bps); bps is the more common unit of measurement. For slower baud rates, one signal represents one bit (in which case baud rate is equal to bps rate); slower modems are often measured in baud rates. For faster baud rates, one signal can represent more than one bit, so faster modems are measured in bps (and baud rates might differ from bps rates). When measuring modem speed by using baud rate, the number of bps will always be equal to or a multiple of the baud rate. The most commonly rated speeds of modems in use today are 14.4 Kbps, 28.8 Kbps, 33.6 Kbps, and 56.6 Kbps. The maximum speed of a modem is often written into the manufacturer's name for the modem.

Because of the sampling rate used by phone companies when converting an analog signal to digital, taking into account the overhead of data transmission (bits and bytes sent with the data that are used to control and define transmissions), the maximum transmission rate that a modem can attain over a regular phone line is about 56,000 bps or 56 Kbps.

The line also often has some disturbance, called *noise*, which can be caused by lines bumping against one another in the wind, fluorescent lighting, nearby radios or TVs, bad wiring, lightning, and so forth. This reduction in line quality is called a dirty or noisy line. A line that consistently produces high-quality results is called a clean line.

Modem standards

The telecommunications industry sets several modem standards to determine modem speed and protocols. The industry-approved standards for international communication were written by Comité Consultatif Internationale de Télégraphique et Téléphonique (CCITT). In 1992, the CCITT organization was incorporated into the International Telecommunications Union (ITU), an intergovernmental organization approved by the United Nations to be responsible for adopting standards governing telecommunications. You might see the standards used by modems referred to as the CCITT standards (more common) or as the ITU standards.

When one modem dials another modem, during the handshake they attempt to establish a communications protocol or standard at the fastest speed that both can support. The receiving modem takes the lead in negotiating these protocols by offering its best solution. If the calling modem doesn't respond to this protocol, the receiving modem continues to offer a slower protocol until they agree on the fastest possible solution common to both. Data-compression and error-checking protocols also are negotiated and agreed upon during the handshake, if both modems can support the same standards for these features.

Modems with 56 Kbps speeds

Before 1998, there were two standards for 56 Kbps transmission, the x2 standard supported by U.S. Robotics and the K56flex standard supported by Lucent Technologies and Rockwell International Corp. These two standards were not compatible with one another. Because of this incompatibility, all three companies agreed to support a third standard for 56 Kbps transmission. This standard, called the V.90 standard for 56 Kbps, was published by ITU in February 1998. If you have a modem that uses either the x2 or the K56flex standard, it's likely that you can upgrade the Flash ROM on the modem card to use the new standard. See the Web site of the modem manufacturer for more information.

Another concern about buying a 56 Kbps modem is that, if your phone line is too noisy, the modem can't attain the high speed. 3Com, a modem manufacturer, offers a way for you to test your phone line to determine if it qualifies, before you buy a 56-Kbps modem. With a modem using the V.34 standard, access the 3Com Web site (www.3com.com/56k/need4_56k/linetest.html) and read and follow the directions to have the 3Com program analyze your line.

Although modems are rated and advertised to transmit at 56 Kbps, this speed is seldom accomplished. When one PC is communicating with another, even if both PCs are equipped with 56K modems and using clean phones lines, most likely the actual attained speed will not exceed 34 Kbps. When a PC is connected to an Internet service provider (ISP), to come close to the 56-Kbps transmission, the ISP's incoming lines must be digital rather than analog. Even so, the transmission from the provider to the PC (called downstream transmission) is only about 53 Kbps, and the transmission from the PC to the provider (called upstream transmission) doesn't exceed 34 Kbps.

Data compression

The modem includes the firmware (permanent programming) housed on the modem, which can perform error correction and data compression. These and other functions of data communication can be performed by either hardware (firmware on the modem) or software (programs on the PC).

When data compression is performed by a modem, it applies to all data that's transmitted by the modem. If data compression is performed by the software on a PC, it applies to single-file transfer operation.

Data compression done by the modem follows either the MNP-5, CCITT V.42, or V.42bis protocol. All three of these protocols also perform error correction. A modem using one of these methods of data compression is communicating to its computer at higher speeds than it's communicating to the phone line. This is because the data is being compressed at the modem and, therefore, there are more bits coming from the local computer into the modem than are transmitted over the phone line (assuming, of course, that few errors occur). This fact might cause the overall speed of the data transmission at the PC to appear much faster than the actual phone line transmission rate.

The compression ratio of MNP-5 is 2:1, and V.42bis can have up to a 4:1 compression ratio. MNP-5 also has more overhead in its compression methods, and sometimes, if a file is already compressed (such as a ZIP file), because of this overhead, the actual transmission time increases because MNP-5. V.42 can determine whether a file is already compressed, and therefore doesn't compress it a second time.

Error correction

The standards that include error correction are MNP-4, CCITT V.42, and CCITT V.42bis. One modem often supports all three standards. If it doesn't, during the handshaking process, the answering modem tries to establish an error-correction protocol with the other modem by first suggesting the fastest, best standard. If the calling modem responds by accepting that standard, then it's used by both. If the calling modem doesn't support the suggested protocol, then the two modems negotiate to find the best protocol they both can use, or they simply decide not to use error correction.

Error correction works by breaking data up into small packets called *frames*. The sending modem performs some calculations on a frame of data and sums these calculations into a checksum. A *checksum* is a summary calculation of data and will later be used to check or verify the accuracy of the data when received. Checksum works somewhat like a parity bit, except that it's a little more complicated and applies to more data. The checksum is attached to the data frame, and they're transmitted together. The receiving modem performs the same calculations and compares its answer to the checksum value received. If they don't agree, then the receiving modem requests a new transmission of the packet. This process does slow down the transmission of data, especially on dirty or noisy phone lines, but accuracy is almost 100 percent guaranteed.

Modem features

In addition to the speed, protocols, data compression, and error correction that are used to rate a modem, there are other features. Some additional abilities you might want to look for in a modem are:

- Caller ID (provided that you subscribe to this service from the phone company) is supported.
- Display readout on external modems provides information about the status of the modem.
- Flash ROM enables you to upgrade your modem to support future standards.
- Plug and Play for Windows 9x makes modem installation more automatic.
- Voice/data capability enables the modem to also serve as a telephone, complete with built-in speaker and microphone.
- Auto-answer makes it possible for the modem to receive incoming calls while you're away from the PC.

Do it!

A-1: Discussing modem properties and features

Question	Answer
1 Define modem.	
2 What type of communication happens in only one direction at a time?	
3 Why is the maximum transmission rate of today's modems limited to 56.6 Kbps?	
4 What's the difference between hardware data compression and software data compression?	
5 Define handshaking.	
6 Name three features you might find on a modem.	

How modems communicate with hardware

Explanation

PCs don't communicate with modems in the same way that modems communicate with other modems. Transmission speeds, error checking, and data format from the PC to the modem (DTE to DCE) are different than they are between a modem and another modem (DCE to DCE). Remember that a modem might be an internal or an external modem. As you study communication between DTEs and DCEs, the concepts are easier to visualize if you think of a PC and an external modem sitting beside it connected by a serial cable. However, the same concepts apply to an internal modem as to an external modem, even though the modem card and the PC aren't connected by a cable.

Transmission speed

Data transmission involves three speeds: the speed between the calling PC and its modem (called the port speed), the speed between the two modems (called the modem speed or the line speed), and the port speed between the answering PC and its modem. The overall speed of data transmission is affected by each of these speeds. As a general rule, port speed should be at least four times as fast as modem speed.

The UART

Recall that the chip responsible for any communication over a serial port is the UART (universal asynchronous receiver-transmitter), sometimes called an ACIA (asynchronous communications interface adapter). The UART controls the port speed as well as other features of serial port communications.

The FIFO (first-in-first-out) buffer is needed by the UART chip to temporarily hold data as it's received or transmitted. If your UART chip has a buffer, you can control its size as well as the port speed from the Modems Properties box of Windows 9x.

If you have a very fast external modem with data compression, but your UART can't support the same speed, the modem can't attain its maximum speed. The solution might be to upgrade your UART or to install an I/O controller card with a fast UART chip. You can use the MSD (Microsoft Diagnostics) utility to determine which UART you have on your PC. When reading documentation about the speed of communication over phone lines, you might see the UART or port speed referred to as the DTE speed, and the modem or line speed called the DCE speed.

External modems connect to a PC by way of a serial port, and therefore use the UART on the system board that controls this serial port. In this case, data from the system board travels over the serial cable to the modem in digital form, so the external modem must have a UART in it to receive the digital data. Sometimes the external modem might combine the UART logic into other chips in the modem.

Internal modems are expansion cards that connect to the system board by way of an ISA or a PCI expansion slot. Internal modems have their own UART on the modem card and provide their own serial port logic to the computer system. This is why an internal modem must be configured to have its own COM port assigned to it for its UART to control. A typical configuration for a PC is to have COM1 assigned to the serial mouse and COM2 assigned to the internal modem. (An external modem doesn't need a COM port assigned to it, because it uses the existing COM port already configured on the system.) The UART on the system board holding the internal modem isn't used by the modem, because the modem isn't using the COM ports on the system board.

Flow control

Three speeds affect the overall speed of data transmission, line speed and the port speeds of the sending and receiving computers. Because each speed can differ, a way is needed to stop the data from flowing when either the DTE or DCE needs to catch up. For example, if the receiving modem is receiving data faster than it can uncompress it and pass it off to its PC, it must stop the flow coming from the remote modem long enough to catch up. Flow control is a method of controlling the flow of data by sending a message to stop data flow. Either the receiving PC or the receiving modem can initiate a flow control message.

There are two methods of flow control: flow control over software channels, called *Xon/Xoff protocol*, and flow control over hardware channels, called *RTS/CTS protocol*. In software flow control, the receiving device transmits a message to the sending device to pause transmission by sending a special control character within the same channel (frequency) in which data is sent. This method is called in-band signaling. The control character to stop the data from flowing, Xoff, is Control-S, sent as an ASCII character with an ASCII value of 19. This method of flow control works well as long as only ASCII data is transmitted, but if data is transmitted in some other coding format, the control characters might be valid data and be mistakenly included in the data stream as regular data, which will cause problems with communication. Another problem with software flow control is that data needs to be continually monitored to detect the signals, and, at the high speeds at which data is transmitted today, the control character might not be detected in time to stop the data.

Instead of embedding signals within data, hardware flow control uses electrical signals from a PC to its modem that aren't part of the data flow channel; this is called *out-of-band signaling*. Hardware flow control is a way for a PC to tell its modem to stop the other modem from sending data. When the first (receiving) modem receives the signal from its PC, it just deactivates the line between the two modems, forcing the other modem to wait.

Additional UART protocols

When a UART chip from a sending device sends digital data to a sending modem, it first prepares the data to be received by the UART chip on the other end. When the UART chip on the receiving end of the transmission receives digital data from its modem, it performs some error checking based on information sent to it from the sending UART chip

Just as the two modems agree to use the same protocols, both the sending and receiving UART chips must have determined to use the same protocol to send and receive data, for communication to take place. The five protocols for digital communication between two PCs, as controlled by their UART chips, are listed in the following table.

Port setting	Description	Common values
Bits per second (port speed)	What will be the speed of transmission in bps?	2400; 4800; 9600; 19,200; 38,400; 57,600; 115,200; 230,400; 460,800; 921,600 bps
Data bits	How many bits are to be used to send a single character of data?	7 or 8 bits
Parity	Will there be error checking, and if so, what will be its format?	Odd, even, or none
Stop bits	What will be the code to indicate that a character (its string of bits) is starting or ending?	1, 1.5, or 2 bits
Flow control	How will the flow of data be controlled?	Xon/Xoff or hardware

Data bits

Historically, when data sent across modems was in ASCII format, the question of how many bits are necessary to send one ASCII character arose. The answer was critical because the maximum number of bits needed to represent one ASCII character is 7 bits, not 8. Therefore, to transmit in ASCII really requires that only 7 bits be used per character. The choice, therefore, for character transmission is either 7 or 8 data bits. Most often today, you should choose 8 data bits unless you know that you're transmitting only in ASCII.

Parity

Parity checking in telecommunications is performed in much the same way that memory on a system board checks parity. When you use 7 data bits, add an extra bit, which can be 0 or 1 to make either odd or even parity. The receiving UART chip compares the parity to its count of odd or even bits to check the data bits for errors. In most cases today, you don't want the UART chip to use parity checking. Error checking as well as error correction can be better performed by the modem.

Stop bits

Whenever the sending UART chip is ready to send a group of data bits (a character) to the receiving UART chip, it puts one start bit in front of the data bits to indicate to the receiving UART chip that a character is starting. In most cases, the UART chip also sends one stop bit to indicate that the character is complete, although two stop bits can be selected.

Do it!

A-2: Examining the modem to hardware relationship

Question	Answer
1 Describe the difference between port speed and modem speed.	
2 Why is a modem required to support more than one standard for transmission speed?	
3 What is the UART chip in an internal modem recognized as?	
4 Do external modems contain UART chips?	
5 During data transmission, what two devices can initiate a flow control message?	
6 Why is hardware flow control better than software flow control?	
7 Why is it best to not have the UART chip perform parity checking?	

Installing a modem

Explanation

Follow these steps to install an internal modem:

1 Read the modem documentation.

2 Determine which serial port is available on your system.

3 Set any jumpers or DIP switches on the modem card. (See your documentation for details about your card. Common jumper and DIP switch settings are for COM ports, IRQ, and I/O addresses, and indicate whether the card will use Plug and Play.)

Jumper bank for
IRQ setting

Jumper bank for COM
port selection

Exhibit 10-5: Modem jumper blocks—use Plug and Play if available

4 Turn off your computer and remove the case. Find an empty slot, remove the faceplate, and save the screw. Mount the card firmly into the slot and replace the screw to anchor the card.

5 Replace the cover. (You might choose to test the modem before replacing the cover.)

6 Plug the telephone line from the house into the line jack on the modem. The second RJ-11 jack on the modem is for an optional telephone. It's used to connect a phone so that you can easily use this same phone jack for voice communication.

For an external modem, follow these steps:

1 You need an RS-232c serial cable to connect the modem to the serial port. If the modem doesn't come with a cable, don't skimp on price here; buy a good quality cable. Connect the cable to the modem and to the serial port.

2 Plug the electrical cord from the modem into a 110V AC outlet.

3 Plug the telephone line from the house into the line jack on the modem. The second jack on the modem is for an optional telephone.

Do it!

A-3: Installing a modem

Here's how

1 Power off and unplug your lab workstation

   Remove the case

2 Locate an available slot for the internal modem

   Remove any blanks that might be in place

3 Configure the modem's jumpers to use an available COM port

4 Gently install the modem into the ISA slot
   (*Warning*: Be careful not to bend the modem from side to side.)

   Secure the modem with a screw

5 Plug in the lab workstation

   Stand clear of the lab workstation and power it on

6 Enter the CMOS Setup program

7 Verify that the modem doesn't conflict with an existing COM port

   If the modem conflicts with a COM port, disable the COM port

8 Save your changes and reboot the PC

9 Power off your lab workstation

   Unplug the power cord

   Replace the case

10 Plug in the power cord

   Stand clear of your lab workstation, power it on, and boot it into Windows 9x

Configuring a modem

Explanation   Turn on your computer and follow these steps to configure the modem under the OS. Begin with Step 1 for Windows NT, with Step 12 for Windows 9x, and with Step 14 for Windows 2000.

1 For Windows NT, choose Start, Settings, Control Panel, and then double-click Modem. The Install New Modem dialog box is displayed. If you want Windows NT to detect and install the modem for you, click Next, and then proceed to Step 3. If you want to provide the installation disk for the modem, select Don't detect my modem: I will select it from the list, and proceed to Step 2.

2 Either select the modem from the list of modems provided by Windows NT or, if you have an installation disk provided with the modem, click Have Disk and provide the location of the files. Go to Step 4.

   Note: Sometimes an installation disk has several directories, one for each operating system it supports. For example, for Windows NT 4.0, look for a directory named \NT40.

3 After the modem is detected, Windows NT requests the location of the Windows NT \I386 directory—which is located on the Windows NT installation CD-ROM—from which it copies the necessary drivers. Place the CD in the drive and tell Windows NT the location of the directory by using the drive letter of your CD-ROM (for example, D).

4 After the modem drivers are installed, the next step is to configure the modem. Choose Start, Settings, Control Panel, and then double-click the Modem icon. The modem Properties box is displayed, which looks and works about the same as it does in Windows 9x. Click the installed modem and then click Properties.

5 Use the properties listed below unless you have a specific reason to do otherwise (such as to compensate for a noisy phone line).

   - Set the modem speed at the highest value in the drop-down list, which is the highest value supported by this modem.

   - Set the port protocol at "8, No, and 1," which is computer jargon for 8 bits, no parity, and 1 stop bit.

   - Use hardware flow control.

6 If you want to use Windows NT to make calls without using other software, then install Dial-Up Networking. Double-click the My Computer icon, and then double-click Dial-Up Networking. Windows NT tells you that you can now install the service.

7 Click Install.

8 Windows NT requests the location of the \I386 directory. Insert the CD-ROM and tell Windows NT the location of the directory.

9 When Windows NT asks you to select the RAS (Remote Access Service, pronounced "razz") device, select the newly installed modem and click OK to continue.

10 When you're asked to select the type of communication protocols that you want to use when connected, select two: NetBEUI and TCP/IP.

11 Reboot the PC. The configuration is now complete for Windows NT.

12 For Windows 9x, turn on the PC. Windows 9x Plug and Play will detect that a new hardware device is present. Allow the OS to identify the modem and install the drivers, or provide your own disk.

13 After the modem drivers are installed, configure the modem. Use the same method as for Windows NT, beginning with Step 4. The Windows 9x installation is now complete.

14 For Windows 2000, the installation is similar to Windows 9x because both OSs use Plug and Play. However, some options in the modem Properties dialog box are slightly different. To configure the modem, click Start, point to Settings, click Control Panel and double-click the Phone and Modem Options icon. When the Phone and Modem Options dialog box opens, click the Modem tab. Select the modem and click Properties. The modem Properties dialog box opens. Configure the modem by using this dialog box.

Testing a modem

The last step after the modem installation is complete is to test the modem by using communications software.

An excellent software utility to use to test a modem is HyperTerminal, which provides a quick and easy way to make a phone call from a Windows 9x PC. Follow these directions to test your modem by using Windows 9x:

1 For Windows 98, choose Start, Programs, Accessories, Communications, Hyperterminal. For Windows 95, choose Start, Programs, Accessories, Hyperterminal.

2 Double-click the Hypertrm.exe icon in the HyperTerminal window.

3 When the Connection Description dialog box is displayed, enter a descriptive name for your connection and select an icon for the shortcut. Click OK.

4 Enter the phone number to dial and select the modem from the list of dial-up devices (most likely it's the only entry). Click OK.

5 Click Dial to make the call. Even if you dial an out-of-service number, you can still hear your modem make the call. This confirms that your modem is installed and configured to make outgoing calls.

Do it!

A-4: Installing modem drivers

Here's how

1 Choose **Start, Settings, Control Panel**

2 Double-click the **Modems** icon

3 If you're not prompted to install a modem, click **Add**

4 Click **Next** to have Windows 9x search for a modem

5 Verify that Windows 9x has detected the correct type of modem. You might have to provide a disk if Windows can't detect your modem

6 Click **Next**

7 Click **Finish**

8 Click **OK**

Topic B: Modem troubleshooting guidelines

Explanation

This section provides a guide to solving problems with modems and communicating over phone lines. Some keys to troubleshooting are to determine what works and what doesn't work, to find out what has worked in the past that doesn't work now, and to establish what has changed since things last worked. Much of this information can be determined by asking the user and yourself questions and by trying simple things first.

Potential problems

Below is a list of problems you might encounter with your modem and suggestions as to how you can proceed.

Unresponsive modem

If the modem doesn't respond:

1   Make sure the modem is plugged into the phone jack.

2   If you're using an external modem, make sure it's plugged into the computer and that the connection is solid.

3   There are two RJ-11 ports on a modem. Check that the phone line from the wall outlet is connected to the line-in port.

4   Plug a phone directly into the wall jack you're using and make sure that there's a dial tone.

5   If necessary, make sure to instruct the modem to dial an extra character, such as 9 or 8, to get an outside line.

6   If this is a new installation that has never been used before, check the following things:

- Make sure the modem is set to the same COM port and IRQ that the software is set to.

- Make sure that no other device is configured to the same COM port or IRQ as the modem.

- For an internal modem, check that the DIP switches and jumpers agree with the modem properties in the OS.

- If you're using an internal modem, try installing it in a different expansion slot. If you're using an external modem by using a serial port card, move the serial port card to a different slot and try to install the modem. If you're using an external modem, substitute a known-good serial cable.

- Check that the software correctly initialized the modem. If you didn't give the correct modem type to the software, it might be trying to send the wrong initialization command. Try AT&F. (Under Windows 9x, click Start, Settings, Control Panel. Double-click Modems. Select the modem and click Modem Properties, Connection, Advanced. A dialog box is displayed. Enter the AT&F command under Extra settings.) Retry the modem.

- Make sure you have enough RAM and hard drive space. Then close all other applications currently running, reboot the PC, and try the modem again.

Modem says there is no dial tone

If the modem says there's no dial tone, even though you can hear it:

1   Make sure the phone cord from the wall outlet is plugged into the line jack on the modem.

2   The modem might not be able to detect the dial tone even if you can hear it. Try unplugging any other equipment plugged into this same phone line, such as a fax machine.

3   Try giving the ATX0 command before you dial. Enter the command under Advanced Settings. If that doesn't help, then remove the ATX0 command.

4   Straighten your phone lines! Don't let them get all twisted and crossed up with other heavy electrical lines.

5   If there has been a recent lightning storm, the modem might be damaged. Replace the modem with one you know works.

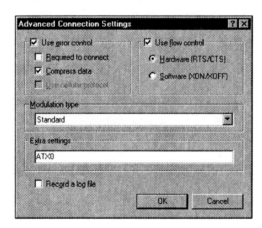

Exhibit 10-6: The Advanced Connection Settings dialog box

Modem says there is a busy signal

If the modem dials and then says that the other end is busy, even when you know that it's not:

1   This can happen with international calls if the modem doesn't recognize the signal as a ring. Try giving the ATX0 command first.

2   Straighten the phone lines and remove extra equipment, as described above.

Slow connection speed

If the sending modem and the receiving modem take a very long time to negotiate the connection:

1 This is probably because of a noisy phone line. Try calling again or using a different number.

2 Remove other equipment from your line. A likely suspect is a credit card machine.

3 Try turning off data compression and try again.

4 Turn off error correction and try again.

5 Try forcing your modem to use a slower speed.

Handshaking restarts during a connection

During a connection, it sounds as if the handshaking starts all over again. Modems normally do this if the phone line is noisy and will cause a lot of data to become corrupted. This is called *retraining*. The problem can resolve itself as the modems renegotiate, compensating for the noisy line. Do the things listed above to clear your line of equipment and twisted phone lines.

Slow file transfers

If file transfers are too slow, make sure your modem is configured to use data compression, if possible.

Lost connections

If the modem loses the connection at odd times or is slow:

1 Check the communications software for the speed assigned to it. Many times people set the communications software speed for the modem speed instead of for what the software is asking for—the port speed, which should be about four times the modem speed.

2 You might have a noisy phone line. Try the connection by using the same brand and model of modem on both lines. If performance is better, the problem is most likely the phone line.

3 Is the phone line from the modem to the jack too long? About four feet is the limit; otherwise, electromagnetic interference might be the problem.

4 Straighten the phone lines and clear the line of any extra equipment.

5 Reinstall the modem. Allow Windows 9x to detect the modem for you and install its own drivers.

Receiving NO CARRIER messages

If the modem drops the connection and gives the NO CARRIER message:

1   Most likely the connection was first dropped by the remote modem. Is someone trying to use a phone extension on this line?

2   Disable call waiting. To do this, enter *70 before the dialing number. Some communications programs give you the option of disabling call waiting. If not, you can enter these characters in the Extra settings box of Advanced Connections Settings.

3   Remove extra equipment from the line and straighten the phone lines.

4   Check the modem settings and make sure "Error control required to connect" isn't checked.

5   Try using a different modulation type under Advanced Connection Settings of your modem properties.

6   The remote modem might not support the high speeds used. Try reducing the port speed to 9600 or lower.

Connection dropped in bad weather

If the connection disconnects often when the weather is bad, the likely cause is a dirty phone line. Remove any extra equipment and straighten the lines.

Data loss during downloading

If some of the data is lost whenever you download large files, make sure that hardware flow control is on and that software flow control is off for the software, the COM port, and the modem. (Use software settings options, the COM port Properties box, and the modem Properties box.)

Connection fails when downloading or uploading large files

If the connection fails whenever large files are uploaded or downloaded, there might be a buffer overflow. Try these things to gain better control of data flow:

1   Make sure that hardware flow control is on and that software flow control is off, for the software, the COM port, and the modem.

2   Is the serial port speed set too high for the UART chip you have? Lower the port speed.

3   For an external modem, try a different serial port cable.

Garbage

If you get nothing but garbage across the connection:

1 Check the port settings. Try 8 data bits, no parity, and one stop bit (8, No, and 1).

2 Slow down the port speed.

3 Slow down the modem speed.

4 Try a different modulation type.

Do it!

B-1: Finding out more about your modem

Here's how	Here's why
1 Choose **Start**, **Settings**, **Control Panel**	
2 Double-click **Modems**	
3 Click the **Diagnostics** tab	

Modems Properties

General | Diagnostics

Windows detected the following ports, and has already installed the following devices:

Port	Installed
COM1	No Modem Installed.
COM2	MDP3880-W Modem
COM3	Xerox W480 FAX

Driver   More Info...   Help

Under Port, click the port that shows the installed modem

Click **More Info**

Use the information listed here to find out more about your modem. Use the space in this column to answer the following questions.

4 What DOS port does the modem use?

5 What interrupt does the modem use?

6 What port address does the modem use?

7 What UART chip is used?

8   What is the highest possible speed supported by the UART chip?

9   What model of modem is installed?

10 List several types of information stored under the Command and Response headings

11 Click **OK**

    Select the **General** tab

    Click **Dialing Properties**

When dialing from here
To access an outside line:
For local calls, dial ☐
For long distance calls, dial ☐
☐ To disable call waiting, dial: ☐
Dial using: ○ Tone dial ● Pulse dial

If you use a business phone, you can tell the computer what to do to access an outside line.

12 Click **Cancel** twice   To close all modem windows.

Topic C: Other communication technologies

Explanation
The speed of communicating data is constantly improving. No matter how fast communication is between the computer and its modem, the speed between one modem and another can be no faster than the limited speed of the regular analog phone lines to which they're connected. The phone company transports voice and data digitally over long distances and then converts it back to an analog signal just before it reaches the customer location, which is usually done at the customer's central office.

Faster than phone lines

The problem with slow analog lines can be greatly improved by making the phone lines digital all the way from one customer to the next. This was first done for large commercial customers. One example of a digital line is called a T1 line, which carries the equivalent of 24 phone circuits and can transmit data at 1.5 million bps. Prices for T1 lines vary and are somewhere around $1,000 per month. These lines are sometimes installed as private circuits connecting two locations of the same company.

A T1 line is too expensive for personal or small business users, so several technologies have emerged to compete for the home and small business market for high-speed data transmission. When referring to digital data communication, data transfer capacity is called *bandwidth*. When referring to analog data communication, bandwidth has a different meaning than it does when applied to digital communication. With analog communication, bandwidth is the range of frequencies that can travel over the analog line. For example, regular telephone lines can accommodate frequencies between 300 Hz and 3,300 Hz, so the bandwidth of a regular phone line is 3,000 Hz.

Technology	Access method	Attainable speeds	Comments
Regular phone line	Dial-up	Up to 53 Kbps	POTS (plain old telephone service)
ISDN	Dial-up	64 Kbps to 128 Kbps	Requires a leased line from phone company. It can be used by a medium-sized business to access an ISP.
DSL	Direct connect	Varies greatly; 1 Mbps upstream and up to 32 Mbps downstream	Requires a leased line from phone company. There are several versions of DSL on the market.
Cable modem	Direct connect	512 Kbps to 5 Mbps	Uses TV cable system to provide home or small business access to ISP.
Satellite	Direct connect	400 Kbps	Works only downstream; upstream transmission requires a dial-up.

Integrated Services Digital Network (ISDN)

A technology developed in the 1980s that uses regular phone lines and is accessed by a dial-up connection was developed by using an accepted international standard called *Integrated Services Digital Network* or ISDN. An ISDN line is fully digital and consists of two channels, or phone circuits, on a single pair of wires. Each line can support speeds up to 64,000 bps. The two lines can be combined so that, effectively, data travels at 128,000 bps, which is about five times the speed of regular phone lines.

Because ISDN lines are designed for small business and home use, the two lines can support voice communication, fax machines, and computers. Logically, the two circuits are two phone lines, which can each have different phone numbers, although most often only one number is assigned to both lines. Because an ISDN line must have little noise on it, only a single jack for the line—which initially connects to one device—is used at a customer location.

In order to use an ISDN line at your business or home, you must have these things:

- An ISDN line leased from the phone company
- An ISDN device on your computer (comparable to a modem for a regular phone line)
- ISDN software on your PC to manage the connection

If you plan to use an ISDN line to access the Internet, then, in order for you to see a performance gain, your service provider must also have an ISDN line. If you plan to use the ISDN line for telecommuting, then your place of business must also have ISDN in order for performance to improve.

The single ISDN device that connects to the ISDN line at your home can be an expansion card inside your PC or can be an external device. Communications software, the OS, and computer hardware relate to an ISDN device for digital phone lines just as they relate to a modem for analog phone lines. The communications software and the OS must support the ISDN device. If the device is external and using the COM port on the computer system, then the UART chip controlling that COM port doesn't make a distinction between communicating with an ISDN device and with a modem, since all its communication is digital in either case. There are three choices as to how you can connect to ISDN:

- Internal card. An internal card is less expensive than the other two choices, but limits the use of the ISDN to when your computer is on.
- External device. An external device requires a connection to your PC. If you connect the device by way of your serial port, you have a bottleneck at the serial port; the device can communicate to your PC only as fast as the serial port speed.
- External device and network card. You can use an external device connected to your PC by way of a network card. The price is higher, but this solution offers the most advantages: the PC doesn't have to be on to use the ISDN line, and the network card is faster than a serial port.

Exhibit 10-7 shows one setup for an ISDN external device. The external ISDN device can also function as a bridge between a LAN in your building and the ISDN line. (In networking, a bridge is a device that connects two networks so that communication can take place between them.) Every PC then connects to the ISDN line by way of its network card, which also is its access to the LAN. Some of these external ISDN devices also supply ordinary phone jacks so that ordinary telephones also can be connected to the ISDN line without having to go through a PC in your building.

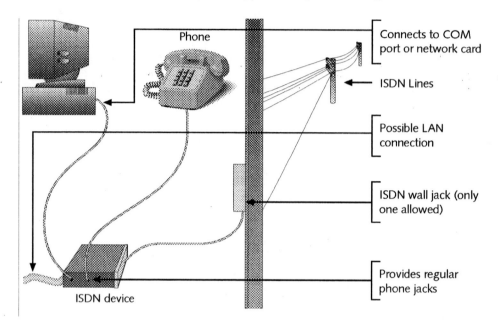

Exhibit 10-7: An external ISDN device connects PCs and telephones

The ISDN device, be it internal or external, in North America is technically an NT1 (network termination 1) device, but the term heard most often in referring to this device is a terminal adapter (TA). The two major manufacturers of TAs in the U.S. are Eicon Technologies and 3Com. (See their Web sites at www.eicon.com and www.3com.com for more information.)

You might hear an external TA called an ISDN modem or an ISDN box. An internal TA might be called an ISDN card or an ISDN modem. Call it a box or a card or a device, but calling it an ISDN modem is not correct! A modem converts digital to analog and analog to digital. An ISDN circuit is digital all the way. No modems are needed.

Cable modems

Regular phone lines and ISDN both require a dial-up connection. In moving to the next generation of data transmission for the home and small business, the choice is a direct connection and speeds measured in Mbps (million bits per second) rather than Kbps (thousand bits per second). A direct connection means that the line is always up rather than establishing it as a connection with a dial-up. Cable modem, a popular technology that's direct connect, uses cable lines that already exist in millions of households in the U.S. Just as with cable TV, cable modems are always connected. Simply turn on the PC and you're up. Cable modems use a technology called *Data Over Cable Service Interface Specifications* (DOCSIS).

With cable modem, you install an Ethernet network interface card in your PC. When the cable company installs the service in your home, they provide an external modem that converts the analog signal coming over the cable to digital before it's sent to the Ethernet NIC in your PC. The modem designed for the DOCSIS interface is likely to be leased to you as part of the cable modem service.

Very few cable companies don't provide upstream service (data flowing from your PC to your ISP) by cable. The connection downstream (data flowing from the ISP to your PC) is a direct connect by cable, but the service upstream is by regular dial-up phone lines. This means that you can receive data over the cable, but to transmit, you must use a regular dial-up. Be sure you understand what you're getting before you lease.

When you lease cable modem service, you're most likely also agreeing to use the service provider as your ISP. The cost for cable modem service, including ISP cost, is in the range of $35 to $90 per month.

Digital Subscriber Line (DSL)

In the race to produce a fast data transmission technology that's affordable for home use and offers a direct connection rather than a dial-up, the telephone industry has developed several technologies, which are collectively called *Digital Subscriber Line* or DSL. ISDN is an early example of DSL.

One prominent version of DSL is *Asymmetric Digital Subscriber Line* (ADSL), which is 50 times faster than ISDN and is direct connect. (Asymmetric refers to the fact that upstream transmission isn't necessarily run at the same speed as downstream transmission.) When using the Internet, most transmission is downstream (downloading Web pages), so the asymmetric technology is a viable option for home use if the emphasis is on using the Internet. ADSL uses a new standard for transmission called G.Lite sponsored by ITU. To have a DSL connection, you must lease the line from the phone company, which provides a converter box on-site. From the box, the line connects to an Ethernet NIC in your PC just like cable modem. The cost of an ADSL line varies greatly, anywhere from $75 to $850 per month, depending on your location. How to connect to the Internet by using DSL is covered in the next chapter.

Satellite

One last way to attain high-speed data transmission is by using satellites. You lease the service from a provider and mount a satellite dish on your premises. One service provider is DirecPC Satellite Service by Hughes (see the Web site www.direcpc.com). Using a satellite connection for downstream transmission of data isn't a good option unless you need high-speed transmission and live in a remote location that doesn't offer other alternatives. The installation can be complicated and requires a dial-up connection for data to travel upstream.

Do it!

C-1: Discussing communication technologies

Question	Answer
1 What is the difference between analog and digital communications?	
2 Define ISDN.	
3 What is the advantage of ISDN over T1?	
4 What is a cable modem?	
5 What is ADSL and is it faster than ISDN?	
6 How do home users take advantage of satellite technology?	

Unit summary: Communicating over phone lines

Topic A You learned how to install a **modem**. A modem converts data from **digital** into **analog** and back again for transmission over phone lines.

Topic B You learned about basic **troubleshooting guidelines** for modems.

Topic C Finally, you discussed communication technologies that offer alternatives to phone lines. You learned about **ISDN, DSL, cable modems**, and **satellite** technologies.

Independent practice activity

1 Change your modem's connection settings:

Following the directions in the troubleshooting guidelines, change your modem's connection settings, so that the modem speaker remains on the entire time that the modem is connected by using the ATM2 command under the Extra settings box of the Advanced Connection Settings dialog box.

Make a call with this setting. After you finish the call, remove the extra setting.

2 Modem troubleshooting:

In the Advanced Connections Settings dialog box, check **Record a log file** (Windows 95) or **Append to Log** (Windows 98). This action causes Windows 9x to create a log file named Modemlog.txt in the folder where Windows is installed. Make a phone call by using the modem and then disconnect. Print the log file that's created.

3 Does your phone line qualify for a 56 Kbps line?

You must have a V.34 standard modem for this project. Determine whether your phone line is clean enough to support a 56 Kbps modem. Access the 3Com Web site at www.3com.com, search the site for "linetest," and follow the directions on the screen. Get a printed screen of your results.

Unit 11

Networking fundamentals

Unit time: 90 minutes

Complete this unit, and you'll know how to:

A Describe different network architectures and topologies.

B Describe basic network hardware.

C Describe common network protocols and popular network applications.

Topic A: Network architectures

Explanation

The three most popular physical network architectures are Ethernet, Token Ring, and Fiber Distributed Data Interface (FDDI). A relatively new type of network is the Asynchronous Transfer Mode (ATM), which is a fast network that works well over both short and long distances. An older type of network is the Attached Resource Computer network (ARCnet), which is seldom used today. Each type of network architecture is designed to solve certain network problems, and each has its own advantages and disadvantages. There are many ways in which network architectures differ from each other. The coverage of some detailed differences is beyond the scope of this book. However, two basic differentiating characteristics—how computers are logically connected and how traffic is controlled on the network—are discussed here.

A network might be either a LAN (local area network, typically a network located in a single building or adjacent buildings, with nodes connected by cables) or a WAN (wide area network, covering a large geographical area, with nodes connected by methods other than just cables, such as microwave signals). Several networks of either type can be tied together, which is called an *internetwork*.

Ethernet

Ethernet is the most popular network technology used today. Ethernet networks can be configured as either a bus topology or a star topology. *Topology* is the arrangement or shape used to physically connect devices on a network to one another. A *bus topology* connects each node in a line and doesn't include a centralized point of connection. Cables go from one computer, to the next one, and the next. A *star topology* connects all nodes to a centralized hub. PCs on the LAN are like the points of a star around a central hub.

The star arrangement is more popular because it's easier to wire and to maintain than the bus arrangement. Also, in a bus arrangement, the failure of one node affects all the other nodes. In a star arrangement, some hubs are called *intelligent hubs* because they can be remotely controlled from a console by using network software. Intelligent hubs can monitor a network and report errors or problems. With intelligent hubs, stations that have problems can be remotely disabled from network access without affecting the rest of the network.

Bus design

Terminator   Terminator
a) Ethernet can be constructed with a bus design.

Star design

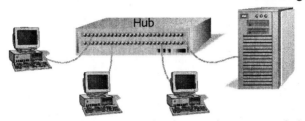

b) Ethernet can be constructed with a star design using a hub.

Exhibit 11-1: Two Ethernet topologies

An Ethernet network is a *passive network*, meaning that the networked computers, rather than a dedicated network device, originate the signals that manage the network. (A *dedicated* network *device* is a device, such as a hub, used solely to support a network. Other devices on the network, such as PCs, have functions other than networking.) Ethernet works much like an old telephone party line, where each computer is like a party line caller. When someone on a party line wanted to use a phone, he or she would pick up and listen. If there was a dial tone (carrier), then the person could make a call. If someone else was talking, the person would hang up and try again later. If two people attempted to make a call at the same time, both calls would fail. They would each need to hang up and begin again. The first one back on the line would be able to make a call.

Similarly, a computer that wants to send packets over Ethernet will first listen on the network for silence. If it hears nothing, it begins to transmit. As it transmits, it also is listening. If it hears something other than its own data being transmitted, it stops transmitting and sends out a signal that there has been a *collision*, which occurs when two computers attempt to send data at the same time. A collision can cause packets that were just sent to be corrupted. Each computer waits for a random amount of time and then tries to transmit again, first listening for silence. This type of network architecture is called a *contention-based* system because each computer must contend for an opportunity to transmit on the network. Computers using Ethernet are said to gain access to the network using the *Carrier Sense Multiple Access with Collision Detection* (*CSMA/CD*) method. The name of the method suggests three characteristics of the way computers communicate on Ethernet:

- A computer must sense that the network is free to handle its transmission before initiating a signal (carrier sense).
- Many computers use the same network (multiple access).
- Each computer must detect and manage collisions (collision detection).

Ethernet can use any one of six cabling systems, which are described in the following table. An example of each of these cables is shown in Exhibit 11-2. The two most popular Ethernet cabling systems are 10BaseT and 10Base2 (Thinnet).

Cable system	Cable & connectors	Description
10Base5 (Thicknet) Speed = 10 Mbps	Thick coaxial cable uses an AUI15-pin D-shaped connector.	Coaxial cable is made of two conductors: a center wire and a metallic braid that surrounds the center wire. Foam insulation separates the two. The maximum segment length of Thicknet is 500 meters.
10Base2 (Thinnet) Speed = 10 Mbps	Thin coaxial cable uses a BNC connector (T-connector).	A less expensive, smaller coaxial cable than Thicknet, with a maximum segment length of 185 meters. Thinnet and Thicknet are sometimes used on the same network.
10BaseT (Twisted pair) Speed = 10 Mbps	Unshielded twisted-pair (UTP) cable uses an RJ-45 connector.	Two wires, each insulated from the other and twisted together inside a plastic casing to lessen crosstalk and outside interference. (Crosstalk is the interference that each wire produces in the other.) There are several grades of UTP. (A lower grade of UTP isn't suitable for 10BaseT and is often used for telephone wire.)
100BaseT (Fast Ethernet) Speed = 100 Mbps	Shielded twisted pair (STP) cable with an RJ-45 connector.	STP costs more than UTP and thin coaxial cable, but less than thick coaxial cable and fiber-optic cable. STP is rigid and thick and has shielding around the twisted wires to protect them from outside interference. (Sometimes a high grade of UTP also can be used for Fast Ethernet for local connections.)
10BaseFL / 100BaseFX (Fiber-optic) Speed = 10 Mbps / 100 Mbps	Optical fiber (fiber-optic cable) uses an ST or SC fiber-optic connector.	These cables use light rather than electricity to transmit signals. A glass or plastic fiber in the center of the cable, about the same diameter as a human hair, transmits the light.

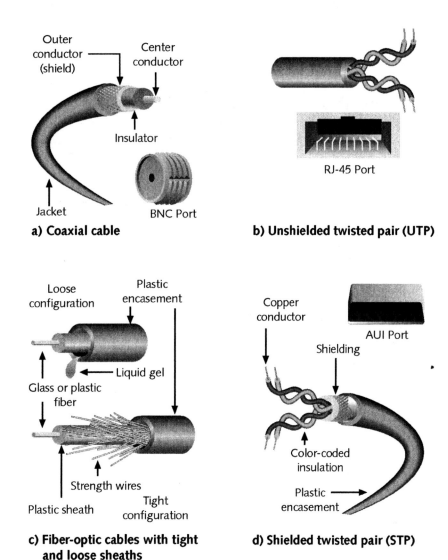

Exhibit 11-2: Networking cables

The "10" in 10BaseT comes from the speed of transmission (10 Mbps). The "Base" comes from *baseband*. Ethernet is a baseband network that carries data over wire one message at a time in digital form. Contrast baseband to a broadband network such as ATM or cable modem that carries multiple messages over wire, each message traveling on its own frequency in analog form. The "T" in 10BaseT stands for twisted-pair cabling.

10BaseT networks use a star topology with each PC on the network connected to a hub, although it's possible to connect two PCs together for a simple 10BaseT network without a hub. 10BaseT networks use RJ-45 connectors, which look like large phone jack connectors.

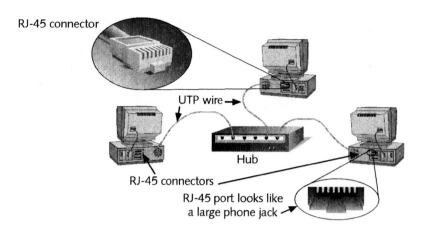

Exhibit 11-3: Ethernet 10BaseT network

Thinnet (10Base2) networks use coaxial cables and BNC connectors, which are shaped like Ts. Thinnet networks use a bus topology with terminators at each end of the bus that screw into the T-connectors at the back of the two end PCs. The BNC port on the network card looks like a cable TV connection.

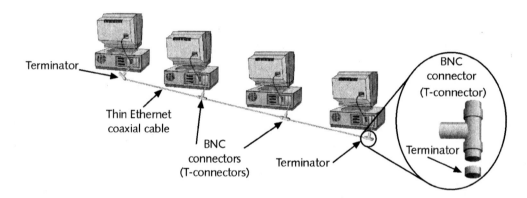

Exhibit 11-4: Ethernet 10Base2 (Thinnet) network

Because signals transmitted over long distances on a network can weaken, devices are added to amplify signals. For example, for a 10BaseT Ethernet cable, if the cable exceeds 100 meters (328 feet), amplification is required. A *repeater* is a device that amplifies signals on a network. There are two kinds of repeaters. An *amplifier repeater* simply amplifies the incoming signal, noise and all. A *signal-regenerating repeater* "reads" the signal and then creates an exact duplicate of the original signal before sending it on.

Each of the cable systems listed in the table can support only a limited number of nodes. As the number of nodes increases, performance speed and reliability can drop for the overall network. One method used to prevent this kind of congestion is *segmentation*. Segmentation splits a large Ethernet into smaller Ethernet segments. Each segment contains two or more computers and is connected to the other segments by a *bridge* or *router*. Stations on a single segment need to contend with only other stations on the same segment to send their packets. The bridge or router transfers packets to other segments only when it knows that the packet is addressed to a station outside its segment. All other network traffic is contained within the segment.

Exhibit 11-5 shows an Ethernet of two segments connected by a bridge. Don't let the two T shapes in part A confuse you; although the Ts exist logically, they don't exist physically. If you were to wire these four PCs and one bridge together, the physical diagram might look like part B.

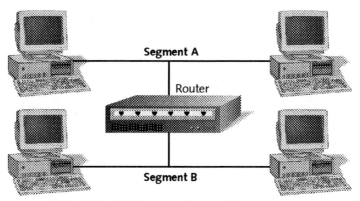

a) Logically, a bridge connects two Ethernet segments.

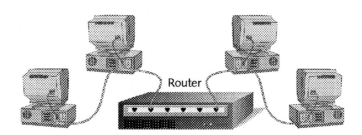

b) Physically, the PCs and bridge can be cabled together in this manner.

Exhibit 11-5: A bridge connecting two Ethernet segments

Do it!

A-1: Reviewing Ethernet networks

Exercise

Discuss the pros and cons of setting up a network with 10base2 (Thinnet) vs. 10baseT (unshielded twisted pair). Would one or the other be better suited for certain environments? Why? Consider some of the following issues in your discussion:

1 The number of computers to be networked

2 The distance between computers

3 Difficulty of setup

4 Physical barriers, building layout, and composition

5 Cost of materials such as routers and amplifiers (assume both cable types cost roughly the same per foot in bulk)

6 The network's purpose

7 Maintenance, administration, and troubleshooting of the network

8 Anything else you think might affect the decision

Token Ring

Explanation

Token Ring networking, which was developed by IBM, is more complex and expensive, but more robust and reliable, than Ethernet. Because of its complexity, it's more difficult to maintain than Ethernet.

Connecting components on a Token Ring

Logically, Token Ring networks are rings. However, physically, stations are connected to the network in a star formation. Each station connects to a centralized hub called a *controlled-access unit* (*CAU*), a *multistation access unit* (*MSAU* or sometimes just *MAU*), or a smart multistation access unit (*SMAU*). Exhibit 11-6 shows one Token Ring configuration using two IBM 8228 MSAUs. Each MSAU shown can connect eight workstations to the network. With this type of MSAU, there can be as many as 33 MSAUs on one Token Ring network. One MSAU can connect to another by a cable called a patch cable. One end of each MSAU has either a Ring In (data flows into the MSAU) or a Ring Out (data flows out from the MSAU) connection. The main ring is composed of the MSAUs and the cables connecting them, which are together referred to as the main ring cable. (The cable connecting the last MSAU Ring Out to the first MSAU Ring In isn't considered a patch cable.) The main ring cable can be fiber-optic.

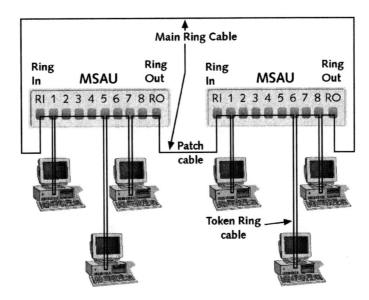

Exhibit 11-6: A Token Ring network

The entire token ring is made up of not only the main ring, but also the cabling to each PC on the token ring. Each workstation contains a Token Ring LAN card with a 9-pin connector for the Token Ring cable, which connects each workstation to an MSAU. Each Token Ring network card has a unique address, which is assigned to it during manufacturing and encoded on the card's firmware. Token Ring cables can be either UTP or STP cables that have two twisted pairs for a total of four wires in the cable.

Looking at Exhibit 11-6, you can see why a Token Ring network is said to be a physical star but a logical ring. All workstations connect to a centralized hub (in this case, two hubs strung together), but you also can follow the ring path around the entire network. The ring path in Exhibit 11-6 goes from the first MSAU down to each PC and back again, across the patch cable to the next MSAU, from this MSAU down to each PC connected to it and back again, and finally, around the main ring cable back to the first MSAU.

Communication on a Token Ring

Communication and traffic on a Token Ring network are controlled by a *token*—a small frame with a special format—that travels around the ring in only one direction. One station receives the token from the preceding station, called its *nearest active upstream neighbor* (*NAUN*), and passes it on to the next station on the ring, called its *nearest active downstream neighbor* (*NADN*). As one station passes the token to the next station, it can attach data in a frame to the token. The next station receives the token together with the data frame and reads this data frame. If the frame is intended for it, it changes two bits in the frame to indicate that the data has been read by the intended station. It then passes the token and the data frame on. When the token and frame are received by the station that sent the frame, it sees that the frame was successfully received and doesn't send the frame on again. In this case, it releases the token by passing it on to the next PC, without a data frame attached. However, if the amount of data requires more than one frame, instead of releasing the token, the PC sends the next frame with the token. In either case, the token is passed on to the next PC, and data is never on the ring without the token preceding it.

Any PC receiving a token with no data frame attached is free to attach a data frame before passing on the token. The token is busy and not released to another PC until the sending PC has received word that the data was successfully received at its destination. In other words, the only PC that should remove a data frame from behind the token is the PC that first attached it.

Do it! ### A-2: Discussing Token Ring networks

Question	Answer
1 Define multistation access unit.	
2 Describe how a computer is connected to a Token Ring network.	
3 Define token.	
4 Describe how traffic is managed on a Token Ring network.	
5 Describe how data frames travel through a Token Ring network.	

FDDI

Explanation

Fiber Distributed Data Interface (*FDDI*, pronounced "fiddy") is a ring-based network like Token Ring, but it doesn't require a centralized hub, making it both a logical and physical ring. FDDI provides data transfer at 100 Mbps, which is much faster than Token Ring or regular Ethernet, and a little faster than Fast Ethernet, which also runs at about 100 Mbps. At one time, FDDI used only fiber-optic cabling, but now it also can run on UTP. FDDI is often used as a backbone network. A *backbone* is a network used to link several networks together. For example, several Token Ring and Ethernet networks can be connected by using a single FDDI backbone.

FDDI uses a token-passing method to control network traffic, but FDDI is more powerful and sophisticated than Token Ring. FDDI stations can pass more than one frame of data along the ring without waiting for the first frame to return. Also, once the frames are transmitted, the sending station can pass the FDDI token on to the next station to use, so that more than one station can have frames on the ring at the same time. With Token Ring, a data frame is only found traveling behind the token. With FDDI, data frames travel on the ring without the token. A PC keeps the token until it sends out its data and then passes the token on. Possessing the token gives a PC the right to send data. A token is released (sent on) when the PC finishes transmitting.

Exhibit 11-7 shows a FDDI network with five stations. There are three frames of data currently on the ring, all sent from Station 1 to Station 5. Because Station 1 is finished sending its data, it passes the FDDI token to Station 2. If Station 2 is ready to send data, it can do so now, even though data from Station 1 is still on the ring. Another optional feature of FDDI is multiframe dialogs. *Multiframe dialogs* enable one station to send a *limited token* to another station. With this limited token, the second station can communicate only with the first station, not with other stations on the network. This "private conversation" provides continuous communication between two stations without interference from other stations. At the same time, the main token can be active on the ring, enabling other frames to be passed among other stations.

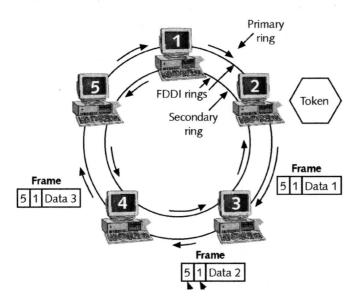

Exhibit 11-7: A FDDI network with three frames of data moving clockwise

One important strength of FDDI is its dual counter-rotating rings. Instead of a single ring, such as the one the Token Ring uses, FDDI has two rings linking each device on the network, a primary ring and secondary ring. Data normally travels on the primary ring. However, if a break occurs on the FDDI ring, any device can switch the data to the secondary ring, which causes the data to travel in the opposite direction back around the ring. When the data reaches the break coming from the other direction, a station switches the data back to the primary ring, and it continues in the opposite direction again. In this way, communication continues even with a break in one FDDI ring.

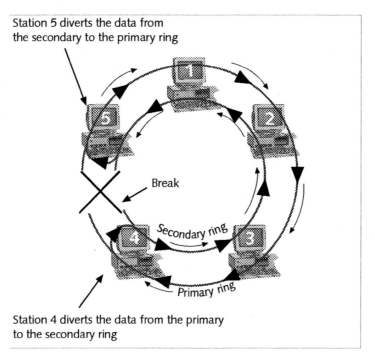

Station 5 diverts the data from
the secondary to the primary ring

Break

Secondary ring

Primary ring

Station 4 diverts the data from the primary
to the secondary ring

*Exhibit 11-8: A break in the FDDI ring causes stations to divert data from one ring to
the other*

Do it!

A-3:   Discussing FDDI networks

Question	Answer
1 Define FDDI.	
2 Define backbone.	
3 How does FDDI differ from Token Ring?	
4 In what type of situation would you use a FDDI network?	

Topic B: Networking hardware

Explanation

Almost all LANs and WANs today are designed by using a Token Ring, Ethernet, FDDI, or possibly ATM architecture. Besides network cards in the PCs and cabling connecting them, several other devices are needed to physically construct a network. It's beyond the scope of this book to cover all the many hardware components needed to make a LAN or WAN work, but this chapter introduces a few common components. Recall that, for a PC, the direct connection to a network is through a network interface card (NIC). Sometimes the logic normally contained on the NIC is on the system board, with a network port coming directly off the system board. This is a common practice for Compaq and Macintosh computers. Hubs are used to provide the centralized location for nodes to connect on a star network. Bridges, routers, and gateways connect one network to another, each performing a slightly different function when connecting like and unlike networks.

Network interface card (NIC)

A *network interface card* (*NIC*) plugs into a system board and provides a port or ports on the back of the card for connection to a network. A NIC manages the communication and network protocol for the PC. A NIC is designed to support Ethernet, Token Ring, or FDDI network topologies, but not all three. However, it might be designed to handle more than one cabling system. Exhibit 11-9 shows some examples of network cards. The network card and the device drivers controlling the network card are the only components in the PC that are aware of the type of network being used. In other words, the type of network in use is transparent to the applications software using it.

Exhibit 11-9: Three types of network cards

A network card sends and receives data to and from the system bus in parallel, and sends and receives data to and from the network in series. Also, the network card is responsible for converting the data it's transmitting into a signal that is in a form appropriate to the network. For example, a fiber-optic FDDI card contains a laser diode that converts data to light pulses before transmission, and a twisted-pair Ethernet card converts data from the 5-volt signal used on the computer to the voltage used by twisted-pair cables. The component on the card that's responsible for this signal conversion is called the transceiver. An Ethernet card commonly contains more than one transceiver, each with a different port on the back of the card, to accommodate different cabling media. This type of Ethernet card is called a combo card.

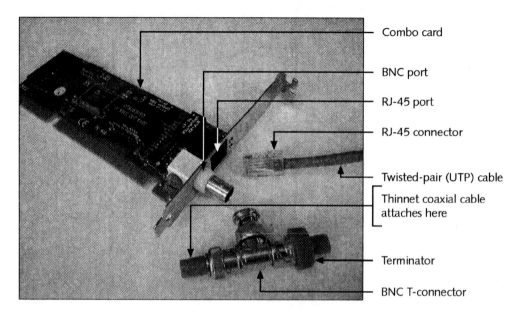

Exhibit 11-10: Ethernet combo card

Different networks have different ways of identifying each node on the network. Ethernet and Token Ring cards have unique addresses hard coded on the card by the manufacturer. Called *media access control* (*MAC*) address or *adapter address*, these addresses are 6-byte hex addresses unique to each card. Part of the MAC address contains the manufacturer, and part of the address is unique to each card; therefore, no two adapters should have the same MAC address.

Network cards require an IRQ, an I/O address, and, for DOS and Windows 9x real mode, upper memory addresses. If the network card is on the PCI bus, then the PCI bus controller manages the IRQ and I/O address requirements. Network cards may be Plug and Play, or they can use jumpers or DIP switches on the card to determine which resources to request. When selecting a network card, three things are important:

- The type of network you are attaching to (for example, Ethernet, Token Ring, FDDI, or a proprietary network standard).

- The type of media you are using (for example, shielded twisted-pair, coaxial, or fiber-optic cable).

- The type of I/O bus you are attaching the card to (for example, PCI or ISA. When selecting the bus to use, recall that PCI is faster than ISA and is the preferred choice. FDDI is much too fast a network for an ISA bus; always use a PCI bus with FDDI cards).

Do it!

B-1:   Installing a network card

Here's how

1 Unplug the power cord

   Remove the case

2 Locate an available slot where you can install the network interface card

3 By using the documentation provided, verify that the network interface card is configured to use the predetermined I/O address and has an available IRQ

4 Gently install the network interface card into the slot
   (*Warning*: Don't bend the card from side to side; move the card only back and forth from end to end.)

5 Screw the mounting screw into place

6 Replace the top of the case

7 Plug in the system unit

8 Power on the lab workstation and boot into Windows 9x

9 If the workstation fails to boot properly, power cycle the PC, and when prompted, choose Safe Mode

Bridges, routers, and gateways

Explanation

When more than one network is connected, the networks form an internetwork. For instance, a large Ethernet network can be broken into smaller, more easily managed segments. A device is needed to bridge the segments. When two networks use different methods of transmission, such as Ethernet and Token Ring, then a device is needed to translate between the two networks. When many networks are interconnected, a device is needed that can choose the best route over these networks.

To satisfy these requirements, bridges, routers, and gateways are used to connect networks and network segments to each other. There are two main reasons for internetworking:

- To extend the geographical area past what a single LAN can support, such as to different floors in a building or to other buildings.

- To decrease the amount of traffic on a single LAN by dividing the LAN into more than one network.

Bridges connect network segments. When a bridge receives signals from one network segment, it makes an intelligent decision as to whether to pass the signals on to the next segment, based on the destination network address. In this way, the bridge limits network traffic across it to only traffic going from one network segment to another, thus making the network more efficient. By using a bridge on a network, you can improve network performance if the bridge is strategically placed in the network so that most traffic remains contained on its own side of the bridge. An example of a strategic use of segmenting a network is to use a bridge to isolate a group of computers that shares the same printers or files. That way the heavy traffic of this group as it communicates within itself doesn't affect the rest of the network.

Routers also connect networks, but are more sophisticated than bridges. Routers are a little slower than bridges because they take the time to make more intelligent decisions about how to route packets to other networks. For example, large networks are often logically divided into many smaller separate networks, and each small network is identified by a logical network name. These smaller networks are sometimes called *subnetworks*, or *subnets*. Now each packet or frame, in addition to having a physical device address, also has a logical network or subnet address. A router can make decisions as to which neighboring network to send a packet to, based on its ultimate destination subnet address.

Routers can be computers with operating systems and special network software, or they can be other dedicated devices built by network manufacturers. Routers hold tables of network addresses, along with the best possible predetermined routes to these networks. These *router tables* also can contain the cost of sending data to a network. The cost can be expressed in one of two ways:

- *Tick count*: The time required for a packet to reach its destination. One tick equals 1/18 second.
- *Hop count*: The number of routers a packet must pass through to reach its destination.

The routing tables are modified every few minutes to reflect changes in the networks. When a router rebuilds its router table, on the basis of new information, the process is called *route discovery*.

A *gateway* connects networks that use different protocols. For example, gateways are used to connect a Token Ring LAN to an Ethernet LAN, or an Ethernet LAN to a mainframe. The gateway translates the incoming network traffic to the protocol needed by the receiving network. Gateways can even function so that a computer on one network that uses one protocol can use data from an application stored on a computer on another network that uses a different protocol. Because of the added overhead of making translations, a gateway is more expensive and slower than a router.

For example, suppose a gateway is a powerful PC that's designed to connect an Ethernet network to a Token Ring network. The PC will have two network cards. One card will be an Ethernet card that belongs to the Ethernet network; the other card will be a Token Ring card that belongs to the Token Ring network. The PC is then the intersection point of the two networks, belonging to both networks.

Do it!

B-2: Discussing bridges, routers, and gateways

Question	Answer
1 What purpose does a bridge serve?	
2 Explain how a router operates.	
3 Define gateway.	
4 What information is stored in a routing table?	

Topic C: Networking software overview

Explanation

In the early 1980s, manufacturers began to make attempts to standardize networking so that networks from different manufacturers could communicate. Two bodies that were leaders in this standardization are the International Organization for Standardization (ISO) and the Institute of Electrical and Electronics Engineers (IEEE).

Proposed new standards are presented to the industry in the form of a *Request for Comment* (RFC), which is assigned a number to identify it. The RFC is publicized and discussed at large and either adopted or rejected by the industry. You can search for and view the many RFCs that pertain to networking and the Internet at this Web site: www.rfc-editor.org.

Open Systems Interconnect (OSI) model

In an effort to identify and standardize all the levels of communication needed in networking, a networking model called the *Open Systems Interconnect* (*OSI*) reference model was developed (as shown in Exhibit 11-11). This model breaks down the communication needed for one user or application to communicate with another over a network into seven logical levels. Each of the seven layers in the OSI model uses different methods of communicating to its counterpart layer. These methods are called protocols. Many different protocols are simultaneously in use when a network is working. The two lowest layers (the physical and data-link layers) are controlled by the firmware on the network cards. However, most of the layers of the OSI model are controlled by the OS managing the network. The three best-known network operating systems in the PC world are the UNIX operating system, NetWare by Novell, and Microsoft Windows NT. In addition to the OS that manages the network, third-party add-on software can be used to provide the top layers of the model. Some examples of this software are Netscape Communicator, Chameleon by NetManage, and Eudora by QUALCOMM. This topic first looks at an overview of all the software components of a network and then looks in detail at several of the more popular products used at the topmost layers of the OSI model, the ones users are most accustomed to seeing and using.

Exhibit 11-11 isn't intended to be comprehensive. There are user and applications services other than the ones listed, and networks other than Ethernet, Token Ring, FDDI, and phone lines. But this exhibit shows how real-life networks map to the OSI model, moving from the lowest level at the bottom to the highest level at the top.

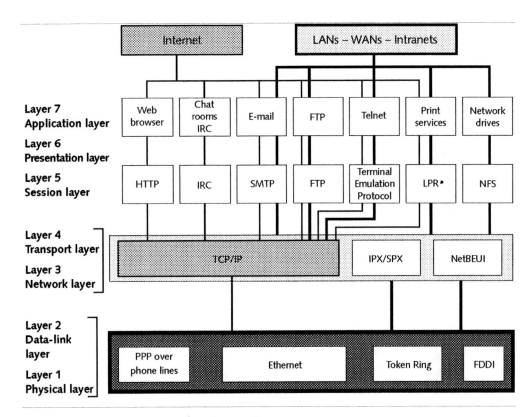

Exhibit 11-11: Overview of networking software

Network protocol

The three network architectures shown in the bottom layer (the physical and data-link layers) of Exhibit 11-11 have already been discussed: Ethernet, Token Ring, and FDDI. Also shown at the bottom layer is *PPP (Point-to-Point Protocol)* over phone lines, which is a protocol by which PCs with modems can connect to a network. The Point-to-Point Protocol is the most popular protocol for managing network transmission from one modem to another. The next level shows the network and transport layers, showing TCP/IP as the protocol used by the Internet. It also is used on LANs, WANs, and intranets. (An *intranet* is a private multiple network used by a large company.) The IPX/SPX protocol is used primarily on Novell LANs. Because TCP/IP is becoming the most popular protocol at this level, Novell also supports TCP/IP as an alternate protocol. Less significant is the *NetBEUI* protocol (*NetBIOS Extended User Interface*, pronounced "net-boo-ee"), a proprietary Microsoft protocol used only by Windows-based OSs (such as Windows for Workgroups) and limited to LANs, since it doesn't support routing. Other proprietary protocols that can be used are XNS, DECnet, Vines, and AppleTalk for Apple and Macintosh computers.

The higher layers in the network model shown also use protocols to communicate with their counterpart services on the receiving node of the network. For example, when you send e-mail across a network, the e-mail is sent by using *SMTP* (*Simple Mail Transfer Protocol*), which operates on the session layer. Network drives use NFS protocol and the World Wide Web on the Internet uses *HTTP* (*Hypertext Transfer Protocol*), both of which operate on the session layer as well. Transferring files across the Internet is most often done by using *FTP* (*File Transfer Protocol*).

Network services

At the highest level of the OSI model are the application and presentation layers. Users access some of these components directly. Others are designed to be interfaces between the network and applications software. Some of the more popular network applications offered at this level are described in the following table.

Item	Description
Web browsers	Provide primary access to the Internet.
Chat rooms	Provide online, interactive communication among several people on the Internet.
E-mail	Provides electronic mail (which consists of text files) across the Internet or other networks.
FTP	Provides a method of transferring files from one computer to another.
Telnet	Provides a console session from a UNIX computer to a remote computer. (In a console session, a window that looks and acts just like the UNIX OS console is displayed on a PC screen, giving the user the opportunity to issue UNIX commands to control the UNIX computer from the PC.)
Print services	Refers to sharing printers across a network.
Network drive	Provides space on one computer on the network and makes it available to another computer as a virtual or logical drive.

Two network configurations

A network can be logically configured either as a peer-to-peer network or as a network using a dedicated server. Exhibit 11-12 shows an example of a peer-to-peer network. Users at each workstation can use shared printers and files on each other's computers. The services on a peer-to-peer network are most often limited to FTP, print services, and network drives. Nodes on a peer-to-peer network can communicate with any other node on the network and access files and other resources on that node, subject to security limitations. Each node is responsible for the security of its own resources.

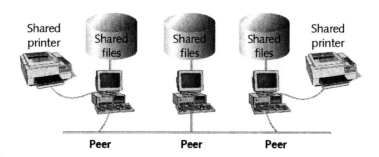

Exhibit 11-12: Peer-to-peer network

A dedicated-server network has at least one computer, or server, on the network that serves the other computers on the network. If the server contains applications software together with data that's shared by other computers on the network (called clients, or workstations), then the network is called a client/server network. The application on the client that makes use of data stored on the server is called the *front end*. The application on the server that processes requests for data is called the *back end*.

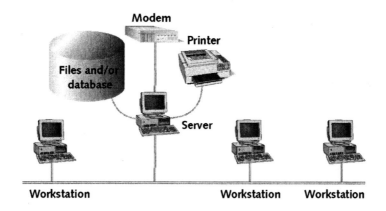

Exhibit 11-13: Dedicated server network

Dedicated-server networks can be used in one of two ways. If data is processed by the front end, and the server holds only the data, processing can be very slow because the client and server need to interact repeatedly. In a true client/server environment, the front end passes all information that's needed to process the data to the back end, and the back end does the processing. When the back end is finished, it can pass a positive response or a calculated answer back to the client. This last method requires less network traffic and is considered to be a better use of the network.

All the programs listed at the application layer can operate on either a dedicated-server or peer-to-peer network. However, the World Wide Web, chat rooms, and e-mail always involve at least one dedicated server. A service that isn't shown in Exhibit 11-11, but that is used in a client/server environment, is the software necessary for an application on a client to pass requests to a server, and for a server to respond with data. This type of software is called *middleware*. One popular example of middleware is Microsoft's Open Database Connectivity (ODBC) software. For example, with ODBC, a front-end application on a client passes a request to update or query a database on the server. The ODBC back-end version of the software processes the request on the dedicated server and returns an answer to the client.

Do it!

C-1: Discussing network configuration

Exercise
Discuss the environments in which you'd rather have a peer-to-peer network, and those that would be better suited to a client/server setup. Consider the following issues in your discussion:
1 The number of users
2 Security concerns
3 Services and applications required by users
4 Hardware cost
5 Anything else you think might matter

Unit summary: Networking fundamentals

Topic A   You learned about some common **networking architectures** and **topologies**—including **Ethernet**, **Token Ring**, and **FDDI**—and about some different cables and connectors used in implementing networks.

Topic B   You learned about the different kinds of PC **network cards**.

Topic C   Your learned about common protocols and network applications and about two different network configurations—**peer-to-peer** and **client/server**.

Review questions

1 What happens if an Ethernet network detects a transmission collision?

2 List and describe three types of cables that can be used on an Ethernet network.

3 What is the function of a router in a network environment? How is a router different from a bridge?

4 What type of connector is used on Ethernet Thinnet? On Ethernet 10BaseT?

5 Describe a client/server network.

6 What is a MAC address or adapter address?

Unit 12

Printers and notebook computers

Unit time: 90 minutes

Complete this unit, and you'll know how to:

A Describe the operation of different printers and troubleshoot printer problems.

B Provide basic technical support for notebook computers.

Topic A: Printers

Explanation This topic explains how printers work and how to support them, including supporting printers on a network. You'll focus on three kinds of printers: the laser printer, the ink-jet printer, and the dot-matrix printer.

Laser printers

Laser printers range from the small, personal desktop size to large network printers capable of handling large volumes of printing on a continuous basis.

Laser printers require the interaction of mechanical, electrical, and optical technologies to work. Understanding how they work will help you support and service them. It also will explain why the safety precautions listed in laser printer user manuals are necessary.

How a laser printer works

Laser printers work by placing toner on an electrically charged rotating drum and then depositing the toner on paper as the paper moves through the system at the same speed the drum turns. Exhibit 12-1 shows the six sequential steps of laser printing. The first four steps use the printer components that undergo the most wear. These components are contained within the removable cartridge, which makes the printer last longer. The last two steps are performed outside the cartridge. Follow the step-by-step procedures of laser printing listed below while you refer to the exhibit:

1 *Cleaning*. The drum is cleaned of any residual toner and electrical charge.

2 *Conditioning*. The drum is conditioned to contain a high electrical charge.

3 *Writing*. A laser beam discharges a high charge down to a lower charge, only in those places where toner needs to be placed.

4 *Developing*. Toner is placed onto the drum where the charge has been reduced.

5 *Transferring*. A strong electrical charge draws the toner off the drum onto the paper. This is the first step that takes place outside the cartridge.

6 *Fusing*. Heat and pressure fuse the toner to the paper.

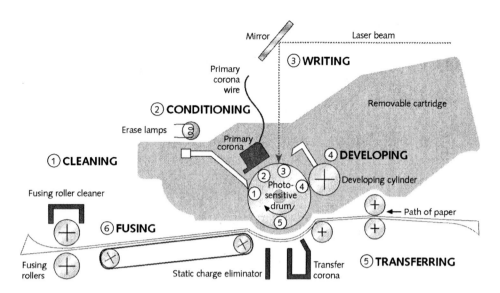

Exhibit 12-1: The six steps of laser printing

Note that the exhibit shows only a cross-section of the drum, mechanisms, and paper. Remember, as you visualize the process, that the drum is as wide as a sheet of paper. The mirror, blades, and rollers in the drawing also are as wide as the paper. Note the location of the removable cartridge in the drawing, the photosensitive drum inside the cartridge turning in a clockwise direction, and the path of the paper, which moves from right to left through the drawing.

Step 1: Cleaning

Exhibit 12-2 shows a clear view of the cleaning step. First, a sweeper strip cleans the drum of any residual toner, which is swept away from the drum by a sweeping blade. A cleaning blade completes the physical cleaning of the drum. Next, the drum is cleaned of any electrical charge by erase lamps (located in the hinged top cover of the printer), which light the surface of the drum to neutralize any electrical charge left on the drum.

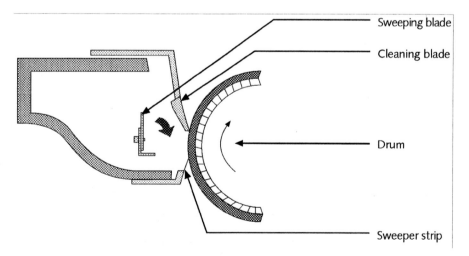

Exhibit 12-2: The cleaning step cleans the drum of toner and electrical charge

Step 2: Conditioning

The conditioning step puts a uniform electrical charge of –600 V on the drive. The charge is put there by a primary corona wire, which is charged by a high-voltage power supply assembly. (A corona is a device that creates an electrical charge.) The primary corona is between the primary corona wire and the drum, and regulates the charge on the drum, ensuring that it's a uniform –600 V.

Step 3: Writing

In the writing step, the uniform charge that was applied in Step 2 is discharged only where you want the printer to print. This is done by controlling mirrors to reflect laser beams onto the drum in a pattern that recreates the image desired. This is the first step in which data from the computer must be transmitted to the printer. The process is outlined in Exhibit 12-3. (1) Data from the PC is received by the formatter and (2) passed on to the DC controller that (3) controls the laser unit. The laser beam is initiated and directed toward the octagonal mirror called the *scanning mirror*. The scanning mirror (4) is turned by the scanning motor in a clockwise direction. There are eight mirrors on the eight sides of the scanning mirror. As the mirror turns, the laser beam is directed in a sweeping motion that can cover the entire length of the drum. The laser beam is reflected off the scanning mirror and (5) is focused by the focusing lens and (6) sent on to the mirror. (7) The mirror deflects the laser beam to a slit in the removable cartridge and on to the drum.

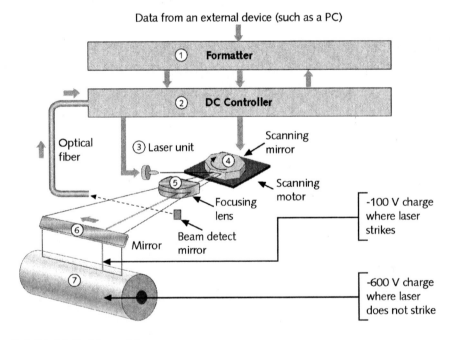

Exhibit 12-3: The writing step

The speed of the motor turning the drum and the speed of the scanning motor turning the scanning mirror are synchronized so that the laser beam completes one pass, or scanline, across the drum and returns to the beginning of the drum to begin a new pass so that the correct number of passes for each inch of the drum circumference is attained. For example, for a 300 dots per inch (dpi) printer, the beam makes 300 passes for every inch of the drum circumference. The laser beam is turned on and off continually as it makes a single pass down the length of the drum, so that dots are written along the drum on every pass. For a 300 dpi printer, 300 dots are written along the drum for every inch of linear pass. The 300 dots per inch down this single pass, along with 300 passes per inch of drum circumference, together accomplish the resolution of 300×300 dots per square inch common to many desktop laser printers.

Note: A laser printer is able to produce better quality printouts than dot matrix printers, even when printing at the same dpi, because it can vary the size of the dots that are printed, creating a sharp, clear image. HP calls this technology of varying the size of dots *RET* (*resolution enhancement technology*).

Note: In a laser printer, where the laser beam strikes the surface of the drum, the drum discharges from its conditioned charge of –600 V down to –100 V where toner will be placed on the drum. Toner will not stick to the highly charged areas of the drum.

Just as the scanning laser beam is synchronized to the rotating drum, the data output is synchronized to the scanning beam. Before the beam begins across the scanline of the drum, the *beam detect mirror* detects the initial presence of the laser beam by reflecting the beam to an optical fiber. The light travels along the optical fiber to the DC controller, where it's converted to an electrical signal that's used to synchronize the data output. The signal also is used to diagnose problems with the laser or scanning motor.

The laser beam writes an image to the drum surface as a –100 V charge. The –100 V charge on this image area will be used in the developing stage to transmit toner to the drum surface.

Step 4: Developing

During the developing step, toner is applied by the developing cylinder to the discharged (–100 V) areas of the drum. Toner transfers from the cylinder to the drum as the two rotate very close together. The cylinder is kept coated with a layer of toner, made of black resin bonded to iron, which is similar to the toner used in photocopy machines. The toner is held on to the cylinder surface by its attraction to a magnet inside the cylinder. (A *toner cavity* keeps the cylinder supplied with toner.) A *control blade* prevents too much toner from sticking to the cylinder surface. The toner on the cylinder surface takes on a negative charge (between –200 V and –500 V) because the surface is connected to a DC power supply called the DC bias.

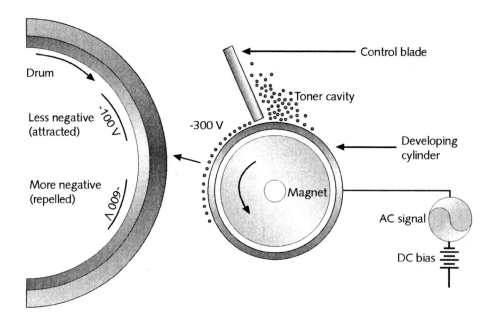

Exhibit 12-4: The developing step

The negatively charged toner is more negative than the –100 V on the drum surface but less negative than the –600 V surface. Because of this fact, the toner is attracted to the –100 V area of the drum surface (the –100 V area is positive relative to the toner). The toner is repelled from the –600 V part of the drum surface, which is negative relative to the toner. The result is that toner sticks to the drum where the laser beam has hit and is repelled from the area where the laser beam has not hit.

Most printers enable you to adjust print density. With laser printers, when you adjust print density, you're adjusting the DC bias charge on the developing cylinder, which controls the amount of toner attracted to the cylinder, which, in turn, results in a change in print density.

Step 5: Transferring

In the transferring step, the transfer corona produces a positive charge on the paper that pulls the toner from the drum onto the paper when it's passed between the transfer corona and the drum. The static charge eliminator weakens the positive charge on the paper and the negative charge on the drum so that the paper doesn't adhere to the drum—which it would otherwise do because of the difference in charge between the two. The paper's stiffness and the drum's small radius also help cause the paper to move away from the drum and toward the fusing rollers. If thin paper is used in a laser printer, the paper can wrap around the drum, which is why printer manuals usually instruct you to use only paper designated for laser printers.

Step 6: Fusing

The fusing step causes the toner to bond with the paper. Up to this point, the toner is merely sitting on the paper. The fusing rollers apply both pressure and heat to the paper. The toner melts, and the rollers press the toner into the paper. The temperature of the rollers is monitored by the printer. If the temperature exceeds a set maximum value (410° F for some printers), the printer shuts down.

The previous steps describe how a black and white printer works. Color laser printers work in a similar way except that the writing process repeats four times, one for each toner color of cyan, magenta, yellow, and black. Then the paper passes to the fusing stage where the fuser bonds all toner to the paper and aids in blending the four tones to form specific colors.

Supporting laser printers

All the mechanical printer components that normally create problems are conveniently contained within the replaceable toner cartridge. So, in most cases, the solution to poor quality printing is to replace this cartridge. Follow these general guidelines:

- If the print is faded, smeared, wavy, speckled, or streaked, the toner might be low. Remove the toner cartridge, gently rock it from side to side to redistribute the toner, and replace it. If this solves the problem, then plan to replace the toner cartridge soon. If not, try replacing the toner cartridge.
- EconoMode (a mode that uses less toner) might be on; turn it off.
- On some laser printers, the mirror can be cleaned. Check the user guide for directions.
- A single sheet of paper might be defective. Try new paper.
- The paper might not be of high enough quality. Use only paper recommended for use in a laser printer.
- Try a different brand of paper.
- Clean the inside of the printer with a dry, lint-free cloth. Don't touch the transfer roller.
- If the transfer roller is dirty, the problem will probably correct itself after printing several sheets. If not, then take the printer to an authorized service center.

Do it!

A-1: Understanding laser printers

Exercise

1 By using the exhibits above, identify and label each of the following components of a disassembled printer cartridge and describe its function:
   - Primary corona
   - Photo-sensitive drum
   - Developing cylinder

2 Power off and unplug your laser printer (If your laser printer has been used recently, cool it down before proceeding)

3 Open your laser printer

4 Identify each of the following components and describe its function:
   - Paper tray
   - Primary corona wire
   - Transfer corona
   - Power supply
   - Sensors (all)
   - Expansion slots
   - Logic boards (all)
   - Fuser

5 Describe each of the six steps of the laser printing process:
   - Cleaning
   - Conditioning
   - Writing
   - Developing
   - Transferring
   - Fusing

Ink-jet printers

Explanation

Ink-jet printers don't normally provide the quality resolution that laser printers do, but these printers are popular because of their small size and their ability to print color inexpensively. Ink-jet printers tend to smudge on inexpensive paper, and they're slower than laser printers. The quality of the paper used with ink-jet printers significantly affects the quality of printed output. Only use paper designed for an ink-jet printer, and to get the best results, use a high-grade paper.

How an ink-jet printer works

An ink-jet printer resembles a dot-matrix printer in several ways. Both printers use a print head that moves across the paper, creating one line of text with each pass. Also, both types of printer put ink on the paper by using a matrix of small dots, although ink-jet printers use much smaller dots than do dot-matrix printers.

Different types of ink jet printers form their droplets of ink in different ways. Printer manufacturers use several technologies, but the most popular is the bubble jet. Bubble jet printers use tubes of ink that have tiny resistors near the end of each tube. These resistors heat up and cause the ink to boil. Then, a tiny air bubble of ionized ink (which means that it has an electrical charge) is ejected onto the paper. A typical bubble jet print head has 64 or 128 tiny nozzles, and all can fire a droplet simultaneously. Plates carrying a magnetic charge direct the path of ink onto the paper to form shapes.

Ink-jet printers come with one or more cartridges of ink. When purchasing an ink-jet printer, look for the kind that uses two separate cartridges, one for black ink and one for three-color printing. If an ink-jet printer doesn't have a black ink cartridge, then it produces black by combining all colors of ink to produce a dull black. There are two advantages to having a separate cartridge for black ink: the black is a true black; and, more importantly, when printing in black, the printer isn't using the more expensive colored ink. You can replace the black cartridge without also replacing the colored ink cartridge.

Exhibit 12-5 shows the two ink cartridges for the Hewlett-Packard DeskJet 712C. The cartridge on the left contains red, blue, and yellow ink (official names are magenta, cyan, and yellow), and the cartridge on the right contains black ink. The print head assemblage is located in the center position because the top cover has been lifted. Normally when the printer isn't in use, the head assemblage sits to the far right of the printing area. This is called the home position and helps protect the ink in the cartridges from drying out.

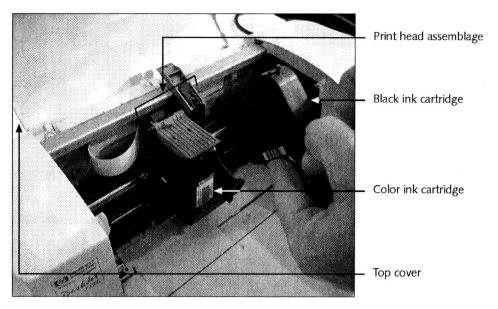

Print head assemblage

Black ink cartridge

Color ink cartridge

Top cover

Exhibit 12-5: The ink-jet cartridges of an ink-jet printer

Photo-quality ink-jet printers

A new generation of ink-jet printers has emerged that can give photo-quality results, especially when used with photo-quality paper. Until this new technology, increasing the quality of an ink-jet printer meant increasing the dpi (dots per inch). Earlier ink-jet printers used 300 dpi, but ink-jet printers today can use as many as 1400 dpi. Increasing the dpi has its drawbacks. Doing so increases the amount of data sent to the printer for a single page, and all those dots on the page can produce a wet page due to the quantity of ink. An improved technology that gives photo-quality results mixes different colors of ink to produce a new color that then makes a single dot. Hewlett-Packard calls this technology PhotoREt II color technology. HP mixes as many as 16 drops of ink to produce a single dot of color on the page, producing up to 30 times as many shades of color as conventional ink-jet printing does. The results are dramatic, and the cost of an ink-jet printer using photo-quality technology isn't significantly different from that of a printer that doesn't use it.

Supporting an ink-jet printer

Sometimes dust or dirt gets down into the print head assemblage, which can cause streaks or lines on the printed page. See the user guide for your printer to see how to clean the print cartridges and their cradles.

Correcting missing lines or dots on the printed page

The ink nozzles on an ink-jet cartridge occasionally dry out, especially when the printer sits for a long time without being used. Symptoms of this problem are missing lines or dots on the printed page. With older ink-jet printers, cleaning the ink-jet nozzles had to be done manually, but now newer printers often have a way to clean the nozzles automatically by using software or buttons on the front panel of the printer. The following section describes how to use supporting software to clean the nozzles on one ink-jet printer. For more information about how to clean the nozzles on your printer, see the printer documentation.

Using software to clean ink-jet nozzles

For the HP 710C series of printers, the software that accompanies the printer offers a way to clean the ink-jet nozzles automatically. When the printer software was installed, it placed a printer toolbox icon on the desktop and several tabs were added to the printer Properties box to support the printer. To clean the ink-jet nozzles, you use the Services tab:

1 Choose Start, Settings, Printers to open the Printers window. Right-click the ink-jet printer icon and select Properties from the shortcut menu.

2 Click the Services tab.

3 Click Clean the print cartridges to clean the ink-jet nozzles automatically.

4 A test page prints. If the page prints sharply with no missing dots or lines, then you're finished. If the page doesn't print correctly, perform the auto-clean procedure again.

5 You might need to perform the auto-clean procedure six or seven times to completely clean the nozzles. If the problem still persists, don't attempt to manually clean the nozzles. Instead, contact the manufacturer or vendor for service.

Correcting ink streaks

Follow the manufacturer's directions to clean the print cartridge assemblage. You need to use clean distilled water and cotton swabs to clean the cartridge cradle and the face and edges of the print cartridge, being careful not to touch the nozzle plate. To prevent the ink-jet nozzles from drying out, don't leave the print cartridges out of their cradle for longer than 30 minutes.

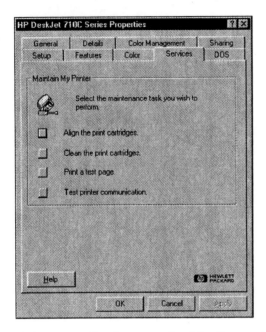

Exhibit 12-6: The Services tab of the Properties dialog box for an ink-jet printer

Dot-matrix printers

Dot-matrix printers are less expensive than other types of printers, but they don't give nearly the print quality. One reason you still see so many of these printers is that they're impact printers and can print multi-copy documents. A dot-matrix printer uses a print head that moves across the width of the paper by using pins to print a matrix of dots on the page. The pins shoot against a cloth ribbon, which hits the paper, depositing the ink. The ribbon provides both the ink for printing and the lubrication for the pin heads.

The ribbon of a dot matrix printer needs occasional replacing, and the print head can wear out. Replacing a print head is probably not cost-effective because it costs almost as much as the printer itself. If the print head fails, buy a new printer. Overheating can damage a print head. Keep the print head as cool as possible so that it will last longer. Keep the printer in a cool, well-ventilated area and don't use it for extended periods without cooling the head down.

Exhibit 12-7: The print head of a dot-matrix printer

Supporting printers

This section includes a brief introduction of how Windows 9x prints, and then moves on to discuss improving printer performance and troubleshooting printer problems.

Printing using Windows 9x

Windows 9x manages print jobs in one of three ways:

- For Windows applications using a non-PostScript printer, the print job data is converted to *enhanced metafile format* (*EMF*). This format embeds print commands in the data to help speed up printing.

- For Windows applications using a PostScript printer, the print job data is converted to the PostScript language. (Recall that a PostScript printer is a printer that uses a special language for data communication called PostScript.).

- For DOS applications, data isn't converted, but sent to the printer as is (this is called raw data).

When Windows 9x receives a print job from an application, it places the job in a queue and prints from the queue, so that the application is released from the printing process as soon as possible. Several print jobs can accumulate in the queue, and you can view them from the Control Panel icon for the printer. This process of queue printing jobs is called *spooling*. (The word "spool" is an acronym for simultaneous peripheral operations on line.) Most printing from Windows 9x uses EMF spooling.

Also, if the parallel port, printer cable, and printer all support bi-directional communication, communication from the printer to Windows is possible. For example, Windows 9x can ask the printer how much printer memory is available and what fonts are installed. The printer can send messages to the OS such as an out-of-paper or paper jam message.

Do it!

A-2: Installing a local printer

Here's how	Here's why
1 Power off your workstation	
2 Attach the printer's parallel cable to the printer and the computer	
Plug in and turn on the printer	
Power on the workstation	Boot into Windows 9x.
3 Double-click **My Computer**	
4 Double-click **Printers**	
5 Double-click **Add Printer**

To start the Add Printer Wizard. |
6 Click **Next**	To advance through the Add Printer Wizard.
7 Select **Local printer**	
8 Select the printer driver	Your instructor will tell you which printer driver to install.
9 Select the printer port	
10 In the Printer Name box, enter **Printer1**	

11 Click **Yes**	To select this printer as your Windows default.
Click **Yes**	To print a test page.
12 Click **Finish**	
13 Close the Printers folder	Click the Close button (the X in the upper-right corner of the window).
Close My Computer	

Improving printer performance

Explanation

The speed of a small, desktop printer is dependent on the speed of the computer as well as that of the printer. If the printer is slow, upgrading the computer's memory or the CPU might help. Printer speed also can be improved by lowering the printer resolution and the print quality.

To speed up a laser printer, besides lowering the printer resolution and print quality (which lowers the RET settings), you can try adding more memory to the printer.

If the bottom portion of a page on a laser printer doesn't print, the problem is that there isn't enough memory, either on the PC or the printer. Upgrading memory on either the PC or the printer might solve the problem.

The quality of the paper you use has a significant impact on the final print quality, especially with ink-jet printers. In general, the better the quality of the paper used with an ink-jet printer, the better the print quality. Don't use less than 20-lb paper in any type of printer, unless the printer documentation specifically says that a lower weight is satisfactory.

Troubleshooting guidelines for printers

When resolving printer problems, begin by determining where the problem is located. It might be with the printer, the PC hardware or OS, the application using the printer, the printer cable, or, in the case of a printer installed on a network, the network. This section first addresses how to isolate the problem and then discusses troubleshooting each of the possible sources of the problem. Problems with printers on a network are covered later in the unit. Follow the steps in the flow chart shown in Exhibit 12-8 to isolate the problem to one of the following areas:

- The application attempting to use the printer
- The OS and printer drivers
- Connectivity between the PC and the printer
- The printer

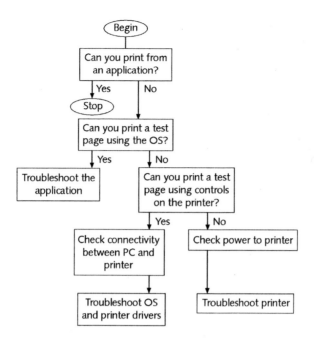

Exhibit 12-8: Isolating a printer problem

Operating system test page

If you can print a test page from the operating system, then you can eliminate every possible source of the problem except for the applications software that is trying to print.

1 To print a test page by using the OS, choose Start, Settings, Printers. The Printers window is displayed.

2 Right-click the icon for the printer you're testing. The printer Properties box is displayed. Verify that the General tab is displayed. Click Print Test Page.

3 The test page that prints isn't the same test page that prints from the printer self-test. This test page contains a list of driver files that the OS is using to communicate with the printer, the port that the OS is using, and the name of the driver being used.

If you can't print successfully, Windows 9x will automatically launch its troubleshooting tool to help you troubleshoot the problem. It will make suggestions and ask questions to help you discover the solution to the problem.

If the operating system test page printed correctly, turn to the applications software and begin troubleshooting there.

Problems with the printer

To eliminate the printer as the problem, print a test page from the printer. If this test page prints correctly, it confirms that the printer works correctly.

Note: When troubleshooting problems with printer drivers, check the Web site of the printer manufacturer to download the latest driver. Also, look for troubleshooting suggestions in the site's FAQs. You might also be able to get help by e-mailing technical support.

Printer self-test page

Follow these steps to print a self-test page:

1 For directions on printing a self-test page, see the user guide for the printer. One example, the HP LaserJet 5L, prints a test page if you hold down the button on the front panel until the front panel lights begin to blink.

2 A printer test page generally prints some text, some graphics, and information about the printer such as the printer resolution and how much memory is installed.

3 Verify that the information on the test page is correct. For example, if you know that the printer should have 2 MB of on-board printer memory, but it reports only 1 MB, then there's a problem with memory.

If the test page doesn't print, or prints incorrectly (for example, there are missing dots or smudged streaks through the page), then troubleshoot the printer until you can successfully print a good test page:

• Turn the printer off and disconnect it from the PC. Turn the printer back on and try to print another self-test page.

• Does the printer have paper? Is the paper installed correctly? Is there a paper jam?

• Reset the printer.

• For a laser printer, check that a toner cartridge is installed. For an ink-jet printer, check that ink cartridges are installed.

• Check that power is getting to the printer.

• Try another power cable.

For some laser printers, if the printer doesn't have enough memory to hold the entire page, an error occurs. For others, only a part of the page prints.

For some HP LaserJet printers that don't have a control panel on the front of the printer, an error message is displayed as a flashing amber error light. For some HP LaserJet printers that do have a control panel, the displayed error message when there isn't enough memory is "20 Mem Overflow." The solution is to install more memory or print only simple pages with few graphics.

Print a self-test page to verify how much memory is installed. Check the user guide for the printer to determine how much memory the printer can support and what kind of memory to buy.

Problem with the printer cable

If the printer self-test worked, but the OS printer test didn't work, the problem might be with the printer cable.

- Check that the cable is firmly connected at both ends.
- Many businesses use a switch box (sometimes called a T-switch) to share one printer between two computers. A printer cable connects to the printer port of each computer. The two cables connect to the switch box. A third cable connects from the switch box to the printer. A switch on the front of the box controls which computer has access to the printer. Switch boxes were built with older dot-matrix printers in mind. Some switch boxes aren't recommended for ink-jet or laser printers that use a bi-directional parallel cable, and can even damage a printer. For these printers, remove the switch box.
- Try a different cable.
- Try printing by using the same printer and printer cable, but a different PC.
- Enter the CMOS setup of the PC and check how the parallel port is configured. Is it disabled? Is it set to ECP or bi-directional? An ECP parallel port requires the use of a DMA channel. Try setting the port to bi-directional.

Problem with the OS or device drivers

If the printer self-test worked, but the OS printer test didn't work, the problem might be with the operating system or device drivers.

- Try rebooting and then attempt to print another OS test page.
- Try printing from DOS. Access a DOS prompt (real-mode DOS, not a DOS box) and print a directory list. Use the command DIR > LPT1. If nothing prints, press the Form Feed button. Sometimes when using DOS, a partial page needs to be ejected by this method before the printer will print.
- If you can print from DOS, but not from Windows, try removing and reinstalling the printer driver. To uninstall the printer driver, right-click the printer icon in the Printers window, choose Delete to remove the printer, and then reinstall the printer.
- Check the configuration of the parallel port in CMOS setup.
- Try another printer driver. It might not print graphics correctly, but if another driver does work at all, then you can conclude that you have a faulty driver. For example, if you have an HP LaserJet 5L, try using the HP LaserJet III driver.
- Verify printer properties. Try lowering the resolution or printing a different document.
- Try printing from Notepad. If you can print from Notepad, then the problem is with the application. Reboot the PC and try to print from the application again.
- Under the printer Properties box, try disabling Check Port State Before Printing.
- Reboot the PC. Immediately enter Notepad or WordPad, type some text, and print.

- If you can print from DOS, but not from Windows, try disabling printer spooling. In the Properties box of the printer, on the Details tab, click Spool Settings, and select Print Directly to the Printer. Spooling holds print jobs in a queue for printing, so if spooling is disabled, then printing from an application can be slower.

- The print spool might be stalled. Try deleting all print jobs in the printer's queue. Double-click the printer icon in the Printers window. Choose Printer, Purge Print Documents.

- Also from the Properties box, on the Details tab, click Spool Settings, and select Disable bi-directional support for this printer. There might be a problem with bi-directional communication between the PC and printer.

- Check the resources assigned to the printer port. Access Device Manager, select LPT1, and click Properties. Verify that the resources are assigned correctly for LPT1 (I/O addresses are 0378 to 037B) and that Device Manager reports "No conflicts."

Problem with the applications software

- If you can print from Notepad or WordPad, but can't print from an application, try closing and reopening the application.

- Verify that the correct printer is selected in the Print setup box.

- Try printing a different application file.

- Try creating new data in a newly created file and printing it. Keep the data simple.

- Try printing from another application.

- If you can print from other applications, but not this one application, consider reinstalling the application.

Do it!

A-3:   Troubleshooting printers

Question	Answer
1 Describe how to replace the fuser in your lab workstation.	
2 During the laser printing process, what determines when the toner sticks to the drum and when it doesn't?	

3 Angie is trying to share her local printer so that Bart can print to it. When she views the properties of the installed printer there isn't a Sharing tab. Explain why Angie doesn't have a Sharing tab for her printer and describe the steps she will need to take in order to share her printer with Bart.

4 Alice has an HP LaserJet 6L at her desk. She is on the phone with you because it won't print. She says that there's a yellow light flashing on the front panel and the printer isn't printing. List at least three things that you would have Alice check to resolve her printing problem.

5 What should you do if an ink-jet printer prints with missing dots or lines on the page?

6 What can you do to help a dot-matrix printer last longer?

7 How can you eliminate the printer as the source of a printing problem?

8 List two possible ways to improve printing speed.

Topic B: Notebook computers

Explanation

Supporting notebook computers is another essential task of a PC technician. This section discusses the special needs of supporting notebooks, including adding memory to a notebook, changing power management options, understanding and supporting PC cards, and using special Windows 98 components available for supporting notebooks.

Notebooks

Notebooks use the same technology as do PCs, but with modifications so as to use less voltage, take up less space, and work when on the move. A *notebook* or *laptop* computer is a computer designed for travel. Notebooks use thin LCD panels instead of CRT monitors for display, compact hard drives that can withstand movement even during operation, and small memory modules and CPUs that require less voltage than regular components.

Notebooks cost more than PCs with similar features, because components are designed to be more compact and to endure movement and even jars when in use. The types and features of notebooks vary widely as they do for PCs. However, notebooks are generally purchased as a whole unit, including both hardware and software, and you aren't likely to upgrade a notebook's hardware and OS, as you would with a PC. In fact, some notebook manufacturers no longer support a notebook that has had the OS upgraded or new hardware components added. Notebook computers can be very proprietary in design, which means the skills needed to support them are brand-specific.

When supporting any notebook, pay careful attention to the stipulations on the warranty that accompanies it. Some warranties are voided if you open the notebook case or install memory, batteries, or a hard drive that wasn't made by, or at least authorized by, the notebook manufacturer. Almost all operating system installations on notebooks are customized by the manufacturer, and a floppy disk comes with the notebook that contains data and utilities specific to the configuration. Read the supporting documentation for the notebook before you consider upgrading or reinstalling the OS.

Exhibit 12-9: A notebook is a computer designed for travel

Windows 98 notebook features

Windows 98 and Windows 2000 Professional offer features designed specifically for notebooks. When choosing between Windows 98 and Windows 2000 Professional for a notebook OS, use Windows 98 for low-end notebooks and Windows 2000 for high-end notebooks that are used in a business environment in which security is important.

- Multilink Channel Aggregation, a feature that enables you to use two modem connections at the same time to speed up data throughput when connected over phone lines. It works on both regular analog phone lines and ISDN. To use the feature, you must have two phone lines and two modem cards that are physically designed to connect two phone lines at the same time. You'll learn more about PC Card modems later in the chapter.

- ACPI (Advanced Configuration and Power Interface) developed by Intel, Microsoft, and Toshiba to control power on a notebook and other devices. ACPI enables a device to turn on a notebook or enables a notebook to turn on a device. For example, if you connect an external CD-ROM drive to a notebook, it can turn on the notebook, or the notebook can cycle up and turn on an external CD-ROM drive. The BIOS of the notebook and the device must support ACPI for it to work.

- Several improvements over Windows 95 for managing power consumption for notebooks. Windows 98 automatically powers down a PC Card modem when not in use, supports multiple battery packs, and lets you create individual power profiles. Power profiles are described in the next section.

- Improved support for PC Cards, adding several new drivers.

- Microsoft Exchange lets a user select what e-mail to download when traveling with a notebook. Downloading large e-mail messages with attachments takes a long time over a modem. You might prefer to leave this e-mail to download when you're later connected directly to the network.

Windows 2000 Professional notebook features

Windows 2000 has stronger power management and security features. Other features new to Windows 2000 include:

- Offline Files, which replaces Briefcase, stores shared network files and folders in a cache on the notebook hard drive so you can use them offline. When you reconnect to the network, Offline Files synchronizes the files in the cache with those on the network.

- Hibernate mode, support for ACPI and APM (Advanced Power Management) has been improved.

- Improved battery support includes the ability to use two batteries and to monitor battery performance with greater control.

- Hot swapping of IDE devices and floppy disk external drives is a new feature.

- Folder redirection lets you point to an alternate location on a network for a folder. This feature can make the location of a folder transparent to the user.

Do it!

B-1: Discussing notebook features

Question	Answer
1 What type of monitor does a notebook use?	
2 Name a Windows 98 feature that is designed especially for notebooks.	
3 What Windows 2000 features are useful to notebook users?	
4 Why are notebooks usually more expensive than PCs with comparable power and features?	

Power management

Explanation

A notebook can be powered by a battery pack or by an AC adapter connected to a power source. The length of time that a battery pack can power the notebook before being recharged varies according to the quality of the battery, the power consumption as determined by the devices being used, and how power is being managed.

Windows 98 has features to help manage power consumption. The goal is to minimize power consumption to increase the time before a battery pack needs recharging. Using Windows 98, to access the power management window, choose Start, Settings, Control Panel and double-click the Power Management icon. Exhibit 12-10 displays the Power Management Properties box for one type of notebook. (Other brands of notebooks might have different tabs showing in the Properties box.) From this Properties box, you can create, delete, and modify multiple power management schemes to customize how you want Windows 98 to manage power consumption.

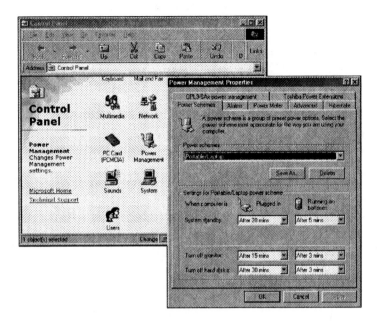

Exhibit 12-10: The Power Management Properties box

For example, one power-saving feature of Windows 98 is the ability to put a notebook into *hibernation*. When a computer hibernates, it stores whatever is currently in memory and then shuts down. When it returns from hibernating, it restores everything back to the way it was before the shutdown. When hibernating, the notebook isn't using power. When you step away from the notebook for a few minutes, if you direct the notebook to hibernate, you save power.

To configure Windows 98 to cause the notebook to hibernate when you close the lid of the notebook, do the following:

1 From the Power Management Properties box, click the Hibernate tab and verify that hibernate support is enabled.

2 Click the Advanced tab.

3 Click the drop-down arrow for "When I close the lid of my portable computer" and select Hibernate from the list.

4 Click Apply and OK to exit the Properties box, saving your changes.

If you need to use the notebook for extended periods of time away from an electrical outlet, you can use extra battery packs. When the notebook signals you that power is low, remove the old battery and replace it with a charged one. See the notebook's user guide for directions. Here's an example of directions for exchanging the battery pack for one notebook:

1 Save your work and turn off the notebook.
2 Remove all cables connected to the notebook.
3 Set the notebook on its back.
4 Slide the battery release panel to the left to expose the battery.
5 Lift the battery out of the computer.
6 Before placing a new battery in the slot, clean the edge connectors of the battery with a clean cloth.

Upgrading memory

Notebooks use proprietary (built by the manufacturer of the notebook) memory modules that are smaller than regular SIMMs or DIMMs. These modules are called *SO-DIMM*s (small outline DIMMs). They have 72 pins and support 32-bit data transfers (as shown in Exhibit 12-11). Before upgrading memory, remember to make sure that you aren't voiding your warranty. Search around for the best buy, but make sure you use memory modules made by the notebook manufacturer and designed for the exact model of notebook you have. Installing generic memory might save you money, but it might also void the notebook's warranty.

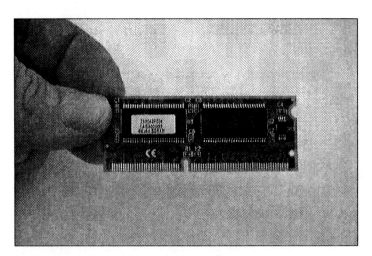

Exhibit 12-11: An SO-DIMM memory module

To install memory, see the notebook's user guide for directions. The following is an example of how to install memory on one notebook. Directions will vary somewhat from one computer to another.

1 Turn off the notebook and remove all cables.

2 Lift the keyboard brace, as shown in Exhibit 12-12.

Exhibit 12-12: Lifting the keyboard brace

3 Turn the keyboard over and toward the front of the notebook. The keyboard is still connected to the notebook via the ribbon cable.

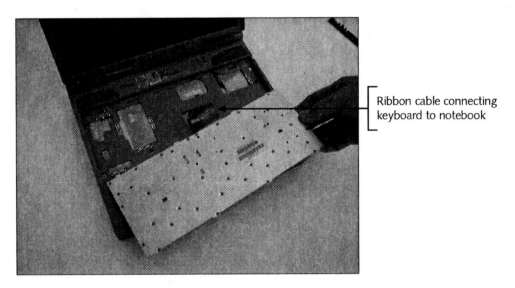

Ribbon cable connecting keyboard to notebook

Exhibit 12-13: Turning over the keyboard to expose memory sockets

4   Lift the plastic sheet covering the memory module socket.

5   Insert the SO-DIMM module into the socket. The socket braces should snap into place on each side of the module when the module is in position.

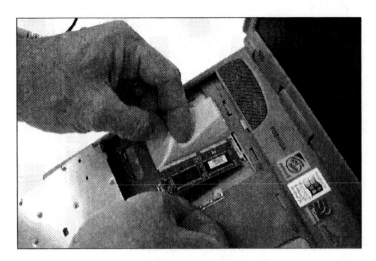

Exhibit 12-14: Installing the SO-DIMM

6   Replace the keyboard and keyboard brace.

7   When you power up the notebook, it detects the new memory.

Connecting peripheral devices to notebooks

A notebook provides several ports on its back, sides, or both. An infrared port is used to connect devices to notebooks or other computers without the need of cabling. A printer, keyboard, microphone, or other device can communicate with the laptop by using an infrared signal over a short distance. With special software, it also is possible for the notebook to communicate with another computer by using the infrared port. The most popular way to add peripheral devices to a notebook is by using PC card slots.

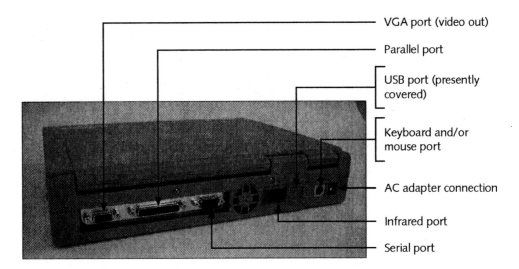

VGA port (video out)

Parallel port

USB port (presently covered)

Keyboard and/or mouse port

AC adapter connection

Infrared port

Serial port

Exhibit 12-15: Ports on the back of a notebook computer

PC cards (PCMCIA cards)

Unlike PCs, notebooks don't have the traditional expansion slots that connect to an I/O bus to enable you to add peripheral devices to a system. Rather, notebook computers contain special bus expansion slots called *PC card slots*, formally called *PCMCIA slots*, which connect to the 16-bit PCMCIA I/O bus on the notebook system board. There are currently four standards developed by the PCMCIA organization (Personal Computer Memory Card International Association) for these slots. Once intended only for memory cards (cards that add additional memory to a notebook), these PC card slots can now be used by many devices, including modems, network cards, CD-ROMs, sound cards, and hard disks. Some docking station PCs also have a PC card slot, so that the device you can use with your notebook also can be attached to the docking station. (A *docking station* is a special device that's designed so a notebook can easily connect to a full-sized monitor, keyboard, and other peripheral devices.) The latest PCMCIA specification is called CardBus and improves I/O speed, increases the bus width to 32 bits, and supports lower-voltage PC cards while maintaining backward compatibility with earlier standards.

Exhibit 12-16: A modem PC card

Three standards for the PCMCIA slots pertain to size and are named Type I, Type II, and Type III. Generally, the thicker the PC card, the higher the standard. A thick hard drive card might need a Type III slot, but a thin modem card might need only a Type II slot. The PC card is about the size of a credit card, but thicker, and inserts into the PC card slot. Type I cards can be up to 3.3-mm thick and are primarily used for adding more RAM to a notebook PC. Type II cards can be up to 5.5-mm thick and are often used as modem cards. Type III cards can be up to 10.5-mm thick, which is large enough to accommodate a portable disk drive. When buying a notebook PC, look for both Type II and Type III PC card slots. Often one of each is included. Also, for improved performance, look for the slots to be 32-bit CardBus slots.

The operating system must provide two services for the PC card, a socket service and a card service. The socket service manages the socket, closing (establishing) the socket when the card is inserted and opening (disconnecting) the socket when the card is removed. The card service provides the device driver to interface with the card once the socket is closed.

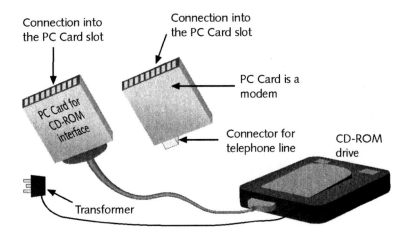

Exhibit 12-17: Two examples of PC cards

The PC card might contain a data cable to an external device, or it might be self-contained. For example, in Exhibit 12-17 the PC card on the left is the interface between the notebook PC and the CD-ROM external drive. Insert the PC card in the PC card slot. The data cable from the PC card connects to the external CD-ROM drive, which requires its own power supply that must be connected into a wall outlet. The PC card on the right is the actual modem. Insert the card in the PC card slot and connect the telephone line to the modem PC card.

One feature you want to have in PC card slots is *hot swapping* (which means you can install a device while a computer is running, and the computer will recognize the device without rebooting). Hot swapping enables you to remove one card and insert another without powering down the PC. For example, if you're currently using a modem in the PC card slot and want to switch to the CD-ROM, first turn off the modem card (open the socket) by using the PC Card icon in the Windows 9x Control Panel. Then remove the modem card and insert the CD-ROM card with the attached external CD-ROM drive.

Exhibit 12-18: Connecting a phone line to a modem PC card

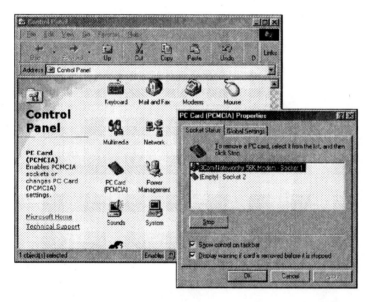

Exhibit 12-19: Stopping a PC card from the PC Card Properties box

Another popular use of a PC card is to interact with a network. Exhibit 12-20 shows an example of a PC card that serves as the NIC to an Ethernet 10BaseT network. The RJ-45 connection is at the end of a small cord connected to the PC card. This small cord is called a *dongle*, and is used so that the thick RJ-45 connection doesn't have to fit flat against the PC card.

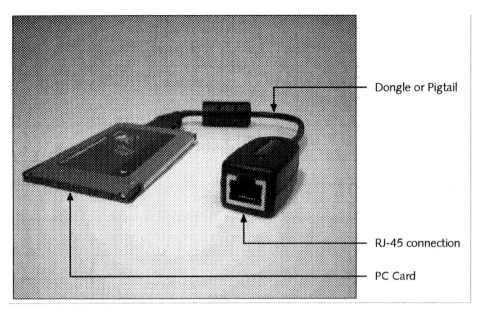

Exhibit 12-20: This PC card serves as a NIC for an Ethernet 10BaseT network

Supporting notebooks

With a few exceptions, notebooks work identically to desktop PCs, and the troubleshooting guidelines in previous units also apply to notebooks. When troubleshooting notebooks, be especially conscious of warranty issues; know what you can do within the guidelines of the warranty. The documentation that comes with a notebook is much more comprehensive than what comes with a PC and most often contains troubleshooting guidelines for the notebook. Remember that the loaded OS and the hardware configuration are specific to the notebook, so you can rely on the notebook manufacturer for support more than you can for a desktop PC. For questions about supporting a notebook that aren't answered in the documentation, see the Web site of the notebook manufacturer.

Manufacturer	Web site
Acer America	www.acer.com
ARM Computer	www.armcomputer.com
Compaq Computer	www.compaq.com
Dell Computer	www.dell.com
FutureTech Systems	www.futuretec.com
Gateway	www.gateway.com
Hewlett-Packard	www.hp.com
IBM	www.ibm.com
Micron Electronics	www.micronpc.com
PC Notebook	www.pcnotebook.com
Sony	www.sony.com
Toshiba America	www.csd.toshiba.com
WinBook	www.winbook.com

Do it!

B-2: Supporting notebook computers

Question	Answer
1 What type of memory module is used in a notebook?	
2 How are battery packs used in a notebook?	
3 When a battery pack discharges and you need to continue working on a notebook, what are your two choices?	
4 What is the small cord sometimes found on the end of a PC card called?	
5 What is a PC card slot?	
6 What types of device cards can be used in a PC card slot?	
7 What is the first step you should take before you consider upgrading or reinstalling the OS in a notebook?	

Unit summary: Printers and notebook computers

Topic A   You learned about the basic functioning of **laser**, **ink-jet**, and **dot-matrix printers**. You also learned how to **troubleshoot printer problems**, and how to **share** network printers with Windows 9x.

Topic B   In this topic, you discussed Windows 98 and Windows 2000 features that are designed for notebook computers. You also learned basic technical support for a notebook computer, including how to use the **hibernation features** of a notebook and how to **upgrade memory**, and how to connect peripheral devices.

Review questions

1   List the six steps used by a laser printer to print a page.

2   What technology makes an ink-jet printer a photo-quality ink-jet printer?

3   What should you do if an ink-jet printer prints with ink streaks on the page?

4 When you are isolating a printer problem, what are the four major possible sources of the problem?

5 What term refers to a PC card you can remove and replace without powering off?

6 What two services must an OS provide for a PC card to work?

A+ Certification: Core Hardware

Course summary

This summary contains information to help you bring the course to a successful conclusion. By using this information, you'll be able to:

A Use the summary text to reinforce what you've learned in class.

B Determine the next course(s) in this series (if any), as well as any other resources that might help you continue to learn about computer hardware maintenance.

Topic A: Course summary

Use the following summary text to reinforce what you've learned in class.

A+ Certification: Core Hardware

Unit 1

In this unit, you reviewed **computer components**, examined the **boot process** in detail, and loaded applications software to observe the **PATH** command. You also discussed the four system resources: **IRQs**, **I/O addresses**, **memory addresses**, and **DMA channels**.

Unit 2

In this unit, you learned about the **system board**, or motherboard. You learned that the **CPU** is the most important component of the system board. You discussed the various types of memory, **ROM** and **RAM**. You also discussed **buses** and **expansion slots** and learned how to install a PCI expansion card.

Unit 3

You examined how a computer **manages memory**. You learned the difference between **physical** memory and **logical** memory. You examined the various types of memory management techniques, such as **swap files**. Finally, you learned how to **install RAM**.

Unit 4

You learned about **floppy drives** and what happens during the **formatting process**. You created an **Emergency Startup Disk** to enable you to start the computer in the event of a hard disk crash. You also learned how to **remove and install a floppy drive**.

Unit 5

In this unit, you were introduced to **hard drive** technologies, specifically **IDE** and **SCSI**. You examined how the hard drive is **organized**. Then, you learned how to **install a hard drive** as well as **remove** a hard drive. You also discussed various ways to **troubleshoot** hard drive problems.

Unit 6

In this unit, you were introduced to the basics of **troubleshooting**. You learned how to **isolate problems to resolve** them. Then, you practiced creating and solving a variety of hardware and software problems. Finally, you learned about **preventive maintenance practices** and how to develop a plan.

Unit 7

In this unit, you examined **I/O devices** and learned the difference between serial ports and parallel ports. You also examined **SCSI devices** in detail and learned how to install one. You also learned how to support I/O devices such as **keyboard, pointing devices, and monitors**.

Unit 8

In this unit, you examined the various types of **multimedia** and its **technology**. In particular, you installed a **CD-ROM driver** and **sound card.** You also learned about **digital cameras** and **DVDs**.

Unit 9

In this unit, you learned about electricity and the **power supplies** that are required for a computer. You learned how to **measure the voltage** and protect against power **surges**.

Unit 10

In this unit, you learned about **communicating** over phone lines. You examined modems in detail and learned how to **install** and **configure modems** and how to troubleshoot modem problems.

Unit 11

In this unit, you discussed the basic fundamentals of **networking**. You learned about the various network **architectures** and the **hardware** required for networking.

Unit 12

In this unit, you learned about **printers**. You examined the various printer devices and drivers. You also learned how to support **notebook** computers and examined the issues specific to these machines.

Topic B: Continued learning after class

It's impossible to learn how to maintain PC hardware effectively in a classroom. To get the most out of this class, you should start performing real tasks as soon as possible. Course Technology also offers resources for continued learning.

Next course(s) in this series

This is the only course in this series. However, a companion course on operating systems is also available:

- *A+ Certification: Operating Systems*
  ISBN: 0-619-17106-5

Other resources

You might also find some of these Course Technology resources useful as you continue to learn about PC hardware maintenance. For more information, visit www.course.com.

- *Enhanced A+ Guide to Managing and Maintaining Your PC, Third Edition Comprehensive*
  ISBN: 0-619-03433-5
- *PC Troubleshooting Pocket Guide*
  ISBN: 0-619-01537-3

Glossary

3D RAM

Special video RAM designed to improve 3D graphics simulation.

32-bit flat memory mode

A protected processing mode used by Windows NT to process programs written in 32-bit code early in the boot process.

Accelerated graphics port (AGP)

A slot on a system board for a video card that provides transfer of video data from the CPU that's synchronized with the memory bus.

ACPI (Advanced Configuration and Power Interface)

Specification developed by Intel, Microsoft, and Toshiba to control power on notebooks and other devices. Windows 98 supports ACPI.

Adapter address

A 6-byte hex hardware address unique to each NIC and assigned by manufacturers. The address is often printed on the adapter. An example is 00 00 0C 08 2F 35. Also called MAC address.

Adapter card

Also called an interface card. A small circuit board inserted in an expansion slot and used to communicate between the system bus and a peripheral device.

ADSL (asymmetric digital subscriber line)

A method of data transmission over phone lines that is digital, provides for a direct connection, and is about 50 times faster than ISDN.

Advanced SCSI programming interface (ASPI)

A popular device driver that enables operating systems to communicate with a SCSI host adapter. (The "A" originally stood for Adaptec.)

Advanced Transfer Cache (ATC)

A type of L2 cache contained within the Pentium processor housing that's embedded on the same core processor die as the CPU itself.

Alternating current (AC)

Current that cycles back and forth rather than traveling in only one direction. Normally between 110 and 115 AC volts are supplied from a standard wall outlet.

Ammeter

A meter that measures electrical current in amps.

Ampere (A)

A unit of measurement for electrical current. One volt across a resistance of one ohm will produce a flow of one amp.

Amplifier repeater

A repeater that amplifies whatever it receives regardless of its source.

Analog-to-digital converter (A/D or ADC)

A component on a sound card that samples and converts analog sound into digital values that can be stored in a file.

ANSI (American National Standards Institute)

A nonprofit organization dedicated to creating trade and communications standards.

Asynchronous SRAM

Static RAM that doesn't work in step with the CPU clock and is, therefore, slower than synchronous SRAM.

AT command set

A set of commands used by a PC to control a modem. AT is the ATtention command, which alerts a modem to prepare to receive additional commands. For example, ATDT means attention and listen for a dial tone.

ATAPI (Advanced Technology Attachment Packet Interface)

An interface standard that is part of the IDE/ATA standards, which enables tape drives and CD-ROM drives to be treated like an IDE hard drive by the OS.

Autorange meter

A multimeter that senses the quantity of input and sets the range accordingly.

Backbone

A network used to link several networks together. For example, several Token Rings and Ethernet LANS may be connected by using a single FDDI backbone.

Backside bus

The bus between the CPU and the L2 cache inside the CPU housing.

Bandwidth

The range of frequencies that a communication cable or channel can carry. In general use, the term refers to the volume of data that can travel on a bus or over a cable.

Bank

An area on the system board that contains slots for memory modules (typically labeled bank 0, 1, 2, and 3).

Baud rate

A measure of line speed between two devices such as a computer and a printer or a modem. This speed is measured in the number of times a signal changes in one second. See bps.

Beam detect mirror

Detects the initial presence of a laser printer's laser beam by reflecting the beam to an optical fiber.

Binary number system

The number system used by computers where there are only two numbers, 0 and 1, called binary digits, or bits.

Binding

Associating an OSI layer to a layer above it or below it.

BIOS (basic input/output system)

Firmware that controls much of a computer's input/output functions, such as communication with the floppy drive, RAM chips, and the monitor. Also called ROM BIOS.

Block mode

A method of data transfer between hard drive and memory that supports multiple data transfers on a single software interrupt.

BNC connector

A connector used on an Ethernet 10Base2 (Thinnet) network. A BNC connector looks like a TV cable connector.

Boot partition

The hard drive partition where the Windows NT OS is stored. The system partition and the boot partition may be different partitions.

Boot record (of hard drives)

The first sector of each logical drive in a partition that contains information about the logical drive. If the boot record is in the active partition, then it's used to boot the OS. Also called OS boot record or volume boot record.

Bootable disk

For DOS, a floppy disk that can upload the OS files necessary for computer startup. It must have the two hidden system files IO.SYS and MSDOS.SYS, and also COMMAND.COM.

Bps (bits per second)

A measure of data transmission speed. (Example: a common modem speed is 56,000 bps or 56 Kbps.)

Bridge

A hardware device or box, coupled with software at the data-link layer, used to connect similar networks and network segments. See Router.

Buck-boost regulator

A line-interactive UPS that offers good line conditioning and has an automatic voltage regulator that decreases ("bucks") the voltage during electrical spikes and boosts it during sags.

Buffer

A temporary memory area where data is kept before being written to a hard drive or sent to a printer, thus reducing the number of writes to the devices.

Burst EDO (BEDO)

A refined version of EDO memory that significantly improves access time over EDO. BEDO isn't widely used today because Intel chose not to support it. BEDO memory is stored on 168-pin DIMM modules.

Burst SRAM

Memory that's more expensive and slightly faster than pipelined burst SRAM. Data is sent as a two-step process; the data address is sent, and then the data itself is sent without interruption.

Burst transfer

A means of sending data across the bus, with one packet immediately following the next, without waiting for clock beats and/or addressing of the information being sent.

Bus

Strips of parallel wires or printed circuits used to transmit electronic signals on the system board to other devices. Most Pentium systems use a 32-bit or 64-bit bus.

Bus enumerator

A component of Windows 9x Plug and Play that locates all devices on a particular bus and inventories the resource requirements for these devices.

Bus mouse

A mouse that plugs into a bus adapter card and has a round, 9-pin mini-DIN connector.

Bus network architecture

A network design in which nodes are connected in line with one another, with no centralized point of contact.

Bus speed

The speed or frequency at which the data on the system board moves.

Cable modem

A method of data transmission over cable TV lines that requires a modem and an Ethernet network interface card to receive the transmission.

Cache memory

A type of fast RAM that's used to speed up memory access because it doesn't need to be continuously refreshed.

Cards

Adapter boards or interface cards placed into expansion slots to expand the functions of a computer, so it can communicate with external devices such as monitors or speakers.

Carrier

A signal used to activate a phone line to confirm a continuous frequency; used to indicate that two computers are ready to receive or transmit data via modems.

Carrier Sense Multiple Access with Collision Detection (CSMA/CD)

A feature used in Ethernet networks whereby packets are sent after the sending node listens for silence, and are resent if a collision is detected.

CD-R (recordable CD)

A CD drive that can record or write data to a CD. The drive might be multi-session, but the data can't be erased once it's written.

CD-RW (rewritable CD)

A CD drive that can record or write data to a CD. The data can be erased and overwritten. The drive might be multi-session.

Chip set

A group of chips on the system board that relieves the CPU of some of the system's processing tasks, providing careful timing of activities and increasing the overall speed and performance of the system.

CHS (cylinders, heads, sectors) mode

The traditional method by which BIOS reads from and writes to hard drives by addressing the correct cylinder, head, and sector. Also called normal mode.

Circuit boards

Computer components, such as the main system board or an adapter board, that have electronic circuits and chips.

Clamping voltage

The maximum voltage that can pass through a surge suppressor, such as 175 or 330 volts.

Clock speed

The speed or frequency that determines the speed at which devices on the system bus operate, usually expressed in MHz. Different components on a system board operate at different speeds, which are determined by multiplying or dividing a factor by the clock speed. The clock speed is determined by a crystal or oscillator located somewhere on the system board.

Cluster

One or more sectors that constitute the smallest unit of space on a disk for storing data (also referred to as a file allocation unit). Files are written to a disk as groups of whole clusters.

Cluster chain

A series of clusters used to hold a single file.

CMOS (complementary metal-oxide semiconductor)

One of two types of technologies used to manufacture microchips (the other type is TTL or transistor-transistor logic chips). CMOS chips require less electricity, hold data longer after the electricity is turned off, are slower, and produce less heat than do TTL chips. The configuration or setup chip is a CMOS chip.

COAST (cache on a stick)

Memory modules that hold memory used as a memory cache. See Cache memory.

Collision

In an Ethernet network, a collision occurs when transmitted packets of data are sent at the same time and collide. Ethernet will first listen for silence before it transmits, and it will stop and resend if a collision occurs.

Combo card

An Ethernet card that has more than one port to accommodate different cabling media.

Common access method (CAM)

A standard adapter driver used by SCSI.

Compressed drive

A drive whose format has been reorganized in order to store more data. A compressed drive is really not a drive at all; it's actually a type of file, typically with a host drive called H.

Computing Technology Industry Association (CompTIA)

A membership trade association that sponsors A+ Certification, a valuable certification for PC technicians.

Configuration data

Also called setup information. Information about the computer's hardware, such as what type of hard drive or floppy drive is present, along with other detailed settings.

Constant angular velocity (CAV)

A technology used by hard drives and newer CD-ROM drives whereby the disc rotates at a constant speed.

Constant linear velocity (CLV)

A CD-ROM format in which the spacing of data is consistent on the CD, but the speed of the disc varies depending on whether the data is reading near the center or the edge of the disc.

Continuity

A continuous, unbroken path for the flow of electricity. A "continuity test" can determine whether internal wiring is still intact.

Control blade

A laser printer component that prevents too much toner from sticking to the cylinder surface.

Controlled-access unit (CAU)

A centralized hub on a Token Ring network. See Multistation access unit.

Conventional memory

Memory addresses between 0 and 640K. Also called base memory.

Cooperative multitasking

A type of pseudo-multitasking whereby the CPU switches back and forth between programs loaded at the same time. One program sits in the background waiting for the other to relinquish control. Also called task switching.

Coprocessor

A chip or portion of the CPU that helps the microprocessor perform calculations and speeds up computations and data manipulations dramatically.

CPU (central processing unit)

Also called a microprocessor. The heart and brain of the computer, which receives data input, processes information, and executes instructions.

Crosstalk

The interference that a signal in one wire might produce in another.

DAC (digital-to-analog converter)

A component that converts digital data back into analog signals just before output from the computer. For example, DAC technology is used to convert digital sound to analog sound just before playback to the speakers.

Data communications equipment (DCE)

The hardware, usually a dial-up modem, that provides the connection between a data terminal and a communications line.

Data compression

Reducing the size of files by various techniques such as using a shortcut code to represent repeated data.

Data line protectors

Surge protectors designed to work with the telephone line to a modem.

Data path

The number of bits of data transmitted simultaneously on a bus. The size of a bus, such as a 32-bit-wide data path in a PCI bus.

De facto standard

A standard that doesn't have an official backing, but is considered a standard because of widespread use and acceptance by the industry.

Demodulation

When digital data that has been converted to analog data is converted back to digital data. See Modulation.

Device driver

A small program stored on the hard drive that tells the computer how to communicate with an input/output device such as a printer or modem.

Diagnostic cards

Adapter cards designed to discover and report computer errors and conflicts at POST time (before the computer boots up), often by displaying a number on the card.

Digital diagnostic disk

A floppy disk that has data written on it that's precisely aligned, which is used to test the alignment of a floppy disk drive.

Digital signal

A signal that has only a finite number of values in the range of possible values. An example is the transmission of data over a serial cable as bits, where there are only two values: 0 and 1.

Digital subscriber line (DSL)

A type of technology that's used by digital telephone lines that direct connect rather than dial-up.

Digital video disc (DVD)

A faster, larger CD-ROM format that can read older CDs, store over 8 gigabytes of data, and hold full-length motion picture videos.

DIMM (dual inline memory module)

A miniature circuit board used in newer computers to hold memory. DIMMs can hold 16, 32, 64, or 128 MB of RAM on a single module.

DIP (dual in-line package) switch

A switch on a circuit board or other device that can be set on or off to hold configuration or setup information.

Direct current (DC)

Current that travels in only one direction (the type of electricity provided by batteries). Computer power supplies transform AC current to low DC current.

Discrete L2 cache

A type of L2 cache contained within the Pentium processor housing, but on a different die with a cache bus between the processor and the cache.

Disk cache

A method whereby recently retrieved data and adjacent data are read into memory in advance, anticipating the next CPU request.

Double conversion

The process by which the inline UPS converts the AC power to battery power in DC form and then back to AC power.

Drop height

The height from which a manufacturer states that its drive can be dropped without making the drive unusable.

Dual ported

When the video chip set (input) and the RAM DAC (output) can access video memory at the same time. A special kind of video RAM is required.

Dual voltage CPU

A CPU that requires two different voltages, one for internal processing and the other for I/O processing.

Dynamic IP address

An assigned IP address that's used for only the current session. When the session is terminated, the IP address is returned to the list of available addresses.

Dynamic RAM (DRAM)

The most commonly used type of system memory, with access speeds ranging from 70 to 50 nanoseconds. It requires refreshing every few milliseconds.

ECHS (extended CHS) mode

A mode of addressing information on a hard drive by translating cylinder, head, and sector information in order to break the 528 MB hard drive barrier. Another name for large mode.

ECP (extended capabilities port)

A bidirectional parallel port mode that uses a DMA channel to speed up data flow.

EDO (extended data output) memory

A type of RAM that might be 10–20 percent faster than conventional RAM because it eliminates the delay before it issues the next memory address.

EEPROM (electrically erasable programmable ROM) chip

A type of chip in which higher voltage may be applied to one of the pins to erase its previous memory before a new instruction set is electronically written.

EISA (extended standard industry architecture) bus

A 32-bit bus that can transfer 4 bytes at a time at a speed of about 20 MHz.

Electrostatic discharge (ESD)

Another name for static electricity, which can damage chips and destroy system boards, even though it might not be felt or seen with the naked eye.

Embedded SCSI devices

Devices that contain their own host adapter, with the SCSI interface built into the device.

EMI (electromagnetic interference)

A magnetic field produced as a side effect from the flow of electricity. EMI can cause corrupted data in data lines that aren't properly shielded.

Energy Star systems

"Green" systems that satisfy the EPA requirements to decrease the overall consumption of electricity. See Green standards.

Enhanced BIOS

A newer BIOS written to accommodate larger-capacity gigabyte drives.

Enhanced IDE technology

A newer drive standard that enables systems to recognize drives larger than 504 MB/528 MB and to handle up to four devices on the same controller.

EPP (enhanced parallel port)

A parallel port that enables data to flow in both directions (bidirectional port) and is faster than original parallel ports on PCs that only supported communication in one direction.

EPROM (erasable programmable ROM) chip

A type of chip with a special window that enables the current memory contents to be erased with special ultraviolet light so that the chip can be reprogrammed. Many BIOS chips are EPROMs.

Error correction

The ability of some modems to identify transmission errors and then automatically request another transmission.

ESCD (extended system configuration data)

A list written to the BIOS chip of what you have done manually to the system configuration that Plug and Play doesn't do on its own.

Ethernet

The most popular network topology used today. It uses Carrier Sense Multiple Access with Collision Detection (CSMA/CD) and can be physically configured as a bus or star network.

Expanded memory (EMS)

Memory outside of the conventional 640K and the extended 1024K range that's accessed in 16K segments, or pages, by way of a window to upper memory.

Expansion bus

A bus that doesn't run synchronized with the system clock.

Expansion card

A circuit board inserted into a slot on the system board to enhance the capability of the computer.

Expansion slot

A narrow slot on the system board where an expansion card can be inserted. Expansion slots connect to a bus on the system board.

Extended memory

Memory above the initial 1024 KB, or 1 MB, area.

External cache

Static cache memory, stored on the system board or inside CPU housing, that isn't part of the CPU (also called level 2 or L2 cache).

FDDI (Fiber Distributed Data Interface)

Pronounced "fiddy." A ring-based network, similar to Token Ring, which doesn't require a centralized hub. FDDI often uses fiber-optic cabling.

Ferroresonant regulator

A UPS device that contains a magnetic coil that can retain a power charge that can be used during a brownout to raise the voltage at switching time.

Field replaceable unit

A component in a computer or device that can be replaced with a new component without sending the computer or device back to the manufacturer. Example: a DIMM memory module on a system board.

File allocation table (FAT)

A table that lists how each cluster or file allocation unit on the disk is currently used.

FireWire

An expansion bus that also can be configured to work as a local bus. It's expected to replace the SCSI bus, providing an easy method to install and configure fast I/O devices. Also called IEEE 1394.

Firmware

Software that's permanently stored in a chip.

Flash memory

A type of RAM that can electronically hold memory even when the power is off.

Flash ROM

ROM that can be reprogrammed or changed without replacing chips.

Flow control

When using modems, a method of controlling the flow of data from a sending PC by having the receiving PC send a message to the sending device to stop or start data flow. Xon/Xoff is an example of a flow control protocol.

FM (frequency modulation) method

A method of synthesizing sound by making a mathematical approximation of the musical sound wave. MIDI may use FM synthesis or wavetable synthesis.

Formatting

To prepare a disk for use by placing tracks or cylinders on its surface to store information (for example, FORMAT A:). Old disks can be reformatted, but all data on them will be lost.

FPM (fast page mode) memory

An earlier memory mode used before the introduction of EDO memory.

Frontside bus

The bus between the CPU and the memory outside the CPU housing.

Full-duplex

Communication that happens in two directions at the same time.

G.Lite

A communications standard sponsored by ITU that is used by ADSL.

Gateway

A device or process that connects networks with different protocols. See Bridge and Router.

Graphics accelerator

A type of video card that has an on-board processor that can substantially increase speed and boost graphical and video performance.

Green Standards

Standards that mean that a computer or device can go into sleep or doze mode when not in use, thus saving energy and helping the environment.

Ground bracelet

An antistatic wrist strap used to dissipate static electricity. Typically grounded by attaching an alligator clip to the computer chassis or to a nearby ground mat.

Ground mat

An antistatic mat designed for electronic workbenches to dissipate static electricity. It often uses a wire attached to the ground connection in an electrical outlet.

Guard tone

A tone that an answering modem sends when it first answers the phone, to tell the calling modem that a modem is on the other end of the line.

Half-duplex

Communication between two devices whereby transmission takes place in only one direction at a time.

Half-life

The time it takes for a medium storing data to weaken to half of its strength. Magnetic media, including traditional hard drives and floppy disks, have a half-life of five to seven years.

Handshaking

When two modems begin to communicate, the initial agreement made as to how to send and receive data. It often occurs when you hear the modem making noises as the dial-up is completed.

Hard boot

Restart the computer by turning off the power or by pressing the Reset button. Also called cold boot.

Hard drive

The main secondary storage device of a PC, a sealed case that contains magnetic coated platters that rotate at high speed.

Hard drive controller

A set of microchips with programs that control a hard drive. Most hard drive controllers today are located inside the hard drive housing.

Hard drive standby time

The amount of time before a hard drive will shut down to conserve energy.

Hard-disk loading

The illegal practice of installing unauthorized software on computers for sale. Hard-disk loading can typically be identified by the absence of original disks in the original system's shipment.

Hardware cache

A disk cache that's contained in RAM chips built right on the disk controller.

Hardware interrupt

An event caused by a hardware device signaling the CPU that it requires service.

Hertz (Hz)

Unit of measurement for frequency, calculated in terms of vibrations, or cycles, per second. For example, a Pentium CPU might have a speed of 233 MHz (megahertz). For 16-bit stereo sound, 44,100 Hz is used.

High-level format

Format performed by the OS that writes a file system to a logical drive. For DOS and Windows 9x, the command used is FORMAT, which writes a FAT and a directory to the drive. Also called OS format.

Host adapter

The circuit board that controls a SCSI bus that supports as many as eight or 16 separate devices, one of which is a host adapter that controls communication with the PC.

Hot swapping

The ability of a computer to use a device, such as a PC Card on a notebook, that's inserted while the computer is running without the computer needing to be rebooted.

I/O addresses

Numbers that are used by devices and the CPU to manage communication between them.

I/O card

A card that often contains serial, parallel, and game ports on the same adapter board, providing input/output interface with the CPU.

IBM-compatible

A computer that uses an Intel (or compatible) processor and can run DOS and Windows.

IEEE 1284

A standard for parallel ports developed by the Institute for Electrical and Electronics Engineers and supported by many hardware manufacturers.

In-band signaling

In modem communication, the name of the signaling used by software flow control, which pauses transmission by sending a special control character in the same channel (or band) that data is sent in.

Inline UPS

A UPS that continually provides power through a battery-powered circuit, and, because it requires no switching, ensures continuous power to the user.

Integral subsystems

In Windows NT, processes used to provide services to the rest of the system and the applications the system supports. (Compare to environment subsystems.)

Integrated Device Electronics (IDE)

A hard drive whose disk controller is integrated into the drive, eliminating the need for a controller cable and thus increasing speed, as well as reducing price.

Intelligent hubs

Network hubs that can be remotely controlled at a console by using network software. These hubs can monitor a network and report errors or problems.

Intelligent UPS

A UPS connected to a computer by way of a serial cable so that software on the computer can monitor and control the UPS.

Interlace

A display in which the electronic beam of a monitor draws every other line with each pass, which lessens the overall effect of a lower refresh rate.

Interleave

To write data in nonconsecutive sectors around a track, so that time isn't wasted waiting for the disk to make a full revolution before the next sector is read.

Internal cache

Memory cache that's faster than external cache, and is contained inside 80486 and Pentium chips (also referred to as primary, Level 1, or L1 cache).

Interrupt handler

A program (either BIOS or a device driver) that's used by the CPU to process a hardware interrupt.

Interrupt vector table

A table that stores the memory addresses assigned to interrupt handlers. Also called a vector table.

IRQ (interrupt request number)

A line on a bus that's assigned to a device and is used to signal the CPU for servicing. These lines are assigned a reference number (for example, the normal IRQ for a printer is IRQ 7).

ISA bus

An 8-bit industry standard architecture bus used on the original 8088 PC. Sixteen-bit ISA buses were designed for the 286 AT, and are still used in Pentiums for devices such as modems.

ISDN (Integrated Services Digital Network)

A communications standard that can carry digital data simultaneously over two channels on a single pair of wires, at about five times the speed of regular phone lines.

Jumper

Two wires that stick up side by side on the system board that are used to hold configuration information. The jumper is considered closed if a cover is over the wires, and open if the cover is missing.

Land

Microscopic flat areas on the surface of a CD or DVD that separate pits. Lands and pits are used to represent data on the disc.

Large mode

A format that supports hard drives that range from 504 MB to 1 GB, mapping the data to conform to the 504 MB barrier before the address information is passed to the operating system.

Legacy

An older device or adapter card that doesn't support Plug and Play, and might have to be manually configured through jumpers or DIP switches.

Limited token

Applies to a FDDI network. A token sent that enables a receiving station to communicate only with the sending station, thus providing continuous communication between the two stations.

Line conditioners

Devices that regulate, or condition the power, providing continuous voltage during brownouts and spikes.

Line protocol

A protocol used over phone lines to provide a connection to a network. Also called a bridging protocol. The most popular line protocol is PPP (Point-to-Point Protocol).

Line-interactive UPS

A variation of a standby UPS that shortens switching time by always keeping the inverter that converts AC to DC working, so that there's no charge-up time for the inverter.

Load size

The largest amount of memory that a driver needs to initialize itself and to hold its data. It's almost always a little larger than the size of the program file.

Loading high

The process of loading a driver or TSR into upper memory.

Local bus

A bus that operates at a speed synchronized with the CPU speed.

Local I/O bus

A local bus that provides I/O devices with fast access to the CPU.

Logical block addressing (LBA)

A method in which the operating system views the drive as one long linear list of LBAs, permitting larger drive sizes (LBA 0 is cylinder 0, head 0, and sector 1).

Logical drive

A portion or all of a hard drive partition that's treated by the operating system as though it were a physical drive containing a boot record, FAT, and root directory.

Logical geometry

The number of heads, tracks, and sectors that the BIOS on the hard drive controller presents to the system BIOS and the OS. The logical geometry doesn't consist of the same values as the physical geometry, although calculations of drive capacity yield the same results.

Logical unit number (LUN)

A number from 0 to 15 (also called the SCSI ID) assigned to each SCSI device attached to a daisy chain.

Low insertion force (LIF)

A socket feature that requires the installer to manually apply an even force over the microchip when inserting the chip into the socket.

Low-level format

A process (usually performed at the factory) that electronically creates the hard drive cylinders and tests for bad spots on the disk surface.

MAC (media access control)

An element of data-link layer protocol that provides compatibility with the NIC used by the physical layer. A network card address is often called a MAC address. See Adapter address.

Master boot record (MBR) on a hard drive

The first sector on a hard drive, which contains the partition table and other information needed by BIOS to access the drive.

Memory

Physical microchips that can hold data and programming located on the system board or expansion cards.

Memory address

A number that the CPU assigns to physical memory to keep track of the memory that it has access to.

Memory bus

The bus between the CPU and memory on the system board. Also called the system bus or the host bus.

Memory cache

A small amount of faster RAM that stores recently retrieved data, in anticipation of what the CPU will request next, thus speeding up access.

Memory mapping

Assigning addresses to both RAM and ROM during the boot process.

MMX (Multimedia Extensions) technology

A variation of the Pentium processor designed to manage and speed up high-volume input/output needed for graphics, motion video, animation, and sound.

Modem

From MOdulate/DEModulate. A device that modulates digital data from a computer to an analog format that can be sent over telephone lines, then demodulates it back into digital form.

Modulation

Converting binary or digital data into an analog signal that can be sent over standard telephone lines.

Multibank DRAM (MDRAM)

A special kind of RAM used on video cards that's able to use a full 128-bit bus path without requiring the full 4 MB of RAM.

Multimeter

Either a voltmeter or an ammeter that also can measure resistance in ohms or as continuity, depending on a switch setting.

Multiplier

On a system board, the factor by which the bus speed or frequency is multiplied to get the CPU clock speed.

Multiscan monitor

A monitor that can work within a range of frequencies, and thus can work with different standards and video cards. If offers a variety of refresh rates.

Multisession

A feature that enables data to be read (or written) on a CD during more than one session. This is important if the disc was only partially filled during the first write.

Multistation access unit (MSAU or MAU)

A centralized hub device used to connect IBM Token Ring network stations.

Multitasking

When a CPU or an OS supporting multiple CPUs can do more than one thing at a time. The Pentium is a multitasking CPU.

Nearest active downstream neighbor (NADN)

The next station to receive a token in a Token Ring.

Nearest active upstream neighbor (NAUN)

The station that has just sent a token to the nearest active downstream neighbor in a Token Ring.

Network interface card (NIC)

A network adapter board that plugs into a computer's system board and provides a port on the back of the card to connect a PC to a network.

Node

Each computer, workstation, or device on a network.

Noise

An extraneous, unwanted signal, often over an analog phone line, that can cause communication interference or transmission errors. Possible sources are fluorescent lighting, radios, TVs, lightning, or bad wiring.

Non-interlace

A type of display in which the electronic beam of a monitor draws every line on the screen with each pass. See Interlace.

Nonparity memory

Slightly less expensive, 8-bit memory without error checking. A SIMM part number with a 32 in it (4 x 8 bits) is nonparity.

Nonvolatile

Refers to a kind of RAM that's stable and can hold data as long as electricity is powering the memory.

North Bridge

That portion of the chip set hub that connects faster I/O buses (e.g., AGP bus) to the system bus. Compare to South Bridge

Object linking

A method where one application can execute a command on an object created by another application.

Octet

A traditional term for each of the four 8-bit numbers that make up an IP address. For example, the IP address 206.96.103.114 has four octets.

On-board BIOS

See System BIOS.

On-board ports

Ports that are directly on the system board, such as a built-in keyboard port or on-board serial port.

Open Systems Interconnect (OSI)

A seven-layer (application, presentation, session, transport, network, data-link, physical) model of communications supported by a network. Refers to only software and firmware.

Out-of-band signaling

The type of signaling used by hardware flow control, which sends a message to pause transmission by using channels (or bands) not used for data.

Overclocking

Running a system board at a speed that isn't recommended or guaranteed by CPU or chipset manufacturers.

P1 connector

Power connection on an ATX system board.

Parallel port

A female port on the computer that can transmit data in parallel, 8 bits at a time, and is usually used with a printer. The names for parallel ports are LPT1 and LPT2.

Parity

An error-checking scheme in which a ninth, or "parity," bit is added. The value of the parity bit is set to either 0 or 1 to provide an even number of ones for even parity and an odd number of ones for odd parity.

Parity error

An error that occurs when the number of 1s in the byte isn't in agreement with the expected number.

Parity memory

Nine-bit memory in which the 9th bit is used for error checking. A SIMM part number with a 36 in it (4 x 9 bits) is parity. Older DOS PCs almost always use parity chips.

Partition

A division of a hard drive that can be used to hold logical drives.

Partition table

A table at the beginning of the hard drive that contains information about each partition on the drive. The partition table is contained in the master boot record.

PC Card

A credit-card-sized adapter card that can be slid into a slot in the side of many notebook computers and is used for connecting to modems, networks, and CD-ROM drives. Also called PCMCIA Card.

PCI (peripheral component interconnect) bus

A bus common on Pentium computers that runs at speeds of up to 33 MHz, with a 32-bit-wide data path. It serves as the middle layer between the memory bus and expansion buses.

PCI bus IRQ steering

A feature that makes it possible for PCI devices to share an IRQ. System BIOS and the OS must both support this feature.

Peripheral devices

Devices that communicate with the CPU but aren't located directly on the system board, such as the monitor, floppy drive, printer, and mouse.

Physical geometry

The actual layout of heads, tracks, and sectors on a hard drive. See Logical geometry.

Pin grid array (PGA)

A feature of a CPU socket where the pins are aligned in uniform rows around the socket.

Pipelined burst SRAM

A less expensive SRAM that uses more clock cycles per transfer than non-pipelined burst, but doesn't significantly slow down the process.

Pit

Recessed areas on the surface of a CD or DVD, separating lands, or flat areas. Lands and pits are used to represent data on the disc.

Pixel

Small spots on a fine horizontal scan line that are illuminated to create an image on the monitor.

Polling

A process by which the CPU checks the status of connected devices to determine whether they're ready to send or receive data.

Port

A physical connector, usually at the back of a computer, that enables a cable from a peripheral device, such as a printer, mouse, or modem, to be attached.

Port settings

The configuration parameters of communications devices such as COM1, COM2, or COM3, including IRQ settings.

Port speed

The communication speed between a DTE (computer) and a DCE (modem). As a general rule, the port speed should be at least four times as fast as the modem speed.

POST (power-on self test)

A self-diagnostic program used to perform a simple test of the CPU, RAM, and various I/O devices. The POST is performed when the computer is first turned on and is stored in ROM-BIOS.

Power conditioners

Line conditioners that regulate, or condition, the power, providing continuous voltage during brownouts.

Power supply

A box inside the computer case that supplies power to the system board and other installed devices. Power supplies provide 3.3, 5, and 12 volts DC.

Preemptive multitasking

A type of pseudo-multitasking whereby the CPU gives an application a specified period of time and then preempts the processing to give time to another application.

Primary storage

Temporary storage on the system board used by the CPU to process data and instructions.

Processor speed

The speed or frequency at which the CPU operates. Usually expressed in MHz.

Proprietary

A term for products that a company has exclusive rights to manufacture and/or market. Proprietary computer components are typically more difficult to find and more expensive to buy.

Protocol

A set of pre-established rules for communication. Examples of protocols are modem parity settings and the way in which header and trailer information in a data packet is formatted.

Pulse code modulation (PCM)

A method of sampling sound in a reduced, digitized format, by recording differences between successive digital samples instead of their full values.

RAM (random access memory)

Temporary memory stored on chips, such as SIMMs, inside the computer. Information in RAM disappears when the computer's power is turned off.

Re-marked chips

Chips that have been used and returned to the factory, marked again, and resold. The surface of the chips might be dull or scratched.

Read/write head

A sealed, magnetic coil device that moves across the surface of a disk either reading or writing data to the disk.

Rectifier

An electrical device that converts AC to DC. A PC power supply contains a rectifier.

Reduced write current

A method whereby less current is used to write data to tracks near the center of the disk, where the bits are closer together.

Refresh

The process of periodically rewriting the data such as on dynamic RAM.

Registry

A database used by Windows to store hardware and software configuration information, user preferences, and setup information. Use Regedit.exe to edit the Registry.

Removable drives

High-capacity drives, such as Zip or Jaz drives, that have disks that can be removed like floppy disks.

Repeater

A device that amplifies weakened signals on a network.

Resolution

The number of spots called pixels on a monitor screen that are addressable by software (example: 1024 x 768 pixels).

Resource management

The process of allocating resources to devices at startup.

RET (resolution enhancement technology)

The term used by Hewlett-Packard to describe the way a laser printer varies the size of the dots used to create an image. This technology partly accounts for the sharp, clear image created by a laser printer

Retension

A tape maintenance procedure that fast-forwards and then rewinds the tape to eliminate loose spots on the tape.

RISC (reduced instruction set computer) chips

Chips that incorporate only the most frequently used instructions, so that the computer operates faster (for example, the PowerPC uses RISC chips).

RJ-11

A phone line connection found on a modem, telephone, and house phone outlet.

RJ-45 connector

A connector used on an Ethernet 10BaseT (twisted-pair cable) network. An RJ-45 port looks similar to a large phone jack.

ROM (read-only memory)

Chips that contain programming code and can't be erased.

Router

A device or box that connects networks. A router transfers a packet to other networks when the packet is addressed to a station outside its network. The router can make intelligent decisions as to which network is the best route to use to send data to a distant network. See Bridge.

Sampling

Part of the process of converting sound or video from analog to digital format, whereby a sound wave or image is measured at uniform time intervals and saved as a series of smaller representative blocks.

Sampling rate

The rate of samples taken of an analog signal over a period of time, usually expressed as samples per second, or Hertz. For example, 44,100 Hz is the sampling rate used for 16-bit stereo.

SCAM (SCSI configuration automatically)

A method that follows the Plug and Play standard, to make installations of SCSI devices much easier, assuming that the device is SCAM-compatible.

Scanning mirror

A component of a laser printer. An octagonal mirror that can be directed in a sweeping motion to cover the entire length of a laser printer drum.

SCSI (small computer system interface)

A faster system-level interface with a host adapter and a bus that can daisy chain as many as seven or 15 other devices.

SCSI bus

A bus standard used for peripheral devices tied together in a daisy chain.

SCSI bus adapter chip

The chip mounted on the logic board of a hard drive that enables the drive to be a part of a SCSI bus system.

Secondary storage

Storage that's remote to the CPU and permanently holds data, even when the PC is turned off.

Sector

On a disk surface, one segment of a track, which almost always contains 512 bytes of data. Sometimes a single wedge of the disk surface is also called a sector.

Segmentation

To split a large Ethernet into smaller segments that are connected to each other by bridges or routers. This is done to prevent congestion as the number of nodes increases.

Sequential access

A method of data access used by tape drives whereby data is written or read sequentially from the beginning to the end of the tape or until the desired data is found.

Serial mouse

A mouse that uses a serial port and has a female 9-pin DB-9 connector.

Serial ports

Male ports on the computer used for transmitting data serially, one bit at a time. They're called COM1, COM2, COM3 and COM4.

SGRAM (synchronous graphics RAM)

Memory designed especially for video card processing that can synchronize itself with the CPU bus clock. They're commonly used for modems and mice, and in DOS are called COM1 or COM2.

Shadow RAM or shadowing ROM

The process of copying ROM programming code into RAM to speed up the system operation, because of the faster access speed of RAM.

Signal-regenerating repeater

A repeater that "reads" the signal on the network and then creates an exact duplicate of the signal, thus amplifying the signal without also amplifying unwanted noise that's mixed with the signal.

SIMM (single inline memory module)

A miniature circuit board used in a computer to hold RAM. SIMMs hold 8, 16, 32, or 64 MB on a single module.

Single voltage CPU

A CPU that requires one voltage for both internal and I/O operations.

Single-instruction, multiple-data (SIMD)

An MMX process that enables the CPU to execute a single instruction simultaneously on multiple pieces of data rather than by repetitive looping.

Slack

Wasted space on a hard drive caused by not using all available space at the end of clusters.

SO-DIMM (small outline DIMM)

A small memory module (designed for notebooks) that has 72 pins and supports 32-bit data transfers.

Socket

A virtual connection from one computer to another such as that between a client and a server. Higher-level protocols such as HTTP use a socket to pass data between two computers. A socket is assigned a number for the current session, which is used by the high-level protocol.

Soft boot

To restart a PC by pressing the Ctrl, Alt, and Del keys at the same time. Also called warm boot.

Software cache

Cache controlled by software whereby the cache is stored in RAM.

Software interrupt

An event caused by a program currently being executed by the CPU signaling the CPU that it requires the use of a hardware device.

South Bridge

That portion of the chip set hub that connects slower I/O buses (e.g., ISA bus) to the system bus. Compare to North Bridge.

Spooling

Placing print jobs in a print queue so that an application can be released from the printing process before printing is completed. Spooling is an acronym for simultaneous peripheral operations online.

SSE (streaming SIMD extension)

A technology used by the Intel Pentium III designed to improve performance of multimedia software.

Staggered pin grid array (SPGA)

A feature of a CPU socket where the pins are staggered over the socket in order to squeeze more pins into a small space.

Standby time

The time before a "Green" system will reduce 92 percent of its activity. See Green standards.

Standby UPS

A UPS that quickly switches from an AC power source to a battery-powered source during a brownout or power outage.

Standoffs

Small plastic or metal spacers placed on the bottom of the main system board, to raise it off the chassis, so that its components will not short out on the metal case.

Star network architecture

A network design in which nodes are connected at a centralized location.

Start bit

A bit that's used to signal the approach of data. See Stop bit.

Startup BIOS

Part of system BIOS that's responsible for controlling the PC when it's first turned on. Startup BIOS gives control over to the OS once it's loaded.

Static RAM (SRAM)

RAM chips that retain information without the need for refreshing, as long as the computer's power is on. They're more expensive than traditional DRAM.

Stop bit

A bit that's used to signal the end of a block of data. See Start bit.

Surge suppressor or surge protector

A device or power strip designed to protect electronic equipment from power surges and spikes.

Suspend time

The time before a Green system will reduce 99 percent of its activity. After this time, the system needs warm up time so that the CPU, monitor, and hard drive

Synchronous DRAM (SDRAM)

A type of memory stored on DIMMs that run in sync with the system clock, running at the same speed as the system board. Currently, the fastest memory used on PCs.

Synchronous SRAM

SRAM that's faster and more expensive than asynchronous SRAM. It requires a clock signal to validate its control signals, enabling the cache to run in step with the CPU.

System BIOS

Basic input/output system chip(s) residing on the system board that control(s) normal I/O to such areas as system memory and floppy drives. Also called on-board BIOS.

System board

The main board in the computer, also called the motherboard. The CPU, ROM chips, SIMMs, DIMMs, and interface cards are plugged into the system board.

System bus

Today the system bus usually means the memory bus. However, sometimes it's used to refer to other buses on the system board. See memory bus.

System clock

A line on a bus that's dedicated to timing the activities of components connected to it. The system clock provides a continuous pulse that other devices use to time themselves.

System disk

A floppy disk containing enough of an operating system to boot.

System-board mouse

A mouse that plugs into a round mouse port on the system board. Sometimes called a PS/2 mouse.

Terminating resistor

The resistor added at the end of a SCSI chain to dampen the voltage at the end of the chain. See Termination.

Termination

A process necessary to prevent an echo effect of power at the end of a SCSI chain resulting in interference with the data transmission. See Terminating resistor.

Thread

A single task that is part of a larger task or program.

Token

A small frame on a Token Ring network that constantly travels around the ring in only one direction. When a station seizes the token, it controls the channel until its message is sent.

Token Ring

A network that's logically a ring, but stations are connected to a centralized multistation access unit (MAU) in a star formation.

Trace

A wire on a circuit board that connects two components or devices together.

Track

The disk surface is divided into many concentric circles, each called a track.

Transceiver

The bidirectional (transmitter and receiver) component on a NIC that's responsible for signal conversion and monitors for data collision.

Translation

A technique used by system BIOS and hard drive controller BIOS to break the 504 MB hard drive barrier, whereby a different set of drive parameters are communicated to the OS and other software than that used by the hard drive controller BIOS.

UART (universal asynchronous receiver/transmitter) chip

A chip that controls serial ports. It sets protocol and converts parallel data bits received from the system bus into serial bits.

Unattended installation

A Windows 2000 installation that's done by storing the answers to installation questions in a text file or script that Windows 2000 calls an answer file so that the answers don't have to be typed in during the installation.

Universal serial bus (USB)

A bus that's expected to eventually replace serial and parallel ports, designed to make installation and configuration of I/O devices easy, providing room for as many as 127 devices daisy-chained together. The USB uses only a single set of resources for all devices on the bus.

Upper memory

The memory addresses from 640K up to 1024K, originally reserved for BIOS, device drivers, and TSRs.

Upper memory block (UMB)

A group of consecutive upper memory addresses in RAM.

UPS (uninterruptible power supply)

A device designed to provide a backup power supply during a power failure. Basically, a UPS is a battery backup system with an ultrafast sensing device.

V.34 standard

A communications standard that transmits at 28,800 bps and/or 33,600 bps.

V.90

A standard for data transmission over phone lines that can attain a speed of 56 Kbps. It replaces K56flex and x2 standards.

VESA (Video Electronics Standards Association) VL bus

A local bus used on 80486 computers for connecting 32-bit adapters directly to the local processor bus.

Video controller card

An interface card that controls the monitor. Also called video card or display adapter.

Video driver

A program that tells the computer how to effectively communicate with the video adapter card and monitor.

Video RAM or VRAM

RAM on video cards that holds the data that's passed from the computer to the monitor and can be accessed by two devices simultaneously. Higher resolutions often require more video memory.

Volatile

Refers to a kind of RAM that is temporary, can't hold data very long, and must be frequently refreshed.

Wait state

A clock tick in which nothing happens, used to ensure that the microprocessor isn't getting ahead of slower components. A 0-wait state is preferable to a 1-wait state. Too many wait states can slow a system down.

Write precompensation

A method whereby data is written faster to the tracks that are near the center of a disk.

Zone bit recording

A method of storing data on a hard drive whereby the drive can have more sectors per track near the outside of the platter.

Index

A

Accelerated graphics port (AGP), 2-25, 2-48
Accelerated Hub Architecture, 2-26
Adapter address, 11-16
Adapter card, 5-4
Amplifier repeater, 11-6
Analog-to-digital converter, 8-24
Applications software, 1-8
    Installing, 5-45
Asymmetric Digital Subscriber Line (ADSL), 10-27
Asynchronous SRAM, 3-7
Audio Modem Riser slot, 2-49
Autorange meters, 9-5

B

Back end, 11-23
Backbone, 11-11
Backside bus, 2-13
Bandwidth, 7-34, 10-24
Bank, 3-15
Baseband, 11-5
Baud rate, 10-5
Beam detect mirror, 12-5
BIOS, 1-9, 7-5
    Incompatibility with hardware, 2-32
    Incompatibility with software, 2-32
    Plug and Play, 2-32
    Total amount in system, 2-30
BIOS manufacturer
    Identifying, 2-30
Bit map files, 8-5
Boot process
    Loading the operating system, 1-16
    Overview of, 1-13
    Power-on self test (POST), 1-14
    Types of, 1-13
Boot record, 5-22, 5-44
Bootable rescue disk, 6-6
    DOS, 6-6
    Windows 9x, 6-7
Booting, 1-9
Break code, 7-30
Bridges, 11-7, 11-18
Buck-boost feature, 9-23
Burst EDO (BEDO), 3-9
Burst SRAM, 3-7
Burst transfer, 5-11
Bus
    Functions of, 2-41

Bus evolution, 2-39
Bus speed, 2-12
Bus topology, 11-2
Bus types
    EISA, 2-43
    FireWire, 2-44
    ISA, 2-42
    Local, 2-45
    PCI local bus, 2-46
    Universal serial bus, 2-43

C

Cable modem, 10-26
Cabling system
    For Ethernet network, 11-4
Capacitor, 9-3
Carpal tunnel syndrome (CTS), 7-28
Carrier Sense Multiple Access with Collision Detection
    (CSMA/CD), 11-3
CD-R drives, 8-13
CD-ROM drives, 8-11
    Adding to Windows 95 ERD, 8-20
    Cache, 8-21
    Inserting, 8-16
    Installation problems, 8-22
    Installing, 8-14
    Interfacing with system board, 8-13
    Testing, 8-19
CD-RW drives, 8-13
Central process unit (CPU) chips
    Attributes of, 2-9
Central processing unit (CPU), 1-2
    Cooling fans, 2-18
    Slots, 2-20
    Sockets, 2-20
    Voltage regulator, 2-23
    Voltages used by, 2-11
Central processing unit (CPU) chips
    Attributes related to bus architecture, 2-10
Checksum, 10-7
Chip sets
    Defined, 2-25
    Types of, 2-25
Circuit board, 1-5
Clamping voltage, 9-19
Cluster, 4-6
Cluster chain, 4-10
CMOS chip
    Configuration information on, 2-54
CMOS settings
    Description of, 2-54

COAST (cache on a stick), 3-4
Collision, 11-3
Combo card, 11-15
Computer case
    Devices inside, 1-5
Computer components
    Overview of, 1-2
Computer terminology
    Defined, 1-3
Contention-based system, 11-3
Control blade, 12-5
Controlled-access unit, 11-8
CPU form factors, 2-19

D

Data
    Compressing, 8-25
Data line protector, 9-19
Data Over Cable Service Interface Specifications
    (DOCSIS), 10-26
Data path, 2-9
Data transmission
    Speed, 10-9
Dedicated network device, 11-3
Demodulation, 10-2
Destructive low-level format, 5-58
Device drivers, 7-6
    Changing, 7-7
    DOS, 8-18
    Windows 9x, 7-6, 8-18
Digital camera, 8-38
Digital diagnostic disks (DDDs), 4-14
Digital signal, 10-4
Digital Subscriber Line (DSL), 10-27
Digital video disc (DVD), 8-40
Digital-to-analog converter, 8-24
Digitizing data, 8-7
DIMM, 2-36, 3-8
Diode, 9-3
Direct memory access (DMA) channels
    Defined, 1-30
Direct Rambus DRAM, 3-10
Directory, 4-9
Display adapter, 1-27
Docking station, 12-27
Dongle, 12-30
Dot pitch, 7-35
Dot-matrix printer, 12-11
Double conversion, 9-23
Double-data rate SDRAM, 3-10
Drive capacity, 5-27
Drop height, 4-23
Dual booting, 5-48
Dual inline pin package (DIPP), 2-21
Dual voltage CPUs, 2-23
Dual-porting, 7-40
Dynamic memory
    Defined, 2-36

Dynamic RAM (DRAM), 3-2

E

ECC (error checking and correction), 3-12
EDO (extended data output) memory, 3-9
EEPROM chips, 3-3
EIDE drives vs. SCSI drives, 5-15
EISA bus, 2-43
Electricity, 9-2
    Components in a PC, 9-3
    Continuity, 9-2
    ESD, 9-4
    Measuring voltage, 9-3
Electromagnetic interference (EMI), 9-4
Electrostatic discharge (ESD), 6-3
ELF emissions, 7-36
Energy Star computers, 9-26
Enhanced IDE (EIDE) drives, 5-8
Enhanced metafile format (EMF), 12-12
EPROM chips, 3-3
Equipment
    Disposing of, 6-37
    Precautions when moving, 6-36
Ergonomic
    Defined, 7-28
Error messages, 4-16
ESCD (extended system configuration data), 2-32
Ethernet network
    Cabling system for, 11-4
    Described, 11-2
    How computers communicate on, 11-3
Expansion buses, 2-39
External cache, 2-13

F

FAT32, 5-25
Ferroresonant regulator, 9-20
Fiber Distributed Date Interface (FDDI) network
    Described, 11-11
    Strength of, 11-12
Field replaceable units, 2-3
File allocation table (FAT), 4-6, 5-23
File allocation unit, 4-6
FireWire bus, 2-44
Firmware, 1-8. See BIOS
Flash memory, 3-4
Flash ROM, 2-33
    Upgrading, 2-34
Floppy disks
    Formatting, 4-3
    Sectors, 4-3
    Sizes, 4-2
    Storing data, 4-3
    Tracks, 4-3
Floppy drives
    Replacing, 4-18
    Supporting, 4-13
Form factor, 2-2

Formatting
   Disks, 4-7
FPM (fast page mode) memory, 3-8
Fragmented file, 4-10
Frames, 10-7
Front end, 11-23
Frontside bus, 2-13
FTP (File Transfer Protocol), 11-22
Full-duplex, 10-4

G

Gateway
   Described, 11-18
General Protection Fault (GPF) errors, 3-12
Graphics accelerator, 7-40
Ground bracelet, 6-3
Ground mat, 6-3

H

Half-duplex, 10-4
Half-life, 4-23
Handshaking, 10-5
Hard boot, 1-13
Hard coded, 1-15, 2-32
Hard drives, 5-2
   Division of, 5-17
   Installing, 5-31
   Partitioning, 5-41
   Technology, 5-2
   Troubleshooting, 5-51
Hardware configuration, 2-54
   Conflicts, 2-30
Hardware interrupts, 1-21
Head, 5-3
Heat sink, 2-19
High-level format, 5-6
   Defined, 5-44
Hop count, 11-18
Host adapter, 5-8, 5-14
   Installing, 7-26
Hot swapping, 2-44, 12-29
HTTP (Hypertext Transfer Protocol), 11-22
Hub, 2-44
Hub Interface, 2-26

I

I/O cards, 4-2
I/O controller card, 7-10
IDE CD-ROM drive
   Configuring, 8-16
IDE technology, 5-4
IDI drives
   Support, 5-7
IEEE 1394, 2-44, 7-19
Ink-jet printer
   Cleaning nozzles, 12-10
   Correcting ink streaks, 12-11
   Correcting missing lines on page, 12-10
   How it works, 12-8
   Photo-quality, 12-10
   Supporting, 12-10
Input/output (I/O) addresses
   Common assignments for, 1-29
   Defined, 1-28
Instruction set, 2-9
Intelligent hubs, 11-2
Interleave, 5-31
Internal cache, 2-10, 2-13
Internetwork, 11-2
Interrupt controller chip, 1-21
Interrupt request number (IRQ)
   Assignment process, 1-22
   Common uses for, 1-21
   Defined, 1-21
Intranet, 11-21
ISA bus, 1-19, 2-42
   Eight-bit, 1-19
   Sixteen-bit, 1-20
ISA expansion slots, 7-22
ISDN, 10-25
Itanium, 2-17

J

Joules, 9-19

K

Keyboard, 7-28
   Connectors, 7-29
Known-good device, 4-16

L

Laptop computers, 12-20
Laser printer, 12-2
   Cleaning step, 12-3
   Conditioning step, 12-4
   Developing step, 12-5
   Fusing step, 12-7
   How it works, 12-2
   Supporting, 12-7
   Transferring step, 12-6
   Writing step, 12-4
Let-through, 9-19
Limited token, 11-12
Line conditioners, 9-20
Local bus, 2-39
   Purpose of, 2-45
Local I/O bus, 2-41
Logical drives, 5-21
Logical geometry, 5-29
Low insertion force (LIF) sockets, 2-21
Low-level formatting, 5-6, 5-58
LUN (logical unit number), 5-9

M

Main directory, 4-11
Make code, 7-30
Master boot record, 5-18
Master boot record (MBR), 1-16, 4-8
Material safety data sheet (MSDS), 6-37
Media access control (MAC) address, 11-16
Memory
    Upgrading on network computer, 12-24
Memory addresses
    Assignment process for, 1-28
    Defined, 1-25
    Uses for, 1-26
Memory bus, 2-12
Memory cache, 2-13
Memory caching, 3-5
Memory technologies
    Described, 2-37
Middleware, 11-24
MIDI technology, 8-25
MMX technology, 8-9
Modem
    Communicating with PC, 10-9
    Configuring, 10-15
    Data compression, 10-7
    Data transmission process, 10-2
    Defined, 10-2
    Error correction, 10-7
    Features, 10-8
    Flow control, 10-10
    Installing, 10-13
    Speed, 10-5
    Standards, 10-6
    Testing, 10-16
    Troubleshooting, 10-18
Modem troubleshooting
    Busy signal, 10-19
    Data loss during downloads, 10-21
    Dealing with unresponsive modem, 10-18
    Garbage, 10-22
    Handshake restarts, 10-20
    Lost connection, 10-21
    Lost connections, 10-20
    NO CARRIER messages, 10-21
    No dial tone, 10-19
    Slow connection speed, 10-20
    Slow file transfers, 10-20
Modulation, 10-2
Monitor, 7-33
    Color depth, 7-41
    CRT technology, 7-34
    Flat panel, 7-36
    Green, 7-36
    Interlaced, 7-35
    Multiscan, 7-36
    Noninterlaced, 7-35
    Resolution, 7-35
    Screen size, 7-34

Mouse, 7-31
    Bus, 7-32
    PS/2-compatible, 7-32
    Serial, 7-32
    System-board, 7-32
MP3, 8-39
Multibank DRAM, 7-43
Multiframe dialogs, 11-12
Multimedia, 8-2
    PCs, 8-5
    Software requirements, 8-4
    Standardization, 8-9
Multimeter, 9-4
Multiplier, 2-12
Multistation access unit, 11-8

N

Nearest active downstream neighbor (NADN), 11-10
Nearest active upstream neighbor (NAUN), 11-10
NetBEUI protocol, 11-21
Network architecture
    Ethernet, 11-2
    Token Ring, 11-8
    Types of, 11-2
Network configurations
    Types of, 11-23
Network interface card (NIC), 11-14
    Selecting, 11-16
    Types of, 11-14
Network services
    Described, 11-22
Networking hardware
    Bridge, 11-17
    Described, 11-14
    Gateway, 11-17
    Network interface card (NIC), 11-14
    Router, 11-17
Networking software
    OSI model, 11-20
    Overview, 11-20
Noise, 10-5
Nondestructive format, 5-58
Nonparity memory, 3-12
Notebook computer
    Connecting peripheral device to, 12-26
    Hibernation feature, 12-23
    Power management on, 12-22
    Supporting, 12-20
    Upgrading memory on, 12-24
Notebook computers, 12-20

O

On-board BIOS, 1-9
On-board ports
    Types of, 2-53
Open Systems Interconnect, 11-20
Operating system (OS)
    Loading during boot process, 1-16

Operating system format, 5-44
Operating system software, 1-8
OS format, 5-6
OSI model, 11-20
Out-of-band signaling, 10-10
Overclocking, 2-16

P

Parallel ports, 7-14
    Configuring, 7-17
    Enhanced, 7-16
    Extended capabilities, 7-16
    Standard, 7-16
Parity, 10-12
Parity bit, 2-35
Parity error, 2-36
Parity memory, 3-12
Partition table, 5-17, 5-41
    Saving, 5-45
Partitions, 5-17
    In a drive, 5-17
Passive network, 11-3
PC card, 12-27
    Services for, 12-28
    Slots for, 12-28
PC card slots, 12-27
PCI bus IRQ steering, 7-21
PCI expansion slots, 7-21
PCI local bus, 2-46
PCMCIA slots, 12-27
Pentium chips
    Classic, 2-14
    Compared, 2-12
    Competitors, 2-16
    Multimedia Extension (MMX), 2-14
    Pentium II, 2-15
    Pentium III, 2-15
    Pentium Pro, 2-14
    Types of, 2-13
Peripherals
    Adding, 7-2
    Connecting to notebook computers, 12-26
Physical geometry, 5-29
Pin grid array (PGA), 2-21
Pipelined burst SRAM, 3-7
Pixel, 7-35
Plug and Play BIOS, 2-32
Pointing devices, 7-31
Polling, 1-23
Port addresses, 1-28
Ports, 1-28
Power conditioners, 9-20
Power management
    Hibernation feature, 12-23
    On a notebook computer, 12-22
Power supply
    For a drive, 9-11
    Measuring voltage, 9-6

Replacing, 9-15
Troubleshooting, 9-13
Upgrading, 9-15
Power-on passwords, 1-13
Power-on self test (POST), 1-13, 1-14
PPP (Point-to-Point Protocol), 11-21
Preventive maintenance
    Guidelines, 6-34
    Keeping records, 6-36
    Moving equipment, 6-36
Printer
    Improving performance of, 12-14
    Operating system test page, 12-15
    Problem with applications software, 12-18
    Problem with cable, 12-17
    Problem with device drivers, 12-17
    Problem with operating system, 12-17
    Self-test page, 12-16
    Troubleshooting guidelines for, 12-14
Printer types
    Dot-matrix, 12-11
    Ink-jet, 12-8
    Laser, 12-2
Printing
    With Windows 9x, 12-12
Processor speed, 2-12
Protocols, 11-20
Pulse code modulation, 8-24

R

Random access memory (RAM), 1-5
    3D, 7-44
Read/write head, 4-4
Reduced write current, 5-3
Refresh RAM, 2-37
Refresh rate, 7-35
Re-marked chips, 3-13
Removable drives, 4-23
Repeater, 11-6
Repetitive stress injury (RSI), 7-28
Request for Comment (RFC), 11-20
Restraining, 10-20
RET (resolution enhancement technology), 12-5
RISC technology, 2-18
RJ-11 connection, 10-4
Root directory, 4-11, 5-23, 5-26
Route discovery, 11-18
Router, 11-7
    Described, 11-18
Router tables, 11-18
RTS/CTS protocol, 10-10

S

Sample size, 8-8
Sampling, 8-6
Scanning mirror, 12-4
SCSI bus, 5-47
SCSI bus adapter chip (SBAC), 5-9

SCSI configuration automatically (SCAM), 5-11
SCSI device drivers, 5-14
    Advanced SCSI Programming Interface (ASPI), 5-14
    Common Access Method (CAM), 5-14
SCSI devices
    Installing, 7-23
SCSI hard drive
    Installing, 5-47
SCSI ID, 5-9
SCSI technology, 5-8
    Embedded devices, 5-9
    Standards, 5-10
    Termination, 5-12
Sector, 4-6
Segmentation, 11-7
Serial ports, 7-10
SGRAM, 7-43
Shadowing ROM, 2-31
Signal-regenerating repeater, 11-6
SIMM, 3-8
SIMM (single inline memory module), 2-36
Single voltage CPUs, 2-23
Slack, 5-25
SMTP (Simple Mail Transfer Protocol), 11-22
SO-DIMMs, 12-24
Soft boot, 1-13
Sound
    Recording, 8-35
    Sampling and digitizing, 8-24
    Storing, 8-25
    Troubleshooting, 8-36
    Windows 9x, 8-32, 8-35
Sound cards, 8-24
    Installing, 8-29
    Installing device drivers, 8-30
Spooling, 12-12
SSE technology, 8-9
Staggered pin grid array (SPGA), 2-21
Star topology, 11-2
Startup BIOS, 1-9
Startup passwords, 1-13
Static electricity. See Electrostatic discharge (ESD)
Static memory
    Defined, 2-36
Static RAM (SRAM), 3-2
Stop bit, 10-12
Subnets, 11-18
Subnetworks, 11-18
Surge suppressors/protectors, 9-18
Synchronous DRAM (SDRAM), 3-9
Synchronous SRAM, 3-7
SyncLink, 3-10
System BIOS, 1-9
System board, 1-5
    Components, 2-3
    Defined, 2-2
    Selecting, 2-6
    Types of, 2-2
System board manufacturers

Web addresses of, 2-7
System buses, 2-39
System clock, 2-8
System resources
    Defined, 1-12
    Summary, 1-31
    Types of, 1-12

T

Technical support calls, 5-46
Terminating resistor, 5-9
Throughput performance, 2-48
Tick count, 11-18
Token, 11-10
Token Ring network
    Communication on, 11-10
    Connecting components of, 11-8
    Described, 11-8
Toner cavity, 12-5
Topology, 11-2
Touch pads, 7-33
Trackball, 7-33
Transceiver, 11-15
Transistor, 9-3
Translation, 5-29
Troubleshooting
    Hard drive, 6-19
    Monitors, 6-24
    Operating system, 6-19
    Perspectives, 6-2
    Power system, 6-15
    Printers, 6-28
    Rules, 6-8
    System board, 6-16
    Tools, 6-4
Troubleshooting tools, 6-2

U

UART chip, 7-13, 10-9
Universal serial bus, 2-43
UPS (uninterruptible power supply), 9-21
    Inline, 9-21
    Intelligent, 9-24
    Line-interactive, 9-23
    Purchasing, 9-24
    Standby, 9-21
USB ports, 7-18

V

VESA (Video Electronics Standards Association) VL bus, 2-45
Video cards, 1-27, 7-38
    Buses, 7-39
    Memory, 7-40
Video controller card, 1-27
Video RAM (VRAM), 7-43
Video-capturing card, 8-40

Virtual file allocation (VFAT), 5-25

W

Wait state, 2-8
Windows 98
  Configuring notebook for hibernation, 12-23
Windows 9x
  Printing with, 12-12
Word size, 2-9
WRAM, 7-44

Write precompensation, 5-3

X

Xon/Xoff protocol, 10-10

Z

Zero insertion force (ZIF) sockets, 2-21
Zone bit recording, 5-6